INTELLIGENCE AND SURPRISE ATTACK

INTELLIGENCE AND SURPRISE ATTACK

Failure and Success from Pearl Harbor
to 9/11 and Beyond

ERIK J. DAHL

GEORGETOWN UNIVERSITY PRESS
Washington, DC

Library of Congress Cataloging-in-Publication Data

Dahl, Erik J.
    Intelligence and surprise attack : failure and success from Pearl Harbor to 9/11 and beyond / Erik J. Dahl.
        pages cm
    Includes bibliographical references and index.
    ISBN 978-1-58901-998-0 (pbk. : alk. paper)
    1. Intelligence service—United States.   2. National security—United States.   I. Title.
JK468.I6D325   2013
327.1273—dc23

2012042488

♾ This book is printed on acid-free paper meeting the requirements of the American National Standard for Permanence in Paper for Printed Library Materials.

15   14   13   9   8   7   6   5   4   3   2   First printing

Printed in the United States of America

CONTENTS

FIGURES

ACKNOWLEDGMENTS

I FIRST BEGAN TO THINK about the subject of intelligence failure and surprise attack during my career as a naval intelligence officer. My greatest goal during that time was to avoid contributing to another failure on the scale of Pearl Harbor, while seeking to recreate the success experienced by an earlier generation of intelligence professionals at the Battle of Midway. In the end neither my failures nor my successes were quite so spectacular, although I had my share of both. But when I retired from active duty and began graduate studies at the Fletcher School of Tufts University, I finally had the time to think systematically about the question: Why does the American intelligence community so often fail to prevent surprise attacks and other disasters?

At the Fletcher School my dissertation adviser Richard Shultz helped me focus my thinking on the project that would become this book. I would also like to thank my other dissertation committee members, William Martel and Anthony Oettinger, for their advice and enthusiastic support. At Fletcher I would also like to thank the staffs of the Ginn Library and of the International Security Studies Program, as well as Beth Ahern, Natasha Bajema, Emma Belcher, Jenifer Burckett-Picker, Beth Chalecki, Josh Gleis, Nathalie Laidler-Kylander, Nicola Minott, Anna Seleney, and Lorenzo Vidino. Among the many others from whom I received valuable advice and guidance in the early days of this project, I would like to thank Frank Stech, who first suggested that I compare the failure of Pearl Harbor with the success of Midway, along with Jim FitzSimonds, Richards Heuer, Art Hulnick, Tom Mahnken, Jim Miller, Fred Parker, and Bob Vickers.

At the Belfer Center for Science and International Affairs at Harvard's John F. Kennedy School of Government, I received wonderful support from Steve Miller, the director of the International Security Program, from my office mate Erica Chenoweth, and from Chuck Cogan, Susan Lynch, and Micah Zenko.

At the US Naval Institute, Janis Jorgensen, Mary Ripley, and Paul Stillwell helped me locate oral histories that were especially useful for my chapters on Pearl Harbor and Midway. At the Naval Historical Center and the Navy Department Library, Linda Edwards and Glen Helm helped me with their invaluable collection of formerly classified cryptologic studies. In Washington, I was able to conduct research using materials on the Day of Terror trial and other terrorism cases through the invaluable assistance of Steven Emerson and the Investigative Project on Terrorism, and I would especially like to thank Ryan Evans and Lorenzo Vidino for going out of their way to help me.

Since arriving at the Naval Postgraduate School in 2008, I have benefited from the support of many colleagues and friends, and for their comments and advice I would especially like to thank Victoria Clement, Mohammed Hafez, Maiah Jaskoski, Jeff Knopf, Sandi Leavitt, Clay Moltz, Brian Pollins, Maria Rasmussen, and Arturo Sotomayor. I have also received valuable advice from Gary Ackerman, Dan Mabrey, and Assaf Moghadam, and from my teaching colleagues at the Center for Homeland Defense and Security, Pat Miller and Bob Simeral. James I. Walsh and Jim Wirtz read several of the book's chapters and provided valuable recommendations.

My editor at Georgetown University Press, Don Jacobs, has been greatly supportive throughout the entire process and provided many important substantive comments and recommendations. The comments from the book's anonymous reviewers were extremely useful. An earlier version of chapter 8 was published in *Studies in Conflict and Terrorism*. The views expressed in this book are my own and do not represent the views of the US government or the Naval Postgraduate School.

Above all I would like to thank my wife, Christa, for the support she has given me in this project and in so many other ways over the years. This book is dedicated to the memory of my mother, Margaret Dahl, and my father, Per Dahl.

INTRODUCTION

Breaking the First Law of Intelligence Failure

WHY DO SURPRISE ATTACKS—whether from terrorists or from conventional military enemies—so often succeed, even though later investigations almost always show that intelligence warnings had been available beforehand? In her classic book about Pearl Harbor, Roberta Wohlstetter provided what is still today the most widely accepted answer to this puzzle. She argued that although there had been numerous warnings of a Japanese threat, the large ratio of extraneous noise to meaningful signals made analysis of the data difficult: "In short, we failed to anticipate Pearl Harbor not for want of the relevant materials, but because of a plethora of irrelevant ones."[1]

Wohlstetter's view—that an excess of noise had drowned out the pertinent intelligence signals and warnings—has since become conventional wisdom, and most major studies of surprise attack and intelligence failure employ the concepts of signals and noise to at least partly explain why intelligence so often fails and surprise attacks succeed.[2] In the words of the intelligence expert Bruce Berkowitz, "This problem of signal-to-noise ratio is so fundamental in the intelligence business that today, if one refers to the 'Roberta Wohlstetter problem,' almost everyone knows exactly what you are talking about."[3]

After the terrorist attacks of September 11, 2001, many scholars and intelligence practitioners cited Wohlstetter's arguments in attempting to explain how the US intelligence community could have missed what after the fact appeared to have been clear warnings.[4] But instead of "signals versus noise," the most convenient shorthand explanation for intelligence failure today has been that the intelligence community failed to "connect the dots." The *9/11 Commission Report* described in detail how the many warnings that had come into the system through the 1990s and up until early September 2001 had never been connected into a coherent narrative that might have convinced the authorities of the need to take effective action against al-Qaeda.[5]

1

The two concepts—signals versus noise, and connecting the dots—are both based on the understanding that intelligence primarily fails through an inability to understand warnings and pieces of information that are already available, rather than through an inability to collect that intelligence in the first place. As James Wirtz has written, "That accurate information on what is about to transpire can always be found within the intelligence pipeline is an important insight that has withstood the test of time and critical scrutiny . . . in fact, it should be considered as the first law of intelligence failure."[6] The terrorism expert Jessica Stern puts it this way: "Surprise attacks do not arise from too little information too late, but from too much information, too soon."[7]

According to most experts, this first law of intelligence failure continues to hold true today, and it has become conventional wisdom that preventing surprise attacks depends largely on the ability of analysts and policymakers to understand and connect the available signals and warnings.[8] This was seen to be the problem that allowed a Nigerian man to board and attempt to blow up a Northwest Airlines flight en route to Detroit on Christmas Day 2009. Reviews by the White House and the Senate Intelligence Committee found that a number of warnings had been missed. President Obama noted, "This was a failure to connect and understand the intelligence that we already had," and he ordered the intelligence community to improve its ability to analyze and understand the information it receives.[9]

This book argues that this conventional wisdom is wrong. When we compare cases of intelligence failure with those of intelligence success, we find that the first law of intelligence failure is broken: Before most surprise attacks or other strategic surprises, the necessary signals were not there; and it is highly unlikely that surprise could have been avoided if only imaginative intelligence agencies and analysts had been able to connect the dots and understand the signals amid the noise. The problem is that most intelligence available before surprise attacks is general and nonspecific, producing what is often termed strategic warning. As a study by the US Central Intelligence Agency (CIA) put it, this strategic intelligence allows policymakers to see the smoke of a growing threat, but not the flames that tell them where and when to take action against it.[10]

This does not mean, however, that surprise—at least in the case of surprise attacks—can never be avoided. This book argues that intelligence can succeed, and surprise attacks can be prevented, but not by increasing the ratio of signals to noise or by improving the ability of analysts to connect the dots. Instead, this book proposes a *theory of preventive action* that helps explain why intelligence can in some cases succeed—and in other cases fail—to foresee and prevent surprise attacks.

Two key factors are required for intelligence to become actionable and useful in preventing attacks. The first is that it must provide very precise warning about the threat, at a level of specificity that many experts might reflexively dismiss as "tactical-level" intelligence and consider not useful in dealing with the most important threats. But this book will show that the specificity of tactical-level intelligence—as opposed to broad, strategic-level intelligence—is much more likely to convince policymakers that there is an imminent threat and that action is thus imperative. This leads to the second critical factor: that the policymakers must be receptive to the intelligence with which they are provided. A more expansive discussion of preventive action follows in chapter 1.

THE CONVENTIONAL WISDOM IS WRONG

What is wrong with the conventional wisdom? This popular view—the first law of intelligence failure—is persuasive, and appears to be based on more than a half century of experience in the United States and elsewhere and a great deal of research and study by academics and practitioners. For example, an intelligence community task force in 1992 went so far as to argue that "all major intelligence warning failures of the past five decades" were the result of a failure to understand and analyze the raw information available, and not the result of a lack of information.[11] But this conventional view is incorrect, largely because most major studies of intelligence failure and surprise attack suffer from two serious limitations.

The first limitation of this literature is that it is based on studies of cases in which surprise attacks succeed and intelligence fails. This means that it can tell us little about what makes intelligence succeed. A second limitation of much existing work is that it results from historians, other scholars, and intelligence experts looking at past failures with 20/20 hindsight, through which missed signals appear to be much clearer than they were perceived at the time. The problem of hindsight bias makes it very difficult for us to understand today just what intelligence officials thought—or should have thought—about the information and warnings they received in the past.

To test the conventional wisdom about intelligence failure, we need to be able to overcome both these limitations. The primary method used in this book is to compare cases of intelligence failure with cases of intelligence success, using in-depth case studies that help us understand for each case what intelligence was available, and what decision makers thought about that intelligence at the time. It is difficult to conduct such a study, because less information is available about intelligence success than there is about failure. The need for the study of success has been recognized, however. Robert Jervis writes, "We—both scholars and members of the IC [intelligence community]—could also learn a lot by comparing intelligence failures with intelligence successes, but for a variety of reasons the latter are rarely studied."[12]

This book is one of few studies examining the subject of intelligence success, and the examples presented here suggest that the type of intelligence available in these cases is, in fact, significantly different from that available when intelligence fails. When intelligence is used to prevent a surprise attack—whether from a conventional military enemy or a terrorist group—it does not happen because an analyst has been able to piece together a lot of little pieces of information that might otherwise appear unimportant, see the big picture, and convince a decision maker of the danger that is coming. The key factor is not the presence or absence of "imagination" or analytical skill. Instead, the critical factor is the collection of very precise intelligence that convinces and enables a decision maker to take the actions needed to prevent an attack.

This book is the first full-length scholarly work to examine conventional military surprise attack and terrorist surprise in the same framework.[13] It builds upon a literature that was developed during the Cold War on the problem of surprise attack, and I attempt here to update that literature to fit today's threats and challenges.

OUTLINE OF THE BOOK

Chapter 1 reviews how previous scholars have answered the puzzle of the intelligence community's frequent failure to prevent surprise attacks, and it explains how those explanations have fallen short. I then propose the theory of preventive action: For intelligence to be actionable and usable in preventing surprise attacks, it must provide precise, tactical-level warning, and it must be combined with a high level of receptivity toward that warning on the part of policymakers who decide how and whether to use it.

Next begins the first major part of the book, examining the problem of conventional surprise attack. In chapter 2 I review the disaster at Pearl Harbor, which at least until 9/11 was the best-known case of intelligence failure in American history. I challenge the conventional wisdom about Pearl Harbor, and argue that the attack was successful not because intelligence analysts and military leaders failed to understand and connect the dots of the intelligence they had available but because of a lack of precise intelligence and receptive decision makers.

The American success at the Battle of Midway has been studied extensively, and the standard view is that the success was a straightforward result of excellent American signals intelligence on the Japanese fleet. But there has been surprisingly little work done comparing the use of intelligence in this case with the failure only six months earlier at Pearl Harbor. This is largely because the two cases have been thought of as something like apples and oranges—two very different situations, one involving decisions and actions before the outbreak of war, the other a case of attempted attack during war. In chapter 3 I explain why I believe such a comparison is in fact valid, and argue that the critical difference at Midway was the presence of specific, actionable intelligence, combined with receptive decision makers.

Chapter 4 tests my argument about preventive action more broadly by reviewing a number of classic cases of conventional surprise attack, including the outbreak of the Korean War, the Tet Offensive in 1968, and the 1973 Yom Kippur War. Because these cases are invariably examples in which intelligence failed and surprise attacks succeeded, I also include several short studies of other cases that represent at least partial intelligence success, including American intelligence predictions of the Arab-Israeli Six-Day War in 1967.

Part II of the book looks at the problem of terrorist attack and begins with chapter 5, which examines the East Africa embassy bombings of 1998. These bombings represent an important case for my argument, because the attacks succeeded despite the presence of a great deal of specific, tactical-level warning beforehand. This chapter argues that the bombings succeeded not because of a lack of intelligence but because senior officials—especially in Washington—were unreceptive to those warnings.

Next, chapter 6 reviews the "Day of Terror" plot in New York City, which was disrupted soon after the first World Trade Center bombing in 1993. This plot was one of the most important thwarted attacks in American history, but it is little remembered today.

Chapter 7 examines the 9/11 attacks, making use of official documents and other information that has become available since the release of the *9/11 Commission Report* to develop the most comprehensive scholarly analysis yet produced on the intelligence available before the attacks. It challenges the conventional wisdom, which holds that whereas the necessary intelligence had been available, it had not been analyzed properly and the dots had not been connected. Instead, I argue that the most convincing explanation for the failure to prevent the 9/11 attacks was that no warning had indicated where or when the terrorists would strike, and worse yet, senior government officials were not receptive toward the intelligence that was available.

In chapter 8 I test my argument using a new data set I have created of unsuccessful terrorist plots against Americans and American targets during the past twenty-five years. This study of "plots that failed" finds that terrorist attacks have been thwarted most often not through the use of imagination but as the result of very specific, tactical-level intelligence—of the sort typically gathered through on-the-ground domestic intelligence collection and surveillance.

In the conclusion I discuss the book's implications for American intelligence and national security today. I argue that much of the recent debate over intelligence reform in the United States has been misguided, because it focuses on organizational reform and on efforts to encourage imagination and long-range, strategic analysis. The history of American efforts to prevent surprise attacks—from both conventional and terrorist enemies—strongly suggests that the intelligence community should instead focus on developing precise, tactical-level intelligence on potential attacks, while at the same time fostering close linkages with senior officials so that when intelligence is developed and warnings are given, policymakers will listen.

CHAPTER 1

WHY DOES INTELLIGENCE FAIL, AND HOW CAN IT SUCCEED?

AMONG INTELLIGENCE PROFESSIONALS, the concept of *intelligence failure* is a sore subject. This is not surprising, because many people assume that when intelligence fails, it is because an intelligence officer or analyst has done a poor job. But for many in the intelligence business and in the academic field of intelligence studies, this is not necessarily the case: Intelligence can fail for many reasons, often despite the best work of intelligence professionals. Former US Marine Corps intelligence director Lieutenant General Paul Van Riper echoed the feelings of many in the intelligence community when he lamented after 9/11: "The Intelligence Community does a damn good job. It troubles me that people always speak in terms of operational successes and intelligence failures."[1]

But whether or not intelligence personnel or organizations are unfairly or too frequently blamed for mistakes, the subject of intelligence failure is widely studied and debated. In the words of one expert, "The study of intelligence failures is perhaps the most academically advanced field in the study of intelligence."[2] Numerous studies have been produced examining various aspects of intelligence failure, such as the inability to provide sufficient warning of surprise attack. Much of this literature leads to the depressing conclusion that—as Richard Betts put it in a classic article—intelligence failures are inevitable.[3]

Intelligence failures can take many forms, but a common theme in major intelligence failures is that decision makers have been *surprised*. For politicians, senior military officers, and other leaders, surprise is usually a bad thing, and they often count on intelligence agencies to help them avoid it. The most significant surprises—the sorts of events that are sometimes called black swans—are known to military and national security analysts as *strategic surprises*. Scholars of strategic surprise have examined the failure of intelligence services to prevent or understand a wide variety of phenomena that pose a threat to national security, such as American intelligence's inability to foresee the fall of the shah of Iran or to understand the nature of Iraq's weapons of mass destruction programs before the United States–led invasion in 2003.

Given the great deal of attention paid to the topic of intelligence failure, it may seem surprising that there is little agreement in the intelligence literature on just what is meant by an "intelligence failure." Mark Lowenthal, a former senior CIA officer, puts the focus on intelligence agencies: "An intelligence failure is the inability of one or more parts of the intelligence process—collection, evaluation and analysis, production, dissemination—to produce timely, accurate intelligence on an issue or event of importance to national interests."[4] Others argue that failures can be committed by policymakers and other senior officials, who either neglect or misuse the intelligence they are given. Abram N. Shulsky and Gary J. Schmitt focus on these officials who receive intelligence, writing: "An intelligence failure is essentially a misunderstanding of the situation that leads a government (or its military forces) to take actions that are inappropriate and counterproductive to its own interests."[5] A better definition of intelligence failure combines these two concepts; failures can involve either a failure of the intelligence community to produce the intelligence needed by decision makers, or a failure on the part of decision makers to act on that intelligence appropriately.

This book focuses on what is by far the most widely studied type of intelligence failure: the failure to detect and prevent a surprise attack from a military, terrorist, or other enemy. But one of the central arguments of this book is that we spend too much time studying and worrying about *intelligence failure*, and we should instead be thinking about *intelligence success*. Before we can get there, however—before we can understand what makes intelligence succeed—we need to better understand why intelligence fails. This chapter reviews the conventional understanding of why intelligence fails, explains how this understanding falls short, and introduces my argument about intelligence and preventive action.

WHY DOES INTELLIGENCE FAIL?

As noted in this book's introduction, most scholars and practitioners who write about intelligence agree that failures usually happen because intelligence agencies and analysts fail to understand signals and warnings that were right in front of them all the time. They refer to this problem as an inability on the part of the intelligence authorities to "connect the dots" of existing information. They conclude that the problem is not in *collecting* the dots—gathering the intelligence in the first place. Instead, for psychological, organizational, or other reasons, intelligence officials—even when they are competent and trying hard—fail to understand the importance of the information (the "dots") they have.

Although this explanation of the problem may seem obvious, other explanations for failure are possible. For example, it could be that intelligence fails to warn of an attack or other disastrous event because there simply are not enough clues to go on—not enough dots to connect. Or it might not matter very much how much intelligence is available, if the responsible officials are incompetent. This latter explanation was a major conclusion of the Joint Congressional Committee that investigated the Pearl Harbor disaster. The committee had set out to answer the question: "Why, with some of the finest intelligence available in our history, with the almost certain knowledge that war was at hand, with plans that contemplated the precise type of attack that was executed by Japan on the morning of December 7—why was it possible for a Pearl Harbor to occur?"[6] The committee answered its own question, finding that the disaster resulted from errors by the military commanders in Hawaii and from organizational deficiencies in the American military.[7]

When Roberta Wohlstetter published her study of Pearl Harbor in 1962, however, she made a different argument, one that has come to be accepted not only as the conventional wisdom about that disaster but also more generally as a broad theoretical explanation for intelligence failures and surprise attacks. She argued that the problem was not that the military commanders were incompetent, or that their intelligence staffs failed in their duties to collect intelligence about the threat from Japan. Instead, the problem lay in the analysis of the intelligence that was available.[8] The signals that could have alerted the American forces to the danger of an attack on Hawaii were lost amid the far larger quantity of unrelated, contradictory, and confusing noise.

Wohlstetter's explanation for intelligence failure remains widely accepted today, and it can be seen in after-the-fact analyses of most failures and disasters, which find that such events could have been prevented if only we had paid better attention to or had been able to better process the volume of information and warnings that were available. This was the conclusion of the White House review after the Christmas Day 2009 attempt to blow up an airliner as it approached Detroit. More recently, after US Army major Nidal Hasan killed thirteen people at Fort Hood, Texas, senators Joseph Lieberman and Susan Collins argued that these deaths could have been prevented. The Department of Defense and the Federal Bureau of Investigation (FBI), they wrote, "collectively had sufficient information to have detected Hasan's radicalization to violent Islamist extremism but failed both to understand and to act on it."[9] Even the turmoil and unrest that rocked much of the Middle East in early 2011, it has been claimed, could have been foreseen if only the warnings from some experts had been listened to.[10]

This is the conventional wisdom about what happens in cases of intelligence failure: It happens despite—and to some extent because of—the presence of abundant clues about the problems on the horizon, as dots are not connected and valuable signals become lost amid the sea of extraneous noise. This explains *what* happens. But to explain *why* intelligence officials and decision makers fail to understand the available intelligence, two primary schools of thought have developed: the traditional school and the reformist school.

The Traditional School

In her book on Pearl Harbor, Roberta Wohlstetter not only established the conventional wisdom about signals versus noise; she also laid the groundwork for what would become the majority view among scholars and practitioners about the causes of intelligence failures. One of the most striking aspects of this view—which I call the traditional school—is its pessimism. Wohlstetter's analysis of Pearl Harbor convinced her that the task of intelligence is intrinsically difficult, and as a result she believed that intelligence performance was not likely to get much better in the future. Writing at the beginning of the computer age, she argued that if anything, future developments in information processing would make surprise attacks even *more* likely: "In spite of the vast increase in expenditures for collecting and analyzing intelligence data and in spite of advances in the art of machine decoding and machine translation, the balance of advantage seems clearly to have shifted since Pearl Harbor in favor of a surprise attacker."[11]

This pessimistic view might sound unsurprising today, when major intelligence failures and surprises seem to arise nearly every year. But Wohlstetter's argument was a sharp corrective to what had until then been a widely held understanding about intelligence and the growing American intelligence system. This earlier view dates back to Sherman Kent, the Yale professor and long-serving senior CIA official who has been described as the dean of intelligence analysis. Kent saw intelligence as a form of academics that could be done well, if performed by the best minds applying rigorous social science methods.[12] But Kent's optimistic view was countered by Wohlstetter's pessimistic analysis, which suggested that intelligence failure might in fact be unavoidable.

Wohlstetter's view became the dominant one among the relatively small community of scholars who studied intelligence matters during the Cold War. Richard Betts made the case for this traditional view in his much-cited 1978 article, in which he wrote that "intelligence failures are not only inevitable, they are natural."[13] And because these failures are natural, traditionalists do not believe that intelligence officials should be held responsible for most failures. Betts wrote that there would always be *some* warning evident as tensions increase before a surprise attack; there are, he wrote in a comment frequently heard among traditional theorists of intelligence failure, no significant "bolts from the blue."[14] But at the same time, these thinkers tend to argue that none of these warnings, even when considered after the fact, can be considered clear and definitive warnings of what was to come; thus it is not surprising that analysts would have missed what later appeared quite clear.

If anyone is responsible for intelligence failure, traditionalists believe, it is policymakers, who too often fail to take the advice given by intelligence professionals. Betts wrote that "the principal cause of surprise is not the failure of intelligence but the unwillingness of political leaders to believe intelligence or to react to it with sufficient dispatch."[15] Michael Handel, another prominent student of intelligence failure, agreed with Betts that the most common culprit was the decision maker. Handel saw intelligence work as divided into the three levels of acquisition, analysis, and acceptance; and in this regard he observed that "historical experience confirms that intelligence failures were more often caused by a breakdown on the level of acceptance than on the acquisition or analysis levels."[16]

For Wohlstetter and other traditionalist scholars who studied the problem of surprise attack during the Cold War, the key problem for intelligence lay in a faulty analysis of the available information and not in the collection of that information in the first place. But why was intelligence analysis so often faulty? Although Wohlstetter did not offer any deeper answer to this question, later scholars in the traditional school found that problems of human psychology and cognition appeared to be at the root of the problem. Betts, for example, studied surprise attacks ranging from World War II through the Korean War to the 1973 Yom Kippur War, and he found that in most cases someone was ringing the alarm but it was not heard. The problem, he believed, was usually that there existed a conceptual consensus among decision makers that rejected the alarm, or else false alarms had dulled the impact of the alarm at the moment of crisis.[17] Handel also felt the most common cause of intelligence failure was based in the psychological limitations of human nature: "Most intelligence failures occur because intelligence analysts and decisionmakers refuse to adapt their concepts to new information."[18] Richards Heuer has offered what may be the most comprehensive statement of this approach in his *Psychology of Intelligence Analysis*, in which he argues that many intelligence failures are caused by mental mindsets and assumptions that are resistant to change, and by cognitive biases—that is, subconscious mental shortcuts and strategies that lead to faulty judgments.[19]

This emphasis on psychological and cognitive factors may help us understand why this school of thought tends to see intelligence failure as largely unavoidable. Just as human nature and patterns of cognition may be resistant to change, psychological limitations on intelligence may be resistant to improvement. Betts, for example, noted that "unlike organizational structure, . . . cognition cannot be altered by legislation."[20] In 1964 Klaus Knorr made an argument that has since been echoed by a number of others: "It seems clear that the practical problem is to improve the 'batting average'—say, from .275 to .301—rather than to do away altogether with surprise."[21] Two decades later Robert Jervis wrote that "for Americans to expect our intelligence community to predict many, if not most, of the non-routine political occurrences in world politics is unrealistic."[22] Several scholars have even expressed the view that because the problem of intelligence failure and surprise attack is so intractable, further studies of it may prove to be of little use. Handel, for example, wrote in 1977 that "studies of military surprise have reached the point of diminishing returns."[23]

The traditional school of thought continues today among many of the most prominent thinkers concerning terrorism and intelligence. Following much the same logic as the earlier literature, these thinkers argue that intelligence failures such as the September 11, 2001, terrorist attacks are largely unpreventable, and that though some improvements to intelligence are possible, the best policy option is to assume that terrorist attacks will succeed and prepare to deal with their effects.[24] These experts believe the US intelligence community has done a generally good job, even in the years and months leading up to 9/11. Betts, for example, points out that the intelligence community was successful in preventing a number of attacks in the years before 2001, and argues that "contrary to the image left by the destruction of September 11, US intelligence and associated services have generally done very well at protecting the country."[25]

Traditional thinkers see the US intelligence community's performance in fighting terrorist threats as having been especially strong in strategic intelligence, which focuses on broad, long-term issues of interest to senior decision makers. In the case of the 9/11 attacks, for example, adherents of the traditional view generally believe that enough strategic warning had been available before the attacks to alert policymakers to the danger from al-Qaeda; but these warnings were either not listened to, or were drowned out by other intelligence and the press of other issues. The US intelligence community has been weak, according to this view, in obtaining tactical, specific intelligence on terrorist plots. But such intelligence is actually rarely, if ever, available—and the traditional school holds that intelligence agencies have erred in trying too hard to gather such tactical intelligence, when they should instead have been concentrating on their broader, strategic intelligence mission.

The Reformist School

Among scholars and analysts who have studied intelligence failure and surprise attack, there is a second broad school, whose members are more critical of the intelligence community but more optimistic about the future than the traditionalists. They tend to believe that the fundamental problems for intelligence lie more in terms of organizational and bureaucratic limitations than analytic or psychological ones, and many of them think that organizational reforms can significantly improve the performance of the intelligence community. These thinkers are fewer in number than the traditionalists, but the reform impulse has been seen prominently in the work of a number of blue ribbon panels and commissions that have studied the US intelligence community in the past half century.[26]

Intelligence reformists tend to agree with the traditional school that intelligence warnings are usually available before major failures. But whereas the traditionalists believe the warnings are missed because of the inherent limits of analysis and cognition, the reformists believe the problem is that intelligence is not sufficiently shared and coordinated within the vast intelligence community and government bureaucracy. The 9/11 Commission, for example, famously argued that the US intelligence community failed to "connect the dots" of the available intelligence that was held by various government agencies and in different, unconnected databases.[27]

For reformist thinkers, the fundamental problem underlying the inability of the intelligence community to share and process information properly lies at the level of structure and organization. A classic expression of this view is Harold Wilensky's *Organizational Intelligence*, in which Wilensky examines the use of intelligence and information in national security as well as business organizations. He argues that "if anything is clear from this book, it is that intelligence failures are built into complex organizations."[28]

Eliot Cohen and John Gooch have used an organizational lens to analyze military and intelligence failure, noting that "as Pearl Harbor and other cases suggest, it is in the deficiency of organizations that the embryo of misfortune develops."[29] Amy Zegart studied the CIA and found that structural and organizational forces worked to make it "one of the weakest links in our national security."[30] These findings by scholars have been mirrored by the results of numerous intelligence reform commissions and studies, dating back to the early days of the Cold War.[31] For example, Zegart examined twelve major studies of the intelligence community conducted between 1991 and 2001, and found that these groups proposed a total of 340 reforms. She wrote that "the vast majority of these recommendations focused on just a few key organizational deficiencies."[32]

What is it about organizations that contribute to disasters such as Pearl Harbor and other surprise attacks? According to this school, it is not merely that intelligence and national security organizations happen to be organized poorly; the problem lies in deeper, more fundamental problems that afflict organizations and bureaucracies. Some writers such as Hastedt argue that the nature of organizations leads to hierarchies, specialization, and centralization, which limit the sharing of information and can all be sources of intelligence failure.[33] Others such as Zegart focus on the difficulty organizations have in adapting to new information and dealing with new problems.

Most reformists tend to be cautiously optimistic about the prospect that changes to the intelligence community, if implemented, could improve the work of American intelligence. Wilensky, for example, writing early in the era of computers and information processing, argued that new information technologies then being developed would likely help the situation. But he noted that "intelligence failures are rooted in structural problems that cannot be fully solved."[34]

Reformists disagree with the traditionalist view that only rarely acknowledges mistakes on the part of the intelligence community. Eliot Cohen has criticized the traditional view as the "no fault" school of intelligence analysis."[35] The title of an op-ed written by Amy Zegart five years after the 9/11 attacks captures the view of many reformists: "American Intelligence: Still Stupid."[36] Zegart believes that the intelligence community is still disorganized, lacks central direction, and duplicates much of its efforts. And in contrast to the traditionalists who believe the intelligence community has done a particularly good job of strategic intelligence, Zegart argues that American strategic intelligence is bad and getting worse.[37]

Challenging the Conventional Understanding: The Contrarian School

There is a third group of scholars and intelligence professionals whose members disagree with both the traditionalist and reformist schools. This smaller, contrarian group argues that disasters such as Pearl Harbor—and more recently the 9/11 attacks—are most often caused by failures of intelligence *collection* rather than by problems of analysis or organization.

This school of thought does not accept the argument of traditionalists that intelligence analysts are talented professionals who simply, and understandably, can become overwhelmed by contradictory data. The view of these thinkers can be seen in the work of the intelligence historian and journalist David Kahn, who writes flatly about Pearl Harbor that "American intelligence had failed."[38] Kahn does not accept the conventional argument that it would have been highly unlikely for the intelligence community to have done any better before Pearl Harbor. More and better-focused collection efforts could have worked, he argues; the United States might have been able to foresee the attack if it had years before put spies in place, flown regular reconnaissance missions against the Japanese Navy, sailed signals interception ships close to Japan, or recruited a network of naval observers to report on Japanese ship movements.

Another challenger to orthodoxy is Ariel Levite, who disagrees with the traditional view that intelligence failures are natural and inevitable and that efforts to reduce surprise are only marginally useful because the problem lies in analytical and cognitive factors that are resistant to improvement.[39] He believes that the literature on intelligence failure dating back to Wohlstetter is wrong in thinking that surprise occurs despite the existence of sufficient warning by intelligence. He argues that "no credible or conclusive warning . . . was available prior to many historical cases of strategic surprise, arguments to the contrary notwithstanding."[40] But he also believes there is good news to be learned from the history of surprise attacks; in those cases in which sufficient intelligence is available, reliable and effective warnings *can* be given, and they can induce the side being attacked to take appropriate defensive actions.

Contrarians also are found among experts on terrorism, who argue that terrorist attacks have succeeded because terrorism presents a dramatically new and different threat for which the United States' intelligence and national security organizations have not been prepared. Many of these writers focus on mistakes by the CIA, especially for failing to collect sufficient human intelligence on terrorist threats. Brian Jenkins expressed the importance of human intelligence in his testimony before the 9/11 Commission: "Using intelligence to prevent terror-ist attacks is very difficult. There are no troop mobilizations to watch for, no ships, no aircraft to track. Knowing what terrorists might do depends largely on human sources—undercover agents and informants. Penetrating small terrorist groups may take months, years."[41]

Although these analysts tend to focus on the limitations of human intelli-gence, they see that the primary problem leading to attacks such as 9/11 is a failure of intelligence collection. They disagree with the two primary schools of thought, which argue that sufficient indicators of the 9/11 attacks were there but were not understood for reasons that were primarily analytic. Instead, these thinkers argue there was not enough intelligence collected to prevent the plot; as *The Economist* wrote, "there were too few useful dots."[42] Writers in this school are often gloomy about the prospect for change in American intelligence, largely because they do not believe the CIA—the agency primarily responsible for human intelligence—is able or willing to make the changes needed.

FAILING GRADE: HOW THESE SCHOOLS FALL SHORT

These schools of thought offer very different assessments about the nature of intelligence failure, and very different prescriptions for the future. The tradi-tional school provides reassurance for intelligence professionals, because it argues that intelligence failures are largely inevitable, resulting from the natural limitations of human cognition. But this view is pessimistic about the prospects for preventing future surprise attacks. Reformist thinkers, conversely, provide less comfort for the intelligence community, which they argue is often guilty of avoidable mistakes and even incompetence. But their view is reassuring to the public because it suggests that if we can fix the problems that produce in-telligence failure, the American intelligence community will be more likely to connect the dots next time and prevent a future terrorist (or perhaps even con-ventional) attack. The contrarian school, conversely, holds a very different view of the reasons for intelligence failure, but it ultimately offers little hope for sig-nificant improvement.

This book challenges all these perspectives, because most of the work on which they are based suffers from two major limitations. The first limitation is that most studies of surprise attacks (with a few exceptions, e.g., Levite) focus solely on cases in which intelligence fails and attacks succeed. These studies fail to consider negative cases—that is, where intelligence has succeeded in preventing surprise attacks. In the terminology of the social sciences, these studies are guilty of "selecting on the dependent variable," or choosing cases to study based on how those cases turned out. For this reason, although existing studies may help us understand some of the many reasons why intelligence can fail, they do little to tell us how it can succeed.

The second limitation is seen most strongly among the adherents of the reformist school; their studies suffer from hindsight bias, also known as "20/20 hindsight." This problem is a familiar one among intelligence scholars, as well as among social scientists in other fields.[43] It is particularly dangerous in studies of intelligence failures and surprise attack, however, because when combined with the first problem—the tendency to study only cases of intelligence failure—it is very easy to find oneself asking, "How could they ever have missed those clues?" Signals and warnings that might have looked weak amid a sea of other data can look strong and clear when viewed afterward and taken out of the full context of the situation that intelligence analysts and policymakers faced at the time.

Scholars and practitioners of intelligence have attempted to compensate for the hindsight bias when evaluating the performance of intelligence. For example, the *9/11 Commission Report* explicitly addressed this problem, noting that the commissioners were aware of and took into account Wohlstetter's caution that it is "much easier *after* the event to sort the relevant from the irrelevant signals."[44] But despite their best efforts, studies such as the *9/11 Commission Report* cannot overcome the hindsight bias as long as they are focusing only on intelligence failures.

As a result of these limitations in the literature, we have fundamentally misunderstood the reason why intelligence fails to help us prevent surprise attacks, failures, and other disasters. The only way to objectively look at intelligence failures is to compare them with successes. For our purposes, we need to examine cases of unsuccessful attack—or seen another way, cases of *intelligence success*. This is particularly hard to do in the field of intelligence studies, because intelligence successes are less well publicized than failures. Though intelligence agencies are not especially happy to talk about their failures, they are even less willing to disclose information about their successes, because those cases can reveal information such as intelligence sources and methods that may still be in use. In addition, successful cases of warning are little known because of what is called the paradox of warning. As Mary McCarthy writes, "Most successful warnings appear to be false alarms," because the warning gets to policymakers in time for them to take action to deter the threat.[45]

As noted above, a few contrarian scholars have studied intelligence success; Levite, for example, has examined the contrast between the intelligence failure at Pearl Harbor and the success at Midway. But as I will describe later in the chapters on these two cases, Levite's findings were not accepted by most scholars of surprise attack, and many historians and intelligence experts see the two situations as "apples and oranges," too dissimilar to warrant close comparison. Arguments about the importance of collection in preventing intelligence failure have remained in the minority; this book is an attempt to revisit those arguments.

Another problem with the literature on intelligence failure and surprise attack is that most of it dates to the Cold War, and thus it needs to be updated for today's era in which surprise attacks can come not only from a conventional military enemy but also from a terrorist group or a cyberenemy. The next section of this chapter examines this problem.

SURPRISE ATTACK: A PROBLEM LEFT OVER FROM THE COLD WAR?

The study of surprise attack burgeoned in the 1980s, as scholars developed theories to explain not only Pearl Harbor but also disasters such as the American intelligence failures in the Korean War and the Israeli surprise in the 1973 Yom Kippur War.[46] But it might appear now that the problem of surprise attack is something of an anachronism—a concern, surely, in the old days when armies attacked at dawn, but why do we need to worry about surprise attacks today? In fact, many national security and intelligence experts argue that the problem of surprise attack is indeed still with us. The threat could come in the familiar form of a conventional military foe; although no one expects to wake up one morning to find an enemy's military on America's shores, countries such as China, Iran, and North Korea certainly have the capability to surprise.[47] An even more likely type of surprise attack could come in the form of a cyberattack. Former CIA director and secretary of defense Leon Panetta warned that "I've often said that I think the potential for the next Pearl Harbor could very well be a cyberattack."[48]

A number of scholars and analysts have noted similarities between the two most notable examples of surprise attacks against America, Pearl Harbor and 9/11.[49] Despite the differences between conventional and terrorist enemies, many intelligence experts—especially those in the traditional school—tend to emphasize the continuity of the challenge more than the difference. That is, they believe the intelligence community today faces problems that are quite similar to those faced in the past. In the words of Richard Betts: "The difference between the world of 2006 and that of 1999 is no more radical than the difference between the worlds of 1999 and 1992."[50]

However, others argue that the challenges are very different today, and that lessons from conventional attacks such as Pearl Harbor can have little to offer for today's struggle against terrorist surprise attacks. For one thing, the nature of the enemy involved is quite different: In the case of Pearl Harbor it was a state-based, conventional military threat, while the problem of terrorism today is primarily one of nonstate actors. Bruce Berkowitz has argued that the analogy between 9/11 and Pearl Harbor is wrong, "because the September 11 intelligence failure was *really a new problem, reflecting the emergence of a new kind of threat.*"[51]

Another potential problem with this comparison is that when faced with different types of threats, the nature of the intelligence problem is different. Former director of national intelligence Mike McConnell noted that with conventional threats the enemy's capability is fairly well understood, while its *intent* is the question. But with terrorism, "it's just the opposite": The intent to commit harm is clear, and the challenge for intelligence is to learn the enemy's capability to do so.[52] Then–CIA director Michael Hayden pointed out another difference between the problems faced by the intelligence community in the Cold War and today: During the Cold War the enemy's forces, such as armies and ballistic missile silos, were relatively easy to find but hard to kill. Today, conversely, "the situation is reversed. We are now in an age in which our primary adversary is easy to kill but hard to find."[53]

Since long before the 9/11 attacks, the authorities on intelligence and terrorism were describing terrorism as a particularly difficult challenge for the intelligence community. Because terrorist groups are usually small and dispersed, and because they do not need to rely on the large infrastructure of a conventional state-based threat, the intelligence community is limited in its ability to use traditional tools and techniques to gain insight into terrorist intentions and capabilities. Nonetheless, good intelligence has been widely perceived as vital if authorities are to be successful in stopping terrorist attacks. In 1996, for example, Bruce Hoffman wrote that "the importance of intelligence to anticipate, preempt, and respond is paramount."[54] More recently, then–CIA director Michael Hayden said that "in the post-9/11 era, intelligence is more crucial to the security of our nation than ever before."[55]

Although the importance of intelligence in combating terrorism is widely understood, ten years after 9/11 there has still been surprisingly little in-depth, empirical work produced on the intelligence aspects of those attacks. Amy Zegart's *Spying Blind* is the first book-length academic study of that intelligence failure to be published, and as Magnus Ranstorp notes, scholars have yet to make extensive use of the *9/11 Commission Report* as a reference.[56] The time lag may not be very unusual in a historical context; after all, Roberta Wohlstetter's seminal study of Pearl Harbor was not published until twenty-one years after the attack.[57] But the current lag does suggest that the 9/11 attacks themselves remain understudied from a scholarly perspective and, more broadly, that additional work is needed on the use of intelligence in counterterrorism.

The question of whether we are facing truly new challenges today is an important one, because it can help us as we search for solutions to today's threats and challenges. If Richard Betts is right, and the challenges for intelligence and security forces today strongly resemble the challenges of the past, then we should be able to find lessons to apply today by looking backward. But if today's terrorist attacks actually present a stark break from the past, then we would be better off tossing out the old rule book and trying to find new methods and new ways of thinking better suited to the new challenge. The problem is that little work has been done to help answer the questions, does terrorism in fact present a truly new problem for intelligence, or are the difficulties being faced today simply echoes of problems seen by earlier generations of analysts and collectors? And are there lessons from the history of conventional surprise attack that can help us deal with the newer problem of terrorist surprise attack? This book attempts to fill this research gap, and it argues that there are indeed important lessons from history that can help us today.

STRATEGIC SURPRISE AND AVOIDING BLACK SWANS

The focus of this book is relatively limited, on what George and Bennett describe as a specified subclass of a general phenomenon: the subclass *surprise attack*, of the broader problem of intelligence failure.[58] Although surprise attacks may be the most disastrous type of intelligence failure, they are only part of a broader category of failure described as *strategic surprise*. The term "strategic surprise" is frequently used to indicate the most serious types of surprise attack—those that achieve a "strategic" level of surprise, as opposed to a merely tactical or fleeting surprise.[59] Others use the term to suggest a broader category of surprise, such as failures by governments, corporations, militaries, or even individuals to foresee future problems and threats.[60] The study of surprise, in fact, has become something of a cottage industry in recent years, with numerous books and articles being published containing advice for how to avoid what are sometimes called "black swans," "wild cards," or "strategic shocks."[61]

Often the advice of these thinkers resembles that of the scholars and experts on intelligence failure and surprise attack we have already reviewed. Several writers have argued that disasters such as the 9/11 attacks could have been predicted, because sufficient warnings had been available. Peter Schwartz, for example, writes that "the terrorist attack that day was perhaps the most forecast event in history."[62] According to Lee Clarke, "The American intelligence community dropped the ball before September 11."[63] These experts, who often come from an economics or business background, focus on the role of leadership in preventing such surprises. Max Bazerman and Michael Watkins list the many warnings that had been given before 9/11 and argue that the message should have been understood by America's political and national security leadership. They believe such failures are *predictable surprises*, which are caused by cognitive, organizational, and even political limitations, and which can be overcome by courageous leaders who recognize the dangers and take steps to mitigate them.[64]

Although some of these thinkers argue that surprises can be avoided, most of the literature on strategic surprise says—as we saw in the literature on intelligence failure—that surprise is inevitable. Leaders may be able to lessen the impact of that surprise by following the principles of risk management, by using one's imagination, or through keeping an open mind; nonetheless, we are told, some amount of surprise is to be expected. And in response, much of this work advises, we must "expect the unexpected."[65] But for a senior government official, or for members of the public, that advice might ring a little hollow. Though this book focuses on the problem of surprise attack, I hope that my theory of preventive action may serve as a building block toward a broader theory of intelligence success, and help intelligence and security officials improve their understanding of how to deal with the challenge of strategic surprise.

HOW CAN INTELLIGENCE SUCCEED?

The literature on intelligence failure and surprise attack is very useful for understanding the *limitations* of intelligence. In fact, experts have often noted that there are more than enough theories and explanations available to help us understand why intelligence so often fails. As Thomas Copeland puts it, "Overall, intelligence failures may be overdetermined."[66] For this reason, scholars have argued that it may not be very useful to continue studying the problem of intelligence failure.[67]

This book rejects this pessimistic view, and argues that scholars may be at a dead end in studying cases of surprise attack because they choose to study only one kind of case—those in which the attacker succeeds and intelligence fails. This problem exists because it is difficult for scholars to find data on intelligence successes such as surprise attacks that were foreseen or prevented. Copeland observes that there are few examples available of failed surprise attacks: "Conceivably there have been cases of failed surprise, where the attacker learned that its intended victim had discovered its plans, and decided not to attack after all; but it is almost impossible to know how often that may have occurred."[68] Other scholars are aware of this weakness. Eliot Cohen and John Gooch have commented, "It is interesting that few of the students of intelligence failure have also discussed at length the nature of successful intelligence work."[69] They observe that this is partly because if intelligence is good enough to anticipate a surprise attack, the attack will likely be called off, writing that "a study of surprise attacks predicted is usually a study of nonevents."[70]

Despite the difficulty of studying intelligence successes, there are data available for study. In the case of conventional military surprise, for example, the Battle of Midway during World War II is often cited as a dramatic intelligence success. More recent history suggests that foiled *terrorist* surprise attacks are relatively common, although they, too, are an understudied phenomenon. The problem of terrorism, in fact, appears to offer the researcher something that conventional surprise attack does not: a universe of cases large enough to encompass a number of failed attacks. This book takes advantage of this opportunity, and thus it is one of the few studies examining intelligence success in preventing both conventional and terrorist surprise attacks.

What do we mean, however, by "intelligence success?" Just as there is little agreement among intelligence scholars and practitioners over what constitutes an intelligence failure, there is debate over how to measure intelligence success.[71]

For example, if intelligence provides warning but policymakers do not act, is that a success, or a failure? Many intelligence professionals would gladly call that an intelligence success. But this book argues that for intelligence to succeed, it is not enough that the intelligence community saw a threat coming and warned about it. As the cases examined here demonstrate, intelligence counts for little if decision makers are not receptive to the warnings they receive.

There is nothing surprising about this argument, because it is a truism among intelligence professionals that intelligence is of no value unless it is produced for some decision maker—whether a president, a senior military officer, or some other customer.[72] But when it comes to defining a situation as an intelligence success or failure, intelligence professionals disagree over whether factors such as policymakers' receptivity should be considered when evaluating the quality of intelligence. For many, the purpose of intelligence is simply to provide accurate information; intelligence failure or success should be defined by what they do, without taking into account the ultimate use or utility of that intelligence by decision makers. Put another way, many in the intelligence community focus only on their own piece of this problem, and argue that their responsibility ends once they offer advice and analysis to policymakers.[73]

I believe this view is shortsighted. This book argues that intelligence professionals and policymakers alike must define intelligence failure and success broadly, and recognize that the goal is to prevent surprise. This means that success is a two-step process. First, intelligence agencies and officials must correctly assess the situation. This is the result of collection and analysis, and my book highlights the importance of collection over analysis. In the second step, intelligence officials must convey their assessments to decision makers and convince them of the importance of the issue. My study also highlights the importance of this step, which I call the receptivity phase.

The argument can be made that I am setting the bar too high; it may seem unreasonable to hold the intelligence community at fault if leaders do not listen. And at the same time it may appear that I am letting decision makers off too easily, if a failure on their part is defined as an "intelligence" failure.[74] My answer is that we need to take a broader view, and realize that the surprise can be just as great, and the harmful effects just as serious, when a surprise attack is successful, whether or not intelligence professionals "called it right."

Intelligence success, then, is the reverse of the definition of intelligence failure provided earlier in this chapter, and requires both that the intelligence community provide the information and analysis required, and that decision makers act on this intelligence appropriately. This definition helps us understand why intelligence success is more difficult to accomplish than failure. A failure can result from a breakdown at either stage of the process, whereas a success requires that both steps must be satisfied.

This analysis may seem pessimistic, and it could appear to bring us back to the argument of the traditional school of intelligence scholarship that sees intelligence failures as inevitable. There is good news, however, because the literature on what is called "actionable intelligence" suggests how intelligence success is possible.

THE ARGUMENT OF THE BOOK: INTELLIGENCE AND PREVENTIVE ACTION

In the field of intelligence, one of the hottest buzzwords today is "actionable intelligence." Military commanders and political leaders say they want it, and intelligence agencies claim they can provide it. After the Christmas Day 2009 airline bombing attempt, for example, US government officials announced that the FBI had "gleaned useable, actionable intelligence" after arresting and interrogating the suspect.[75]

Although actionable intelligence appears to be something that everybody wants, there is little consensus on just what it is or how to get it. The term is used often by intelligence professionals and others to simply describe intelligence that is useful and desirable for decision makers. But while definitions of the term tend to be rather general, they often include two key factors. The first factor is *precision*: a common theme in many discussions of actionable intelligence is that in order for intelligence to be useful, it must be specific.[76] But precision and specificity alone are not necessarily helpful, and can be counterproductive. An example of such unhelpful precision is often told about Operation Desert Storm, during which General Norman Schwarzkopf received a report that a certain bridge had been 52 percent destroyed. That level of precision was not useful to the general, who merely wanted to know whether the bridge could be used.[77]

The second factor is that in order for intelligence to be actionable, it must be linked to the immediate and specific needs of the decision maker. This factor is not surprising, because most experts believe that in order for intelligence to be worthwhile, it must have some value to action and policy. A deputy director of the CIA, for example, once defined intelligence as "knowledge and analysis designed to assist action."[78] Similarly, in the words of the British intelligence expert R. V. Jones, "The ultimate object of Intelligence is to enable action to be optimized."[79] But scholars of intelligence have argued that the link between intelligence and decision makers is especially important in the case of actionable intelligence designed to prevent surprise attacks. James Wirtz, for example, describes actionable intelligence as "information of immediate and direct use to policymakers."[80]

In order to build on these two key factors and develop a more general understanding of what makes intelligence actionable and useful in preventing attacks, we need to first better define what we mean by these two factors, and how we would recognize them if we saw them. This book defines the first factor of precision to mean intelligence that provides specific warnings in terms of targets being threatened or attacks being planned.[81] This type of precise intelligence is sometimes considered to be "tactical," as opposed to "strategic," and it is important to understand how these terms are used by intelligence professionals and scholars. Military planners and intelligence officers typically make a three-level distinction among strategic, operational, and tactical levels.[82] But warnings about possible surprise attacks usually occur at either the strategic or tactical level, and the two terms are usually defined this way:

> ➤ *Strategic intelligence* tends to be longer-term, broader in focus, and of interest to senior-level policymakers who make decisions concerning the most important national and international issues.
> ➤ *Tactical intelligence* is shorter-term, more narrowly focused (often on specific events), and most likely to be used by junior-level officials engaged in planning or directing individual operations.

As a general rule, *strategic* intelligence warning is the kind most highly sought after by policymakers, and it is what most intelligence officials would like to provide. Conversely, many experts dismiss tactical intelligence as not useful in preventing surprise attacks or dealing with the most important, strategic-level threats.[83] In the words of Melvin Goodman, "Far too much attention is given to current and tactical intelligence and insufficient attention to the big-picture needs of strategic intelligence."[84] Paul Pillar has argued that because terrorist plots typically involve small numbers of people operating in secrecy, "Good, plot-specific intelligence on terrorism will always be rare," and the intelligence community should instead focus on strategic intelligence, which he describes as involving the broad assessment of threats.[85]

This book argues, however, that the American intelligence and national security communities face what might be called the *paradox of strategic warning*.[86] As we will see in the case studies examined here, strategic-level intelligence and warnings are surprisingly easy to acquire and are often readily available before major attacks. But they are unlikely to be acted upon by decision makers, and in any case are too general to be useful in preventing attacks. Tactical-level intelligence is much harder to acquire, but when available it is much more likely to be useful and actionable. This is largely because surprise attacks, even when they have strategic-level consequences, are essentially tactical events, involving relatively few decision makers and occurring in a relatively confined space and time.

Figure 1.1 provides examples of the different types of warnings that may be available before a surprise attack, and whether they would be considered strategic or tactical. As the figure makes clear, the critical difference is that tactical-level warning as defined in this book means specific, precise intelligence on particular threats.

The second factor, the utility of intelligence for decision makers, is a challenging one to define, measure, and analyze. After the fact—after an attack is prevented, for example—it may be easy to point to a particular warning and

Figure 1.1 Strategic versus Tactical Intelligence

	Strategic intelligence	Tactical intelligence
Examples of conventional surprise attack	Warning that war is approaching	Location of enemy forces in position for attack
	General indications of hostile intent	Interception of attack plans
Examples of terrorist surprise attack	Unspecific threats made by terrorist group	Specific details of a plot being planned
	"Chatter" of increasing terrorist activity	Identification of individual or facility being targeted

recognize that it was useful. But what factors or conditions can we identify that help us measure the utility of intelligence for policymakers, without simply waiting to see how it all turns out?

There is unfortunately no single formula for determining what leaders want from intelligence, or for ensuring that they will listen to the warnings they receive. Stephen Marrin writes that "policymaker satisfaction with intelligence analysis is a notoriously fickle and idiosyncratic metric."[87] The most important predictor of the utility of intelligence may be the degree to which a policymaker is *receptive* toward the warning he or she receives. Does the decision maker pay attention to the intelligence? Even if the intelligence is not acted upon, is it considered? Does the decision maker ask questions or show other signs of interest in the information? I argue that intelligence is most useful when policymakers are receptive to it, and *policymaker receptivity* is the second factor necessary for actionable intelligence. But receptivity is more than simply a willingness to listen to intelligence. Receptivity exists when, through a combination of *belief in the threat* and *trust in intelligence*, a decision maker is willing to act on the basis of the intelligence they are provided.

With these definitions and variables understood, this book proposes a preliminary *theory of preventive action*: In order for intelligence to be actionable and usable in preventing surprise attacks, it must provide precise, tactical-level warning, and it must be combined with a high level of receptivity toward that warning on the part of policymakers who will decide how and whether to use it.[88] To put it another way: If intelligence authorities are able to develop specific, tactical-level intelligence, and if policymakers believe the threat and trust the intelligence, then surprise attacks are more likely to be disrupted. But if these two conditions do not exist, then it is highly unlikely that a well-planned major surprise attack will be disrupted.

Support for the importance of these two variables—precise intelligence and receptive policymakers—can be found in the literature on the relationship between intelligence and policy. This work indicates that policymakers prefer to make decisions based on facts rather than analysis, and on the basis of certainty rather than ambiguity—and yet intelligence warnings are usually analytical and ambiguous.[89] The more hypothetical and theoretical the analysis, the less policymakers are inclined to act on it. In particular it appears that policymakers are inclined to discount intelligence products that offer what appear to be predictions and opinions from intelligence analysts.[90] Thus it is little wonder that general, strategic-level warnings of potential surprise attacks—if not backed up with specific data on targets and timing—are unlikely to generate aggressive action on the part of government officials.

The literature on intelligence–policy relations also suggests that a closer relationship between intelligence officials and policymakers can help improve the quality of assessments and analysis and make it more likely that intelligence will be listened to.[91] But most of this work appears to take policymaker receptivity for granted: It is assumed that if sufficiently good intelligence is available (presumably at the strategic level), officials will naturally take the appropriate actions based upon it. The cases examined in this book, however, demonstrate that this does not always happen. Even when precise intelligence is plentiful, such as during the months leading up to the Battle of Midway, and when decision makers are supporters of intelligence, it may take a great deal of effort on the part of intelligence staffs to convince leaders to pay attention. There has been little empirical work in this area, and this book is one of the first comparative studies to examine the impact of the intelligence–policy relationship on intelligence success or failure.

This understanding of the decision-making preferences of senior government decision makers suggests that brilliant analysis, bold imagination, and creative efforts to connect the dots of disparate intelligence information are not enough to prevent surprise attacks. If the analysis is not accompanied by specifics, and if the decision maker does not trust the analysis of the intelligence staff, warnings are likely to be disbelieved or discounted.[92] This argument may sound like a tautology—how could good tactical intelligence and policymaker willingness to listen *not* result in foiled attacks? But the theory of preventive action actually runs counter to many scholarly and professional assumptions about intelligence, and this book tells us much more about policymaker receptivity than we knew before, for instance that a big-picture, strategic-level warning—which is usually believed to be the most important kind of warning—is unlikely to convince leaders to listen.

DEVELOPING THE ARGUMENT

To develop this argument, this book looks separately at two types of surprise attack—conventional and terrorist—and for each type it takes two different approaches. The first approach is to use the tools of process tracing and structured, focused comparison to conduct an in-depth case study comparing cases of success and failure.[93] For each case we will consider whether the information that had been available was primarily strategic or tactical, and whether decision makers were receptive to the warnings they received. Then, because these case studies represent a relatively small sample of the surprise attacks potentially available for study, the second approach is to conduct a broader examination of a larger set of "mini-cases" of surprise attack.

If the conventional wisdom is correct—that there is always sufficient intelligence warning of surprise attacks, and failures occur when those warnings are not understood or heeded—then we would expect to find that the intelligence picture differs little between cases of success and failure. We should find that intelligence warnings are no more numerous or evident in cases of success—in which surprise attacks are foiled, for example—than in those of failure. Instead, in cases of success we should expect to find that the available warnings were analyzed and understood by intelligence and policy officials with the ability and imagination to connect the dots. The critical factor should not be the type or number of warnings, but how those warnings were processed or analyzed.

On the other hand, if the theory of preventive action is correct, then we should find that the intelligence warnings available in the cases of intelligence success is more specific, and that decision makers were more receptive to those warnings. The critical factor would not be the presence or absence of brilliant analysts, or the organization of intelligence agencies, but rather the availability of precise intelligence and receptive policymakers.

Figure 1.2 illustrates the relationship between these factors, and the results that would be predicted by the theory of preventive action, in a simple 2-by-2 table. Cases involving low policymaker receptivity and the presence of strategic (but not specific or tactical) warning, in the upper-left-hand quadrant, would most likely result in a successful attack and an intelligence failure. The combination of high receptivity and specific warning, in the lower-right-hand quadrant,

Figure 1.2   Theory of Preventive Action: Predicted Relationship among Variables

	Low policymaker receptivity	High policymaker receptivity
Strategic warning	*(Attack most likely to succeed)*	
Specific warning		*(Attack most likely to be prevented)*

would be most likely to result in an attack being prevented. We will revisit this table in the conclusion, where I will use it to show that the cases examined in this book suggest both factors—precise, tactical intelligence, and strong policymaker receptivity toward intelligence—are necessary for the prevention of a surprise attack, and neither, on its own, is sufficient.

PART I

THE PROBLEM OF CONVENTIONAL SURPRISE ATTACK

CHAPTER 2

PEARL HARBOR

Challenging the Conventional Wisdom

T HIS CHAPTER EXAMINES what has been considered—at least until the September 11, 2001, terrorist attacks—to be the greatest intelligence failure in American history: the Japanese attack on Pearl Harbor. It challenges the conventional wisdom about this failure, and by extension it also challenges one of the most widely accepted understandings in the intelligence studies literature: that in cases of failure, sufficient intelligence is virtually always present, and the primary failure lies in improper analysis of that intelligence.[1]

Pearl Harbor remains important today not only because of its historical significance but also because it has been widely seen as exemplifying a type of intelligence failure that still remains with us. For example, many intelligence professionals and scholars argued after the September 11, 2001, terrorist attacks that the two situations were eerily similar: Despite years of warnings of a growing threat, in both 2001 and 1941 the world's most capable intelligence community failed to properly understand the danger and prevent a surprise attack that many saw coming.

The case of Pearl Harbor, especially since Roberta Wohlstetter published her classic book *Pearl Harbor: Warning and Decision* in 1962, has been the paradigmatic example that helped to establish the conventional wisdom about how such intelligence failures can happen.[2] That conventional view typically sees intelligence failure as occurring when important warning signals are available but are lost amid a background of extraneous noise. But as Jack Levy has noted, this was not always believed to be the case: "Prior to the 1960s, it was widely believed that the primary source of strategic surprise was insufficient information. Had the United States possessed ample information, it would have anticipated (and possibly avoided) the Japanese attack on Pearl Harbor. That hypothesis was seriously weakened by Wohlstetter's (1962) single case study of the American intelligence failure at Pearl Harbor. She demonstrated that the United States had ample

29

information of the impending attack but that the information was lost in a noisy international environment and blocked by parochial bureaucratic interests."[3]

This chapter argues, however, that the conventional wisdom about the role of intelligence in that disaster, first established by Wohlstetter, is mistaken. The surprise attack on Pearl Harbor did not succeed despite the existence of sufficient warning; instead, the failure occurred because the two key factors needed for preventive action were lacking: a precise, tactical-level warning, and decision makers who were receptive to that warning.

The rest of this chapter proceeds as follows. Because the case of Pearl Harbor is so well known, the chapter does not provide background or details of the attack itself. Instead, it begins with a review of the conventional explanations that have been put forward for why America was so thoroughly surprised on December 7, 1941, despite the abundance of warnings of approaching hostilities in the Pacific. Next is an overview of the types of intelligence information that had been available to American decision makers leading up to the attack, followed by a detailed examination of the various strategic and tactical indications and warnings that had been received before the attack. The subsequent section reviews how receptive American decision makers were toward that intelligence, first at the strategic level, and then the tactical and operational level. The chapter concludes by discussing the lessons that this analysis offers.

EXPLANATIONS FOR FAILURE

What went wrong at Pearl Harbor? More than half a century after the event, and nearly fifty years since Roberta Wohlstetter published what remains the primary academic study of the failure, it is remarkable on how little historians, intelligence experts, and others can actually agree concerning the reasons behind the disaster. Even among mainstream scholars, who generally reject the most extreme revisionist and conspiracy-minded theories, no single overall explanation has been completely accepted. Although many experts believe a failure of intelligence was to blame, they disagree on whether the roots of that failure were organizational, psychological, or analytical. Others argue that the real problem lay not with the intelligence community but with the military commanders who were unprepared for the Japanese attack; or with the American policymakers who pushed the nation to war; or with the Japanese enemy who devised a brilliant plan of deception and surprise.

No fewer than eight official boards and commissions investigated Pearl Harbor in the five years following the attack, culminating in the Joint Congressional Committee that conducted the most comprehensive study in 1946.[4] That committee's thirty-nine-volume report included the texts of the previous investigations,[5] and it determined that the disaster resulted from "supervisory, administrative, and organizational deficiencies which existed in our Military and Naval establishments in the days before Pearl Harbor."[6]

The underlying assumption that runs through the Joint Committee's report is that there had been sufficient intelligence and warning of impending Japanese hostilities, but those in charge—principally the military commanders in Hawaii—failed to take the proper actions. The committee's strongest language came in finding that errors by Admiral Husband E. Kimmel and Lieutenant General Walter C. Short, the senior navy and army officers in Hawaii, had contributed significantly to the disaster: "They failed to defend the fortress they commanded."[7] Its list of recommended reforms, conversely, is not so sharply worded, and reminds the reader of the recommendations made in the *9/11 Commission Report*. It begins with an organizational change—a call for greater centralization of authority of American intelligence—but is mostly filled with rather commonplace advice such as warnings against complacency and procrastination, and encouragement for the greater use of imagination.

The Joint Committee's recommendations for greater intelligence community centralization served as the impetus for the formation of the Central Intelligence Agency as part of the National Security Act of 1947.[8] But it was not until Roberta Wohlstetter published her book in 1962 that an overarching theoretical understanding of the failure at Pearl Harbor became accepted widely enough to be considered conventional wisdom. Her study, based largely on the Joint Committee's report, found that the problem was not that the military commanders were incompetent or that there had been a lack of intelligence. Instead, Wohlstetter wrote that if anything, American intelligence collection had been *too* good: "Never before have we had so complete an intelligence picture of the enemy."[9] The problem was rather in the *analysis* of that intelligence.

Wohlstetter argued that many vital signals had been available that could have alerted the American forces to danger. Some of these signals were known to the military commanders in Hawaii, such as changes to Japanese radio call signs and war warnings sent from Washington by army and navy leaders.[10] Leaders in Washington had even more information at their disposal, including intelligence gained from the breaking of Japanese diplomatic codes that was not always shared with Hawaii. Policymakers in Washington also had the advantage of their inside knowledge of American policies and planning concerning Japan, and Wohlstetter noted that such information was itself an important part of the signals picture.[11] Although these signals did not provide specific warning of the Japanese plan to attack Pearl Harbor, Wohlstetter argued that they should have been enough to alert officials to the danger and to cause them to take precautions against an attack. But the significance of these signals was lost amid the far larger quantity of noise—of contradictory and otherwise confusing intelligence that indicated, for example, that Japan was preparing to attack toward the South China Sea: "In short, we failed to anticipate Pearl Harbor not for want of the relevant materials, but because of a plethora of irrelevant ones."[12]

Wohlstetter's book served to solidify what I have called the traditional view of intelligence failure as the predominant set of explanations for Pearl Harbor among scholars and intelligence experts who have studied the disaster.[13] But not all writers have accepted the Wohlstetter view.

Much of the vast literature that continues to be published about Pearl Harbor focuses on the question of who was to blame, and argues either to indict or to clear someone or some group from guilt. Most prominent here are the revisionists, many of whom make an argument that has not been accepted by most mainstream scholars: that American leaders knew about the imminent attack but let it happen in order to bring America into the war.[14] Another group makes the less sensational argument that sufficient intelligence on the Japanese threat was available in Washington, but through neglect and incompetence it was not forwarded to Hawaii. These authors, including Edwin Layton and Edward Beach, write in part with the goal of clearing the reputations of Kimmel and Short.[15] A final argument in this category holds that America's prewar leaders—FDR in particular—are responsible for having neglected intelligence and thus becoming blind to the growing Japanese threat.[16]

Most scholarly critics of the Wohlstetter thesis, however, avoid blaming individuals. Eliot Cohen and John Gooch do find that the primary problem was a failure on the part of the operational commanders to take reasonable defensive precautions that would have mitigated the effect of the attack; it was "an operational failure, not solely or even primarily an intelligence failure."[17] But they do not assign guilt to any specific individuals involved, finding rather that the roots of the operational failure can be found in organizational problems—especially a lack of coordination between the army and navy in Hawaii.

Irving Janis argues that even when one takes into account the ambiguous nature of the intelligence available before December 7, 1941, it is puzzling why the American military commanders failed to consider at least the *possibility* of Japanese attack: "After all, military leaders are supposed to be constantly vigilant and to have contingency plans ready in order to cope with low probability events."[18] He finds that the concept of "groupthink," in which a small group of officials in Hawaii developed a set of firmly shared beliefs, helps to account for the lack of vigilance among the navy commanders at Pearl Harbor.

Although these various explanations differ on the reasons for failure, most agree that someone failed to understand or make proper use of the intelligence that was available. Intelligence *collection* before Pearl Harbor, by most accounts, was a relative success. But David Kahn disagrees, arguing that Wohlstetter was wrong—the failure was not one of analysis but of collection, for there were not enough data for anyone to conclude that the Japanese were going to attack Pearl Harbor: "Sufficient indications of an attack simply did not exist within the mass of American intelligence data. Not one intercept, not one datum of intelligence ever said anything about an attack on Pearl Harbor or on any other possession."[19] This argument has also been made by Ariel Levite, who writes that

Wohlstetter—and just about everyone who has studied Pearl Harbor since her work—is mistaken in believing that the United States had sufficient warning of an attack.[20]

Several other scholars have made an argument related to that of Kahn and Levite, that the key to the failure at Pearl Harbor was skill and deception on the part of the Japanese. Alex Robert Hybel has made this point: "The United States failed to avert surprise because Japan chose a strategy of surprise that was successful in exploiting the image the American leaders had of Japan's capabilities, behavioral style, and approach to calculating political action."[21]

These contrarian views have not made much impact on the conventional wisdom, and Levite's book received largely negative reviews from other scholars of surprise attack.[22] The most widely accepted explanation for the American failure to anticipate Pearl Harbor continues to be that first described by Wohlstetter: The intelligence was available, but it was not understood or believed. This is the conclusion of Gordon Prange, the author of *At Dawn We Slept*, perhaps the most careful and even-handed study of Pearl Harbor since Wohlstetter. He argues that in 1941 the future course of Japanese action had been made clear to American leaders from sensitive codebreaking intelligence, known as Magic: "Make no mistake about it, Japan was going to war, and those with access to Magic knew it."[23] But having the intelligence was not the same thing as believing it. The root cause of the failure at Pearl Harbor, according to Prange, lies in "the stark disbelief that such an attack was possible."[24]

A PRIMER ON SOURCES OF INTELLIGENCE BEFORE PEARL HARBOR

Before we examine the specific pieces of information that were available to American intelligence agencies and decision makers before Pearl Harbor, it is useful to briefly review where this information came from. What were the principal sources and types of intelligence available on the Japanese threat in 1941?[25]

The most important source of tactical- and operational-level intelligence—intelligence of use to military commanders, focusing on the locations and actions of Japanese forces—was derived from the interception of Japanese communications (known as communications intelligence, or COMINT). Most famously, this included codebreaking, or what is more technically known as cryptanalysis or cryptology.[26] The most secret Japanese code was used primarily for Japanese diplomatic dispatches, and was known by the Americans as Purple. In what David Kahn has called "the greatest feat of cryptanalysis the world had yet known," US Army codebreakers led by William F. Friedman had cracked the code by actually constructing a copy of the machine used by the Japanese to encipher their messages—known as the Purple machine.[27]

Before the outbreak of war, US Navy communications intelligence processing for the Pacific was conducted in three main centers. Central coordination as well as a share of the actual processing work was done from Washington, in the navy staff office known as OP-20-G, which was also referred to as Station Negat. The Pacific Fleet's communications intelligence unit was at Pearl Harbor, and was commanded by Lieutenant Commander Joseph Rochefort. It was code-named Station Hypo, although it was later renamed the Fleet Radio Unit Pacific, or Frupac. And a third center at Corregidor in the Philippines, primarily supporting the small Asiatic Fleet, was known as Cast.[28] Each office was responsible for supporting different sets of operational commanders, and they did not all work on the same Japanese code systems; but cryptanalysts at different centers who were working on the same codes were able to coordinate their efforts and share their results with each other. The American codebreakers also coordinated with the British codebreaking office in Singapore, the Far East Combined Bureau.[29]

The intelligence derived from the Purple code was known as Magic, and was one of the most closely guarded secrets of the time; in January 1941 the army and navy intelligence chiefs drew up a list of those cleared to see Magic, and only ten men were on it, including the president; the secretaries of state, war, and the navy; the army chief of staff; and the chief of naval operations.[30] The army and navy commanders in Hawaii were not on the list, although Washington did send them the intelligence they were believed to require, without identifying it as coming from codebreaking and usually attributing it to "highly reliable sources."[31]

Magic intercepts, however, revealed only what Japanese diplomats were being told by Tokyo, and this included little about actual military and strategic planning. For that, US intelligence attempted to break the Japanese military codes, but here they had less success than with the diplomatic Purple code. Hypo in Hawaii focused on the Japanese Navy's "flag officers' system," which Kahn has described as "the Japanese Navy's most difficult and the one in which it encased its most secret information."[32] This code had provided most of the US Navy's information on the Japanese fleet from 1926 until late 1940, but in early December 1940 a new version had been introduced that proved difficult to break.[33]

The other major Japanese Navy system was called JN-25 by US intelligence. OP-20-G in Washington and Cast in the Philippines worked on it, as did the British Far East Combined Bureau. This code had come into use in 1939, and the cryptanalysts at OP-20-G were beginning to make progress in late 1940. But then, on December 1, 1940, the first JN-25 version was superseded by a new version, dubbed JN-25B, and from that point on little progress was made before the attack on Pearl Harbor.[34]

Although codebreaking has received the bulk of attention in accounts of intelligence before Pearl Harbor, most of the US Navy's day-to-day communications intelligence effort was actually devoted to two other endeavors: direction-finding and traffic analysis. *Direction-finding* is a method used to locate radio transmitters; two or more receivers take bearings on the same radio signal, and the point at which their lines of direction cross marks the position of the transmitter. Because ship call signs are often transmitted in the clear, or can otherwise easily be determined, "DF'ng" was a very useful way to keep track of the location of Japanese ships. In 1941 the navy used a string of direction-finding stations throughout the Pacific and East Asia to keep track of Japanese naval and merchant shipping. The second technique is *traffic analysis*; by analyzing the "external" features of a message such as the call signs of the sender and receiver to determine who is talking to whom, and by studying how much radio traffic is being transmitted, a trained operator can develop a fairly good picture of naval and military operations.[35]

Other intelligence on the Japanese fleet was gained from reports gathered from coastal observers in Asia, naval attachés, and captains of merchant fleets.[36] In Hawaii, both the FBI and military intelligence spied on the Japanese consulate. Once war had begun, additional sources of intelligence would be gathered from the interrogation of prisoners of war and from captured documents. And American leaders also could benefit from press reporting about Japanese political and diplomatic affairs.[37] But none of these sources proved useful in anticipating the Japanese attack on Pearl Harbor.[38]

STRATEGIC-LEVEL INTELLIGENCE AND WARNING

Historians and other scholars of the Pearl Harbor tragedy have pointed to a number of key pieces of intelligence and warning that were available before the attack, arguing that the commanders at the time should have recognized the seriousness of these warnings and taken better precautions to prevent a Japanese surprise attack. Many of these pieces of intelligence can be categorized as strategic warning, often derived from high-level communications systems that were processed and analyzed mostly in Washington. This section of the chapter divides these warnings into three types: assessments resulting from military planning and exercises, some of which were extraordinarily accurate; specific reports from strategic-level intelligence sources; and general assessments produced by key intelligence organizations and individuals.

Military Plans and Exercises

Beginning at least as early as 1936, war games and military exercises in Hawaii had been planned on the basis of war with Japan (which was referred to as "Orange"). In many scenarios the conflict began with a Japanese surprise attack on Pearl Harbor, and three documents written by senior military officers during these years read today as eerily prescient.[39] Although these reports were not intelligence products, they were likely inspired by intelligence estimates of the situation, and they have been frequently cited as crucial warnings missed in the period before the attack.

The first report was the Bloch memo, prepared by Rear Admiral Claude Bloch, commandant of the Fourteenth Naval District, which included Hawaii. On December 30, 1940, Bloch sent a memo to the chief of naval operations in Washington, via Admiral James Richardson, who preceded Kimmel as commander of the US Fleet in Hawaii, on the subject of the security of the fleet. Bloch wrote, "Aircraft attacking the base at Pearl Harbor will undoubtedly be brought by carriers."[40] This memo received Admiral Richardson's endorsement, and inspired Rear Admiral Turner, the navy's war plans chief in Washington, to prepare a letter for Navy Secretary Knox's signature that Prange describes as "one of the most historic Knox ever signed." That letter—sent to Hawaii in January 1941 after Kimmel had taken command—warned that "if war eventuates with Japan, it is believed easily possible that hostilities would be initiated by a surprise attack upon the Fleet or the Naval Base at Pearl Harbor."[41]

The second document, which has become known as the Martin-Bellinger Report, was a study by the army and navy air chiefs in Hawaii on military planning in the event of an attack. This report, dated March 31, 1941, stated that an Orange (meaning Japanese) attack force could arrive without warning from intelligence, and that "it appears that the most likely and dangerous form of attack on Oahu would be an air attack. It is believed that at present such an attack would most likely be launched from one or more carriers which would probably approach inside of three hundred miles."[42]

A third report, "Study of the Air Situation in Hawaii," was signed by Major General Martin, head of the Hawaiian Army Air Corps, but Prange writes that it was largely the work of Colonel William E. Farthing, commander of the Fifth Bombardment Group at Hickam. Prange refers to this as the Farthing Report, and it was even more accurate in its forecast, stating that "our most likely enemy, Orange," could probably employ a maximum of six carriers against Oahu, and an early morning attack was the best plan for the enemy. The report argued against complacency: "It has been said, and it is a popular belief, that Hawaii is the strongest outlying naval base in the world and could, therefore, withstand indefinitely attacks and attempted invasions. Plans based on such convictions are inherently weak and tend to create a false sense of security with the consequent unpreparedness for offensive action."[43]

Strategic Intelligence Indicators

Japanese call sign changes. On November 1 and again on December 1, 1941, the Japanese changed their 20,000 radio call signs, making it much harder for the US intelligence specialists to read their message traffic. Rochefort said that two changes in such rapid succession had never happened before, and they made identification of Japanese ships very difficult.[44] The change was also seen as an indicator of preparations for hostile activity; the Fourteenth Naval District daily intelligence summary for December 1 reported that "the fact that service calls lasted only one month indicates an additional progressive step in preparing for active operations on a large scale."[45]

Loss of contact on carriers. Partly because of the call sign changes, and partly because the Japanese fleet kept radio silence while other elements of the Japanese Navy transmitted deceptive radio traffic, American analysts lost track of the Japanese aircraft carriers in mid-November, and disagreed on where they were likely to be located.[46] Some believed they were all still near Japan, while others thought one division was near the Marshalls.[47] The Fourteenth Naval District summary for December 2, 1941, reported, "Almost a complete blank of information on the Carriers today."[48]

The "winds" messages. In November 1941 Tokyo sent dispatches to its Washington embassy establishing a code to be used on the daily Japanese language short wave news broadcast if Japan's diplomatic relations were becoming dangerous. The coded signals would be inserted at the end of the daily weather forecast, and the specific wording to indicate that Japan–United States relations were in a state of emergency was "east wind rain." American cryptanalysts translated the dispatches establishing this code, and on November 28 naval communications in Washington directed Hawaii to monitor all Japanese shortwave broadcasts 24 hours a day for the coded signal (which became known as a "winds execute" message).[49]

There has been a continuing controversy over whether the Japanese ever sent such an "execute" message. Captain Laurence F. Safford, head of the Navy Department's Communications Security Unit in Washington, later testified that he had seen a winds execute message, but no other key personnel remembered seeing one.[50] Rochefort testified that his unit had never intercepted such a message, and Prange believed it unlikely that one was ever sent. Even if it had been sent, it would not have been a warning of an attack on Pearl Harbor; but as Wohlstetter notes, the mere fact that the Japanese had set up such a system of coded messages was a warning that they thought a breakdown in diplomatic relations was possible.[51]

Deadline messages. Another set of warnings that were later described as missed signals of war were six messages sent by Tokyo to its embassy in Washington in November 1941. These reports, intercepted and translated through Magic, warned Japanese diplomats that a deadline had been set of November 25 (later extended to November 29) for the conclusion of negotiations with the United States. Tokyo reported ominously that after this deadline, "things are automatically going to happen."[52]

Japanese code burning. On December 1 and 2, Tokyo ordered a number of its diplomatic posts in Asia and those in Washington and London to destroy most of their codes and code machines. Information about these messages was sent to Hawaii on December 3. Intelligence officials in Hawaii also learned on December 6 from the FBI that the local Japanese consulate had been burning papers for the last two days.[53]

Last-minute Japanese signals. Just before the attack on Pearl Harbor, the Japanese government sent four last-minute cables to its embassy in Washington, and these have been considered crucial missed warning signals. The first, known as the "pilot message," was sent on December 6 alerting the embassy that Tokyo would be sending a reply to the latest American proposal in fourteen parts. This pilot message was intercepted by the navy early in the morning of December 6. The first of the fourteen parts of the actual message began coming in to the navy intercept station on Bainbridge Island near Seattle that same morning, and the various parts were forwarded to Washington by teletype as they came in, mostly in order, throughout the morning and into the afternoon. Part fourteen did not come in to Bainbridge until 3:00 a.m. Washington time on December 7. Then came what has later been dubbed the "one o'clock message," telling the Japanese ambassador to submit the reply to the US government at 1:00 p.m. Washington time on December 7. This was intercepted at 4:30 a.m., Washington time, at Bainbridge, and it was followed by the last message of the series—a message ordering the Japanese embassy to destroy its code machines and secret documents after deciphering the incoming messages.[54]

Strategic-Level Intelligence Assessments

Senior army and navy intelligence officials in Washington, who had the benefit of all the available reporting, saw clearly that war was coming in the Pacific—but they did not expect it would come against the United States. They expected Japan to attack either to the south, such as against Thailand, or to the north against Russia. As an example of such assessments, on November 2, 1941, the army's Military Intelligence Division (MID) stated that Japan wished to avoid military conflict with the American, British, and Dutch powers, and that although it might make military moves, it would not "at present" attack US territories such as the Philippines.[55] On November 27, the MID issued a more alarming report that Japan had "completed plans for further aggressive moves in Southeastern Area," but still there was no hint of aggression against Hawaii.[56] Then on December 5, the MID issued a prophetic report that described Japan as being pushed toward war as a result of economic crisis—although it mistakenly stated that Japan would most likely move first to occupy Thailand.[57]

Navy intelligence reached largely the same conclusions as the army: War was coming, but it would likely begin with a Japanese attack to the south toward Thailand. On December 1, the Office of Naval Intelligence reported, "Deployment of naval forces to the southward has indicated clearly that extensive preparations are underway for hostilities."[58] Also on that date Commander Arthur

McCollum, the chief of the Office of Naval Intelligence's Far Eastern Section, sent a memo to the director of naval intelligence assessing that Japanese army, navy, and diplomatic activity over the previous two months indicated the "principal preparatory effort" by the Japanese was directed toward control or occupation of Thailand, followed almost immediately by an attack against British possessions, possibly in Burma and Singapore.[59] McCollum felt so strongly about the growing threat that he met with the chief of naval operations, Admiral Stark, and others in Stark's office on December 1 and warned that in his opinion either war or a rupture of diplomatic relations was imminent. He asked whether the fleets had been alerted, and he even prepared a warning dispatch of his own, but it was not sent—evidently because his superiors felt that the warnings that had been sent in previous days were sufficient.[60]

TACTICAL-LEVEL INTELLIGENCE AND WARNING

Although most of the intelligence and warning available before the attack on Pearl Harbor was of a long-range, strategic nature, there were also a number of more specific, tactical warnings of the potential for hostile action on the part of the Japanese Navy against Pearl Harbor. This section reviews first the specific tactical-level intelligence indicators, and then the assessments that intelligence officials in Hawaii drew from those indicators.

Specific Indicators of a Threat to Pearl Harbor

Ambassador Grew's extraordinary report. One of the most intriguing reports of the Pearl Harbor story is the telegram sent by Joseph Grew, the American ambassador in Tokyo, on January 27, 1941. He reported that the Peruvian minister to Japan had heard a report that seemed "fantastic": that should trouble break out between Japan and the United States, the Japanese intended to make a surprise attack on Pearl Harbor "using all of their military equipment."[61] Grew himself discounted this report at the time, and the consensus of historians who have studied it is that though it turned out to be prescient, it had no basic in fact. The source of the rumor has never been confirmed.[62] If the rumor was just someone's lucky guess, it was an extraordinarily timely one, as the rumor originated at nearly the same time that Admiral Yamamoto was finishing up his original plan for the Pearl Harbor attack.[63] Richard Betts has described it as "a curious example of a 'perfect' warning that was really unjustified."[64]

"The Bomb Plot message." On September 14, 1941, the Japanese Foreign Ministry sent a message to its Honolulu consulate asking for detailed reporting on the ships at Pearl Harbor. The message was translated by US Army intelligence on October 9, and delivered to the Office of Naval Intelligence with a mark indicating it was of interest.[65] A later message, on November 15, directed that

these reports were to be made twice a week, and were to divide the waters of Pearl Harbor into five smaller areas and report on warships and carriers at anchor.[66] Washington intelligence agencies did not inform the military commanders in Hawaii about this November 15 message. After the Pearl Harbor attack it became known as the "bomb plot" message, and was cited by the congressional investigations as an important missed warning.[67]

The USS Ward *contact.* At about 4:55 a.m. on December 7, the USS *Ward*, a destroyer patrolling the entrance to Pearl Harbor, was notified by one of two minesweepers operating in the area that it had spotted a submerged submarine. The *Ward* was unable to get a contact, and neither ship reported the incident. Then at 6:45 a.m. the *Ward* reported that it had spotted the conning tower of a submarine, and it had opened fire. This information was reported up the chain of command to the commandant of the Fourteenth Naval District, Admiral Bloch, and above him to Admiral Kimmel. But none of the senior officers saw any immediate threat, either because they understood that Captain Outerbridge, the commanding officer of the *Ward*, believed he had sunk the submarine, or because they wanted confirmation that it had actually been a submarine.[68]

The Opana radar plot. The army operated an Aircraft Warning Service (AWS) on Oahu, with mobile, truck-mounted radars set up at various points around the island. One position was on the northern tip of Oahu, at Kahuku Point, which was also called Opana. On December 7, the radars were to be manned from 4:00 a.m. to 7:00 a.m., but the operators at Opana decided to remain on duty past 7:00 a.m. At 7:02 a.m. they began seeing something unusual on their screen: a group of aircraft that first appeared 137 miles north of Oahu. They called the AWS information center at Fort Shafter, and after several minutes spent trying to reach anyone in charge, they were able to speak to Lieutenant Kermit Tyler, an Air Corps officer in training who had the shift from 4:00 a.m. to 8:00 a.m. He thought the aircraft were probably a flight of American B-17 bombers due back from the mainland that morning, and told the two privates to forget about it. They decided to keep tracking the contact anyway, continuing until 7:30 a.m. At about 7:55 a.m. Tyler stepped outside his office to see what he thought was "navy bombers in bombing practice over at Pearl Harbor."[69]

Tactical-Level Intelligence Assessments

The senior navy intelligence officers in Hawaii felt confident that war with Japan would come soon, but much like their Washington-level counterparts, they did not suspect that the Japanese Navy was capable of launching an attack against Pearl Harbor. This disbelief was most poignantly expressed in an exchange between Admiral Kimmel and his fleet intelligence officer, Lieutenant Commander Edwin Layton. On December 1, Kimmel had told Layton to prepare a report setting out the locations of the Japanese fleet units. This was a difficult task, Layton later stated, because the Japanese Navy had just changed its call signs, and especially because for the previous several days there had been no radio transmissions noted to or from the Japanese carriers. Most analysts believed the carriers were probably in home waters, but with nothing specific to report, he wrote down for the carriers "Unknown—home waters?"

Layton took the report to Kimmel on December 2, and he later described Kimmel's reaction: "He read it through, very carefully, then said, 'What! You don't know where the carriers are?' And I said, 'No, sir.' . . ."

"He said, 'You mean to say that you are the Intelligence officer of the Pacific Fleet and you don't know where the carriers are?' And I said, 'No, sir, I don't.' He said, 'For all you know, they could be coming around Diamond Head, and you wouldn't know it?' I said, 'Yes, sir. But I hope they'd have been sighted by now.' He kind of smiled and said, 'Yes, I understand.'"[70]

Layton later testified, "I did not at any time suggest that the Japanese carriers were under radio silence approaching Oahu. I wish I had. I did not so consider at the time."[71]

Rochefort, who commanded the Pacific signals intelligence unit, was no better informed, and thus he estimated in November that the missing Japanese ships were headed south, not east toward Hawaii.[72] Nor did the army's intelligence organization in Hawaii (known as G2) suspect that an attack on Pearl Harbor was likely. In October, however, the G2 office provided an "Estimate of International (Japanese) Situation" that at least left the door open for a surprise somewhere. The assessment, signed by Lieutenant Colonel George Bicknell, the assistant head of G2, advised that "it is highly probable that Japan will, in the near future, take military action in new areas of the Far East." The assessment stated that attacks would most likely be against Russia, French Indochina, Thailand, or British possessions, but a simultaneous attack on America and its allies in the Pacific "cannot be ruled out." The assessment warned, "there remains the possibility that Japan may strike at the most opportune time, and at whatever points might gain for her the most strategic, tactical, or economic advantages over her opponents."[73]

RECEPTIVITY TOWARD INTELLIGENCE WARNING

What did military and government decision makers think of these intelligence indicators and assessments? What messages did they take from the warnings of impending conflict with Japan? In this section we examine, first, what military leaders in Washington, who had access to all the available intelligence (including Magic), thought about the Japanese threat; next, the views of President Franklin Delano Roosevelt and his closest advisers; and finally, the views of American military commanders on the scene in Hawaii.

What Did Military Commanders in Washington Think?

It is clear that some senior military officials in Washington had thought about and imagined the possibility of a Japanese surprise attack on Pearl Harbor. We have seen that Navy Secretary Knox had warned Admiral Kimmel in January 1941 about the danger of a surprise attack. Only a short time later, on February 7, 1941, the army chief of staff, General George Marshall, wrote to General Short upon his taking command in Hawaii, cautioning him that "the risk of sabotage and the risk involved in a surprise raid by air and by submarine, constitute the real perils of the situation."[74]

But even as Knox and Marshall were warning of the possibility of a surprise attack on Hawaii, other military leaders were discounting the threat. On February 1, 1941, Admiral Harold Stark, the chief of naval operations, wrote a memo to the commander in chief of the Pacific Fleet that was titled "Rumored Japanese Attack on Pearl Harbor." Stark passed on the information reported by Ambassador Grew in Tokyo, and then wrote that "the Division of Naval Intelligence places no credence in these rumors. . . . No move against Pearl Harbor appears imminent or planned for in the foreseeable future."[75]

By the fall of 1941, it appears that concern over a possible surprise attack had faded completely. The senior leaders of the army and navy knew that war with Japan was likely to come soon, and they were concerned that their forces needed more time to prepare.[76] But they did not expect the first Japanese attacks to be against US possessions, either in Hawaii or farther west. General Marshall, the army chief of staff, and Admiral Harold Stark, the chief of naval operations, sent a memo to the president on November 27, 1941, that estimated Japan would most likely move against either the Burma Road or Thailand—but it would be deterred from attacking the Philippines by the strength of US forces there, and from attacking Russia because of Russia's strength. They did not mention a risk to Hawaii.[77]

It was against this background—the expectation of war in the Pacific, but no expectation of a threat to Hawaii—that the navy and army sent out a series of warning dispatches on November 24, 27, and 28. The middle dispatch of this series was sent by the navy and began with the famous phrase, "This dispatch is to be considered a war warning."[78] In these messages the service chiefs warned of a possible Japanese "surprise aggressive movement in any direction" (November 24); of an amphibious expedition against "either the Philippines, Thai, or Kra Peninsula or possibly Borneo" (November 27); and that "Japanese future action unpredictable but hostile action possible at any moment" (November 28).[79] But despite their ominous wording, these messages were actually quite ambiguous, and did not suggest the possibility of an attack against Pearl Harbor.

Receptivity at the Diplomatic and Political Levels

There is little evidence to support the conspiracy theorists' charge that the president knew about the Japanese plans or was willing to provoke such a disaster in order to bring America into the war. Alvin Coox, for example, has provided a useful debunking of these arguments as they pertain to FDR and his senior advisers.[80] But what did FDR and his key advisers know, and what did they believe was possible, in the months before the Pearl Harbor attack?

Although FDR never made his innermost thoughts and intentions clear even to his closest aides, the available evidence suggests that though he and his inner circle felt that war with Japan was likely, they did not consider an attack on Pearl Harbor to be a realistic threat. Ambassador Grew's report in particular was discounted and does not appear to have influenced FDR. John K. Emmerson, a Foreign Service officer in Tokyo, later confirmed that an attack on Hawaii was considered beyond the bounds of possibility. A Japanese move into Southeast Asia was considered possible at the time, according to Emmerson: "In our minds, however, a direct assault on American territory was insane and therefore unthinkable."[81] It appears that FDR was following a policy of attempting to contain or restrain Japanese expansionism, understanding the risk of war but hoping to delay it until America was ready. As Waldo Heinrichs has described the situation, FDR intended in particular to drain Japan's oil supply and thus its capacity for war, while building up America's own military capability in the region. But he did not want to take abrupt action that would push Japan toward war: "He wanted a drying up of Japanese oil supplies rather than a formal severance of trade, a sobering realization not a sudden shock."[82]

The president's desire for a middle policy between overt confrontation and outright appeasement may explain the awkward and confusing way in which the US oil embargo was placed on Japan. In July 1941, Japanese military moves in southern Indochina, and, perhaps more important, Magic intercepts of Japanese offensive plans, convinced Roosevelt and his advisers that further action would be necessary to deter Japan. FDR issued an executive order freezing all Japanese funds and assets in the United States; under the order, a limited amount of oil and gas would be allowed to be exported, but it would require an export license. FDR left Washington for the secret meeting with Churchill that would be known as the Argentia Conference, and while he was absent government officials rejected all applications for gas and oil export licenses—implementing what was in effect a total ban. FDR later approved (or at least decided not to overturn) this decision, and the ban stood. Although scholars have debated whether this sequence of events was planned by FDR or was the work of overzealous junior officials, its effect was clearly to help convince Japan that conflict with the United States was becoming inevitable.[83]

FDR and his advisers appear to have drawn their clues from the same Magic and other intelligence sources that the Washington military leadership was seeing, which indicated that the only question was, in which direction would Japan make its first move—to the north, or the south? During the summer of 1941, reports from southern Indochina had suggested that an attack would most likely be directed south. Then, in October, intelligence from Chinese military sources predicted an imminent attack against Russia, and FDR wrote Churchill on October 15 that he thought the Japanese were "headed north."[84]

By November the consensus had once again shifted, as widespread reporting of Japanese troop buildups in Indochina convinced most decision makers that the Japanese move would indeed come in the south. This was the situation when, on November 26, FDR and Secretary of State Cordell Hull decided that efforts to establish a modus vivendi with Japan had failed. Hull presented the Japanese with a comprehensive proposal that called for a total Japanese withdrawal from Indochina—not likely to be accepted—and wrote the next day to Secretary of War Henry Stimson, "I have washed my hands of it and [the situation] is now in the hands of you and Knox, the Army and Navy."[85]

What Did the Operational Commanders in Hawaii Think?

Despite the history of war games and drills focusing on the threat of a Japanese surprise attack, neither Kimmel nor Short considered the threat of attack on Hawaii to be serious. Instead, they focused their energies on preparing the US Fleet for offensive action when war broke out (Kimmel), and defending against the threat of sabotage (Short). As we saw with Kimmel's exchange with Layton about the "missing" Japanese carriers, Kimmel was aware of at least the remote possibility of a Japanese attack. But he appeared to reflect the confidence that his war plans officer, Captain Charles "Soc" McMorris, expressed on November 27 when Kimmel turned to McMorris and asked, "What do you think about the prospects of a Japanese air attack?" McMorris replied, "None, absolutely none."[86]

Most senior staff and operations officers appear to have shared this confidence, and thus they were dismissive toward anyone who expressed greater concern. This view was captured in an incident described by Layton. On Saturday, November 29, a week before the Pearl Harbor attack, Layton arrived late at the wardroom mess for lunch. When someone asked his opinion of the situation, he replied that he thought he would be back in his office the next day, Sunday—clearly suggesting that he expected a crisis was imminent. But that Sunday passed peacefully, and on the following Monday he was greeted with jeers and cries of "What happened to your crisis, Layton? Layton and his Sunday crisis."[87] Kimmel and his senior advisers were so confident in disregarding the possibility of a surprise attack that, in Wohlstetter's words, "the only signal that could and did spell 'hostile action' to them was the bombing itself."[88]

EXPLAINING PEARL HARBOR

The problem before Pearl Harbor was not a lack of imagination; for as we have seen, a number of American military leaders, including the secretary of the navy and the chief of staff of the army, did consider the possibility of a Japanese surprise attack on Hawaii and warned their subordinates about it. Nor was the problem a failure of long-range, strategic intelligence on the Japanese threat; for leaders both in Washington (where they had access to all available intelligence, including from Magic) and in Hawaii (where they did not) understood that war was coming between Japan and the United States.

What was lacking before December 7, 1941, was specific, tactical intelligence that indicated the Japanese Navy was planning a surprise attack against Hawaii. Although a Japanese attack had been envisioned by a number of planners and strategists, there was no hard evidence to suggest that such a thing was likely or even possible. Intelligence officials charged with estimating the threat—with the occasional exception, such as the after-the-fact testimony of Captain Wilkinson, the director of naval intelligence—did not believe the Japanese would be capable of launching such a long-distance attack.[89] And when the experts scoffed, those responsible for protecting the fleet in Hawaii, and for making national policy in Washington, focused their attention elsewhere.

Edwin Layton and Frederick Parker, among others, have argued that American intelligence could have produced specific indicators of the attack on Pearl Harbor if they had been given more support from Washington.[90] In particular, Layton and Parker have written that if the codebreakers in Hawaii had been allowed to work on the Japanese operational code JN-25, they might have been able to break enough of it anticipate the attack.[91] Although this argument amounts to a counterfactual that can never be proven, there is evidence supporting it: American intelligence did in fact intercept thousands of messages in JN-25 during the months leading up to the attack, but could not read them. Those messages were finally decrypted and translated in 1945 and 1946, and still later this collection was declassified and made available to scholars. A total of 188 messages were found to have pertained to December 7; though none specifically referred to Pearl Harbor, there were references to shallow-running torpedoes and training in conducting aerial attacks, which might have been enough to alert Hawaii.[92]

However, there was a second factor missing before Pearl Harbor that helps to explain the disaster and also suggests that even additional intelligence might not have been enough to change the course of history. This factor was a lack of belief in the seriousness of the threat on the part of key American decision makers. James Forrestal, secretary of the navy later in the war, noted the problem of the fundamental disbelief: "Although the imminence of hostile action by the Japanese was known, and the capabilities of the Japanese Fleet and Air Arm were recognized in war plans made to meet just such hostile action, these factors did not reach the state of conviction in the minds of the responsible officers . . . to an extent sufficient to impel them to bring about that implementation of the plans that was necessary if the initial hostile action was to be repelled or at least mitigated."[93]

In part, this lack of belief and conviction in the threat appears to have occurred because of the lack of specific, tactical warning. But there appears to have been more at work: a general lack of receptivity toward intelligence on the part of many senior leaders. Frederick Parker, for example, has written that intelligence from cryptography and traffic analysis, which was particularly important in determining Japanese intentions, was not trusted by military commanders: "The lack of confidence in such intelligence made traffic intelligence from the Pacific during the last half of 1941 more an elaborate rumor than trustworthy source material. Commanders at the theater level and in Washington, through lack of early training or insight, were not prepared to exploit the intelligence provided by this source, particularly when the messages themselves could not be read."[94]

The conventional explanation for Pearl Harbor is that sufficient intelligence indicators had been available, but they were misunderstood or ignored as a result of faulty analysis. But this chapter's examination of the intelligence picture before the attack supports the views of Kahn and Levite that the principal intelligence failure was one of collection, not analysis. The problem, however, was not just a lack of specific, tactical intelligence on the Japanese threat; there was also a failure of receptivity toward intelligence on the part of key decision makers. This lack of receptivity made it unlikely that even better intelligence would have convinced policymakers to take the actions that would have been needed to prevent the Japanese attack.

At Pearl Harbor a lack of tactical intelligence and poor receptivity toward intelligence on the part of decision makers combined to allow the Japanese Navy to carry out a disastrous surprise attack for which the American military had spent years planning, and which American strategists had warned might happen. We can never know how the situation might have been different if either of these key factors had been changed. But within six months of Pearl Harbor, Japan was to attempt another surprise attack, against another US island possession in the Pacific. This time the result was quite different. The next chapter examines this case, the Battle of Midway.

CHAPTER 3

THE BATTLE OF MIDWAY

Explaining Intelligence Success

ALTHOUGH THE BATTLE OF MIDWAY has not generated as much controversy and public fascination as Pearl Harbor, it remains today nonetheless the subject of a steady stream of books and articles. In part this interest stems from a desire on the part of naval personnel and veterans to remember a great victory and turning point in the war in the Pacific; the US Navy, for example, began several years ago to commemorate the battle each year with celebrations and speeches.[1] But among historians and military analysts, a number of debates continue to be waged over operational aspects of the battle, such as to what extent failures on either the Japanese or the American side contributed to the outcome.[2]

Despite the growing literature on Midway, however, few recent works focus on intelligence issues.[3] This may be a reflection of the fact that although the outcome of the battle was far from assured—as indicated by the titles of two well-known books on the battle, *Incredible Victory* and *Miracle at Midway*—it has been almost universally seen as an outstanding example of the successful use of intelligence.[4] Admiral Chester Nimitz, for example, expressed the prevailing view when he wrote that "Midway was essentially a victory of intelligence."[5]

The important role played by intelligence at Midway, and the fact that the story of that role has been widely told, begs the question: If the intelligence available to the US side was so good, is there anything left to study, and are there any lessons applicable to situations in which the available intelligence is less adequate? Richard Betts has suggested there may not be, writing that "it is difficult to think of cases in which the intelligence needed for decision was more adequate than it was in regard to Midway."[6] The case is close to tautological, according to Betts: When the warning is nearly perfect, it will not be disregarded by decision makers, and surprises will be avoided. This chapter argues, however, that there are indeed important lessons still to be learned from the use of intelligence at Midway. As we will see, even with this superb intelligence, not only was the battle a close-run matter operationally, but key decision makers up until the time the battle began were divided in their belief in the utility of that intelligence.

Surprisingly, little work has been done to compare the use of intelligence in the cases of Pearl Harbor and Midway. The two cases would appear to lend themselves to a comparative analysis, attempting to answer the question: How could the same US intelligence system—one that failed tragically before Pearl Harbor—recover only six months later, in time to produce a dramatic success and help turn around the war in the Pacific? But historians and scholars of intelligence and surprise attack have seen the two cases as representing very different circumstances, and have argued that there is little merit in comparing the failure at Pearl Harbor with the success at Midway. I disagree with this assessment, and this book argues that the two cases in fact represent a natural experiment that can help us understand the difference between failure and success, and can offer lessons for today in the effort to prevent future surprise attacks.

The first section of this chapter reviews the question of whether a comparison between Pearl Harbor and Midway is worthwhile. Next, because the details of the Midway story may not be as familiar to readers as those of Pearl Harbor, is a description of the main events leading up to the battle, focusing on how American intelligence developed its picture of what the Japanese were planning. This is followed by a review of the intelligence available to American decision makers at the strategic and tactical levels, and then of policymakers' receptivity at the same levels. The concluding sections note that the success of American intelligence at Midway was due to the combination of precise, tactical-level warnings together with receptive policymakers; and that by comparison, the intelligence failure at Pearl Harbor can be seen even more clearly as resulting from an absence of these key factors.

WHY COMPARE PEARL HARBOR AND MIDWAY?

Although both Pearl Harbor and Midway continue to be studied and debated, and books and articles on each are published every year, only one book-length study has been published comparing the use of intelligence in the two events: Ariel Levite's *Intelligence and Strategic Surprises*.[7] One reason for this lack of comparative work may be, as Arthur Hulnick has suggested, that intelligence failure is heralded, whereas intelligence success is quickly forgotten and little studied: "Everyone alive then or who has studied World War II remembers clearly that the Japanese attack on Pearl Harbor was probably the worst US intelligence failure of the twentieth century, while few can recall that Nimitz's defeat of Admiral Yamamoto's battle fleet at Midway was perhaps one of the greatest victories for intelligence ever."[8]

But a more significant reason for the lack of comparative studies is that although both cases involve surprise attacks in the Pacific during World War II, they have been seen as very different situations that may not merit close comparison. This criticism was leveled against Levite when his book was published. Richard Betts, for example, argues that comparing the two cases is like comparing "peacetime apples" with "wartime oranges."[9] The stakes and risks involved in decisions about whether an enemy will go to war, Betts writes, are very different from those about where and when the enemy will strike during a war. In particular, political considerations are much more important in decisions about going to war than in decisions made during a war. And a major consideration before the outbreak of war is that one's responses to warning could be unnecessary or even counterproductive; but once war has begun, that is no longer a consideration.[10] Betts argues that before Midway, several of the most difficult questions for intelligence and policymakers had already been settled, such as whether war would come, and how operationally and tactically the Japanese might strike. In addition, after the war had begun decision makers no longer needed to be as concerned about the potential costs of reacting to warning. The remaining questions—where and when the attack might fall—had both been answered with near certainty as a result of codebreaking, making the intelligence-warning process easier than it had been before Pearl Harbor.[11]

In response, Levite argues that the distinctions between the two cases are not as great as Betts describes them. For example, before Pearl Harbor it was clear to American political and military leaders that Japan was heading to war and that the United States would be involved, meaning that the important question of whether war would come had already been settled.[12] In addition, Levite holds that the differences between the cases are not as important as their similarities, notably that the same two countries are involved, in the same geographic region, and in roughly the same period of time. In fact, the similarities between the two cases are so great, he argues, as to create "what functionally approximates a controlled experiment."[13]

Uri Bar-Joseph, in a very detailed critique of Levite's book, makes what is essentially the opposite argument against comparing the two cases: that although the two situations are very similar to each other, they are otherwise unique and hard to use in making generalizations. The primary failure in both cases, Bar-Joseph writes, was the inability of one side—the United States at Pearl Harbor and Japan at Midway—to locate the other side's fleet. This problem is unique to navies, Bar-Joseph argues, and is less likely to occur today as a result of improvements in intelligence-gathering capabilities.[14]

Critics are correct to argue that the nature of the surprise was different in the two cases. The Pearl Harbor attack was a strategic surprise, shocking America into war and shaking its understanding of its security and its place in the world, whereas at Midway the surprise was more tactical, concerning where and when the enemy would attack in the middle of an ongoing conflict. But Pearl Harbor was both a tactical surprise and a strategic shock, and at the tactical level the similarities between the two cases are indeed striking, supporting Levite's point that they can serve as a type of natural experiment. Similarly, it is true that the characteristics of the two cases are not identical. The primary difference is that one case involves decisions and actions before the outbreak of war, whereas the other is a case of attempted attack during war. As Van Evera notes, differences between cases can make case comparison a weak method for testing a theory; but even so, such a comparison can be useful in generating new hypotheses, which is my goal here.[15]

I have chosen to compare these cases in part because of their intrinsic importance as classic examples of intelligence failure and success, but also because they offer an opportunity for study using the "method of difference": The two cases are quite similar in many ways, but they provide different values on the dependent variable (success or failure in preventing an attack).[16] The same US intelligence system that failed to detect and warn of the Japanese attack on Pearl Harbor was successful, only six months later, in detecting and warning of a follow-up attack on Midway. The adversaries were the same, the geography was the same, and the intelligence organizations, sources, and methods were the same. Several of the principal decision makers were different, but it would be difficult, I believe, to find a better comparison to use in attempting to determine the factors that make the difference between failure and success in preventing a surprise attack.[17]

BACKGROUND TO THE BATTLE

During the first few months after the attack on Pearl Harbor, Japanese strategy was directed to the south, aimed at seizing territory in Southeast Asia and the Southwest Pacific. But by mid-March 1942, planning by the staff of the Combined Fleet, commanded by Admiral Isoroku Yamamoto, began to focus on the tiny island (actually two tiny atolls) some 1,000 miles northwest of Hawaii called Midway. At a series of meetings from April 2 to 5, the Naval General Staff discussed Yamamoto's proposal for an operation aimed at Midway. Several senior officers were strongly opposed to the idea, arguing that Midway was of little strategic value. Yamamoto was not present at the meetings, but when his staff officers reported that he threatened to resign if his plan was not adopted, the General Staff accepted a version of the plan that included a diversionary operation against the Aleutians.[18]

The Japanese Combined Fleet and Naval General Staff continued to haggle over the details of the plan for the next several weeks, until on April 18 all debate was quickly brought to an end when American Lieutenant Colonel James Doolittle led an air strike from the carrier *Hornet* in a surprise attack on the Japanese homeland. The Doolittle raid steeled the determination of Japanese planners to press for an early execution of the Midway operation, and the plan was soon completed. On May 5, Admiral Nagano issued Imperial General Headquarters Navy Order No. 18, which directed the commander in chief Combined Fleet to "carry out the occupation of Midway Island and key points in the western Aleutians in co-operation with the Army."[19]

Although the Midway operation was partially designed to seize the tiny atoll for use as a base for future operations against Hawaii and to extend Japan's defensive perimeter, the Japanese high command believed its principal value was to draw the American fleet out into what would be a climactic battle. The plan was built around an assault on Midway carried out by three major Japanese naval forces. A Striking Force, centered on four aircraft carriers, would approach from the northwest and attack Midway from the air under the command of Vice Admiral Chuichi Nagumo, who six months earlier had led the attack on Pearl Harbor. This force was also called the Mobile Force, or the First Air Fleet. An invasion force, also called the Midway Occupation Force, would approach from the west with transports bringing landing troops intended to occupy the island. And a Main Battle Force of three battleships and escorts under the command of Admiral Yamamoto himself would be held in reserve to combat the main US fleet once it sortied from Pearl Harbor in response to the attack. In addition, while all this was taking place, a Second Carrier Striking Force would execute a diversionary strike against the Aleutians, conducting air strikes against Dutch Harbor in the eastern end of the island chain and landing 2,500 men to occupy the western islands.[20]

CONVENTIONAL EXPLANATIONS FOR THE AMERICAN VICTORY

Historians and scholars of intelligence are nearly unanimous in describing the Battle of Midway as a great success for American intelligence. James Wirtz, for example, has described Midway as one of the rare examples in which decision makers are able to get what he calls "the Holy Grail of intelligence: accurate and timely indications of exactly when, where, how, and why an opponent will strike."[21] The US intelligence community regularly touts Midway—and especially the famous prediction made by Nimitz's intelligence officer, Captain Edwin Layton, of when and where the Japanese fleet would appear—as an outstanding example of the use of intelligence.[22] An article that won the Naval Intelligence Essay Contest in 2003 described the story of Layton's prediction, calling it "a glorious page in the history of our Navy."[23] In particular, Midway has been seen as a victory for the codebreakers of the US Navy. As David Kahn puts it, "The codebreakers of the Combat Intelligence Unit . . . had turned the tide of a war. They had caused a Rising Sun to start to set."[24]

Admiral Nimitz gave credit to intelligence, writing in an after-action report: "Had we lacked early information of the Japanese movement, and had we been caught with Carrier Task Forces dispersed, possibly as far away as the Coral Sea, the Battle of Midway would have ended far differently."[25] Nimitz has himself also received a great deal of credit for his judicious use of intelligence. Admiral Raymond Spruance later told Gordon Prange that "the credit must be given to Nimitz. Not only did he accept the intelligence picture but he acted upon it at once."[26] Samuel Eliot Morison, in his official history of the US Navy in World War II, also credits the victory both to the intelligence available, and to the use of it, especially by Nimitz: "But for this early and abundant information and (what was equally important) the prompt and intelligent use of it, the Pacific Fleet would have had only a slim chance of winning."[27]

Nonetheless, despite the Americans' superior intelligence, the Battle of Midway was by all accounts a near failure for the US Navy, and not all historians have given the primary credit to intelligence. John Keegan is the most prominent historian who has taken issue with the consensus view. In his book *Intelligence in War*, he argues that although "the exactitude of the intelligence available to Nimitz and his subordinate commanders about the Midway attack was indeed extraordinary," the outcome was still not preordained, and "contingencies and chance were critical determinants of victory."[28] Victor Davis Hanson agrees that the work of intelligence personnel was a key factor, but he argues that the broader reason for American success was the American culture of individuality, innovation, and spontaneity: "Far better than luck, surprise, or accident, the power of the individual himself explains the Americans' incredible victory."[29]

Several authors argue that the most important question is not why the Americans *won* but why the Japanese *lost*. One factor frequently cited is that following their victory at Pearl Harbor, the Japanese succumbed to what has been called the "victory disease," as their early successes encouraged them to plan too aggressively. Mitsuo Fuchida and Masatake Okumiya, the authors of the standard English-language Japanese account of the battle, call this a malady of over-confidence. They argue that because Japan had been able to achieve a surprise at Pearl Harbor, Japanese planners assumed they would also be able to take the Americans by surprise at Midway.[30] More generally, Fuchida and Okumiya believe the root cause of the Japanese defeat "lies deep in the Japanese national character," and in an inherent irrationality and impulsiveness that leads to haphazard and often contradictory actions.[31] Parshall and Tully argue the Japanese defeat occurred as a result of widespread failures throughout the entire Japanese Navy, stemming from the fact that the navy was a parochial institution that had failed to adapt to the modern world.[32]

Few works on Midway have explicitly argued that there was a relationship between the failure at Pearl Harbor and the success at Midway. To the extent that scholars have considered this relationship, however, the conventional wisdom is that the earlier failure helped produce the later success. Michael Handel has written: "If not for the Pearl Harbor disaster, which had shaken Naval Headquarters and Naval Intelligence, Nimitz and his intelligence advisers might not have enjoyed the same degree of success in asserting their views over those prevailing in Washington."[33]

Despite a few dissenting opinions, then, the conventional account of the Battle of Midway—at least as far as intelligence is concerned—appears to be clear: American intelligence organizations, inspired by their failure to anticipate the attack on Pearl Harbor, were able to break the Japanese codes and predict exactly when and where the next major attack would come. Admiral Nimitz used this information to expertly position his fleet to meet the Japanese attack, and though ultimate victory required a combination of luck and valor on the American side, the victory could not have been obtained without the initial advantage assured by intelligence.

This conventional story of Midway is compelling but it is too simplistic. When we look more closely at the issue of intelligence and Midway, to try to unpack which people, organizations, or types of intelligence deserve credit, and how the critical intelligence was produced and used, the story becomes less clear. The next sections examine the intelligence warnings that were available to American decision makers before the Battle of Midway, first at the strategic level and then at the tactical and operational levels.

STRATEGIC-LEVEL INTELLIGENCE AND WARNINGS

Although the Japanese attack on Pearl Harbor had answered many questions for American strategic planners—such as when the war they were expecting would come—it told them little about where and when they should prepare to meet the next Japanese assault. In the immediate weeks and months after the attack, the Japanese effort was clearly devoted to expanding their area of control in the Southwest Pacific and Southeast Asia. But where would they turn after that?

The traditional sources of strategic-level intelligence, such as diplomatic communications, were of little use in answering questions that called for an assessment of Japan's future military plans. But that did not mean there was a lack of predictions and estimates for what the Japanese would do next. During the early months of 1942, navy intelligence officials in Washington at times predicted a Japanese assault on the Aleutians, while Admiral King sometimes suspected Hawaii might be the target for a repeat attack and at other times believed the Japanese would continue to focus on the South Pacific. Meanwhile, the US Army Air Force worried about the chance of an air raid on San Francisco, while Secretary of War Henry Stimson was more concerned about an attack on the Panama Canal than a new attack on Hawaii.[34] There were, however, two incidents that provided broad, strategic-level indications that the Japanese might be planning something big in the Pacific. The first was an action by the Japanese, and the second was an assessment by American intelligence.

Operation K: The "Second Attack on Pearl Harbor"

On the night of March 3–4, 1942, the Japanese provided the Americans with a strong indication that they might be planning to launch another attack against Pearl Harbor. In what Japan called Operation K, two long-range flying boats took off from Wojte in the Marshall Islands, touched down briefly at the French Frigate Shoals to refuel from a waiting submarine, and then continued on to make a nighttime reconnaissance flight over Oahu. The pilots apparently intended to drop four bombs on Pearl Harbor—for what Prange has described as "strictly for terrorist purposes," and which the standard Japanese account says was for "psychological effect"—but because of overcast conditions mistakenly dropped them harmlessly into the Punch Bowl crater near Honolulu.[35]

Although this operation was not intended as a prelude to any immediate follow-on attack on Hawaii, it had the effect of warning American leaders that a second attack was possible.[36] The operation also alerted the Americans to take precautions against a similar small-scale raid, and when a reconnaissance flight over Midway was attempted on March 9–10, American fighters were able to shoot the Japanese aircraft down.[37]

But Operation K was to have an even more significant result for the Japanese. The plan for the Midway invasion depended greatly on the element of surprise, and to ensure that the American forces were not alerted ahead of time, another reconnaissance mission was scheduled over Hawaii only a few days before the Japanese fleet launched its assault on Midway. Admiral Nimitz, however, responded to the March 4 operation by ordering that an observation patrol be maintained at French Frigate Shoal, where he suspected the Japanese aircraft might have refueled. When a Japanese submarine arrived at the shoals on May 31 in preparation for refueling a follow-on to Operation K, it found two US ships already there. The reconnaissance mission had to be called off, leaving the Japanese attack force without the critical information that much of the American fleet had already gone to sea.[38]

Admiral King's Request for an Estimate

In April Admiral King, the commander in chief of the US fleet, sent a request directly to Rochefort, commander of the signals intelligence unit in Hawaii, asking for his estimate of Japan's future intentions. It was unprecedented for King to ask for such information directly, and Rochefort said later, "We were a little surprised that he would ask us what our views were. I personally felt that he was not even aware of our existence."[39] Rochefort and his team went to work immediately, and sent back an assessment that stated they believed the Japanese had completed operations in the Indian Ocean. They estimated that Japan had another operation planned in the vicinity of eastern New Guinea (which later developed into the Battle of the Coral Sea); that Japan had no intention of invading Australia; and that another operation was being planned for the future, but they knew only it was to be in the Pacific and was to be a major operation. All this turned out to be correct, and the major operation they foresaw was to be the assault on Midway.[40]

SPECIFIC, TACTICAL-LEVEL INTELLIGENCE AND WARNING

It would ultimately be cryptologic intelligence—codebreaking—that made the difference by providing specific intelligence on Japan's plans against Midway. But in the immediate days and weeks after the attack on Pearl Harbor, the naval intelligence unit in Hawaii lapsed into what Frederick Parker has called "an eclipse that lasted until late January 1942."[41] The personnel in the communications intelligence unit, which was named Hypo, felt they had failed, and for a time they were hesitant to offer analysis and assessments in their intelligence reporting, sticking instead to the bare facts.

In addition to the sense of failure, a continuing problem was a lack of personnel. This problem began to be addressed when Durwood K. (Texas) Rory, a chief master at arms (the navy version of a military policeman) for the Fourteenth Naval District, was assigned the task of recruiting workers for Hypo from the new personnel arriving in Hawaii. Parker writes that "his success rate became legendary" after he selected and assigned the band members from the battleship *California*, which had been sunk in the attack.[42] David Kahn writes that the band members "proved above average and some exceptional in their new tasks," and Rochefort later commented, "They were pretty good as a matter of fact."[43] In addition Nimitz, likely acting on Rochefort's advice, knew the radio unit at Hawaii was desperately short of manpower, and requested additional personnel for Hypo in February, in April, and again in May. In May he urged an increase from 170 to more than 400.[44]

Early Progress on JN-25

The most critical pieces of intelligence were to come from the efforts of Rochefort and his team to crack the Japanese Navy operations code, known to the Americans as JN-25. But before the cryptologists in Hawaii could break the code, they had to be assigned the task of working on it. Before the war the Combat Intelligence Unit in Hawaii had been given the primary task of working on the Japanese flag officers' code, on which they were never able to make much progress, and under the existing distribution of assignments between Washington, Hawaii, and Corregidor, Hawaii did not work on JN-25. Three days after the attack on Pearl Harbor, however, as part of a reorganization of cryptologic responsibilities directed by Washington, Hypo was told to discontinue work on the flag officers' code and begin working on JN-25, which was thought to be more likely to provide useful intelligence.[45] This order, changing priorities for intelligence collection as well as analysis, would turn out to be the key to solving the puzzle of determining the Japanese Navy's intentions.

Forrest R. Biard, who worked under Rochefort at Hypo, has described the change that began to come over Hypo after they were given permission to start working on JN-25. Within a few weeks after the attack, "our small group changed from an essentially ineffective unit to one of the nation's most important wartime assets."[46] Working together with codebreakers in Washington and the Philippines, Hypo began the painstaking effort to break the Japanese code. They began making significant headway, according to Rochefort, by January and February.[47] By mid-April JN-25 messages were being routinely intercepted, decrypted, translated, reenciphered, and disseminated by Hypo to Washington and other users within six hours of their original transmission.[48] Although some authors have credited OP-20-G (naval intelligence headquarters in Washington) with a major share of the credit for cracking the JN-25 code, it appears clear that the key work on the code was done by the cryptologists at Hawaii—a unit that before the attack on Pearl Harbor had not been allowed to work on it.[49]

Indications of a Moresby Campaign

The Japanese military used two- and three-letter codes—which American intelligence called digraphs and trigraphs—to refer to geographical place names. On March 25, 1942, an intercepted Japanese message referred to an upcoming offensive against "RZP," which had been tentatively identified as Port Moresby, an Australian base on the southeastern coast of New Guinea.[50] This was the first specific indication of Japanese intentions in that direction, and further intercepts in April confirmed that the Japanese planned to seize Port Moresby.[51] By April 29, Admiral Nimitz had enough intelligence to commit his forces, and on that date he dispatched the carriers *Lexington* and *Yorktown* to the Coral Sea under Admiral Frank Jack Fletcher to meet the Japanese fleet. The resulting Battle of the Coral Sea was tactically a draw, but strategically it was the first setback for the Japanese in the war; and it was a significant triumph for US communications intelligence. As a National Security Agency (NSA) historian later wrote: "Comint passed its first test under fire and proved it could provide accurate, timely intelligence."[52]

Identifying Midway as the Target

In early March 1942, a new digraph, "AF," began to appear in Japanese message traffic.[53] Then, on March 9, Tokyo sent out a message to its air group commanders giving a two-day forecast of wind force and direction for AF. Rochefort thought it could be a reference to American island bases within range of the Marshalls, and this message turned out to be the first indication that AF could be Midway.[54] Further evidence that Midway could be the target of upcoming operations came from traffic analysis by the codebreakers at Corregidor.[55]

In the first week of May, traffic analysis indicated that the Japanese Navy might be preparing for a new operation that included almost all of Japan's major aircraft carriers. In a message on May 2, the chief of staff of the Japanese Second Fleet directed commanders on the island of Saipan to make preparations to receive what he called the A Force and the Striking Force in Truk for a period of about two weeks after June 20.[56] Clearly the Japanese were planning something big—but what and where?

Then, in the middle of May came several intercepted messages that confirmed for Rochefort and Layton that Midway was the target of the upcoming operation. On May 13, a message referred to "AF ground crews," which indicated both that AF was an air facility, and that AF was involved in the upcoming operation.[57] On May 14, Rochefort called Layton to tell him he had something "so hot here it's burning the top of my desk," which was probably the message about AF ground crews.[58] Then the communications intelligence indicators began to fill in the picture of the upcoming operation. In a message sent on May 16 and read by navy cryptologists on May 18, the First Air Fleet wrote "on the day of the attack we will endeavor to—at a point 50 miles NW of AF and move pilots off as quickly as possible."[59] Although not all of the message had been decrypted, the inference was clear: The Japanese pilots would launch their attack on Midway from a point 50 miles northwest of the island.

By breaking the Japanese codes, American intelligence analysts were able to figure out a great deal about the upcoming Japanese offensive. But to understand the full scale of the operation, they also needed other sources of information, such as traffic analysis. And because even decrypted messages were not always self-explanatory, the job of analysis was not finished once the messages could be read. For example, Rochefort later said that he had been able to conclude that the Japanese intended to do more than just conduct an air attack against Midway, not because their message traffic said so but because it said they were bringing refrigeration vessels and seven or eight transports with about 15,000 troops. "These people are there for a purpose. For what purpose? The purpose of occupying the islands," said Rochefort.[60]

However, communications intelligence and cryptography provided the most crucial pieces of the puzzle. On May 20, a message was intercepted saying the occupation force for MI—which was a new code replacing AF—was to depart Saipan on the 27th.[61] To cap it all off, another message was intercepted that appeared to indicate clearly the state of mind on the Japanese side: "The next address of the 14th Air Ron [squadron] will be AF."[62]

Confirming Midway as the Target: The AF Ruse

Although senior intelligence officials in Hawaii were certain by the middle of May 1942 that the Japanese were planning a major attack on Midway, not everyone was convinced. The navy's cryptologic headquarters in Washington,

OP-20-G, did not believe that "AF" necessarily meant Midway, and the navy's war plans department also had its doubts.[63] To convince the doubters—especially those in Washington—intelligence officials in Hawaii came up with a plan for what was to become one of the most famous incidents in American intelligence history.

To confirm that "AF" really did refer to Midway, a message was sent to the garrison on the island via an undersea cable that could not be intercepted by Japan. The message directed Midway to report in an *uncoded* radio transmission that they were having trouble with their desalination plant and were running short on water. Sure enough, within a few days after Midway sent such a report, a Japanese message was intercepted and decrypted that reported that "AF" was running low on water.[64]

Although the "AF ruse" has become an important part of American intelligence lore, the two principal actors in the drama have both downplayed its importance. Both Layton and Rochefort have argued that the ruse was not intended to confirm that the Japanese were planning to attack Midway, because they were each already convinced of it. Nor was it to persuade Nimitz of the threat, because he, too, had become a believer by then. Instead, the reason for the ruse was to prove the doubters in Washington wrong—and even then, it did not convince everyone. Rochefort later dismissed the significance of the ruse, saying that he did not remember whether he had thought it up, or Layton had. "A lot of people have made much to do about that, and I honestly see no reason," he said.[65]

According to Rochefort, simple logic had already made it clear that AF meant Midway. By knowing that the Japanese referred to air searches being conducted from AF, and through analysis of other aspects of Japanese message traffic, it was obvious that they could only be referring to Midway. But not everyone, he said, could understand this: "And the amazing part of this whole thing is that many people could not accept this line of reason. There was no other line of reason, just none at all. Therefore, we were quite impatient at Station Hypo that people could not agree with our reasoning, because they had the same information that we had, and they should have without any particular stress on their brain come up with the same answers."[66]

A number of questions remain about this ruse, including exactly who thought it up and just when it was carried out. Three of the best-known accounts of the incident give the credit to Rochefort; the cryptologic historian David Kahn, for example, writes that Rochefort "cooked up the idea."[67] But it appears that the original idea came from one of Rochefort's assistants, Jasper Holmes, who described the episode in his memoirs. Holmes had earlier worked at the University of Hawaii and had become familiar with the problems of getting fresh water on Midway, and one morning he and two other analysts, Thomas Dyer and Joseph Finnegan, were at Rochefort's desk. Holmes suggested that the potential for a water shortage could be used to construct a ruse; Finnegan built on the idea, and Rochefort liked it, but that was the last Holmes heard of it at the time. It was only after the war that Holmes learned about the ruse taking place, and he asked Rochefort, who confirmed that they had in fact done it.[68]

Questions also remain about when the ruse was carried out. The NSA historian Henry Schorreck notes, "The exact date has never been precisely documented."[69] Several writers have described the episode as occurring around May 10–12.[70] No record has been found of the cable sent to the island's defenders, but it appears likely that it was sent on approximately May 19. According to Layton, the plan was for the island to follow up its plain-language message with another, using a "strip cipher" that the Japanese were known to have captured on Wake Island, making the fresh water crisis even more urgent by stating that an explosion had damaged their fresh water tanks. It is not clear whether such an encrypted message was ever sent, but on May 21 Tokyo naval intelligence sent a message stating that the "AF Air Unit" had reported "at the present time we have only enough water for two weeks. Please supply us immediately."[71]

The ruse had been a complete success—so much so, that it fooled even some of the American analysts. Thomas Dyer, one of the codebreakers at Hypo, had not been involved in carrying out the ruse (but by Holmes's account, may have been present at its early stage), and he first learned about it when he came across the Japanese message reporting the Midway transmission. "And I said, 'Those stupid so-and-sos, why did they send this in plain language?' not knowing that they'd been told to."[72]

Rochefort Breaks the Date-Time Cipher

By now it had become clear, at least to officials in Hawaii, that the Japanese were planning a major assault on Midway. But they still did not know when the attack was planned, because the date and time of the operation had been enciphered separately within the Japanese coded messages. Rochefort said this had been only the third time this special coding system had been used, "so we had nothing in which to prove or disprove our assumptions as to June 4th or June 8th or June 10th or whether it was July the 19th. We had no way of knowing."[73]

The answer came finally on the night of May 26, when all of the navy's Pacific codebreaking units—Hawaii, Corregidor, and Washington—coordinated their efforts to crack the date-time cipher used in a lengthy Japanese message that turned out to be Admiral Yamamoto's operations plan for the entire Midway assault. As Rochefort recalled, "by concerted attack by everybody concerned" they were able to figure it out, although their estimate "was rather shaky."[74] Rochefort had been summoned by Nimitz to a staff meeting first thing in the morning, but he remained in his office until he was sure the decryption was correct. Layton described the scene when Rochefort eventually appeared at the meeting: "Joe finally turned up half an hour late, looking disheveled and bleary-eyed from lack of sleep. Well aware that he had kept the commander in chief waiting, he could not escape the icy gaze that greeted his brief apology."[75]

Rochefort's tardiness was forgiven, however, when he explained that they now had not only the planned date and time for the Japanese assault but also the enemy's plan of battle. The intelligence information was so complete, in fact, that it raised suspicions on the part of some staff officers, both in Hawaii and in Washington, that the Japanese might be conducting a ruse themselves. Why else would they send such sensitive information on a circuit we could intercept and decode? Writes Potter: "The exposure of Admiral Yamamoto's purported plan, instead of convincing the doubters at CinCPac [Commander in Chief, Pacific Fleet] headquarters, merely deepened their suspicions."[76]

As it turned out, the Japanese were indeed aware of the possibility that their codes could be compromised, and on the same day, May 27, they introduced changes to their codes that made their message traffic unreadable to the Americans until after the Battle of Midway. But the damage had already been done. On May 27, Nimitz issued his own operational plan for the upcoming battle, stating that "the enemy is expected to attempt the capture of Midway in the near future."[77]

Layton's Prediction

The final bit of intelligence available to American commanders before the Battle of Midway has become famous as one of the most critical pieces of tactical intelligence analysis in American history. The analysis was made by Layton, who was summoned by Nimitz as the admiral was planning the disposition of the American fleet in the upcoming battle. His question for Layton was simple: When would the Japanese attack come?

In an oral history interview conducted by Nimitz's biographer, E. B. Potter, Layton described the encounter this way: "As a matter of fact, he had asked for a specific date and time and I had said, 'I have a very difficult time being very specific.' He said, 'I want you to be specific. After all this is the job I have given you—to be the admiral commanding the Japanese forces, and tell me what you're going to do.' I said, 'All right then, Admiral. I've previously given you intelligence that the carriers will probably attack on the morning of the 4th of June, so we'll pick the 4th of June for the day. They'll come in on northwest or bearing 325 and they will be sighted about 175 miles from Midway and the time will be about 0600 Midway time.' "[78]

Later, when the first sighting reports on the approaching Japanese carriers came in, Nimitz went to his operations plot room to check the location on the maps. Once he had, Nimitz turned to Layton and remarked to him with a smile, "Well, you were only five minutes, five degrees, and five miles out."[79]

Like much else in the Midway story, the timing of Layton's prediction to Nimitz is not clear.[80] In his book Layton indicates it happened the day before Rochefort showed up late for the staff meeting, May 26.[81] Most other accounts place Layton's prediction as having been made in late May.[82] But it appears that it actually happened in even more dramatic fashion, on June 4, only an hour before the first report came in of a US reconnaissance plane sighting the attacking Japanese carrier force.[83]

RECEPTIVITY TOWARD INTELLIGENCE WARNING

What was the effect of Pearl Harbor on the receptivity of decision makers? Rather surprisingly, we do not see any *direct* relationship between the intelligence failure at Pearl Harbor and the success at Midway. As Levite has noted, the effect that existed was negative at first: "The immediate impact of the Pearl Harbor debacle was to shatter confidence in intelligence and discredit intelligence organizations and products. Under these circumstances, the receptivity of policymakers at all levels to intelligence warning was lower than before."[84] According to the NSA historian Schorreck, senior officials were especially doubtful about communications intelligence, both because it was new and because it had failed to warn of the attack on Pearl Harbor.[85]

Operation K, the "second attack on Pearl Harbor," was an example of how even after the attack on Pearl Harbor, when we might expect that American decision makers would be primed to respond to further warnings, good intelligence was not always listened to. Rochefort had warned that the Japanese might attempt a seaplane reconnaissance, but his warnings had not been taken seriously. Rochefort was bitter about the episode later, saying, "the next morning Com 14 [the Navy's regional commander] sent for me and was quite irritated because these people had appeared and had flown more or less unmolested over the island of Oahu. It was actually incredible."[86]

Admiral Nimitz: Receptive but Skeptical

From the moment he first arrived in Hawaii after the attack on Pearl Harbor, Nimitz was a strong supporter of intelligence. An indicator of that support was the fact that he kept Layton on when he took command, and Layton was the only officer besides Nimitz himself who remained attached to CinCPac headquarters throughout the war.[87] But this was not because Layton had asked to be kept on. When Nimitz came on board, Layton said later in an oral history interview, "I told him I wanted to go to sea in command of a destroyer, if possible, and kill Japs. He told me that he wanted me to stay on; that he had confidence in me and that I could kill more Japanese sitting in my chair on his staff, than I ever could kill by commanding a destroyer."[88]

Layton has written that once Nimitz came on board as CinCPac, he encouraged Layton to come to his office at any time with new information: "Apart from his flag secretary, I was the only one accorded this privilege. Nimitz clearly appreciated and understood that good intelligence is essential to sound strategic decisions."[89] But that did not mean Nimitz believed everything he was told by his intelligence staff. According to Gordon Prange, "In his early days at Pearl Harbor, Nimitz had not been too much impressed with Hypo and was quite skeptical of its value. If radio intelligence was all that efficient, how had the attack of December 7, 1941, been possible?"[90] When the admiral took his first tour of the Hypo facility soon after arriving, he asked only a few questions and left, suggesting that he had not been impressed.[91] Nimitz also was not at first convinced by the intelligence he received from Layton and Rochefort that indicated the Japanese were planning to attack Midway; he later told Prange that he had been concerned that the Japanese might have been setting a trap.[92]

An early indicator of Nimitz's interest in Midway came on May 2, when he made a surprise inspection visit to the atoll. The official Marine Corps history of this visit makes it clear Nimitz was concerned about a Japanese assault. After a hard day of touring the atoll, the admiral asked the senior marine officer on the island, Colonel Harold D. Shannon, to state what he would need to hold Midway against a major attack. After hearing what Shannon would need, Nimitz said, "If I get you all these things you say you need, then can you hold Midway against a major amphibious assault?" Colonel Shannon replied, "Yes, sir."[93]

Although Nimitz's concern about Midway might appear to indicate he was acting on warnings from intelligence, it appears more likely that he was merely taking prudent precautions concerning what was, after all, a US outpost lying directly between Hawaii and Japan. Evidence that this was the case can be seen in a message Nimitz sent to Admiral King on April 29 stating that he was concerned about the ability of Midway to withstand a major attack—but citing no specific warnings—and that he intended to conduct an inspection of Midway on May 2.[94] This was also the assessment of Nimitz's biographer, who described the trip as more the result of a hunch about the danger to Midway, rather than a reasoned belief.[95] Layton argues that Nimitz made the trip to Midway in response to King's concern about defense of Pacific island outposts, "and not, as many historians have wrongly suggested, because of his anticipation of the Japanese attack, which had yet to be revealed."[96]

Even as the intelligence reporting on the Japanese plans became more specific as the battle drew nearer, Nimitz was only partially convinced that Midway was going to be the next target. Nimitz "had not rushed to buy the whole package as Layton and Rochefort saw it," thinking it could be a trap set by the Japanese, Prange writes.[97] On approximately May 8, Layton went to Nimitz to warn him about the growing evidence pointing toward Midway as the target. As Layton later related the story, he told the admiral it was important enough that he needed to see the various pieces of intelligence at first hand: He needed to come down to the Combat Intelligence Unit for a personal, in-depth briefing. Nimitz said he was too busy, and would believe what Layton was telling him: "And I said, 'It isn't that. I want you to see it and be as convinced as I am.'"[98]

Nimitz agreed to send Captain Lynde D. McCormick, his war plans officer, to review the raw data. McCormick also told Layton he was too busy, but he finally agreed to set aside two hours. When they arrived in the Hypo offices, Rochefort had spread his intercepts of Japanese communications out on a make-shift table of planks and sawhorses. He carefully showed McCormick how they all fit together. According to Lord, "McCormick was fascinated. In the end, he spent not two but three and a half hours poking around, flipping the material, asking a thousand tough, show-me questions." Ultimately, "McCormick came away completely convinced, and to sell McCormick was to sell Nimitz. From that day on, the Admiral was the staunchest ally Rochefort and Layton could hope to have."[99]

The Battle of the Coral Sea: A Critical Victory for Intelligence

As we have seen, after the disaster of Pearl Harbor senior officials were disinclined to pay attention to intelligence. Ronald Lewin has written, "What FRUPac urgently needed, therefore, was a manifest and credible success."[100] The Battle of the Coral Sea turned out to be just such a success, as Rochefort's prediction to Admiral King of an upcoming Japanese operation in the Southwest Pacific was shown to be accurate. Coral Sea was an important victory for intelligence especially "because it persuaded Nimitz to trust Rochefort over and above the often conflicting assessments being made by naval intelligence in Washington."[101]

Nimitz Becomes a Believer

Admiral Nimitz was becoming more and more convinced of the threat to Midway, but as the middle of May approached many dissenting voices continued to be raised, both in Hawaii and in Washington. Lieutenant General Delos C. Emmons, the commanding general of the army's Hawaiian department, was naturally concerned for the threat to Hawaii. He forwarded to Nimitz a critique prepared by army intelligence that argued it was more prudent to plan on the basis of everything the enemy was capable of doing—and the army warned that Japan had proven itself capable of attacking Hawaii.[102] In addition, OP-20-G in Washington continued to disagree with the assessments from Layton and Rochefort, arguing that the invasion might be aimed at Johnston Island instead.[103]

In response to these complaints, Nimitz assigned another member of his staff, Captain James Steele, the task of reassessing the intelligence and playing the role of devil's advocate, challenging the data and making Rochefort and Layton back up every point of their argument. According to Lord, "Steele really threw himself into the job. Layton rued the day it ever happened, but from Nimitz's point of view the assignment served two very useful purposes." First, it was a response to Emmons' letter, and second, it was a check just in case they were all wrong.[104]

The end result of all these developments—the intelligence success at Coral Sea, the careful investigations by McCormick and Steele, and the close relationship that Nimitz had with his intelligence officers—was that Nimitz had become a believer both in the value of intelligence and in the warnings that Midway was the target of the next Japanese offensive. But even then, he was careful not to express too much confidence in the intelligence picture. On May 16, Nimitz's Command Summary assessed that the Japanese would attack Midway and raid Oahu in the first part of June, adding cautiously that "unless the enemy is using radio deception on a grand scale, we have a fairly good idea of his intentions."[105]

Receptivity in Washington

Convincing the military's leadership in Washington of the threat to Midway was an even harder task than convincing Nimitz. Forrest Biard, who was a member of the Hypo team, later complained that in mid-May the leadership in Washington had not been listening to them: "While the Dungeon (Rochefort, Finnegan, Lasswell, and Layton) were crying 'Midway! Midway!' Washington was stoutly maintaining that we were 'Wrong! Wrong! Wrong!'"[106] According to Donald M. Showers, a young naval officer assigned to Hypo in February 1942, "Washington was assuming that the target was bigger than a small atoll in the mid Pacific."[107]

On May 14, King, not yet convinced that the target was Midway, directed Nimitz to declare a state of "Fleet Opposed Invasion." He cited four possible enemy actions: attack Midway-Oahu, the Aleutians, Nauru, or to the southeast of New Guinea.[108] Within a few days, however, King had come around to Hawaii's assessment that the Japanese were planning to attack Midway and the Aleutians, and he sent a message to Nimitz saying he agreed.[109] But still OP-20-G and the navy war plans staff under Admiral Richmond K. Turner saw it differently, and a May 15 message, apparently from Turner, argued that an offensive was pending against northeast Australia, New Caledonia, and Fiji, starting in mid-June.[110]

It does not appear that President Roosevelt or other civilian leaders played a significant role in the decision making leading up to Midway. In part this could be because most of the critical intelligence was coming from intercepted communications; as Christopher Andrew has described, FDR was mostly uninterested in signals intelligence, even after the disaster of Pearl Harbor. "Despite its enormous importance to the war effort, SIGINT [signals intelligence] failed to capture the president's imagination. Roosevelt continued to find spies and secret operations more appealing than codebreaking."[111] David Kahn has also examined the question of FDR's use of SIGINT, and concluded that there is little evidence that FDR made any use of information from decrypted messages during World War II. Only a few such messages can be shown to have been given to him, and there is no evidence he took any actions based on them.[112]

Rear Admiral Theobald: How the Best Intelligence Can Be Disbelieved

Amid the general picture of successful use of intelligence by the Americans at Midway, there is one glaring exception. The story of Rear Admiral Robert Theobald is an illustration of how even very good intelligence can be dismissed and failure result, if the decision maker decides not to believe it.

Because the intercepted Japanese plans indicated that the Midway assault would include a feint toward Alaska, Nimitz in late May sent Theobald to the Aleutians in command of a small task force of ships. Theobald was told—but without being given details about where the information came from—that intelligence indicated the Japanese intended to invade Attu and Kiska islands, at the far western end of the Aleutian chain. He was also told that the Japanese were considering mounting an air strike strictly as a diversion against the more significant American air field at Dutch Harbor, farther to the east and closer to the mainland. Theobald was skeptical about this intelligence; what possible reason could the Japanese have for invading such distant and desolate spots as Attu and Kiska? He concluded that the intelligence reports were likely a deception, and Japan instead intended to attack Dutch Harbor in strength. He then deployed his forces 400 miles south of Kodiak, far to the east—where they were of little use in countering the main brunt of the Japanese attack, when it came as predicted against the outer Aleutians.[113]

EXPLAINING MIDWAY

The American victory at the Battle of Midway was to a great extent the result of outstanding intelligence. But just as the ultimate outcome of the battle was far from assured, the successful acquisition and use of intelligence was more nearly a failure than the conventional accounts suggest.

The most critical factor was the assignment of Rochefort and his team following Pearl Harbor to work on the Japanese fleet operations code, JN-25. The breaking of this code ultimately revealed the secrets of the Japanese plan that enabled the American forces to meet the attack. The JN-25 code was cracked by the coordinated efforts of units in Washington, the Philippines, and Hawaii, but the record clearly indicates that without the work of Rochefort and Hypo, and without the success of Rochefort and Layton in convincing Nimitz to believe the intelligence, the outcome of the battle and perhaps the war in the Pacific would have been quite different. The story of Midway, however, is much more than the story of a broken code.

The failure at Pearl Harbor, far from encouraging military commanders to pay more attention to intelligence, had the effect of making them more likely to dismiss the products of their intelligence staffs. Even Admiral Nimitz, who was inclined to listen to his intelligence officer, needed to be convinced—especially when the intelligence came from the obscure world of codebreaking, and he was receiving assessments at the same time from Washington that conflicted with those of his own staff in Hawaii. The most striking example of this lack of receptivity toward intelligence following Pearl Harbor came in March 1942, when Rochefort's warnings about the possibility of a Japanese seaplane reconnaissance mission fell on deaf ears—until the "second attack on Pearl Harbor" showed that he had been correct. Only when early successes at the Battle of the Coral Sea showed what intelligence could do did Nimitz and others fully begin to put their trust in the work of the cryptologists. And only when Rochefort and Layton were willing and able to give Nimitz the precise predictions of Japanese actions he needed did he commit US forces to meet the coming threat.

Layton demonstrated this uncertainty in commenting on the relief both he and Nimitz felt when the Japanese fleet was finally sighted: "So we were very glad indeed to see them at the point where they were sighted. There had been those who did not profess to believe Midway to be the objective; some even thought the Japanese 'AF' operation to be a huge deception for an attack on Oahu or the West Coast of the US. He [Nimitz] said, 'This will clear up all the doubters now. They just have to see this to know that what I told them is correct.' "[114]

CONCLUSION: EXPLAINING THE DIFFERENCE BETWEEN PEARL HARBOR AND MIDWAY

The comparison between the use of intelligence in the two cases of Pearl Harbor and Midway supports my argument that the key factors are precise, tactical-level intelligence, and a high level of receptivity toward intelligence on the part of decision makers. In the months before Pearl Harbor, there was a great deal of long-range, strategic intelligence on the Japanese threat, but no specific information on a planned attack on Hawaii. Even if such intelligence had been developed, it is not clear that the military commanders on the scene or in Washington would have acted on it, because they were united in their belief that such an attack was impossible.

After Pearl Harbor the strategic threat from Japan was of course clear. But strategic warning was not enough to defend against another surprise Japanese attack, this time against Midway. The American commanders had only limited naval assets, and they needed specific intelligence to know where best to station their forces. The American intelligence officers—primarily in Hawaii—were able to obtain this intelligence by breaking the Japanese codes and learning the details of the Japanese assault plan.

The Americans' codebreaking success was made possible because the attack on Pearl Harbor resulted in a shake-up of cryptologic responsibilities, and the

Hawaiian unit was told to stop working on one code that had resisted all efforts and begin work on another that appeared more promising. But even after that code was broken, the American commanders had to be convinced that the intelligence could be trusted, and that the US fleet should be stationed in position to meet an attack on Midway at the possible expense of leaving undefended Hawaii, areas of the Southwest Pacific, or even the American West Coast. Admiral Nimitz ultimately was convinced, but only after intelligence proved its value at the Battle of Coral Sea. Rear Admiral Theobald, conversely, was not told about the source of the intelligence he was given, and he did not trust it, which led to failure in the Aleutians.

The case of Midway suggests that in order for preventive action to be possible, the intelligence authorities need to be able to focus attention on a specific problem. The intelligence failure at Pearl Harbor had the effect of providing this focus. In addition, Pearl Harbor convinced the American leaders that the Japanese threat was much graver than they had anticipated; Japan was capable of mounting a much longer-range and more devastating attack than had been believed. However, whereas the decision makers now believed in the threat, they did not yet trust in intelligence. For that, an intelligence success was required.

Decision makers need to both believe in the threat they face and trust in the intelligence they are given. The disaster of Pearl Harbor confirmed the reality of the threat, whereas the early intelligence successes at the Battle of the Coral Sea and the close relationship between Nimitz and his senior intelligence officers encouraged the development of that trust.

CHAPTER 4

TESTING THE ARGUMENT

Classic Cases of Surprise Attack

THE PREVIOUS TWO CHAPTERS have examined the intelligence failure at Pearl Harbor and the success at Midway and developed a tentative hypothesis to explain the difference in outcomes between these two cases. My argument is that intelligence can lead to preventive action when a specific warning about an attack (typically found at the tactical level) is made available to policymakers who are receptive to that warning. In particular, these two cases strongly suggest that strategic intelligence and warning—the long-range, big-picture intelligence that is most often demanded by policymakers and is considered the goal of most intelligence agencies—is not enough to prevent surprise attacks.

To fully test the concept of preventive action would involve examining a large data set of surprise attacks—preferably including both successful and unsuccessful attacks—and determining whether the factors of precise intelligence and receptive policymakers appear to explain the results better than other available explanations. Such a study is beyond the scope of this book, at least partly because such a data set of surprise attacks does not exist. Although a great number of books and articles have been written about the problem of surprise attack, and the list of successful surprise attacks is long, surprisingly little is known about cases in which surprise attacks have been foiled.

Instead, this chapter is intended as an initial step toward testing the concept of preventive action, through the use of what might be called "mini–case studies" of conventional surprise attack. The goal is to conduct a relatively brief review of several of the best-known cases, to determine whether the presence or absence of the two factors of precise warning and receptive policymakers helps to explain the outcomes. This chapter is modeled on comparable chapters in works by Richard Betts and Richard Posner. The nine cases examined in this chapter include all of the post–World War II cases discussed by Betts and Posner, with the addition of two prominent cases not covered by them.[1]

Although all these cases are well known, the argument here is that the model of preventive action does more to explain the outcome than do more traditional accounts. Four of these cases are frequently cited as classic examples of intelligence failure to foresee surprise attack: the outbreak of the Korean War in June 1950, the intervention by China in Korea later that year, the 1968 Tet Offensive in Vietnam, and the 1973 Yom Kippur War in the Middle East. The remaining five cases may be even more interesting, because they are cases in which American intelligence agencies and analysts have been credited with at least warning of the potential for surprise attack: the 1956 Israeli attack on Egypt, the Arab-Israeli Six-Day War in 1967, the 1968 Soviet invasion of Czechoslovakia, the 1979 Soviet invasion of Afghanistan, and Iraq's invasion of Kuwait in 1990. As this chapter explains, most of these cases are not true intelligence successes as described in this book, because in most cases the attack was successful and American policymakers were surprised despite having been warned. But all these cases add to our understanding of how it is that surprise attacks so often succeed.

THE OUTBREAK OF THE KOREAN WAR, JUNE 1950

The attack by North Korea against South Korea on June 25, 1950, came as an utter shock to most American policymakers, military commanders, and intelligence agencies. Officials in Washington were preoccupied with the larger problems of the Cold War, and had assumed that North Korea would only act with the approval of the Soviet Union—and because the Soviets surely knew such a step could lead to world war, they would never condone it. At General Douglas MacArthur's Far East Command in Tokyo, there was little concern about the threat from the clearly inferior North Korean military. And within the intelligence community, few agencies or assets were focused on such a secondary area of concern. As an article in the CIA journal *Studies in Intelligence* put it, "No one in the US Government seemed worried about Korea."[2]

There were, however, a number of warnings that the North might be preparing to attack, and in many ways the outbreak of the Korean War was a classic case of intelligence failure and surprise attack. It was a case in which, to use Wohlstetter's later phrase, the available warning signals were lost amid a sea of other noise. Strategic, nonspecific warnings, such as propaganda statements from the North and incidents along the border, were common, but as Richard Betts describes, they only "served to dull sensitivity more than to heighten it."[3] The problem of decision maker misperception was clearly evident, as American leaders held strongly to their beliefs even in the face of evidence of a threat. As an example, in March 1950, MacArthur's headquarters sent a report warning that an attack would come in June, but added the comment, "We don't believe this statement."

Another classic problem illustrated in Korea is the dilemma between capabilities and intentions; one can often gain a good understanding of an enemy's capabilities, but its intentions are much more opaque. CIA reporting during the spring of 1950 noted a North Korean troop buildup, and a report on June 20 concluded that the North had the capability to invade the South at any time. But other CIA reports during the same period made the argument that the North, a "firmly controlled Soviet satellite," would never act on its own.[4]

The case of Korea in June 1950, then, can be explained by most of the conventional explanations for intelligence failure to anticipate surprise attack. But the case also can be explained by the concept of preventive action, for both of the key factors that can make intelligence actionable—precise warning, and receptive decision makers—were absent.

Specific, tactical-level intelligence on the coming North Korean attack was not available, partly because the North made a deliberate effort during the weeks leading up to the invasion to reduce its troop activity and adopt a more conciliatory diplomatic stance. But in any case, American intelligence was not looking very hard for warnings of war in Korea. Little effort was put on monitoring the North's communications; as a National Security Agency (NSA) historical study noted, "the North Korean target was ignored."[5] For its part, the CIA had few of its own sources on information on North Korea, and most of its reports before the outbreak of the war were derived from State Department, military, or open source press reporting.[6]

There is debate among experts today about whether the primary intelligence failure in Korea in June 1950 was one of analysis or of collection.[7] Richard Mobley has argued convincingly that the lack of clear, tactical indications of the North's preparations for attack showed that the primary failure lay in terms of intelligence collection.[8] But even if more intelligence had been gathered, it is not at all clear that American decision makers—either political or military—would have paid much attention. They were unreceptive. The primary problem was that few, if any, American leaders or senior intelligence officials felt there was any danger of an attack in Korea.[9] As Mobley puts it, even a more urgently written warning would not have been likely to convince American leaders to take action: "Even had it been packaged differently, the key decision makers would have wanted more compelling evidence that an attack was imminent instead of just possible."[10]

CHINESE INTERVENTION IN KOREA, NOVEMBER 1950

The intervention of Chinese troops into the conflict in Korea in the fall of 1950 presented a second great shock to American leaders and intelligence officials, and it has been seen by historians as an even more puzzling intelligence failure. Although the warnings of war in June had been muted and came mostly at the broad strategic level, the intelligence on the threat from China later that year was much clearer, and came at both the strategic and tactical levels. The Chinese sent strong diplomatic signals, such as a warning conveyed through the Indian ambassador to China that the People's Republic of China (PRC) would intervene if the Americans crossed north of the 38th parallel. And there was a steady drumbeat of reporting in October and November that massive numbers of Chinese troops were moving toward the Korean border. Why, then, did American officials once again fail to understand the warnings of an attack in Korea?

Several experts have argued that intelligence agencies did a good job of collecting and reporting on the threat from China. An article in the NSA's classified journal, for example, noted that there had been many warnings in communications intelligence about the threat of Chinese involvement, and argued that "no one who received COMINT [communications intelligence] product, including MacArthur's own G-2 in Tokyo, should have been surprised by the PRC intervention in the Korean War."[11] The CIA warned soon after the war had begun in June that Chinese forces could become involved. But though on the one hand the CIA was providing worrisome tactical reporting—such as that Chinese units composed of ethnic Korean soldiers appeared to be prepared to become involved—on the other hand it was providing more reassuring strategic analysis that there were no indications that the Soviets intended to have China intervene. As an article in the CIA in-house journal notes, this type of balancing act "became the preferred art form for most Agency reporting through late November."[12] Even after the US amphibious landing at Inchon in September, and in the face of its own reporting that increasing numbers of Chinese troops were assembling near the border, the CIA assessed that a full Chinese intervention "is not probable in 1950."[13]

South Korean troops began coming into contact with Chinese forces beginning on October 25, when the Chinese began what they called their First Phase Offensive. Chinese prisoners of war—interrogated by US Army intelligence officers—told of a large Chinese presence in Korea. But intelligence assessments, both from the CIA and from MacArthur's command, continued to judge that there was no major Chinese intervention under way. In November American forces started engaging Chinese troops, and by the middle of the month twelve Chinese divisions had been identified in Korea. Nonetheless, a National Intelligence Estimate issued on November 24 stated that whereas China had the capability for large-scale offensive operations, there were no indications that such an offensive was taking place.[14] On that same day the Chinese began a second major offensive, and by November 28, MacArthur had been forced to recognize that he faced a completely new war.

This was indeed a classic case of an attack that came as a complete surprise despite the presence of ample warning. Experts such as Grabo have described the failure as an example of the difficulty in determining enemy intentions.[15] For Betts, the bulk of the blame lies with American policymakers and senior military officials, who through a "mix of hubris, wishfulness, and miscalculation" did not believe that China would invade and refused to accept the warnings they received.[16] Here the crucial factor missing was receptivity to the intelligence on the part of decision makers. The intelligence should have been actionable given its specificity, but the crucial ingredient of receptivity was lacking. As an example of how resistant American military leaders were to warnings about the Chinese, there are reports that MacArthur's intelligence chief, Major General Charles Willoughby, deliberately manipulated intelligence reports to exclude the threat from China.[17]

THE 1956 ISRAELI ATTACK ON EGYPT

The 1956 Arab-Israeli War began with an attack by Israel into the Sinai Peninsula on October 29, 1956. This attack, known as Operation Kadesh, was an operational success that stunned Egyptian leaders. Even though Israel had not revealed its plans to the United States, the US intelligence community had been able to assess the situation correctly and warn American leaders of the impending operation. Yet the Israeli attack still came as a shock to American policymakers, making this case an outstanding example of how policymakers can be surprised, even though they have been warned.[18]

The Egyptian leader Gamal Abdel Nasser nationalized the Suez Canal in July 1956, and US intelligence assessments published soon afterward did not foresee that Israel would take any major military action. On July 31, a Special National Intelligence Estimate stated that Israel would "view with satisfaction" the growing rift between Egypt and the West, but it added, "We do not believe, however, that Israel will attack Egypt, at least during the early phases of this crisis."[19]

By late October, however, the warning signs were increasing. On October 26, the director of the National Indications Center wrote a memo titled "Possibility of Israeli Raid on Egypt." The memo noted that the members of the Watch Committee, the organization responsible for such top-level warnings, "generally agree that the likelihood has increased of major Israeli reprisals, probably against Egypt in the near future." But the memo added that Israel did not appear to be making a full mobilization, and was not believed to be preparing for general hostilities.[20] Other reports of an Israeli mobilization came to Washington from the army attaché in Tel Aviv, who reported that mobilization was on a larger scale than anything since the 1948–49 war.[21]

Then, on October 28, a "Special Watch Report of the Intelligence Advisory Committee" was published, reporting "new evidence of heavy Israeli mobilization" that could permit Israel to invade either Jordan or Egypt. It stated that the scale of Israeli mobilization and other factors "all provide a favorable opportunity for a major attack," and advised that developments "indicate the attack will be launched against Egypt in the very near future."[22] Also on that same day, the director of the National Indications Center sent another memo to the Intelligence Advisory Committee, summarizing the evidence that supported the special watch report. This memo was titled "Evidence Bearing on the Possibility of an Israeli Attack on Egypt."[23]

American intelligence, then, had provided both long-range strategic warning of the crisis between Israel and its Arab neighbors, as well as specific, tactical-level reporting on Israeli preparations for military action. A later CIA assessment noted that the Watch Committee had "provided several days of advance warning of the imminent possibility of Israeli-Egyptian hostilities and 24 hours' specific warning of Israel's intention to attack Egypt with French and (initially) tacit British support."[24] According to an expert on the NSA, "In the weeks leading up to the 1956 Arab-Israeli War, SIGINT [signals intelligence] proved to be a critically important source of intelligence indicating that war was imminent."[25]

Nonetheless, the Israeli attack surprised President Eisenhower and other American leaders, who did not believe the warnings they were given. This lack of receptivity came in part because Eisenhower had trusted the personal assurances he had been given by the Israeli leaders that Israel would not become involved in the dispute over the Suez Canal. In addition, the president and other senior American officials had been taken in by an Israeli deception campaign that suggested any action would come against Jordan, rather than Egypt. As an article in the CIA's *Studies in Intelligence* notes, "the British-French-Israeli deception perpetrated on the United States during the Suez Crisis was one of the most successful operations of its kind ever undertaken."[26]

THE 1967 SIX-DAY WAR: AN AMERICAN INTELLIGENCE SUCCESS

Israel launched another surprise attack in 1967, beginning the Six-Day War with an offensive against Egypt on June 5. The American intelligence community's performance in this case has been often cited as an example of an outstanding intelligence success, providing what has come to be remembered as a near-perfect estimate: that it would take the Israelis from seven to nine days to recapture the Suez Canal. In the event, the war actually lasted six days. According to the director of national intelligence, "Community all-source analysts correctly forecast the timing, duration, and outcome of the Arab-Israeli crisis. Their pithy, well-reasoned product enabled the president to modulate US involvement and avoid a larger US-Soviet confrontation."[27] The CIA proudly noted that "through analytic rigor, the agency made a near-perfect forecast of the 1967 Mideast War."[28] And former acting director of the CIA Richard Kerr writes, "The 1967 Six-Day War is a case study of how US intelligence 'got it right.'"[29]

The CIA's assessments were actually slightly less precise than they are sometimes remembered as being, but the Six-Day War still deserves to be seen as one of the few cases in American history when excellent strategic and tactical warning combined with policymaker receptivity to produce unmistakable intelligence success. It was an even greater American intelligence success than in the 1956 Israeli attack on Egypt, because in this case the president listened to the CIA's warnings, and the war did not come as a surprise to American leaders.[30]

There were actually two predictions, and in both cases the intelligence community, led by the CIA, got it right. The first and best known was about the result of the war that everyone expected would come between Israel and its Arab neighbors: Would Israel be able to survive on its own, or did the United States need to get actively involved? The second was a question of timing: When would Israel strike?

As president, Lyndon Johnson had not been particularly interested in reports he received from the intelligence community; as an article in the CIA's in-house journal put it, "Johnson was a hard sell."[31] But the director of central intelligence, Richard Helms, pushed the CIA to be ready to respond when needed, and as tensions in the Middle East rose in 1967, he set up a task force to monitor the situation. That proactive posture paid off on May 23, when Johnson told Helms he wanted an assessment of the situation in the Middle East—and Helms was able to respond within four hours, in time for one of LBJ's famous Tuesday lunches. One of the two memos Helms provided that day stated that Israel would be able to defend itself successfully and would win the coming war.

A later paper produced by the Board of National Estimates titled "Military Capabilities of Israel and the Arab States" has become famous as the estimate that called the war right. Although early drafts had said that Israel would need seven to nine days to reach the Suez Canal, the final paper was not so precise, estimating that Israel could breach Egypt's forward lines in the Sinai within "several" days.[32] But that was enough information for Johnson, who accepted the assessment and decided not to publicly support Israel or send it military aid.

Having answered the question of who would win, Helms was also able to warn the president about when the war would begin. On June 1, Helms met with a senior Israeli official, who told him that Israel could no longer delay making a decision about what to do. When that official was recalled to Israel the next day, Helms immediately warned the president that war was imminent.[33] Then on June 3, the CIA task force issued a memorandum warning that "all reporting from Israel shows mounting pressure for a 'decision,'" and on June 4, the day before the Israeli offensive began, the NSA reportedly decoded an intercept that revealed the Israelis intended to attack Egypt within 24 hours.[34]

The key factor in this case was that LBJ was receptive to the information Helms was giving him, even though it contradicted the more dire warnings (and requests for assistance) he was receiving from Israeli officials. His receptivity was not a result of any close relationship he had with Helms.[35] Nor does it appear to be the case that he was responding to particularly brilliant or imaginative intelligence analysis.[36] In this case what worked is that the CIA had prepared extensively to be able to answer questions quickly, that the problem was a relatively clear one, and that analysts had been able to devote considerable time to collect-ing and analyzing information. In addition, American intelligence officials bene-fited to some extent from the insights provided by their Israeli counterparts (especially about the timing of the Israeli attack); and when they were able to produce an unambiguous and unanimous assessment, it happened to align with the policy desires of the administration—that Israel would be able to win without American help.

THE TET OFFENSIVE, JANUARY 1968

Less than twenty years after the twin shocks of the Korean War, American leaders were again surprised by an attack coming from the northern half of a divided Asian nation. The failure to anticipate the Tet Offensive was yet another classic case in which numerous warning signals and intelligence reports were ignored, and in two ways it closely resembled the second surprise attack in Korea, the failure associated with the Chinese intervention. First, just as in Korea during the fall of 1950, there was a great deal of warning in 1967 and 1968 from both strategic and tactical intelligence about what the enemy was preparing to do. But American intelligence officials and commanders in Saigon and in Washington—with a few exceptions discounted the warnings, and were surprised when the North launched a major offensive.

Second, and more unusually, the surprise of Tet did not come at the begin-ning of a war, but rather during an ongoing conflict. As James Wirtz describes in his book on the intelligence failure of Tet, we might expect that intelligence agencies and policymakers would be less likely to suffer from a major surprise in the middle of a war, when the identity of the enemy is clear and all attention is focused on the problem of identifying what might happen next.[37] And yet in the case of the Tet Offensive, as with the Chinese intervention in Korea, America was indeed deeply surprised.

North Vietnamese leaders decided in July 1967 to launch an offensive during Tet, the beginning of the Lunar New Year and the most important Vietnamese holiday. From that point until the actual start of the offensive on January 31, 1968, American officials missed many indications about the developing threat. One important strategic indicator whose importance was missed was the publi-cation in September 1967 of an article by General Giap, North Vietnam's defense minister, titled "The Big Victory, The Great Task." In this article—which was hardly a secret, as it was broadcast publicly by Radio Hanoi—Giap provided a general description of the Tet Offensive to come.[38]

Tactical intelligence was also obtained on many of the details of the coming offensive, including the discovery that the Viet Cong had placed weapons caches around Saigon. As the Tet holiday neared, communications intelligence revealed increasingly specific information about North Vietnamese activity. But despite these and many other indications, the US commander General William Westmoreland and his staff at Military Assistance Command, Vietnam, did not believe there was any significant threat to the southern part of the country. The conventional wisdom was that an offensive, if it came, would concentrate near the Demilitarized Zone rather than in the urban areas to the south.[39] As Wirtz writes, American commanders were not receptive: "Although Americans received an ever-increasing amount of detailed information about the targets, tactics, and even timing of the Tet attacks, they generally downplayed the threat posed against urban areas, government installations, ARVN units [i.e., units of the Army of the Republic of Vietnam—the South Vietnamese Army], and US facilities during December 1967 and January 1968."[40]

Although important (and, it was later realized, accurate) warnings and intelligence reports were issued from the CIA station in Vietnam and from the NSA, policymakers in Washington and military commanders in Vietnam refused to believe them. A study by the CIA's Center for the Study of Intelligence later found that "the most important cause of American surprise was the deliberately optimistic mindsets" of key policymakers leading up to Tet, and there was a "pronounced gulf between their beliefs and reality."[41] After Tet the intelligence community produced a postmortem report that attempted to determine what went wrong. The report was generally favorable about the performance by intelligence agencies, noting that a considerable amount of warning had in fact been produced. But it acknowledged that even so, the overall scope and scale of the offensive came as a surprise, because "most commanders and intelligence officers, at all levels, did not visualize the enemy as capable of accomplishing his stated goals as they appeared in propaganda and in captured documents."[42]

In Vietnam before the Tet Offensive, the key problem was a lack of receptivity toward warning intelligence on the part of military commanders, policymakers, and even senior intelligence officers. The lack of receptivity appears to have been greatest in Washington, and less evident among officials in Saigon, at least in part because analysts and officials in Vietnam made greater use than Washington did of captured North Vietnamese documents that provided a relatively clear picture of the offensive to come.[43]

THE SOVIET INVASION OF CZECHOSLOVAKIA, AUGUST 1968

The case of the Soviet invasion of Czechoslovakia on August 20, 1968, is a clear demonstration of how timely warning and perceptive analysis is not enough to avoid surprise unless it is accompanied by policymaker receptivity. American leaders knew that a Soviet invasion was possible in response to the liberal policies of the "Prague Spring" under Alexander Dubček. The US intelligence community provided extensive warning of the Soviet buildup of forces. And the CIA director even warned President Johnson personally that an invasion was likely. But still the assault came as a surprise to LBJ, who learned of it not from the CIA but from the Soviet ambassador.[44]

In this case long-term, strategic warning was just about as good as it can be. The official NSA history, for example, writes of this case that the "strategic warning was impeccable."[45] At a symposium in 2010 on intelligence and the invasion, one scholar said, "In terms of strategic warning, they did a very good job."[46] That warning began early, as a postmortem of the intelligence community's performance found that the community had first begun to suggest that a Soviet military intervention into Czechoslovakia "was a real possibility" in late March 1968.[47] In July the CIA reported that the possibility of an invasion existed, but it cautioned that "we know of no way of foretelling the precise event in Czechoslovakia which might trigger such an extreme Soviet reaction."[48]

American intelligence agencies never received warning of a Soviet decision to intervene, but as the invasion neared they did collect specific, tactical-level warning of extensive Soviet preparations. On August 2, a CIA memo reported that five Soviet field armies were poised near the Czech border, and "it appears that the Soviet high command has in about two weeks' time completed military preparations sufficient for intervening in Czechoslovakia if that is deemed necessary by the political leadership."[49] Not all sources of intelligence were available during this period; during the weeks leading up to the invasion, the CIA did not have the support of photoreconnaissance satellites. A satellite was in orbit, but its canister was not recovered until after the invasion, and Donald Steury writes that "when it was, the film showed Soviet forces deployed to invade—airfields packed with aircraft, Soviet military vehicles painted with white crosses to distinguish themselves from identical Czech equipment."[50] But signals intelligence was available, and shortly before the invasion analysts at the NSA intercepted communications that convinced them the Soviets were about to act. On August 19, the NSA issued an alert, warning that Soviet radio traffic indicated that the USSR was about to invade.[51]

This case is a vivid example of how a brilliant analysis and the ability to "connect the dots" will do little good if decision makers are not willing to listen. On the morning of the invasion, Director of Central Intelligence Richard Helms met with several of his senior officials. They had just learned from a wire service report that the Soviet leaders had been summoned to Moscow for an urgent Politburo meeting. Such a meeting was unusual, and taken together with the Soviet military activity, Helms decided this most likely meant that the invasion of Czechoslovakia was imminent. Helms had already been scheduled to meet with LBJ that day, and he conveyed his warning to the president personally. But the president rejected Helms's conclusion, saying, "Dick, that Moscow meeting is to talk about us."[52] LBJ knew that the Soviet Union and the United States were about to make a major announcement about upcoming strategic arms limitation talks, and he believed—wrongly—that this was what the Kremlin meeting was about.[53]

How much warning would have been enough? American decision makers knew that the Czech government's actions had provoked Moscow (strategic warning), and they knew of the Soviet troop buildup and preparations for an attack (tactical warning). President Johnson had even been warned by his top intelligence official that an invasion was imminent. But even then, there was no proof of what the Soviets actually intended to do, and LBJ and other senior officials did not think they would invade. According to several accounts the only warning that could have convinced American leaders of what was about to happen would have been intelligence on the Soviet decision to launch an attack. The CIA postmortem, for example, found that warning of a Soviet decision to invade "was not given and could not have been given under the circumstances and with the information available at the time."[54]

Without such intelligence on Soviet intentions, policymakers were left with what were ultimately ambiguous warnings, and that was not enough to convince them to take the threat seriously. But the case of Czechoslovakia in 1968 helps confirm the assessment of experts such as Cynthia Grabo that warning of the enemy's decision to attack is very rarely available and is too much for policymakers to expect.[55] And even when it is available, such as before Midway, leaders are as likely to suspect deception as they are to act on the intelligence. What can be useful, however, is specific, tactical-level intelligence on the enemy preparations for attack; but for it to be effective, policymakers must be receptive. In the case of Czechoslovakia, the intelligence community called it right, but LBJ and other leaders disregarded the call.

THE YOM KIPPUR WAR, OCTOBER 1973

The October 1973 Yom Kippur War, also known as the October War, began with a surprise attack by Egypt across the Suez Canal into Israel. Although the Israeli military was able to recover and mount a successful counterattack, the initial surprise was seen as a great blow to Israel's pride and an intelligence failure ranking with Pearl Harbor, Korea, and Tet.

But the Israeli intelligence agencies were not the only ones that failed to anticipate the Yom Kippur War: US intelligence was also watching Israel's Arab neighbors, and it failed to warn of the attack that threatened the very existence of one of America's closest allies. In the words of Richard Betts, "American intelligence, with its vast panoply of sophisticated intelligence collection mechanisms, made virtually all the same mistakes as the Israelis."[56] In fact, the story is even worse: Despite an abundance of information on impending hostilities, US intelligence agencies not only failed to see an attack coming but actually predicted that there would be no war.[57]

Charles Allen was a CIA official at the time and served later in a number of senior intelligence community positions, including as the national intelligence officer for warning and as the Department of Homeland Security's intelligence chief. He has said that "even today, I feel personally seared by my failure and the Agency's failure to warn of the Middle East War of October 1973. The indicators were there, but we failed to act on what were painfully obvious indicators—which we saw clearly ex post facto—that major conflict was about to erupt in the Middle East."[58]

There had been many warnings, at both the strategic and tactical levels, but even so most intelligence reporting judged that an attack was unlikely. An example was a report from the CIA on October 5, the day before the attack began: "The exercise and alert activities under way in Egypt may be on a somewhat larger scale and more realistic than previous exercises, but they do not appear to be preparing for a military offensive against Israel."[59]

An intelligence community study of the failure found that the information available should have been enough to lead analysts to warn that an attack had been imminent; the intelligence "was not conclusive but was plentiful, ominous, and often accurate."[60] The study listed a number of pieces of specific intelligence that had been available—most of which were blacked out in the version made public—and noted in a strongly worded rebuke, "there is no gainsaying the judgment that, whatever the rationale, the principal conclusions concerning the imminence of hostilities reached and reiterated by those responsible for intelligence analysis were—quite simply, obviously, and starkly—wrong."[61]

Where did American intelligence professionals go wrong in 1973? Many factors contributed to their failure, including preconceptions on the part of analysts who did not believe that Arab militaries were as capable as those of Israel. This belief was partly the result of ill-informed bias, but it was also to some extent correct: Egypt did in fact lack the military capability it needed to win a war against Israel, and thus the analysts assumed that Egyptian leaders knew that and would act rationally.[62] American officials also relied too heavily on the overly optimistic assumptions of their Israeli counterparts; as the State Department's intelligence chief, Ray Cline, said, "Our difficulty was partly that we were brainwashed by the Israelis, who brainwashed themselves."[63] And American intelligence was also fooled, as were the Israelis, by deception on the part of the Egyptians. Ultimately, however, the problem was a familiar one: For all these reasons, senior American policy officials as well as intelligence officers were unreceptive to the warnings that in hindsight, at least, appear obvious.

THE SOVIET INVASION OF AFGHANISTAN, DECEMBER 1979

Although the invasion of Czechoslovakia demonstrated that good warning is not enough to avoid surprise attack, the later Soviet invasion of Afghanistan was an even more striking example of how difficult it can be to avoid surprise even when excellent strategic and tactical warnings are available. Throughout 1979, American intelligence reported frequently on the deteriorating security situation in Afghanistan. As an insurgency grew against the Soviet-backed government early in the year, intelligence reporting at first assessed that the Soviets were unlikely to insert combat forces. During the summer and fall Soviet military activity in and around Afghanistan increased, but according to a CIA postmortem investigation and a study by former CIA deputy director for intelligence Douglas MacEachin, most analysts continued to believe it unlikely that the Soviets would move large numbers of troops into the country.[64]

Soviet military activity near Afghanistan increased dramatically in December, however, and on December 19 an Alert Memorandum was issued, warning that "the USSR has significantly changed the nature of its military commitment in Afghanistan and is now capable of conducting multibattalion combat operations."[65] On December 22 the NSA director, Bobby Ray Inman, called the national security adviser, Zbigniew Brzezinski, and the secretary of defense, Harold Brown, to tell them that there was "no doubt" the Soviets would begin a major military intervention within the next seventy-two hours, and then on December 24 he called them again to say that the move would begin within the next fifteen hours.[66]

But despite these warnings, the invasion still came as a shock to American policymakers—including President Jimmy Carter—and to many intelligence officials, who had not expected the Soviets to actually mount a major invasion.[67] Even after the invasion had begun, it was difficult for many in the intelligence community to accept that the Soviets had taken a step that would clearly be against their best interests. Intelligence reporting on December 26 and 27, for example, assessed that the forces being deployed into Afghanistan were likely to be used in small-scale operations to help prop up the Afghan regime.[68] When even most intelligence officials did not really believe the warnings about the possibility of a major Soviet invasion, it is easy to understand why senior American leaders were unreceptive to the intelligence reports they were receiving.

This case demonstrates the importance of the distinction between assessing *capabilities* and *intentions*. As several studies of the episode have concluded, the problem was not a lack of warning about what the Soviets were *capable* of doing but a failure to assess what they *wanted* to do. A later CIA study of intelligence failures found that "in hindsight, the intelligence community accurately estimated the advantages and disadvantages of intervention. . . . We had a clear understanding of their capabilities, but we misjudged their intentions."[69]

For the American intelligence community, this intelligence operation was a called a success in the sense that policymakers were warned repeatedly during the fall of 1979 that the Soviets might intervene in force. Through imagery, signals intelligence, and other sources, American intelligence had been able to track most of the Soviet Union's buildup near Afghanistan. In its postmortem study, the CIA stated that "the Intelligence Community's analysts met their basic responsibility in a situation of this sort by providing sufficient prior reporting to assure that no key policymaker should have been surprised by the invasion."[70] The official NSA history of the period is even more positive in its assessment: "This time there was no 'intelligence failure.' "[71]

These official assessments present a far too rosy picture of the intelligence community's performance in 1979. Intelligence officials do deserve some credit for at least hedging their bets—they reported the warning signs of a possible Soviet invasion, even though many analysts did not truly believe the warnings themselves. But this book argues that intelligence warnings count for little if decision makers are not receptive. American leaders, receiving contradictory reports from intelligence, were not convinced of the reality of the Soviet threat, and the invasion of Afghanistan was ultimately a failure for American intelligence.

IRAQ'S INVASION OF KUWAIT, 1990

The Iraqi invasion of Kuwait on August 2, 1990, may be the most dramatic example of a case in which all the strategic and tactical indicators of an attack were present and the intelligence community warned that an attack was imminent—yet once again policymakers were unreceptive, which resulted in strategic surprise.

As far as the intelligence community is concerned, this was a clear case of success. The CIA has stated, for example, that it "offered accurate and timely warning of Saddam Hussein's 1990 invasion of Kuwait."[72] The intelligence community had been closely monitoring Iraq beginning at least in early 1990, as Saddam's belligerent rhetoric against his neighbors increased.[73] In January the National Warning Staff reviewed key indicators of an Iraqi attack against Kuwait and Saudi Arabia, and in April the Department of Defense's intelligence agencies stepped up their collection, formally establishing what was called an Iraq "regional warning problem."[74] By July Iraq's financial situation was growing dire, as it faced huge international debts and saw the price of oil falling. Saddam began making public accusations that Kuwait was siphoning oil from the oilfield that lay underneath the Iraq-Kuwait border, and on July 15 he moved several divisions of Republican Guard troops to the border.

On July 25 Charles Allen, the national intelligence officer for warning, issued a "warning of war" memorandum that assessed Iraq had nearly achieved the capability to mount a corps-sized operation, and rated the chance of invasion at better than 60 percent.[75] Then on August 1, after satellite imagery and other sources revealed that Iraqi forces had moved into attack positions, Allen personally phoned senior officials at the National Security Council, the Vice President's Office, the State Department, and the Pentagon to give them what he called a "warning of attack," telling them that he could promise no further warning after that—the Iraqi military was ready to move.[76] Despite these warnings, however, when the invasion came it was a shock to American leaders, who had not expected Saddam to actually carry through on his threats. Allen writes that although the intelligence community had assessed the indicators correctly, "the warning messages of the NIO [national intelligence officer] for warning—for warning of war and warning of attack—were not heeded, either by senior intelligence officials or policymakers."[77]

What went wrong? Part of the problem was that even in this case, in which Iraq's military preparations were closely monitored and Saddam made no effort to hide his aggressiveness, intelligence could not know what actions Iraq would actually take. Much of the intelligence reporting during the weeks before the invasion argued that although Iraq was capable of mounting a major assault, it was not likely to do so. On July 25, for example—the day Charles Allen issued his forward-leaning "warning of war" memo—the top-level *National Intelligence Daily* published a more ambiguous article titled "Iraq-Kuwait: Is Iraq Bluffing?"[78] And also on that day the Defense Intelligence Agency released a Defense Special Assessment that seemed to argue both sides of the question: "Although unlikely to use military pressure, Iraq is marshaling forces sufficient to invade Kuwait," and could occupy all of Kuwait in five days.[79] As late as August 1, when Allen was warning that an attack was imminent, other senior intelligence officials were assessing that a major attack was unlikely.[80]

For American leaders, however, there was an even greater problem than just gauging the distinction between capabilities and intentions. In deciding what to think about the situation, many senior officials relied heavily on the views of their counterparts in the Middle East. As Robert Gates, then the deputy national security advisor, later remembered thinking, "Who knows Saddam Hussein better? King Fahd, the Amir of Kuwait, or a GS-15 analyst out in Langley, Virginia?"[81] The problem was that these foreign leaders, who reassured American officials that Iraq was merely posturing in order to pressure Kuwait over oil production levels, were completely wrong. King Hussein of Jordan, for example, assured President George H. W. Bush in a July 31 phone call that the crisis would be resolved without fighting.[82]

Because of the inherently ambiguous nature of the available intelligence, and because they were receiving more optimistic assessments from elsewhere, American officials were not receptive when they were warned that Iraq was about to invade Kuwait. Allen later commented, "I did sound the warning bell, and, surprisingly, there were very few listeners on the other side. I was accused of being an alarmist."[83] As Mary McCarthy put it, "The warners warned, but the rest of the Community equivocated. Thus, policymakers were not persuaded that the threat was real."[84] General Lee Butler, then the senior plans officer (J-5) on the staff of the Joint Chiefs of Staff and later the commander in chief of the US

Strategic Command, said starkly, "We had the warning from the intelligence community—we refused to acknowledge it."[85]

CONCLUSION

One lesson that stands out from these cases is that the problem of avoiding a surprise attack can be just as challenging during war as it is at the outbreak of war. In Korea in the fall of 1950, for example, the warnings of Chinese intervention were much stronger and came from many more sources than had the warnings prior to the North's invasion in June. And yet the second surprise was just as strong as the first. Similarly, US leaders were surprised by the Tet Offensive in 1968, even though it came during wartime, when presumably the threat was well understood and all available intelligence assets were focused on determining what the North planned to do.

These cases show that long-range, strategic warning is not enough to convince decision makers to take action to prevent surprise attacks. But they also demonstrate that even very accurate, tactical warnings may not be enough. As Steve Chan has noted, the accuracy of intelligence forecasts and warnings is not in itself a determinant factor in preventing surprise attacks. Accuracy in warning may be a necessary, but not a sufficient, condition for a successful warning.[86] An accurate warning may come too late to be effective, or it may not be believed by the decision maker, especially when he or she is receiving contradictory assessments from other sources.

The most important factor in producing actionable intelligence to prevent a conventional surprise attack is policymaker receptivity—but this chapter shows how difficult it is to determine what makes a leader receptive toward intelligence. Decision makers fail to listen to the warnings from intelligence professionals for a variety of reasons. In some cases, such as 1973, policymakers are unreceptive because they assume that the attacker will act in a rational manner. In other cases, they do not listen because of fixed preconceptions about the way events will play out, or because they prefer to rely on assessments they receive from other sources such as counterparts overseas. And as we have seen here, even when leaders receive dire warnings that an attack is coming, there is always another, more ambiguous report available to which they can instead choose to listen.

What factors help encourage receptivity? The case of the Tet Offensive suggests that proximity to the threat may be a factor in producing receptivity, given that officials in Saigon were more willing to believe threats of an upcoming offensive than were leaders in Washington. But the clearest case of intelligence success in this chapter—that of LBJ and American assessments of the Six-Day War in 1967—shows just how difficult it can be to predict intelligence receptivity. President Johnson was not predisposed to pay attention to intelligence, and it took a combination of factors to convince him to trust the advice he was given. In the end the deciding factor may have been that the intelligence assessments were in line with the policy he wanted to follow anyway—to stay out of the conflict and let Israel win on its own.

It is not surprising that in the case of conventional surprise attacks, receptivity should be the most critical limiting factor. As these cases have demonstrated, the other key factor for preventive action—specific, tactical-level warning—is often available, because modern national intelligence systems are well suited to detecting the sorts of preparations that a nation-state must make when getting ready to mount a major assault. In several of the cases examined in this chapter, the intelligence picture was about as clear as it could ever be—except that the one piece of information American intelligence did not know was what the enemy intended to do. Assessing the intention of a conventional enemy is much more an art than a science, and convincing decision makers to pay attention to such assessments is often the most difficult part of the intelligence process. The history of American intelligence successes and failures indicates that even when intelligence gets it right—even when intelligence agencies and analysts feel strongly that an enemy is about to attack—their assessment is of little use because policymakers are unreceptive.

In the case of surprise attacks from terrorists, however, the situation is different. National intelligence systems are often unable to gather the same level of warning about actions from nonstate actors as they can from conventional military forces, and the challenge of determining enemy intentions is different as well. Part II of this book explores the problem of preventing terrorist attacks.

PART II

THE PROBLEM OF TERRORIST SURPRISE ATTACK

CHAPTER 5

THE EAST AFRICA
EMBASSY BOMBINGS

Disaster Despite Warning

IN NOVEMBER 1997 an Egyptian man named Mustafa Mahmoud Said Ahmed walked into the US embassy in Nairobi and told the authorities a remarkable story. He said he was part of a group that was planning to blow up the embassy building by detonating a bomb-laden truck in the underground parking garage. The attack, he claimed, would involve several vehicles and the use of stun grenades, and he said he had already taken surveillance photos of the embassy. But when CIA officials interviewed him, they were skeptical about his claims. They gave him a lie detector test, which he failed. They were told by Israeli intelligence that Ahmed was not to be trusted. And according to some reports, they learned he had made similar claims about other embassies before. Eventually, the CIA sent several warnings to the State Department, and the embassy in Nairobi increased its security for a short time, but nothing else was done about his warnings. Ahmed was turned over to the Kenyan authorities, which deported him.

Less than a year later, on August 7, 1998, the embassy in Nairobi was attacked by two men who attempted to drive a truck bomb into the garage below the building. When the Kenyan security guards would not let them in, the attackers began shooting and threw a stun grenade at the guards before detonating the explosives. A total of 213 people were killed, including 12 Americans, and an estimated 4,000 were injured. At almost exactly the same time, another attack was made against the US embassy in Dar es Salaam, killing 11 people. They were the first attacks planned and executed by al-Qaeda under the direct supervision of Osama bin Laden and his chief lieutenants.

The CIA's decision to disregard Ahmed's warning can be seen in hindsight as an understandable mistake—after all, he could have been simply trying to make some money in exchange for peddling his story. But Ahmed the walk-in was not the only warning that the US authorities received before the bombings of the US embassies in Kenya and Tanzania in 1998. Almost all the elements needed for preventing a surprise attack had been present: Intelligence collection and analysis were good, there were ample intelligence warnings at both the strategic and tactical levels, and local officials on the scene were quite receptive to those warnings. But despite the warnings, the al Qaeda cell in East Africa was able to carry out the attacks.

What went wrong? To help answer this question, this chapter begins with the background to the embassy bombings, describing al-Qaeda's lengthy planning process and how its operatives conducted the attacks.[1] It next describes how the bombings have been explained by the official commission that investigated the attacks and by others, and then turns to a study of the intelligence that had been available before the bombings, first at the strategic and then the tactical levels. Next is a review of the receptivity of US officials in Nairobi and Dar es Salaam, and officials in Washington, toward those warnings. The chapter concludes by analyzing the facts of this case in terms of the model of preventive action.

BACKGROUND

Although the embassy bombings were apparently the first terrorist attacks to be directly planned and carried out by al-Qaeda itself, Osama bin Laden had been calling for attacks against the United States and other Western countries since at least 1991, when he moved from Saudi Arabia to Sudan. Some of his early efforts involved coordination with and support from Iran. Al-Qaeda and Iranian representatives met in Sudan in late 1991 or 1992 and came to an informal agreement to cooperate in providing support for actions against Israel and the United States. Senior al-Qaeda operatives and trainers then traveled to Iran to receive training in explosives, and in the fall of 1993 another al-Qaeda delegation went to the Bekaa Valley in Lebanon for more training in explosives and in intelligence and security. According to the *9/11 Commission Report*, "Bin Ladin reportedly showed particular interest in learning how to use truck bombs such as the one that had killed 241 US Marines in Lebanon in 1983."[2]

During the early and mid-1990s al-Qaeda focused on providing funds, training, and weapons for attacks carried out by other groups.[3] In 1993 al-Qaeda members provided military training and weapons to Somali warlords fighting against US forces in Somalia, and al-Qaeda members later boasted that their assistance led to the October 1993 shooting down of two US Black Hawk helicopters and the later withdrawal of US forces from Somalia.[4] Much of this support for the Somalia conflict was provided out of a cell established in Nairobi—a cell that was to develop into the organizational base for the planning and staging of the embassy attacks.

Ali Mohammed: An Al-Qaeda Agent in America

The first concrete steps in planning the East Africa embassy bombings were taken in 1993 by a former Egyptian army officer named Ali Abdelsoud Mohamed. But Ali Mohamed was much more than just an al-Qaeda terrorist planner; he was also a key source of information on al-Qaeda for the CIA. His story illustrates the ability of al-Qaeda to insert a sleeper agent within American society, and thus it represents a major missed opportunity for US intelligence preceding the embassy bombings.[5]

Mohamed had been a major in the Egyptian army, reportedly serving in Special Forces and protecting Egyptian diplomats overseas. He had secretly joined the extremist Islamic Jihad movement, however, and was forced out of the army in 1984 because of his fundamentalist leanings. In that year he walked into the Cairo station of the CIA to offer his services, and he was sent to Germany to be an agent infiltrating mosques. But his employment with the CIA was terminated soon afterward, when he told clerics at one mosque that he had been hired by the CIA to spy on them. Unknown to him, the mosque had already been penetrated by other American agents who reported him to the CIA as a double agent.

But by the time the CIA fired him, he had already traveled to California, reportedly on a CIA visa waiver program.[6] On the flight to the United States he met an American woman, and soon they were married. He later became an American citizen, and signed up as an enlisted man in the US Army, becoming a sergeant assigned to supply duties at the Special Warfare Center at Fort Bragg, North Carolina. While there, he also served as an instructor, teaching troops about Middle Eastern culture.[7] Also while assigned to Fort Bragg, he once took several weeks' leave, telling friends he wanted to join the mujahideen in Afghanistan and kill Russians. On returning he told stories of having taken part in combat. His behavior was suspicious enough that he was reported to army intelligence, but he does not appear to have been the subject of any serious concern; in 1989 he was cast as the star in a series of army training videos designed to teach soldiers about how Islamic radicals saw the world. In that same year he left military service, obtaining an honorable discharge and joining the army reserve.[8]

Mohamed moved to Santa Clara, California, but he traveled extensively and at some point became associated with bin Laden. He also became associated with the Alkhifa Refugee Center in Brooklyn, and he was a friend of El Sayyid Nosair, the man who was convicted in 1990 in the assassination of the Jewish militant Rabbi Meir Kahane.[9] By 1991 he had become a top aide to the al-Qaeda leader, and was given the assignment of coordinating bin Laden's move that year from Afghanistan to Sudan.[10]

At some point Mohamed again approached the CIA, but it was no longer interested in him. The FBI, however, became interested when he offered to provide it with information on the smuggling of illegal aliens. He may have sought the position as an FBI source in order to shield himself from further suspicion, because the authorities were then beginning to learn of his ties to al-Qaeda. He reportedly provided some information about bin Laden and al-Qaeda, including when he was interviewed by US counterintelligence specialists in San Jose, California, in 1993.[11] But he was not arrested; nor were serious efforts apparently made to enlist him as a double agent.

Ali Mohamed in Nairobi

In late 1993, Ali Mohamed traveled to Nairobi to lead a team of al-Qaeda operatives who were to conduct surveillance of potential targets for attack.[12] The team set up a makeshift laboratory for developing surveillance photographs in an apartment that belonged to an al-Qaeda member named L'Houssaine Kherchtou. Their equipment included state-of-the-art video cameras obtained from China and from dealers in Germany, and they conducted surveillance in Nairobi as well as in Djibouti of American, British, French, and Israeli targets. The American embassy in Nairobi appeared to be an inviting target, at least in part because a car bomb could be parked close by, and Mohamed spent four or five days taking pictures of it, watching the traffic patterns, and noting the rotations of the guards. He drew up a plan of attack, which he put on an Apple PowerBook 140 computer.[13]

Mohamed went to Khartoum to make a presentation to bin Laden and other senior al-Qaeda leaders, who examined his surveillance files and photographs as well as diagrams prepared by another member of the surveillance team, a computer specialist. Mohamed later testified that bin Laden pointed to a picture of the embassy and indicated where a truck bomber might strike.[14] But at this point planning for the embassy attacks appears to have been delayed, for reasons that are not completely clear. The 9/11 Commission suggests that it was due to operational disruptions that are discussed later in this chapter; Lawrence Wright argues that once the international community withdrew from the relief operation in Somalia, the excuse for attacking the embassy was eliminated. In any case, as Wright describes the situation, "the plan was not forgotten, however; it was only filed away."[15]

Why Were These Targets Chosen?

It is also not clear why bin Laden chose these embassies to attack. It appears that the embassy in Nairobi was chosen at least partly because Kenya had been a logistics base for the American relief effort in Somalia in 1992 and 1993. Bin Laden later said in an interview that "the brutal US invasion of Somalia kicked off from there."[16] Ali Mohamed gave the same reason, saying in his plea agreement with the US government that he had traveled to Nairobi in order "to retaliate against the United States for its involvement in Somalia."[17]

But other reasons have also been suggested. One of the members of the al-Qaeda cell in Nairobi described several different reasons for the choice when he was interrogated after being captured following the attacks. He explained that he had been told the embassy was chosen because it had a large American presence; because the ambassador was a woman, which would result in a great deal of publicity for the bombing if she were killed; because personnel from the embassy worked in Sudan; because there were a number of Christian missionaries at the embassy; and because the ease of access to the embassy made it an easy target.[18] At other times bin Laden reportedly offered even more explanations, including that the genocide in Rwanda had been planned in these US embassies.[19]

Mohamed Odeh Arrives in Mombasa

In about August 1994, a Jordanian man named Mohamed Saddiq Odeh arrived in Mombasa from Pakistan.[20] He married a local woman and bought a fishing boat. For the next three years he worked as a fish merchant, traveling to ports up and down the Kenyan coast to buy fish from local fisherman and transport the catch back to Mombasa to resell it there. In 1997, after his wife had a baby boy, his wife's uncle gave them a small, mud-walled house in the small town of Witu, north of Mombasa. He started a carpentry shop, hoping to make furniture, but his relatives told reporters that he seemed to know little about carpentry, and the family lived in poverty.[21]

Odeh was not really a carpenter. He would later admit to Pakistani officials when he was captured after the bombing that he was a member of al-Qaeda who had met bin Laden while fighting against the Soviets in Afghanistan in 1990. The money to buy the fishing boat had been provided by al-Qaeda, and while he traveled up and down the coast buying fish from fishermen, he had also been gathering and transporting bomb-building components.[22] He would eventually build the bomb used in Dar es Salaam.

Other al-Qaeda members also began setting up operations in Kenya in 1994 and 1995. Wadih el Hage, an American citizen who had been a secretary for bin Laden in Sudan, moved from Khartoum to Nairobi and set up several businesses. These included a gem business called Tanzanite King, and a Muslim charity organization called Help Africa People.[23] Also in Kenya was Abu Ubaidah al-Banshiri, a former Egyptian policeman who was a top bin Laden aide and the operational commander of the East Africa cell.

Planning Is Delayed

In 1996 and 1997, planning for the East Africa attacks was delayed by several different developments. A key factor was that in 1995, bin Laden began to have difficulties in Sudan. International pressure was mounting on the Sudanese regime to expel him, and at the same time several of bin Laden's companies began losing money and he was forced to cut back on expenses. In May 1996, he returned to Afghanistan and was, in the words of the 9/11 Commission, "significantly weakened, despite his ambitions and organizational skills."[24]

The next major delay occurred in about May 1996, when Banshiri, the cell's commander, drowned in a ferryboat accident on Lake Victoria. To replace him bin Laden sent Harun Fazul, a Kenyan citizen who had been with al-Qaeda since at least 1990. Fazul arrived in Nairobi in 1997, and he shared a house with Wadih el Hage.[25]

Then, as described by the 9/11 Commission, "in August 1997, the Kenya cell panicked," after a British newspaper reported that Madani al Tayyib, the former head of al-Qaeda's finance committee, had been taken into custody by Saudi authorities. This much was correct; but the newspaper also reported incorrectly that the Saudis were sharing his information with the British MI6 and the CIA.[26] Al-Qaeda members around the world, including in East Africa, began telephoning each other to ask if anyone knew what Tayyib was saying; at one point a member of the Kenya cell warned another operative in Hamburg to stop calling because the lines were being tapped.[27]

Then, several weeks later, US and Kenyan officials searched Wadih el Hage's house in Nairobi, confirming for cell members that they were under suspicion and that el Hage's telephone was likely being tapped. El Hage returned to the United States the next month (September 1997), when he was brought before a grand jury investigating bin Laden. Fazul, who had been left in charge of the operation in Kenya, then sent a fax to several al-Qaeda sites warning that cell members were in "grave danger" because "America knows . . . that the followers of [bin Laden] . . . carried out the operations to hit Americans in Somalia."[28]

Final Planning Begins

By February 1998, the difficulties of the past two years had been overcome, and bin Laden was ready to begin final planning for the attacks. On February 23, he issued a public fatwa that ordered Muslims worldwide to kill Americans and their allies wherever possible, and soon afterward, the teams that were to carry out the two attacks began to be assembled. In May an Arabic-language newspaper in London published a new fatwa stating that it was the duty of Muslims to carry out holy war against the enemies of Islam and to expel the Americans from the Gulf region. The fatwa had been issued by a group of sheiks in Afghanistan, but it was sent to London by al-Qaeda. Later in May, bin Laden gave a videotaped interview to ABC News sending essentially the same message, adding that "we do not differentiate between those dressed in military uniforms and civilians; they are all targets in this fatwa." While he was being interviewed, bin Laden was sitting in front of a large map of Africa.[29]

In Nairobi and Dar es Salaam, cell members rented homes to be used as bases for operational planning. In May, Fazul paid cash for a lease on a villa in an exclusive section of Nairobi, and in June, one of the Tanzania plotters, Khalfan Khamis Mohamed, rented a house in a low-income neighborhood of Dar es Salaam.[30] Cell members purchased bomb-making materials and bought vehicles for transportation. An explosives expert was brought in to assist in putting the weapons together, and a hotel room was rented in Nairobi for visiting operatives. In late June or July, the conspirators bought the vehicles to be used in the suicide attacks: a Toyota Dyna truck for use in Nairobi, and a Nissan Atlas truck in Dar es Salaam.[31]

By August 1, members of the cells not directly involved in the attacks had mostly left East Africa, but at least one of the would-be suicide bombers did not arrive in Nairobi until August 2. This was Mohamed Rashed al Owhali, a Saudi Arabian militant who had trained at several al-Qaeda camps in Afghanistan and had fought alongside the Taliban against the government of Afghanistan. A considerable amount is known about him because he was captured after the bombing and gave lengthy interviews to the American authorities; he and three other plotters were eventually convicted in a 2001 federal trial in New York City.[32]

Owhali had been scheduled to arrive in Nairobi from Pakistan on August 1, but he missed a connecting flight, so he did not arrive in Nairobi until Sunday, August 2. On that day a number of the Nairobi plotters—apparently not including Owhali—met at the Hilltop Hotel, an inexpensive hotel in downtown Nairobi that catered to Arabs. Fazul led the meeting and warned that everyone except for the bombers themselves needed to leave the country before the attacks. The next day, August 3, Owhali met with Abdullah Ahmed Abdullah, who was also known as Saleh, and learned for the first time exactly what his mission would be. Saleh, who had been a well-known soccer player in Egypt before joining the forces opposing the Egyptian government, was a trusted bin Laden associate who was the coordinator of the East African cell.[33]

The following day, August 4, Saleh took Owhali to the embassy building and showed him where the bomb truck was to be driven. Saleh explained to him that the time of the attack—on a Friday between 10:30 and 11:00 a.m.—had been chosen because most Muslims would be at the mosque at that time and not in danger. By August 6, the day before the attacks, everyone had left the country except the bombers and a few operatives who would stay behind to remove evidence.[34]

The Tanzanian Operation

Although the overall planning for the East Africa operation was conducted out of Kenya and took several years, specific planning and preparation for the Tanzanian bombing required only a few months. Of the five men later indicted for a direct role in that attack, only one, Khalfan Khamis Mohamed (KK Mohamed), is in US custody, and testimony about him during the 2001 trial provides the fullest account available of how that bombing was organized.

Raised in a village on Zanzibar Island in Tanzania, KK Mohamed had dropped out of high school and sought to fight with al-Qaeda. He received training in Afghanistan in the early 1990s but was not given an assignment, and he eventually returned to Tanzania and began a fishing business. He was working as a grocery clerk in the spring of 1998 when he received a call in the middle of the night asking, "Do you want to do a jihad job?"[35] The request came from a man named Hussein, who was also known as Mustafa Fadl. Hussein had been appointed by Saleh to be in charge of the al-Qaeda cell in Dar es Salaam, and the jihad job would turn out to be assisting in the attack on the US embassy there.

KK Mohamed was assigned to arrange transportation of bomb components and rent the house where the bomb could be constructed. On the day of the attack, his job would be to drive part of the way with the man who would actually drive the suicide truck. That man was known as "Ahmed the German," but he was actually a fair-skinned Egyptian who did not speak the local language and might need some help finding the way.[36]

Al-Qaeda members referred to the Kenya attack as the Holy Kaaba operation, after the site in Mecca that is the holiest in the Muslim world; the Tanzanian attack was codenamed Operation al-Aqsa, after the mosque in Jerusalem.[37] Although it is not clear that the attacks were timed to take advantage of the anniversary, the date of the attacks—August 7, 1998—came eight years after US troops were ordered to Saudi Arabia as part of Operation Desert Shield.

The Attacks and Identifying the Bombers

On August 7, 1998, at 10:30 a.m. local time, Owhali and Azzam drove their truck to the US embassy building in Nairobi and attempted to enter the rear basement garage. The local-hire guards refused to let them in, and the attackers began shooting and threw a flash grenade in an attempt to stun the guards before detonating the explosive. Of the 213 people killed, 44 were embassy employees and 12 were Americans. An estimated 4,000 at the embassy and in the vicinity were injured.[38]

The nearly simultaneous attack in Dar es Salaam was carried out by Ahmed the German. When he was unable to get into the embassy perimeter, Ahmed detonated his explosive about 35 feet from the outer wall of the chancery. A water truck blocked the chancery building from the full brunt of the explosion, but the building was still damaged enough to be unusable afterward. The ambassador's residence, 1,000 yards away and vacant at the time, suffered roof damage and collapsed ceilings. The death toll was not as great, with 11 people killed—none of them Americans—and 85 injured.[39]

Within days 375 FBI agents and investigators had arrived in East Africa, and the investigations into the two blasts—given the codenames KENBOM and TANBOM—became the FBI's largest deployment of personnel in its history to that point, with more than 900 special agents deployed around the world.[40] In coordination with the local authorities, they were soon able to find and arrest a number of suspects with links to bin Laden.[41]

Additional intelligence personnel also arrived, and the *9/11 Commission Report* noted that "unusually good intelligence, chiefly from the yearlong monitoring of al-Qaeda's cell in Nairobi," quickly fixed responsibility for the bombing on bin Laden's group.[42] Reportedly, this intelligence included one al-Qaeda message intercepted by the National Security Agency (NSA) after the bombing complaining that too many Africans and not enough Americans had been killed.[43] Al-Qaeda also claimed responsibility for the attacks; on August 7 and 8, a London-based organization sent faxes to media outlets claiming responsibility on behalf of the group.[44]

US district judge Royce C. Lamberth, who was then the chief judge of the Foreign Intelligence Surveillance Court, was called at his home at 3:00 a.m. on August 8 to approve five wiretaps, including one for Wadih el Hage in Texas.[45] At both bomb sites, agents combed the rubble for auto parts—looking especially for the vehicle identification number (VIN) of the delivery vehicles. In Dar es Salaam the FBI painstakingly reconstructed the bomb truck, found the VIN, and was able to trace it back to the manufacturer in Japan. They then followed a trail of ownership that ran from a Japanese dealership to the truck's first owner, and then to the exporter who shipped the used vehicle to Tanzania. The path first led to a local importer, then to the broker who peddled the truck, and eventually to the cell member who had bought it.[46] In Nairobi, FBI investigators were also able to identify the type of vehicle used.[47]

Investigators were fortunate because two of the key plotters were captured soon after the bombings and revealed a great deal about the plot. One was Saddiq Odeh, who left Kenya on August 6, the day before the attacks, on a flight to Karachi bound for Afghanistan. Pakistani immigration officials were immediately suspicious: Odeh, who had shaved off his beard and had a slight build, looked very little like the heavyset, bearded man in the photo in his passport. The passport was a forged Yemeni one, which the cell leader Saleh had given Odeh after Odeh had failed to get his own Jordanian passport renewed in time.[48]

For three days Pakistani security officers interrogated Odeh, and he was apparently interrogated roughly; according to *Newsweek*, he initially refused to talk, but "then he was handed over to the Army's Inter-Services Intelligence Directorate, in whose hands he finally broke down." He later claimed he was coerced into confessing, but Pakistani officials say he boasted of his feat to them. By the end of the week a team of CIA and FBI agents had secretly escorted him back to Nairobi, where he confessed after being confronted with evidence found in his home.[49]

The second plotter captured was Owhali, one of the two in the truck that attacked the embassy in Nairobi. Luckily for investigators, he did not die in the blast. He got out of the truck and ran away seconds before the explosion, and was wounded. He checked himself into a local hospital, and on August 12 was arrested by Kenyan officials and turned over to the FBI.[50]

A third conspirator, Dar es Salaam cell member KK Mohamed, was also apprehended later. After the bombings he fled Tanzania for Cape Town, where he was eventually arrested and turned over to the FBI. As noted above, his confession provided considerable information about the Tanzanian operation.[51]

CONVENTIONAL EXPLANATIONS FOR WHAT WENT WRONG

The official US government investigations into the embassy bombings were conducted by two accountability review boards, whose members were selected by the secretary of state and the director of central intelligence. Admiral William J. Crowe Jr. was chairman of both boards, which were known collectively as the Crowe Commission. The two boards released a joint report covering both bombings, referred to here as the Crowe Commission Report.[52]

The Crowe Commission reported that it was "most disturbed at two interconnected issues: first the inadequacy of resources to provide security against terrorist attacks and, second, the relative low priority accorded security concerns throughout the US government." Although the commission did not blame any individual member of the US government for the disaster, it argued that "there was a collective failure by several Administrations and Congresses over the past decade to invest adequate efforts and resources to reduce the vulnerability of US diplomatic missions around the world to terrorist attacks."[53]

The commission argued there had been no intelligence failure, because no specific intelligence had been missed. Admiral Crowe said at a press conference that the boards found "intelligence provided no immediate tactical warning of the August 7 attacks," and added that with the state of intelligence today, "it's just not within our reach to have tactical warning."[54] But the commission did criticize the intelligence community for attempting to rely too much on tactical intelligence. Although past experience with terror attacks had indicated that immediate, tactical warnings would not likely be available, the report argued, "both the intelligence and policy communities relied excessively on tactical intelligence to determine the level of potential terrorist threats to posts worldwide."[55] In the absence of warning from tactical intelligence, the threat level was assumed to be lower than it really was.[56]

Other Studies of the Bombings

Other studies of the bombings generally agree that poor physical security at the embassies contributed to the disaster.[57] But several scholars have disagreed with the Crowe Commission's findings concerning intelligence.[58] The staff of the

Institute for the Study of Diplomacy at Georgetown University conducted an extensive investigation into the intelligence that was available before the bombings, and their study agreed with the commission's finding that too much emphasis had been placed on tactical intelligence.[59] But unlike the commission, the Georgetown study found that enough *strategic* intelligence had been available that intelligence and policy officials should have understood the terrorist threat to the embassies. The critical intelligence, the study argued, was "strategic warning—the massive body of intelligence showing that a terrorist group that was dedicated to killing Americans, and that had in fact already been engaged in doing so, had a key operational component in Nairobi."[60]

Other studies of the bombings have reached similar conclusions—that enough warnings had been available before the bombings that officials should have taken more preventive and defensive action than they did.[61] The 9/11 Commission found that in the years leading up to the embassy bombings, the US intelligence community failed in terms of strategic intelligence analysis on al-Qaeda. There was a great deal of intelligence available on the threat from al-Qaeda, the commission reported. But that intelligence was held by individual organizations and elements of the intelligence community, and "the reams of new information that the CIA's Bin Ladin Unit had been developing since 1996 had not been pulled together and synthesized for the rest of the government."[62]

Journalists who have written about the bombings are more direct in their criticism of the American intelligence community. Some argue that the intelligence failure was in not making a sufficient effort to gather intelligence on the plot. James Bamford, for example, writes that the CIA had been too focused on Afghanistan and Pakistan rather than on other areas of the world such as Africa, and it had not done enough to place operatives inside al-Qaeda: "Once again, the CIA was caught totally by surprise. Because the agency had spent most of its time and money on its band of Afghan soldiers of fortune, and no effort trying to actually penetrate the group, in Afghanistan or elsewhere, it picked up not a whisper of the long-planned and complex plot."[63]

Others have criticized the intelligence community for not being able to make sense of the intelligence warnings that had been available, and the bombings have been described as "a textbook example of intelligence failure."[64] John Miller and Michael Stone write that clues to the East Africa plot had been known beforehand to the FBI, the CIA, the State Department, and the Israeli and Kenyan intelligence services, and "the embassy attacks thus represented law enforcement's most egregious failure to date to protect the lives and interests of Americans and American allies against bin Laden's vicious holy war."[65] They describe the failure to prevent the bombings as a puzzle they could not solve: "The failure of US intelligence to anticipate, much less interdict, the embassy bombings elicited some of the most troubling questions in our writing of *The Cell*. We asked virtually every source we spoke to from top administration and intelligence officials to line investigators: What went wrong in East Africa? We never got a satisfactory explanation."[66]

WHAT STRATEGIC WARNING HAD BEEN AVAILABLE?

Earlier attacks on US diplomats and embassies, and in particular the 1983 and 1984 bombings of the US embassy buildings in Beirut, had made it clear to the US government that its diplomatic posts were at risk from terror attacks. Following the Beirut bombings former CIA deputy director Admiral Bobby Ray Inman chaired a commission that studied the problem of embassy security, and in 1985 the commission issued a broad set of recommendations that became accepted as security standards.[67] A number of these recommendations focused on physical security, such as the distance embassy buildings should be set back from the street. But because the embassies in Nairobi and Dar es Salaam had been occupied before these standards were adopted, they were not required to meet them.[68]

Early Intelligence Warnings

As early as 1995, the NSA was reportedly gaining "very useful information" by monitoring bin Laden's telephone traffic that was routed through a ground station outside Khartoum.[69] But intelligence on al-Qaeda was otherwise quite limited. In 1996 the CIA set up a bin Laden unit—a "virtual station" with a dozen officers focusing on analyzing intelligence on and planning operations against bin Laden.[70] But while members of this unit became strongly convinced of the danger posed by bin Laden, the rest of the intelligence community was not so sure. Members of the bin Laden unit later told the 9/11 Commission staff "they felt their zeal attracted ridicule from their peers."[71] Even within the CIA's Counterterrorist Center, which was focused more broadly on the problem of terrorism, bin Laden was seen mostly as an "extremist financier" rather than as a planner and organizer of terrorist operations himself.

The Attacks in Saudi Arabia

In November 1995, a car bomb exploded outside a US–Saudi joint facility in Riyadh that was used for training the Saudi National Guard and killed five Americans. The Saudi authorities eventually captured four suspects, who claimed to have been inspired by bin Laden, and they executed them. There was no proof that bin Laden had ordered the attack, but intelligence reports did indicate that al-Qaeda had shipped explosives to Saudi Arabia for the purpose of attacking Americans.[72] Then, in June 1996, a bombing attack on the Khobar Towers residential complex for US Air Force personnel in Dhahran, Saudi Arabia, killed 19

Americans and wounded 372. A massive investigation by the FBI revealed evidence that the operation had been conducted by Saudi Hezbollah, an organization supported by the government of Iran. There were indications that al-Qaeda had been involved, but this could not be confirmed.[73]

Developments in Sudan

In 1996, two developments in Sudan, the country where bin Laden had been based since 1991, dramatically changed the ability of US intelligence to collect on al-Qaeda. The first served to reduce that ability, whereas the second increased it.

The first development was that in early 1996, the deteriorating security situation in Sudan forced the United States to close its embassy there—and with it, to shut down the CIA station. The closure was driven by a series of warnings the embassy had been receiving of terrorist threats to US personnel and their children in Khartoum. The CIA station chief had reportedly urged that Americans be pulled out, after he and his staff had found themselves under surveillance and had been attacked twice—once with a knife, and once with claw hammers.[74] In late 1995, the CIA realized that the informant who had been the primary source of the threat warnings had been a fabricator. But concerns about security remained high, especially when a second source warned that Sudan was intending to assassinate the national security adviser, Anthony Lake, who was a strong critic of the regime in Khartoum.[75] In early 1996, the embassy was closed, and in his memoir CIA director George Tenet says that in retrospect the closure can be seen as a mistake: "We lost a valuable window into the burgeoning terrorist environment there as a result."[76]

A second development in 1996 proved beneficial to the intelligence community in its efforts to learn more about bin Laden: The al-Qaeda leader was expelled from Sudan and moved his operation to Afghanistan. Human intelligence collection was easier in Afghanistan; not because American operatives were able to infiltrate terrorist cells themselves but because CIA officers were able to reestablish the local contacts they had made years earlier while supporting the anti-Soviet forces. The chief of the bin Laden unit told the 9/11 Commission that the move to Afghanistan had been "a stroke of luck" for US intelligence, and the chief of the Counterterrorist Center at the time said that CIA's local assets were "near to providing real-time information about Bin Ladin's activities and travels in Afghanistan."[77]

Signals intelligence collection was also easier in Afghanistan, because the country's primitive telecommunications infrastructure forced al-Qaeda members to use satellite phones that the NSA could track relatively easily. According to one analyst, during this period the NSA was monitoring "virtually all satellite phone calls coming in and out of Afghanistan."[78] One particularly good source of intelligence was an Inmarsat satellite telephone that a bin Laden operative living in the United States bought in November 1996. For two years this phone was the primary means of communications bin Laden used to keep in touch with operatives around the world—and American intelligence was listening.[79]

Assessing the Threat

At least one agency of the intelligence community made what reads today as a prescient forecast about the growing threat from bin Laden. In July 1996, the State Department's intelligence unit produced a report stating that bin Laden might be preparing to take a more active role than as a mere financier of terrorism by others. The report, which was written at a time when bin Laden was understood to have left Sudan and was reportedly on the run, stated that recent press interviews with bin Laden "reveal an increasingly confident militant leader." If bin Laden were to move back to Afghanistan, the report said, that country could provide "an ideal haven" for him which "could prove more dangerous to US interests in the long run than his three-year liaison with Khartoum."[80]

Although these developments indicate the US intelligence and national security communities were gaining an increasing sense of the threat from international terrorism, the record also shows that terrorism remained a relatively low priority for American intelligence. In January 1997, the CIA published its *Annual Report on Intelligence Community Activities*, an unclassified report to Congress evaluating the intelligence community's performance during 1996 in terms of the administration's priorities.[81] Terrorism was not at the top of the list, which was headed by concerns about rogue states, the changes occurring in China and Russia, and the proliferation of weapons of mass destruction.

Jamal al-Fadl

By 1996, the American intelligence community had begun to understand the rising threat from radical Islamic terrorism, but it had little hard information on bin Laden and his al-Qaeda group. But in June of that year this situation began to change, when a former al-Qaeda member named Jamal al-Fadl turned up in the visa line at the US embassy in Asmara, the capital of Eritrea. He told the clerk that he had vital information for the US national security—and over the next several years he would become the most important source of intelligence on al-Qaeda.[82]

Fadl had been born in Sudan and had immigrated to New York after high school. After a while he went to Afghanistan to join the war against the Soviets, and eventually he became one of the first members of al-Qaeda and a close associate of bin Laden. But he became disappointed by his relatively low status—Saudis and Egyptians tended to get the best jobs in al-Qaeda and were paid more—and he began taking kickbacks for himself. In 1995, his scams were discovered, and he went into hiding until he appeared at the US embassy in Eritrea.

CIA officials debriefed him for a month and a half after he turned himself in, and then in the fall of 1996, the CIA flew him from Eritrea to a US military base in Germany, where they handed him over to the FBI for further interrogation.[83]

By 1997, the bin Laden unit at CIA had "recognized that Bin Laden was more than just a financier. They learned that al-Qaeda had a military committee that was planning operations against US interests worldwide and was actively trying to obtain nuclear material."[84] But although this new information may have sharpened the views of the CIA officers assigned to the bin Laden unit, it does not appear to have led to changes in the overall, national-level intelligence assessment of the threat from his group, which continued to see bin Laden as primarily a financier of terrorism. An intelligence community assessment in 1997 expressed this view, stating that "Iran and its surrogates, as well as terrorist financier Usama Bin Ladin and his followers, have stepped up their threats and surveillance of US facilities abroad in what also may be a portent of possible additional attacks in the United States."[85]

Warnings from Bin Laden

The 1997 assessment was to be the last national-level intelligence estimate of the terrorist threat produced before 9/11.[86] But there were a number of other warnings concerning al-Qaeda during this period, including several delivered by bin Laden himself. In March 1997, he gave his first television interview with a Western broadcaster, to Peter Arnett of CNN, declaring "the concentration at this point of jihad is against the American occupiers."[87] In May 1998, he held a press conference in Afghanistan that was attended by a few Pakistani and Chinese journalists. He said there would be "good news in the coming weeks," and that a group called the International Islamic Front had been formed "to do jihad against the crusaders and Jews." He added that "by God's grace, the men . . . are going to have a successful result in killing Americans and getting rid of them."[88]

As a result of these threats, the State Department issued a warning on June 12, 1998, that stated, "The United States continues to receive information from other sources which indicates planning for an attack against Americans in the Persian Gulf." It announced that the United States was increasing security at government facilities in the Middle East and Asia, but the warning did not mention Africa.[89] The State Department had earlier, in March 1998, issued a worldwide warning about the threat from bin Laden against American military and civilians, but that warning also did not identify any special threat to East Africa.[90]

Other indications of an increased threat to American personnel came in the summer of 1998. In June a plot against the US embassy in Albania was disrupted. Although little information is available about this operation, it apparently led to the capture of several al-Qaeda-related operatives.[91] Also in June, the federal grand jury in New York issued a sealed indictment against bin Laden. Sometime during the summer of 1998, the intelligence community received information indicating that bin Laden was interested in publicity and attacks involving mass casualties; and on July 29, the CIA's Counterterrorist Center issued an alert about a possible chemical, biological, or radiological attack by bin Laden. But none of these reports warned about his plans in Africa.[92]

WHAT SPECIFIC WARNING HAD BEEN AVAILABLE?

From sources such as al-Fadl's testimony, signals intelligence intercepts, and human intelligence assets in Afghanistan, the American intelligence community was able to develop a general, if rather fuzzy, strategic-level picture of the threat posed by bin Laden's organization. But gaining specific, tactical-level intelligence on the al-Qaeda cell in East Africa was a very different problem. The cell based in Nairobi was a hard target for intelligence, largely because its members made careful use of denial, deception, and other counterintelligence tactics. Members used false names when communicating with each other; Ali Mohamed, for example, testified in his plea agreement that he had used the name "Jeff" in Nairobi, while el Hage used the name "Norman."[93] After he was captured, Odeh told his interrogators that the group had used code words, such as using "potatoes" to mean hand grenades.[94] They established sleeper cells including false businesses, and married and acquired local families.[95] Despite these difficulties, however, American intelligence was able to get a better tactical-level picture of the al-Qaeda threat in East Africa than it had in many other areas of the world.

Signals Intelligence

Just as in Afghanistan, signals intelligence proved to be a fruitful source of intelligence in East Africa. In late 1996, a joint NSA-CIA Special Collection Service team operating from the US embassy in Nairobi began intercepting phone calls and faxes associated with al-Qaeda in Nairobi.[96] The number of phone calls available for monitoring increased dramatically after the arrest in Saudi Arabia of Sidi Tayyib created panic among the conspirators.[97]

Phone conversations were apparently being tapped until the bombings in 1998, and a number of intercepts were introduced into evidence during the 2001 federal trial in New York City. Not all of this intercept data was able to be translated and analyzed in real time, however; according to press reports, after the bombings an intercept was found to have involved a group of known bin Laden associates in Africa who said they thought "something bad was going to happen," and that they were "going to get out of the area."[98]

The Al-Haramain Foundation

One of the first specific indications of a terrorist threat against the embassy in Nairobi appears to have begun to develop in the summer of 1997, when the intelligence service of another country turned over an informant to the CIA. The informant said that the Nairobi branch of an Islamic charity, the Al-Haramain Foundation, was plotting terrorist attacks against Americans. He eventually warned that the group was plotting to blow up the American embassy in Nairobi.[99] The circumstances of this case are not clear; according to a different report, the tip came from an informant who walked into the Nairobi embassy in September 1997, claiming that seven Arabs who worked for a local Islamic charity had connections to bin Laden.[100]

On October 31, 1997, the Kenyan authorities arrested nine Arabs who were connected to Al-Haramain and seized the group's files. The CIA took this threat seriously enough that it sent a team from Langley to Nairobi to investigate. The members of the team went through the files but could find no evidence of a bomb plot. They wanted to question the group members in jail, but this set off an internal CIA dispute. The station chief in Nairobi refused to ask the Kenyans for access, arguing that he had pushed his local counterparts far enough; senior officials at CIA urged him to reconsider, but ultimately the decision was up to the station chief, and American officials did not interview the suspects. Because there was no evidence of a plot, the original informant was deemed not credible, and Kenya ordered the nine deported. But some members of the counterterrorism team were furious, and blamed the decision to not talk to the suspects on the fact that the station chief was from the CIA's analytical arm, the Directorate of Intelligence, rather than from the Directorate of Operations, and he was on his first overseas espionage assignment.[101]

Wadih el Hage

An important source of intelligence on al-Qaeda's Kenya operations was Wadih el Hage, who, as noted above, had been an early member of the East Africa cell. He was born into a Catholic family from Lebanon and converted to Islam at fourteen. He lived in the United States several times, and he attended the University of Southwestern Louisiana from 1978 to 1986, receiving a bachelor's degree in urban planning. He married an American Muslim woman and the couple settled in Tucson. In 1989, he became a US citizen. Sometime around 1992 he received an offer to become bin Laden's personal secretary, and for the next two years he lived in Sudan. In 1994, he and his family moved to Nairobi.[102]

American intelligence agencies knew about el Hage and his connection to al-Qaeda in part from their debriefings of Fadl. In early 1997, they began bugging his Nairobi phone—an action considered especially sensitive because he was a US citizen. The wiretap apparently did not result in much hard intelligence on what the cell was up to, largely because el Hage spoke in code.[103] Eventually, the American authorities decided to take stronger action to disrupt the al-Qaeda organization. On August 21, 1997, FBI officials stopped el Hage at the Nairobi airport as he was returning from a trip to Afghanistan. They told him they knew of his activities and suggested that he return home to the United States, where they could keep a closer eye on him.[104] The next month he and his family flew to New York, where he was greeted at the airport by federal agents. He was interrogated overnight and was brought before a grand jury in the morning. He denied just about everything and was let go.[105] He eventually settled in Arlington, Texas, where the authorities monitored his movements.

Although intelligence officials were not able to learn much from el Hage himself, on the day they stopped him at the Nairobi airport they also searched his house and found an Apple Power Book 140 laptop computer.[106] Experts were later able to recover several documents that had been deleted, including a letter written by Harun Fazul, one of the leaders of the Nairobi cell who had stayed in el Hage's house.[107] In the letter, which was evidently written to other al-Qaeda members, Fazul wrote, "We can now state that the security position on the cell is at 100 percent danger." He warned "my brothers in East Africa" that they should know "there is an American-Kenyan-Egyptian intelligence activity in [Na]irobi aiming to identify the names and residences of the members who are associated with the Shaykh [meaning bin Laden]." The letter did not include any information about upcoming operations, and in fact, Fazul wrote, "We, the East Africa cell members, do not want to know about the operations plans since we are just implementers." But his letter clearly implied that some sort of operation was being planned: he said recent facts "leave us no choice but to ask ourselves are we ready for that big clandestine battle?"

Although the information on el Hage's computer confirmed that al-Qaeda had an active cell in East Africa, American officials did not know what the group was up to. They concluded that whatever was going on, it was a low-end operation, and the exposure of el Hage had stopped whatever activities might have been in the planning stage.[108]

It appears that some of the documents that had been downloaded from el Hage's computer were not analyzed promptly. According to the Georgetown University study of the bombings, a CIA official testified to the Crowe Commission in 1999 that documents taken from the computer had been shipped to CIA Headquarters, but because of a shortage of translators most of these documents were not translated until after the embassy bombings.[109] Some of the material was, however, translated on an ad hoc basis, and at least one analyst integrated this information with other intelligence and produced what the Georgetown study called "a comprehensive picture of the organizational structure, operational objectives, and record of attacks for the Al-Qaeda organization." This analysis was produced months before the embassy bombings, but it was still in draft form at the time of the bombings because the analyst's supervisor did not allow its dissemination.[110]

Ahmed's Warning

The most critical piece of tactical intelligence on the embassy plots was described at the beginning of this chapter: the warning in 1997 from an Egyptian man named Mustafa Mahmoud Said Ahmed, who told embassy officials that he was involved with a group planning to blow up the embassy's underground parking garage.[111] Although he claimed he had already taken surveillance photos and described the future attack in some detail, CIA analysts judged him to be unreliable.[112] Ahmed was let go and returned to Tanzania, where he was later charged by the Tanzanian authorities with being involved in the bombing in Dar es Salaam. But the charges were eventually dropped, and he was released in 2000 and deported to Egypt.[113]

Gary Berntsen, who headed the CIA team sent to Tanzania after the bombings, has written about encountering a source shortly after the attacks who appears to be Ahmed. In his book *Jawbreaker*, Berntsen writes that on August 14, 1998, an Egyptian named Mustapha entered the embassy "of a close ally of the United States" and said that he had information to sell about the attacks that had just occurred. The same man had visited the embassy the year before and tried to sell information about a planned attack; he had provided data, some of which was confirmed, but some was false, and "he was branded a fabricator and sent on his way. Unfortunately, the tip he gave about the bombing of the US embassy in Nairobi proved to be correct." Berntsen says that he then met with Mustapha, but the rest of his description of "Mustapha" and the information he provided have been redacted from his book by the CIA.[114]

RECEPTIVITY TOWARD WARNING

The warnings about terrorist threats were received very differently in East Africa than they were in Washington. The American ambassador in Nairobi, Prudence Bushnell, was extremely receptive to the warnings she received from the intelligence community, but she found that she had little authority to act on those warnings. In Washington, where the authority rested to make major security improvements, there was less of a sense of urgency, and less receptivity.

Receptivity in Nairobi

Soon after arriving in Kenya in 1996, Bushnell had become concerned about the embassy's security. She was briefed in early 1997 by intelligence officials on what was known about the presence of al-Qaeda in Kenya, but was told there was no evidence of a specific threat against the embassy or American interests in the country.[115] In the summer of 1997, after the CIA station in Nairobi learned of the possible threat connected to the Al-Haramain Foundation, Ambassador Bushnell was assured that any threat had been eliminated. But she was evidently not told that some CIA officers had believed the investigation had not been thorough enough.

Bushnell and her staff do not appear to have been shown all the available intelligence, such as reports from wiretaps and the interrogation of el Hage.[116] But what she did see was enough to cause her to send urgent requests to Washington asking for increased security. On December 15, 1997, she sent a report to the State Department warning that the embassy's location made it "extremely vulnerable to a terrorist attack," and that it had to be replaced with a more secure building. On December 24, she cabled Washington again, emphasizing the extreme vulnerability of the embassy due to lack of standoff distance, and asking for Washington's support for building a new chancery and for a comprehensive review of the embassy's security status.[117] In January 1998, the State Department responded that the post's current security rating of medium was appropriate, and no new office building was being contemplated. It offered to send a team to review the embassy's security assessment, which had last been updated in 1994.[118]

General Anthony Zinni, commander of the US military's Central Command, had visited Nairobi, and warned that the embassy would be a tempting target for terrorists. He offered to send his own specialists to review the security situation, but the State Department turned him down, preferring to send its own team instead.[119] The State Department team arrived in March 1998, and found the embassy was in compliance with security standards for a post facing a medium terrorist threat. It did recommend about $500,000 in new security measures, including the installation of new fences and increased perimeter surveillance, but it filed no written report. Improvements based on these recommendations were under way but had not been completed by the time of the attack. The Crowe Commission noted that the improvements would have made no difference in mitigating the blast, nor would they have deterred the terrorists from getting as close to the chancery as they did.[120]

In April 1998, Ambassador Bushnell sent letters to the secretary and undersecretary of state restating her concerns. She was also lobbying visiting senior American officials and members of Congress who came to Nairobi, telling them, according to an American official, "How do you like our building? I think it's terrible."[121] But terror threats were not the only security concern; during this time most US officials saw crime as the key security threat to embassy personnel in Kenya. In early 1998, the CIA's deputy station chief in Nairobi had been mugged near the embassy, and at about the same time the ambassador had been told about a plot to kill her. Local police refused to guard the embassy, and they would sometimes beat political dissidents right in front of the building.[122]

In response to the threats in Nairobi, the embassy had increased the number of roving guards, added more vehicle and perimeter searches, and conducted additional security drills.[123] But Ambassador Bushnell's efforts to increase security and to get the attention of Washington led to tensions between Nairobi and Washington. As a result, for the first time in her long career, Bushnell received a mediocre performance review; just weeks before the bombings she was chided for her excessive preoccupation with security and her "tendency to overload bureaucratic circuits."[124]

Receptivity in Dar es Salaam

Although the embassy in Tanzania had not been the target of as many threats, it appears that officials there took the terrorist threat seriously. Security procedures at the embassy were quite good and often exceeded the State Department's requirements. Blast-resistant 4-millimeter Mylar film, which was not required by security regulations, had been added to all windows. The regional security officer at the embassy, John DiCarlo, had only arrived on July 22, 1998, but had already tightened procedures even further, for example, by ensuring that vehicles were screened outside the compound before being allowed to enter. A drill to exercise the post's procedures in case of a package bomb was conducted just 30 minutes before the terrorist attack; but no drill had been held or planned to contend specifically with vehicle bombs.[125]

Receptivity in Washington

As we have seen above, until at least 1996 few officials in Washington realized the danger that Osama bin Laden and his organization presented. After the threat began to become clear, in 1997, the focus of most Washington agencies involved in the antiterrorist effort was at the broad, strategic level of action against bin Laden himself, rather than on local, tactical-level efforts to reduce the risk of attacks by his organization. The effort was uncoordinated, as each agency pursued its own effort against bin Laden. The CIA's Counterterrorist Center was developing a plan to capture and remove him from Afghanistan; the Justice Department was moving toward indicting him; and the State Department was focusing on reducing nuclear tensions between India and Pakistan, ending the Afghan civil war, and limiting the Taliban's human rights abuses, rather than on driving out bin Laden. The US military does not appear to have been actively involved in these efforts, and General Zinni, head of Central Command, reportedly shared the State Department's view that the right tools to be employed were primarily diplomatic.[126]

With their focus on bin Laden and the top level of the al-Qaeda organizations, Washington-level officials appear to have been unresponsive toward warnings about specific threats in particular places. To some extent this view was unsurprising. In East Africa, for example, CIA and State Department security officials believed that the greatest threat to Americans was from crime, not from terrorism. And the US government was taking steps to deal with bin Laden's organization where it knew it existed, such as in Kenya. Beginning at least a year before the embassy attacks, the CIA was actively involved in what was described in press accounts as a "disruption operation," which is typically conducted when officers believe someone or some organization is involved in terrorism but they do not have specific information on what is going on.[127] Harassment and searches of Wadih el Hage in connection with Kenyan officials were part of that operation.

However, when specific threat information materialized, neither the State Department nor the CIA responded aggressively, despite Ambassador Bushnell's frequent calls for additional security. We have seen above how the State Department did not acknowledge the likelihood of an al-Qaeda threat to the embassy in Nairobi, refused to plan for a new building, and turned down an offer of security assistance from General Zinni of Central Command. The CIA, too, could have taken additional steps that could have helped break up the terrorist cell or deter the attacks. After Ahmed walked into the embassy in November 1997 and provided details about a planned attack, the CIA could have assigned a special countersurveillance unit, known as a "snapshot team," to the embassy to watch for terrorists who might be casing the building. But instead it only sent out a mildly worded report warning that while Ahmed was probably a fabricator, he could have been telling the truth.[128]

CONCLUSION

The embassy bombings case is a dramatic example of how, even when warning is available, carefully planned terrorist attacks can be very difficult to prevent. The problem was not a lack of strategic intelligence on the threat from al-Qaeda, because by the summer of 1998 warnings from bin Laden himself and from other sources had made the threat clear to American policymakers. Nor was the problem a lack of tactical-level intelligence on the specific threat to the embassies, because more than one source had warned American officials in Nairobi that the embassy there was being targeted.

Neither intelligence collection nor analysis was faulty. The answer to the puzzle of the East Africa bombings is that the other key element needed for preventive action was missing: There was a lack of receptivity toward the warnings of intelligence, most critically among State Department officials in Washington who had the authority to do something about the threat. The American ambassador in Nairobi strongly believed in the threat but could not get senior officials in the State Department to listen. The embassy security officer in Dar es Salaam believed in the threat enough to strengthen security measures and even hold an antiterrorism drill on the morning of the attack, but those measures were not sufficient. Although we cannot know what efforts would have prevented the attacks of August 7, 1998, it is likely that a combination of intelligence, law enforcement, and protective measures would have been needed either to break up the al-Qaeda cell or to prevent the attacks from succeeding. Some of those measures would have been expensive, such as the building of new embassies, or difficult, such as gaining Kenyan cooperation for more aggressive measures to either penetrate or dismantle the al-Qaeda cell. Taking these actions would have required the approval of senior-level American officials, probably in Washington—but it was at that level that receptivity toward the warnings of intelligence was lacking.

The findings of this chapter run counter to the findings of the Crowe Commission and other studies of the embassy bombings. The conventional wisdom has been that decision makers had been paying too much attention to tactical-level intelligence and should instead have paid more attention to the growing broad, strategic-level intelligence on the threat from al-Qaeda. But this chapter suggests just the opposite: The critical intelligence warnings were there at the tactical level, and the greatest failure of policymakers, especially at the Washington level, was in not paying enough attention to those warnings. Certainly, more could have been done to analyze the strategic-level threat. But it seems highly unlikely that any additional strategic intelligence product or assessment, any reshaping of the information already available, would have convinced officials in Washington to take specific action on the warnings coming out of East Africa. For preventive action, what was needed was a combination of precise tactical warning and receptivity among the decision makers who could take action against the threat. The first part of that equation was available, but not the second, and the result was a disaster despite warning.

CHAPTER 6

NEW YORK CITY

Preventing a Day of Terror

ONE OF THE FIRST and most successful cases of terrorism prevention in American history is also one of the least known. In June 1993, only four months after the first World Trade Center bombing, a group of men was arrested while preparing to bomb a number of targets in the New York City area, including the UN Headquarters, the Lincoln and Holland tunnels, and the George Washington Bridge. The men had been organizing and training since 1989 for what the US government later called a conspiracy "to levy a war of urban terrorism against the United States."[1] The plotters were eventually convicted following what remains today the longest and most complex international terrorism trial in American history. Federal Judge Michael B. Mukasey said the planned attacks would have caused destruction on a scale "not seen since the Civil War" and would have made the earlier World Trade Center bombing "seem insignificant."[2]

The case of the "Day of Terror plot" is important not only because of the massive destruction that was prevented but also because it offers lessons for counterterrorism and preventing surprise attacks today. It was one of the first major radical Islamist terrorist plots thwarted in the United States, and it resembles in a number of aspects several more recent plots that have been foiled since the September 11, 2001, terrorist attacks. But despite its significance for today, this case has not been widely studied by academics or terrorism analysts.[3] This chapter examines the Day of Terror plot and argues that it was thwarted by the same combination of precise, tactical-level intelligence and strong policymaker receptivity toward intelligence that had more than half a century earlier prevented the Japanese from being successful in their attempted surprise attack at Midway.

The chapter begins with an overview of the Day of Terror plot, including a description of how the conspirators were linked to the men who carried out the earlier bombing of the World Trade Center. The primary reason why the authorities were able to break up the plot was that the FBI had an informant in the group, and the next section reviews how this informant had come to be there, and how challenging it was for the New York authorities to manage him. The subsequent two sections examine more closely the intelligence that was available to the authorities concerning the plot. First, at the strategic level: Before the 1993 attack on the World Trade Center, there was little strategic, long-term warning that such an attack was possible. And second, at the tactical level of specific information on the plot itself: Who was the government informant, and how did he come to work for the FBI?

Next, the chapter reviews how receptive policymakers were toward the strategic- and tactical-level warnings they received. It argues that officials in New York City were receptive to the tactical intelligence available from the FBI informant—but only after the first World Trade Center bombing served as a focusing event that convinced them that the informant's information could be worth the money and effort required. The conclusion argues that the Day of Terror plot is significant not only because it provides lessons about how terrorist attacks can be prevented; it is also important because in many ways this case serves as an early model of the threat that America continues to face today from ad hoc groups of loosely affiliated extremists who come together to plan a major terrorist attack.

THE PLOT'S BACKGROUND

The conspiracy that eventually became the Day of Terror plot first began to take shape in January 1989, when a group of men including El Sayyid Nosair and Clement Hampton-El met at John F. Kennedy International Airport in New York.[4] In July of that year the two men, along with several others who would later be convicted of participating in the World Trade Center bombing, trained together at a shooting range in Calverton, on Long Island. On at least three weekends they fired AK-47 assault rifles and semiautomatic pistols—and all the while they were under surveillance by the FBI, which had been led to the men after getting a tip that a group of Palestinians associated with the al-Kifah Refugee Services Center in Brooklyn was planning to set off bombs in Atlantic City casinos.[5]

The FBI agents conducting the surveillance found no evidence of a plot against US citizens, so they were not particularly worried about the training activity. It was considered an "open secret" in law enforcement at the time that a number of mosques were sponsoring such training for recruits who wanted to join the mujahideen fighting the Soviet Army in Afghanistan. The FBI's main concern was that the group could be violating federal neutrality laws, which prohibit Americans from waging war on countries with which the United States is at peace, and therefore the training was not disrupted.[6]

But the members of the group were not training to fight in Afghanistan; they were training to conduct attacks within the United States, and they were doing so under the direction of the radical Egyptian sheik Omar Abdel Rahman, the "Blind Sheik." Abdel Rahman was in Egypt during this time, but the plotters spoke to him by phone about the progress of their military training and about the construction of camps for further training. Abdel Rahman's group made tape recordings of these conversations for distribution among the Blind Sheik's followers, and in one conversation Nosair told Abdel Rahman, "we have organized an encampment, we are concentrating here."[7] The Blind Sheik arrived in the United States in July 1990, and his preaching quickly drew a following at mosques in Jersey City and Brooklyn.[8]

The Killing of Rabbi Meir Kahane

The reality that this group was training for violence in the United States became clear on November 5, 1990, when one of the men who had participated in the paramilitary training, Nosair, shot and killed Rabbi Meir Kahane, a founder of the ultraconservative Jewish Defense League, in New York City. Kahane was a militant Zionist who advocated expelling Arabs from Israel. After making a speech at the Marriott East Side Hotel in New York, Kahane was talking with members of the crowd when two shots were fired that hit him in the neck and chest. Nosair was arrested after he attempted to flee and was shot by a uniformed postal police officer.[9]

When police and FBI agents searched Nosair's house in New Jersey, they found sixteen boxes of files that included bomb-making manuals, maps of New York landmarks such as the Statue of Liberty and World Trade Center, and training manuals from the US Army Special Warfare School at Fort Bragg.[10] A few investigators, including Neil Herman, the supervisor of the New York City Joint Terrorism Task Force, and a policeman named Eddie Norris, thought Nosair might be involved in a wider conspiracy to commit a more deadly act of violence. But the official investigation of the Kahane killing concluded that Nosair had acted alone, and the files taken from Nosair's house went into storage, apparently without being studied for possible clues to further plots and attacks.[11]

Nosair was sent to Rikers Island prison awaiting trial, and while there he began receiving regular visits from his cousin, Ibrahim El-Gabrowny, and several other members of the group of plotters. As was later revealed in federal court, during these visits he suggested various terrorist operations that the group should carry out. His trial lasted from November to December 1991; and although he was acquitted of Kahane's murder, he was found guilty on weapons charges and sentenced to prison.[12] He was transferred to the maximum-security Attica prison, where the visits by the plotters continued, as did his recommendations for future attacks. Among the plans Nosair urged that they carry out were the murders of the judge who had sentenced him to prison and of Dov Hikind, a Jewish New York City assemblyman.[13]

In late spring 1992, Nosair made his most ambitious proposal of all. When one of the group's members, Emad Salem, visited Nosair at Attica together with Sheik Ali Shinawy, an administrator at the Abu Bakr Mosque in Brooklyn, Nosair proposed a plot to bomb twelve "Jewish targets" at once, including the judge and Hikind. While they rode back to New York City in a bus after the meeting, Salem and Shinawy talked about how to build the twelve bombs and set them off at locations frequented by Jews.[14]

The First World Trade Center Bombing

During most of 1992, the group of plotters around Sheik Abdel Rahman was only loosely organized, and they appear to have made little headway toward implementing the plans proposed by Nosair from prison. But that changed in September 1992, when Kuwaiti-born Ramzi Yousef arrived in the United States. American officials were to learn later that Yousef was the nephew of Khalid Sheikh Mohammed, the key planner of the 9/11 attacks, and would go on to help plan "Operation Bojinka," which was to have involved simultaneously blowing up twelve airliners over the Pacific, along with other plots. There is a great deal about Yousef that is still unknown—for example, although the name on his passport is Abdul Basit Karim, some terrorism experts believe he may actually be someone else.[15] But those events were still years away, and in New York in late 1992 and early 1993, he appears to have quickly become associated with the circle of plotters around Abdel Rahman, and his participation dramatically changed the dynamics of the plot that was being developed.

Ramzi Yousef appears to have become the de facto leader of the cell, and he was successful in professionalizing what had until that point been a group of mostly inept plotters. Even more dangerously, he radically increased the scale of their ambition. He had much bigger plans than to bomb twelve Jewish locations in a series of explosions; he wanted to build a bomb big enough to topple the World Trade Center.[16]

In late 1992, members of the group began seeking detonators, "clean" guns that had never been involved in criminal activity, and military training. They rented a storage shed and started purchasing the supplies—including 1,000 pounds of urea, a chemical compound often used as a fertilizer, and 1,500 pounds of nitric acid—that would go into making the bomb used against the World Trade Center.[17] At the end of 1992, they resumed paramilitary training at a location in New Bloomfield, Pennsylvania, and in January 1993, an FBI surveillance team observed the men practicing martial arts, sniper firing, and rappelling at a farm near Harrisburg, Pennsylvania.[18]

On February 24, 1993, one of the members of the group, Mohammed Salameh, rented the van that would be used in the World Trade Center bombing.

For identification he used a New York driver's license in his own name, and he gave the home address of Ibrahim El-Gabrowny. The next day he reported the van as stolen. On February 26, the van was exploded in the parking garage underneath the World Trade Center, causing six deaths and massive destruction.[19]

Investigators were quickly able to trace the explosion to Salameh. On what remained of the van they found a C-VIN, or confidential vehicle identification number, which is a coded number hidden in places where car thieves might not know to look. They matched the C-VIN to the real vehicle ID number, which belonged to a Ryder rental van. They learned that the van had been rented by a Ryder outlet in New Jersey to a man named Mohammed Salameh. And when officials contacted the rental company, they were surprised to learn that Salameh had been calling Ryder every day since he reported the van stolen, trying to get his cash deposit back.

An FBI agent was inserted at the rental agency, posing as a Ryder "loss prevention" representative. When Salameh showed up, the FBI agent met him to discuss his claim. Salameh said he wanted his $400 back, but he was told that $200 was the best they could do. He thanked the FBI agent and walked out of the rental agency, where an FBI SWAT team arrested him.[20] Because Salameh had used El-Gabrowny's address, El-Gabrowny's apartment was searched; and when El-Gabrowny resisted the search, he too was arrested. Over the next several months El-Gabrowny remained in prison, held without bail, as the other plotters planned the Day of Terror bombings.

A New Plan Is Developed

In the years since the group of plotters around Sheik Abdel Rahman had first organized in 1989, its members continued to conduct training, both in a remote area near Harrisburg, Pennsylvania, and at a public park in Jersey City. As former US prosecutor Andrew McCarthy later testified, "The paramilitary training we are talking about was no amateur hour." The training was led by men who had military experience, including a former Egyptian Army major named Ali Mohamed who would later play a key role in the planning of the 1998 East Africa embassy bombings. In addition to the use of firearms, the training included commando tactics, the construction of explosives, the neutralization of sentries, and more.[21] By early 1993 the training seemed to be under the leadership of a man named Siddig Ibrahim Siddig Ali, a Sudanese who was a translator for Abdel Rahman, and Clement Hampton-El. The participants had a cover story: They were preparing to fight in the former Yugoslavia on behalf of Bosnian Muslims. But Siddig Ali explained to one of the members of the group—who turned out to be a government informant—that the real reason was to be ready for future terrorist actions that would be approved by Abdel Rahman.[22]

In March 1993, Egyptian president Hosni Mubarak was scheduled to visit New York, and members of the group saw it as an opportunity to assassinate him. Siddig Ali described the plan to Abdo Mohammed Haggag, an Abdel Rahman confidant who later cooperated with the Egyptian and United States authorities. But the plan did not come off, because Haggag informed the Egyptian government about the plot, and the New York leg of Mubarak's trip to the United States was canceled.[23] Siddig Ali also proposed to the members of the group that they bomb a state armory. In a conversation recorded by the informant in the spring of 1993, Siddig Ali asked, "Can't we conduct an operation over here? At military places? Do you know the places that are called—their reserve places?"[24]

Then, in a conversation on May 10, 1993, Siddig Ali suggested that the group bomb the United Nations headquarters. He said he had friends in the Sudanese UN Mission who could get them official license plates so they could drive a car bomb into the UN's underground garage.[25] A code name was agreed on to be used when talking about the UN: the Big House. On May 12 one of the members of the group, Salem, met with Siddig Ali, and told him he had found a garage in Queens that could be used for bomb making; what Siddig Ali did not know was that Salem was an informant for the FBI, and that the FBI had rented the garage and equipped it with surveillance monitoring equipment.[26]

On May 21, as the group's plans proceeded, Siddig Ali and Salem went to Attica to visit Nosair in prison and get his blessing for the operation. Nosair told them he approved of the plan, and he suggested additional acts of terrorism they could commit.[27] The next step was to get Sheik Abdel Rahman's approval. But here the group was not able to get such a simple answer.

Salem met with Abdel Rahman on May 23 and asked his opinion about the plan to bomb the UN. Abdel Rahman told him, "It is not illicit; however, [it] will be bad for Muslims."[28]

"Find a plan, find a plan," continued Abdel Rahman.

"Yes," replied Salem.

Abdel Rahman went on: "To inflict damage, inflict damage on the American Army itself."

Salem told him that Siddig suggested the second target would be the FBI office at 26 Federal Plaza. "What do you think of this one?" he asked.

Abdel Rahman answered, "By God, I mean, wait for a while, wait for a while, we will talk about this later."

This cautious expression of support was apparently enough for the conspirators, and they began refining their plans and making surveillance trips by car to the target sites. On May 27, Siddig Ali introduced Salem to two other men, Amir Abdelgani and Fares Khallafalla, and together they went to the safe house where they talked about the bombing plans. Siddig Ali indicated he wanted to bomb the UN and the Lincoln and Holland tunnels; he outlined a plan for three explosions five minutes apart, sketching on a piece of cardboard. Over the next few days, Siddig Ali and Abdelgani, together with Salem on one occasion, drove to the tunnels, the UN, and the Federal Building in Manhattan to scout the targets and examine the traffic conditions. At the UN Siddig Ali commented that a bomb could topple the building. During one of these trips Abdelgani suggested that they consider bombing the diamond district in Manhattan because that would be like "hitting Israel itself." Siddig Ali told him, "It is full of diamonds, all of them are Jews."[29]

On a trip on the night of May 29, Salem asked Siddig Ali about the plot, and which tunnel was he planning, the Lincoln or the Holland? Siddig Ali responded "both of them," along with the "Big House"—UN headquarters. Siddig Ali went on to explain how blowing up a car bomb in the lowest point of the tunnels would flood them.[30]

On June 4, 1993, Siddig Ali arranged to go with Salem to meet Mohammed Saleh, who Siddig Ali explained was an important supporter of jihad activities and the owner of two gasoline stations in Yonkers, just north of New York City, who might assist in the bombing campaign. During dinner at Saleh's house, Siddig Ali explained the plan to Saleh, showing him and Salem a list of proposed targets he had written down in a notebook. Once Siddig Ali felt Saleh understood the plan, he ripped the paper out of the notebook and gave the list to Salem, asking him to eat it—which Salem did.[31]

During the next few weeks, the group began to collect items needed to prepare the bombs, including detonators, fertilizer, fuel, and stolen cars. On June 19, in Siddig Ali's apartment, Siddig Ali, Salem, and Abdelgani talked about how to conduct the Hudson River tunnel bombings. They would stop their cars in the tunnel, raise the hoods to indicate engine trouble, and then flee before the explosives would detonate. "The water will be going everywhere—everything will be broken into smithereens, everything," said Siddig Ali. "The World Trade Center, compared with this, will be like a dwarf."[32] In another conversation on the night of June 21–22, they talked over the plans to bomb the UN, and learned that the parking for UN headquarters is not in an underground garage but is above ground. Siddig Ali said that after parking the Lincoln Town Car, "press the button and walk away. After half an hour or 45 minutes, it is going to sing for them."[33]

On June 22, after buying five 55-gallon steel barrels from a Newark drum business, Siddig Ali and Abdelgani went to Saleh's gas station to get fuel for the bombs. They filled two of the drums, and an employee of Saleh's made out a receipt on which he recorded the license plate of the van. Siddig Ali wrote a phony signature on the receipt. The next day, the 23rd, Abdelgani and his cousin Fadil Abdelgani returned to fill the remaining three drums with diesel fuel, while Siddig Ali and Salem bought fertilizer for the bombs.[34]

On June 23, Siddig Ali drove through the Holland and Lincoln tunnels with Salem, videotaping the tunnels and discussing where the bombs would be placed. Siddig Ali explained to Salem that he wanted to put the bomb close to the wall of the Holland Tunnel next to a blue sign at the midpoint between the two states.[35] Siddig Ali asked Salem, who was operating the video camera, to film the police booth at the entrance; Siddig Ali told Salem that because the police were watching for hazardous materials, not bombs, they would not notice them.

That evening the conspirators began mixing the fuel and fertilizer at the safe house. At about 2 o'clock in the morning of June 24, FBI agents raided the safe house and arrested the defendants; a few hours earlier they had arrested Saleh at his apartment in Yonkers. The Day of Terror plot had been foiled.[36]

HOW THE PLOT WAS FOILED

The fundamental reason for the success of security officials in foiling the plot is clear: the presence of an FBI informant, Emad Salem, among the plotters. US Attorney Mary Jo White later testified that "the Day of Terror Plot . . . was fortunately foiled by the New York FBI and the JTTF [Joint Terrorism Task Force] because they had been able to infiltrate the terrorist cell operating in the New York–New Jersey metropolitan area with an informant posing as an explosives expert. As a result, the plot could be—and was—carefully monitored and stopped before it could come to fruition."[37] Time magazine reported soon after the arrests that "the case might never have been cracked without the help of Salem."[38]

But how did this informant happen to be there? If Salem's presence had been simply good luck, then the Day of Terror plot might offer few lessons for future counterterrorism efforts. But government officials argued the success of the case was due to more than just luck or coincidence, but rather the result of a long-standing cultivation of contacts among the Muslim community. "There was some damn good police work involved," said one FBI agent.[39]

The next two sections of this chapter consider what sort of information was available to FBI and other officials concerning the threat of terrorism, and the Day of Terror plot in particular, in the months and years leading up to the foiling of the plot.

WHAT INTELLIGENCE HAD BEEN AVAILABLE AT THE STRATEGIC LEVEL?

A reader of the US government's strategic-level terrorism threat assessments in the years before the 1993 World Trade Center bombing and the Day of Terror plot would have received little warning that an amorphous group of radical Islamic extremists was already forming within the country's borders and would soon attempt to launch devastating attacks. The US State Department, for example, reported in its Patterns of Global Terrorism report for 1991 (released in April 1992) that the primary international terrorist threat was from state sponsors, in particular from Iraq, Libya, and Iran. The major developments noted in the report were echoes of terrorist attacks and crises from years past. After a world-wide investigation, the US and British authorities had developed evidence linking Libya to the 1988 bombing of Pan American Flight 103. Nine Western hostages had been freed during the previous year from captivity in Lebanon, but two German hostages remained. Iran continued to provide support to Palestinian terrorist groups and Islamic militant organizations. And Iranian agents were suspected in the murder of the dissident former Iranian prime minister Shapour Bakhtiar in Paris in August.[40]

Similarly, when Robert Gates, the director of central intelligence, testified before the Senate Armed Services Committee on January 22, 1992, he noted that "terrorism remains a threat in many countries," with separatist and insurgent groups posing a threat to American lives and property abroad. But he noted that while new, ethnic-based terrorist groups might arise in the upheaval following the fall of the Soviet Union, "most would be unlikely purposely to attack US targets."[41]

The threat of domestically based terrorism was also seen as low. In its assessment of the terrorist threat published in 1992, the FBI reported that although 127 acts of terrorism had been recorded within the United States from 1982 to 1986, the total from 1987 to 1992 had been only 38.[42] In that report the FBI even felt compelled to ask the question, "Is terrorism still a threat?" It answered its own question by stating: "The simple answer is, Yes! The threat of terrorism is dynamic and ever-changing. It will not go away."[43] And elsewhere in the same report, the FBI noted presciently: "During the past few years there has been growing concern about extremist elements surfacing in the Islamic fundamentalist movements."[44] But the overall message of that year's report was upbeat: "The US counterterrorism program is successful because it has taken a very consistent, aggressive, and proactive approach to the problem of terrorism. Terrorists can count on being relentlessly pursued and prosecuted if they choose to operate in the United States or target Americans."[45]

Even *after* the World Trade Center was attacked, official US assessments of the terrorist threat conveyed little sense of increasing concern. The 1992 edition of *Patterns of Global Terrorism* was released in April 1993, after the World Trade Center bombing and the killing of two CIA employees outside CIA headquarters. But it noted with a sense of assurance that "despite these worrisome trends, there is some good news to report. International terrorism in 1992 fell to the lowest level since 1975."[46]

WHAT INTELLIGENCE HAD BEEN AVAILABLE AT THE TACTICAL LEVEL?

The FBI was able to gather information about the Day of Terror plot from several confidential informants, but the key source of intelligence was the informant named Emad Salem. This section examines this man's background and considers how he came to work for the FBI. The story of Salem turns out to be a complex one: He first began infiltrating Muslim extremist groups in New York City in 1991, but was dropped by the FBI shortly before the World Trade Center bombing in 1993. After that attack he was brought back on the payroll, and he was quickly able to infiltrate the group that was planning the Day of Terror attacks. This chain of circumstances strongly suggests that without the World Trade Center attack, Salem would not have penetrated the Day of Terror plot, and that second group might well have succeeded in carrying out its plan.

Who Was Emad Salem?

The US government's primary source of intelligence on the Day of Terror plot was a former Egyptian military officer who immigrated to the United States in 1987. Emad Salem was a burly, bearded, enigmatic figure, who worked as a private investigator and who also supported himself as a jewelry designer. During the trial in 1995, the *New York Times* described him as "a commanding presence. His bald pate is tanned and his rim of neatly trimmed black hair slicked back. He tends toward expensive suits, especially double-breasted models that cover an expanding bulk."[47] Another account described him as "handsome, muscular, meticulously well groomed, and quite the charming actor."[48] He appears to have been something of a chameleon, at times dressing in Islamic robes, at other times in jeans and T-shirts; to some he appeared to be a religious man, but to others he came across as not religious at all.[49]

According to press accounts, Egyptian officials said Salem had entered the Egyptian Army as a private and was "pensioned out" as an officer eighteen years later, while continuing a relationship with Egyptian military intelligence. He arrived in New York City from Cairo on September 25, 1987, leaving behind a wife and two children in Egypt. According to press accounts citing US government sources, he had agreed to report to Egyptian authorities on any contacts with Egyptian military personnel who failed to return home after receiving training in America.[50]

Within a week after his arrival in the United States, Salem met a woman named Barbara Rogers, a secretary at Mount Sinai Medical Center. They met at a karate school, where they were introduced by a girlfriend of a cousin of Salem's, and they were married only six weeks later, in a Muslim ceremony on November 8, 1987. Salem told Rogers that he had been an intelligence officer in the Egyptian Army, and he had been in charge of security for the president of Egypt—stories that he would later repeat to his FBI handlers but would eventually admit were lies. In his trial testimony in 1995, he said he had actually been a radar officer in Egypt.[51]

During his first several years in the United States, Salem worked as a security guard at several different stores, including Bergdorf Goodman and Henri Bendel.

He drove a cab briefly, but quit when an angry passenger threw a two cent tip in his face. His wife explained to a newspaper reporter that such an insult was difficult for a proud man to take. "You have to understand," she said. "This man had his own driver in Egypt." From 1991 to early 1993, he made several trips to Egypt, including at least once with his wife. He and Rogers separated in 1990, and he later moved into the apartment of a jewelry designer, Karen Ohltersdorf. He became an American citizen in August 1991, and soon afterward he and Rogers began divorce proceedings. In late 1991, he married Ohltersdorf, although he was still married to Rogers; he and Rogers were eventually divorced in 1993.[52]

Salem Becomes an Informant

Salem first came to the attention of the FBI in August 1991, when he was in charge of security for the Best Western Woodward Hotel in Manhattan. FBI agent Nancy Floyd visited the hotel as part of a program in which she went to second-rate hotels, hoping to find misbehaving Soviet diplomats who might be willing to share secrets. Salem turned out to be able to provide leads on just the sort of people for whom Floyd was looking, and she later used him to gain information on Russians suspected of gun smuggling and selling counterfeit green cards.[53]

Salem then indicated to Floyd that he could provide information about the Blind Sheik, Abdel Rahman, so Floyd introduced him to John Anticev and Louie Napoli of the New York City Joint Terrorism Task Force (JTTF). The New York JTTF, the first to be established in the nation, had been formed in 1980 in response to incidents of domestic terrorism.[54] Anticev and Napoli attempted to recruit Salem to be an undercover informant, offering to match his hotel salary of $500 a week, but at first Salem hesitated, telling them he already had a full-time job.

In October 1991 Salem was injured at work, falling off a stepladder and hitting his head when he was trying to adjust a boiler. The manager of the hotel later said that Salem's behavior changed after the accident; he began shirking work, and other employees started complaining about him. He apparently was let go from his job at the hotel.[55] As Salem told the story later during the trial, he found himself out of work for a while because of his injuries, and when the FBI agents came back in November to renew their offer, he decided to take them up on it.[56]

Salem insisted, however, on one condition: that his identity could never be disclosed. The FBI agents told him that if he wore a wire (secretly recording his conversations), he might have to testify sometime down the line, so he told them he refused to wear a microphone. They agreed to his condition, telling him that they would use him purely as an intelligence asset, and if surveillance was necessary to develop trial-worthy evidence, other agents would move in to conduct it.[57] This condition would later play a critical role when Salem was terminated as an informant in 1992—not long before the World Trade Center was attacked.

The Nosair Trial

Soon after they brought him onto the government payroll, Salem's FBI handlers approached him with a request. The trial of El Sayyid Nosair, suspected in the murder of Rabbi Kahane, was beginning in New York, and Nosair had developed quite a large circle of admirers and supporters among radical Islamists and others. Would Salem be able to infiltrate the group of followers around Nosair, and help the FBI keep tabs on what they were up to? Salem agreed, and he quickly turned out to be very good at undercover work. A source told the journalist Peter Lance that "we had given him six weeks to get under. He did it in two days."[58]

Salem began to attend the trial and visit mosques, and he befriended Nosair's cousin, Ibrahim El-Gabrowny, a vocal supporter of Nosair who headed a fundraising committee and called for support from mosques and Muslim associations. At one point during the trial, El-Gabrowny introduced Salem to Nosair, describing Salem as "a new member in the family."[59] Soon El-Gabrowny told Salem that he and some friends were assembling materials for a bomb. He was vague about what their target might be, but Salem thought he sounded serious, and when El-Gabrowny asked him to join the group, he accepted.[60]

Before the Nosair trial ended, Salem was invited for dinner at El-Gabrowny's house. During dinner, El-Gabrowny indicated that he was concerned about being bugged by the FBI and turned up the television, and then discussed building high-powered explosives. El-Gabrowny asked Salem if he knew how to make bombs, and Salem indicated that he did, because of his army experience in Egypt.[61] By early 1992 Sheik Abdel Rahman, too, had welcomed Salem into the group, and Salem even traveled to Detroit with Abdel Rahman and others to attend a conference on the Islamic economy.[62]

"Don't Call Me When the Bombs Go Off"

By June 1992, Salem still had not learned what the group was planning to do, but he had been told that the operation would involve twelve bombs, and that guns would be needed in case they encountered police.[63] But in early July 1992, a dispute developed between Salem and the FBI—a dispute that would result in Salem being released as an undercover informant.

The problem arose when the agents in charge of the Salem case—Napoli and Anticev—gave their superiors a briefing on the progress they had made and were told it was now time to build a case that could be taken to court. To do this, Salem would need to wear a wire, which he had previously said he would never do. At about the same time, another problem arose for Salem: The FBI agents asked him to take a polygraph examination, apparently because they were suspicious that he might be working for Egyptian intelligence. He was given three tests during the spring and summer of 1992, and although the agent who administered the tests believed he had passed, when experts in Washington reviewed the results they determined that he had lied on at least one of the tests.[64] In June or July 1992, Salem went to the FBI's New York City headquarters to meet with senior officials Carson Dunbar and John Crouthamel. They told Salem that he would need to wear a wire and be prepared to testify in court about the plot that was developing, but he continued to refuse.[65]

In July 1991, Salem was fired as an informant, but he continued to get his weekly salary of $500 to tide him over until he found another job. To explain his disappearance to the conspirators, Salem told El-Gabrowny that he needed to go to Spain to take care of a problem in his jewelry business.[66] Nancy Floyd continued to meet with him, to give him the cash, at a Subway sandwich shop near the FBI's New York office. Salem warned her that something was going on with the Blind Sheik's cell, and he told her that the FBI should be keeping track of the cell members.[67]

In September, in an effort to shake up the plotters and attempt to find out the extent of the conspiracy, the FBI had subpoenas issued to El-Gabrowny and several dozen others—including to Salem, who was included in the group in order to maintain his cover. On September 15, some twenty men reported to 26 Federal Plaza, where they were questioned, fingerprinted, and confronted with surveillance photos from the Calverton shooting range. But no one confessed to anything, and they were allowed to leave with no charges filed.[68]

Floyd had her last meeting with Salem in early October 1992, and again he warned her that the FBI should be worried about what was going on. She told him she had been transferred to another job and was no longer involved in the case. As he left the Subway shop, he turned toward her and said, "Don't call me when the bombs go off."[69]

After the World Trade Center Bombing, Back on the Payroll

On the afternoon of the day the World Trade Center was bombed, Salem called Nancy Floyd in a panic from a room at Saint Clare's Hospital in Manhattan, where he had been admitted for an inner-ear infection. He told her he was worried that no one had listened to him, and now they might think he had been involved. She told him they had done all they could, but she would talk to her supervisor to see what could be done. She called her boss in the FBI's Foreign Counter Intelligence Division, who said that it would be up to the Terrorism Section to handle Salem if they wanted to. So she called Napoli and told him that Salem wanted to talk.[70]

At 1:00 a.m. later that night, Napoli and Anticev were in a meeting in the office of the FBI's New York assistant director. Running the meeting was Mary

Jo White, who had recently been appointed the US attorney for Manhattan. Napoli mentioned they had an asset who "was very close to these people," and told White about Salem. White said she wanted to meet him, but Napoli answered, "Well, we were paying him like five hundred a week. This time, you know, considering what's happened, he's probably gonna want—a million dollars." At which White answered, "I don't give a damn *what* he wants. If he can deliver, give it to him."[71]

After weeks of negotiation between Salem and lawyers and agents representing the FBI, it was agreed that the government would pay Salem more than $1 million to once again become an undercover source, to be a witness at any future trial, and to be put into the witness protection program afterward. It did not take long for the decision to rehire Salem to pay off. In April 1993, Salem told Detective Louie Napoli that he had been approached by Sheik Abdel Rahman's translator, Siddig Ali, who said he was planning a series of simultaneous bombings against four major New York City landmarks: the Lincoln and Holland tunnels, the UN, and 26 Federal Plaza, the location of the FBI's New York offices.[72]

Although the FBI was already involved in the massive investigation into the World Trade Center attack that had been codenamed TRADEBOM, an investigation was now begun into the new plot, dubbed TERRSTOP. The FBI's Special Operations Group outfitted Salem with an array of listening devices, including two recorders in the trunk of his car and a specially designed pair of pants with an electronic chip in them that recorded voices. Salem got back in touch with Siddig Ali and began providing supplies to the conspirators, including a video camera for surveillance and a van that the FBI had wired for sound.[73]

The investigation was almost exposed in May, when Siddig Ali confided to Salem that there were additional plans to assassinate several political figures sympathetic to Israel, including US senator Alphonse D'Amato and Brooklyn assemblyman Dov Hikind. The authorities informed the officials about the threats against them, but stressed how sensitive the information was; because only a few of the conspirators knew about these plans, it was felt that Salem might be exposed as the source if the information on the threats became public.

Despite the FBI's efforts, however, the threat to Hikind leaked to the press, and on May 25, the *New York Post* ran headlines announcing this new, second terrorist plot. Salem believed his cover had been blown. He later told his ex-wife, Barbara Rogers, that when Siddig Ali heard the news, he lined up Salem and several others who knew about the plot against Hikind and put a revolver to each man's head. "Allah is going to tell us who the traitor is," Siddig Ali said. But luckily for Salem and the FBI, when no one confessed Siddig Ali concluded that it might have been a coincidence, or that the FBI could have gotten its information through some sort of surveillance of the group.[74] The FBI and the JTTF continued monitoring the plot until the group had begun to actually mix the explosives that would go into their bombs on the night of June 23–24. It was then that the safe house was raided and the Day of Terror plot was foiled.

For Salem, the stress involved in living a double life as terrorist conspirator and government informant brought on an asthma attack, and after the FBI raided the bomb factory he ended up in the emergency room of Mount Sinai Hospital, seeking treatment under a false name.[75] But he recovered and prospered from his role in the case. At the 1995 trial it was revealed that the government had agreed to pay Salem a total of $1,056,200 for his work as an informer; and until he received that payment, he was given $7,000 a month. Before that, as mentioned above, his payment as a government informant had been $500 a week, plus expenses. The federal witness protection program, which reportedly moved him fourteen times from the time he entered it in June 1993 until the trial, also paid him $2,600 a month for living expenses.[76]

Other Government Informants

Although Salem was by far the most important confidential informant involved in the Day of Terror plot, he was not the only one. The government also received information from Garrett Wilson, a source on the fringe of the plot as it was developing. Wilson was a former army ranger who worked as a military police officer at a naval base in Philadelphia, and who had gotten to know a number of militant Black Muslims while attending martial arts conferences in the New York area. Conspirator Clement Hampton-El had approached Wilson in an effort to obtain detonators and guns, but he did not know that Wilson was a cooperating witness for the US Naval Investigative Service. Wilson later testified for the government at the trial.[77]

In addition, two members of the conspiracy had apparent changes of heart after the plot was broken up and offered to make deals with the government. One was an Egyptian named Abdo Mohammed Haggag, who had taken part in the paramilitary training from late 1992 to early 1993 and had been a close confidant of Sheik Abdel Rahman. He had been providing information secretly to the Egyptian government, and after going to jail he offered to tell the FBI what he knew.[78] The second conspirator to help the prosecution was the key plotter Siddig Ali. Shortly after the trial began, he pleaded guilty and became a cooperating witness. He never testified at the trial, and the details of the information he provided are not known, but in October 1999 he was sentenced to eleven years in prison—considerably less than the sentence he could have received—after the court received a letter from US Attorney Mary Jo White describing his extensive assistance in the case.[79]

The Case Goes to Trial

Soon after the June 24 arrests, it was discovered that the terrorist conspirators were not the only ones Salem, the informant, had been secretly spying on and tape recording. He had also been making secret recordings of his conversations with government agents, going back at least to the Nosair trial. He apparently wanted the tapes as an insurance policy in case the government backed away from its promises of money and protection. These "bootleg" tapes came to light when Salem hurriedly left his West Side Manhattan apartment after the plot was broken up, leaving behind cassettes of the secret recordings. Judge Mukasey allowed the transcripts of the hundreds of hours of tapes to be given to the defense lawyers, ordering that they be kept secret. But the New York Times obtained a copy of the transcripts and their existence became public. Eventually, the transcripts of the tapes were introduced into evidence during the trial.[80]

The tapes revealed some new details about the terrorist plot, as Salem could be heard saying that the conspirators also discussed bombing Grand Central Terminal, the Empire State Building, and Times Square.[81] But more significantly, they showed how sensitive and troubled the relationship was between Salem and his FBI handlers; and how at some points FBI officials appeared to be encouraging Salem to push the cell's members to make incriminating statements and possibly entrap themselves.

The original indictment in the case was superseded in August 1993 with a new indictment that included for the first time charges against Sheik Omar Abdel Rahman for leading the conspiracy. The new indictment also for the first time linked together the 1990 killing of Kahane, the World Trade Center bombing, and the Day of Terror plot, charging the plotters with seditious conspiracy, based on a little-used law that forbids efforts to overthrow the US government.[82] The trial opened in New York federal court in January 1995, and it ended nine months later after the jury heard testimony from more than two hundred witnesses and listened to more than a hundred hours of tape recordings that Salem had secretly made. The jury deliberated for seven days before pronouncing all ten defendants guilty of attempting to carry out a campaign of terrorism.

RECEPTIVITY TOWARD WARNING

Before the World Trade Center bombing in 1993, there was little concern among government officials about the threat of international terrorism, particularly radical Islamist terrorism, on American soil. This lack of concern reflected a lack of strategic-level intelligence warnings about such a threat, and it appears to have been particularly felt at the senior levels of the police and FBI, where there was less emphasis on the terrorist threat than there was among lower-level FBI agents and police.

A scene described by Miller and Stone illustrates this difference of view. In the summer of 1992, the chief of the New York FBI's Criminal Division called into his office two agents who had been involved in terrorism investigations and told them that "terrorism was dead." From then on, he told them, they would be working on gang investigations. Another FBI agent, Neil Herman, objected to this reduction in effort and tried to convince an official in the New York Police Department to assign more police detectives to take up the slack. But the police official said that the department did not have any more detectives to spare.

"What happens when the big one goes down?" Herman asked.

"When the big one goes down, I'll send you five hundred detectives," the police official replied.[83]

After the World Trade Center was attacked, the FBI agents and police detectives tracking the terrorist threat did indeed get the help they needed. But that help was not in the form of five hundred detectives: It was one well-placed informant, and the story of Emad Salem strongly suggests that he would not have been brought back on the government's payroll if the World Trade Center attack had not energized the authorities into reaching out for whatever sources of intelligence they could find.

CONCLUSION

The Day of Terror case remains important today because it demonstrated several techniques that have been shown to be critical in the fight against terrorism. These techniques include the use of human intelligence—in this case, in the form of a government informant—and of electronic surveillance and secret wiretaps, as much of the evidence introduced in the case came from secret wiretaps, some of which were authorized by the Foreign Intelligence Surveillance Court. The plot also remains useful for study because it provided an early model or template for how a group of loosely affiliated extremists can come together, train, plan, and very nearly carry out a terrorist attack inflicting wide-scale death and destruction. The conspiracy described in this chapter proceeded through a number of distinct stages, including member recruitment, group training, target selection, and weapons acquisition. Similar patterns can be seen in a number of terrorist plots that have been foiled since then, which suggests that such a template may prove useful in analyzing and preventing complex terrorist plots in the future.[84]

This case is most significant for this book, however, because it provides a successful test of the theory of preventive action. The Day of Terror plot was not thwarted because law enforcement officials or intelligence analysts were able to "connect the dots" and piece together clues about the growing conspiracy. Nor was it foiled because officials had been alerted by strategic-level intelligence assessments of the terrorist threat; as we have seen, even after the World Trade Center had been bombed, national-level assessments portrayed the problem of international terrorism as being in decline.

What might have been America's most devastating terrorist attack before 9/11 was foiled because an FBI informant provided the authorities with precise, tactical-level intelligence on the plot as it was developing. But the history of the Day of Terror plot suggests that even such precise intelligence is not necessarily enough to prevent a terrorist attack. The intelligence must lead to action, and in order to be *actionable*, precise intelligence needs to be combined with receptive policymakers.

The FBI and the New York JTTF had originally recruited Emad Salem as a confidential informant in the fall of 1991, but senior officials were not receptive to the information he was providing. This was partly because they did not trust Salem's motives, but it was also a reflection of the conventional assessment of the terrorist threat in America at that time. Terrorism was seen as a primarily international problem, caused by hostile states such as Libya; though there was a limited domestic threat from disgruntled or deranged individuals, domestic terrorism was seen as much less threatening.

Against the strenuous objections of the working-level agents who were handling Salem, senior FBI officials ordered that he be dropped as an informant in the summer of 1992. When the World Trade Center was bombed, that attack served as a focusing event—a wake-up call—that convinced officials of the seriousness of the threat posed by loosely connected groups of individuals such as the one Salem had penetrated. He was brought back on the payroll, and he was soon able to uncover information that prevented the Day of Terror attacks and also helped convict Abdel Rahman and nine others of conspiracy in the plot.

CHAPTER 7

THE 9/11 ATTACKS

A New Explanation

O NE OF THE MOST ENDURING QUESTIONS surrounding the 9/11 attacks is: Why, when American intelligence agencies and others had been warning for years about the threat from bin Laden and international terrorism, were the attacks not anticipated and prevented? James Wirtz puts the puzzle this way: "Even accounting for hindsight, it is difficult to understand how the government, the public, and the scholarly community all failed to respond to the threat posed by al-Qaeda, in a way that is eerily similar to the failures that preceded Pearl Harbor."[1]

The consensus of the two major official investigations and of many scholars, journalists, and others who have investigated the attacks follows the conventional wisdom about how intelligence fails: There had been warning signals about the threat from bin Laden and al-Qaeda, but these warnings were misunderstood or ignored in an intelligence failure unmatched by any in American history since Pearl Harbor. The reasons behind this failure—the reasons why the warnings were ignored—have been hotly debated. But the standard argument, expressed in the report of the 9/11 Commission, is that intelligence and national security officials lacked the imagination to "connect the dots" and make sense of the information that was available.[2]

In addition to the failure of imagination, the standard explanation holds that before 9/11 the US intelligence community was too focused on the tactical level, and did not produce enough broad, long-range, strategic-level intelligence assessments on the threat from bin Laden and al-Qaeda. If intelligence agencies had done a better job of assembling the available warning signs into such assessments for senior policymakers, this argument runs, the attacks might have been prevented.

This chapter makes an argument that is essentially the opposite of this widely accepted view. The problem was not too much intelligence and insufficiently imaginative intelligence analysts, but too little precise warning and insufficiently receptive policymakers.

Although the conventional view holds that the intelligence community failed in providing strategic warning, in this chapter I argue that strategic-level intelligence assessments of bin Laden and al-Qaeda were in fact remarkably good. Years of intelligence assessments and briefings alerted American policymakers to the rising threat of international terrorism, to the danger from al-Qaeda, and even to the threat that terrorists might use commercial airliners in their attacks. But why, if strategic-level intelligence assessments of al-Qaeda were so good, did 9/11 happen? Because strategic warnings—long-term, big-picture assessments of threats such as were available before September 11, 2001—are not enough to prevent failure and surprise.

Terrorist attacks such as those of 9/11 can have long-term, strategic consequences, but they are actually *tactical* events. In order to prevent them, policymakers require specific, *tactical*-level intelligence, such as where and when a certain plot is planned and who is involved. And it was here that American intelligence failed: It failed to gain tactical intelligence on the 9/11 plot and to give specific warning about the attacks being planned. Rather than being too focused on the tactical level, the intelligence community before 9/11 had *not been focused enough* on gathering and analyzing specific, tactical-level intelligence on al-Qaeda and the threat of international terrorism.

But there is more to the failure of 9/11 than just a failure of tactical-level intelligence. The history of American intelligence failures demonstrates that in order to be useful in preventing major terrorist attacks, intelligence must be received and understood by decision makers who have the ability to act. Intelligence can lead to preventive action when it provides specific warning and is received by decision makers who are receptive to it. But in the years leading up to 9/11, national-level decision makers were insufficiently receptive to the warnings they received about the threat from bin Laden. This suggests that even if tactical intelligence on the threat had been available, it is unlikely that policymakers would have been prepared to listen and take the actions necessary to stop the attacks.

This chapter begins with an overview of the official investigations into 9/11 and of the conventional view of what led to the intelligence failure. Next is an outline of the primary sources of intelligence that were available on bin Laden and al-Qaeda. The subsequent section reviews the warnings that were available from intelligence and from other sources, first at the strategic level and then the tactical level.[3] Next is an examination of the receptivity that existed toward these warnings, first in the Clinton administration and then in the Bush administration. The conclusion returns to the question of whether the attacks could have been prevented, and considers how the findings of this case study fit into the broader theory of intelligence failure and success developed in this book.

HOW THE 9/11 ATTACKS HAVE BEEN EXPLAINED

The first major official study of the 9/11 attacks was the Congressional Joint Inquiry, completed in December 2002.[4] It concluded that while there was no specific intelligence information available before the attacks that could have identified the time, place, or precise nature of the attacks, there was significant information available that the intelligence community did not handle properly. The Joint Inquiry found that the intelligence community's understanding of al-Qaeda was hampered by insufficient analytic capability, especially in terms of "the strategic analysis needed to develop a broader understanding of the threat and the organization."[5] The Joint Inquiry produced a detailed report whose findings in many ways foreshadowed the later report of the 9/11 Commission, and its report, staff statements, and public hearings remain useful to 9/11 researchers today. But the rambling, 858-page report attracted little public attention when it was published.[6]

The primary narrative and explanation of the 9/11 attacks is that of the 9/11 Commission, whose report has become so widely accepted among Americans—although not by all academics and policy experts—that it can be considered conventional wisdom. The *9/11 Commission Report* used a broad brush to argue that the blame needed to be shared widely throughout the American government, the press, and even the American public. But much of the report, and its recommendations for reform, focused on failures of intelligence analysis and assessment.

The commission found that intelligence reporting on bin Laden and terrorism had been particularly weak at the level of broad, strategic analysis, with no overall assessment of the threat from al-Qaeda produced from 1998 to 2001.[7] Although American intelligence agencies had provided many reports and briefings documenting specific threats and warnings from al-Qaeda, there were no reports describing bin Laden's broad strategy or summarizing the lessons that could be learned from al-Qaeda's involvement in past attacks.[8] In the absence of such an authoritative depiction of the threat, the commissioners found, there was a lack of understanding at the top levels of the government about just how dangerous al-Qaeda was. Although presidents Clinton and Bush and their senior advisers all had said they understood the danger from bin Laden, the commission wrote that "at some level that is hard to define, we believe the threat had not yet become compelling."[9]

Other Official Investigations

In addition to the Congressional Joint Inquiry and the 9/11 Commission, two other important official investigations have examined the use of intelligence by the FBI and the CIA.[10] The first to be released to the public was an investigation by the Justice Department's inspector general of the FBI's use of intelligence before 9/11.[11] The report argued that a major problem at the FBI was a lack of strategic intelligence analysis, and "a striking example of the FBI's failing" in terms of strategic analysis was that before 9/11 it had not performed a comprehensive national-level assessment of the risk of terrorist attack, even though in 1999 it had promised Congress that it would conduct such an analysis.[12]

The second investigation to be made public was conducted by the CIA's inspector general in response to a directive by the Congressional Joint Inquiry to determine whether CIA employees deserved either rewards or blame for their performance before 9/11. It was completed in 2005 but kept secret until 2007, when Congress passed a bill requiring that an unclassified summary be made public.[13] The report found there had been neither a "single point of failure" nor a "silver bullet" that could have enabled the intelligence community to predict or prevent the 9/11 attacks.[14] But it argued that before 9/11 the CIA had failed to develop a comprehensive strategic plan for responding to the threat from al-Qaeda, and its strategic analysis on al-Qaeda was poor, with analysts focusing primarily on current and tactical issues, rather than big-picture, strategic-level threats.[15]

A more favorable account of the CIA's efforts against al-Qaeda and bin Laden can be found in a CIA internal study that was released with many redactions in June 2012 in response to a Freedom of Information Act request by the National Security Archive. That study argued that the CIA had in fact been able to provide American policymakers with strategic warning of the rising threat from al-Qaeda, but it had been unsuccessful in obtaining specific, tactical warning. In the case of 9/11, as in other terrorist attacks, the report said, "we saw the smoke but could not see the flames directly."[16] As the rest of this chapter shows, this relatively positive assessment does not reflect the conventional wisdom about the intelligence community's performance before the 9/11 attacks. But it is actually a remarkably good (and even poetic) description of what really happened.

The Conventional Wisdom about 9/11

Some experts, especially from within the American intelligence community, have argued that the 9/11 attacks were actually not the result of any failure of intelligence. Then–director of central intelligence (DCI) George Tenet testified in 2002 that the 9/11 attacks had not represented a case of intelligence failure: "When people use the word 'failure,' 'failure' means no focus, no attention, no discipline—and those were not present in what either we or the FBI did here and around the world."[17]

Other analysts and scholars from outside of the intelligence community take a macro view, arguing that blame for 9/11 must be assigned more widely than just to the intelligence community. Joshua Rovner, for example, has written, "September 11 was not an intelligence failure, it was a national failure."[18] And still others take a micro view, that the attacks were the result of individual incompetence or bad decisions. Former White House counterterrorism adviser Richard Clarke, for example, has charged that President Bush "failed to act prior to September 11 on the threat from al-Qaeda despite repeated warnings."[19] Some even attribute the disaster to more ominous forces, charging that there may have been some sort of conspiracy—or at least an extraordinarily high level of incompetence—among high-level government officials before 9/11.[20]

But despite this wide variety of arguments and theories, the view expressed in both the Congressional Joint Inquiry and the 9/11 Commission Report has become broadly enough accepted to be called conventional wisdom. The disaster of 9/11 was largely (although not entirely) an intelligence failure, as intelligence agencies and national security officials lacked the imagination to connect the dots about the growing threat of international terrorism and al-Qaeda.

SOURCES OF INTELLIGENCE ON BIN LADEN AND AL-QAEDA

In the years leading up to the 9/11 attacks, the US intelligence community gathered intelligence on bin Laden and al-Qaeda from a variety of sources and methods. This section provides a brief overview of the primary sources, and serves as a primer to aid in understanding the specific pieces of intelligence discussed later in this chapter.[21]

Imagery intelligence—the collection of satellite photos and imagery from other sources—was a backbone of American intelligence collection during the Cold War. More recently it proved valuable in helping to identify terrorist training camps and providing targeting data for cruise missile strikes and other military operations (planned as well as actually conducted), but in the intelligence effort against al-Qaeda it has largely taken a back seat to other collection methods.[22] Open source intelligence, including statements made by bin Laden and information gathered from the monitoring of foreign media, provided important information on al-Qaeda's growth and bin Laden's intentions. Other intelligence was supplied to American agencies through liaison relationships with foreign governments and intelligence services.

The most important intelligence on al-Qaeda, however, came from two sources: signals intelligence (SIGINT) and human intelligence (HUMINT). Although SIGINT does not usually receive as much attention in the literature on intelligence and terrorism as does HUMINT, it appears that SIGINT, coming largely from the National Security Agency (NSA), was actually a very lucrative source. Richard Clarke told the Congressional Joint Inquiry in a closed session that before 9/11 "eighty to ninety per cent of our quality intelligence came from the NSA."[23] One student of the American SIGINT community, Matthew Aid, writes that "SIGINT was the US intelligence community's principal source of 'actionable' information about terrorist activities prior to September 11, 2001."[24]

It has been widely reported that before 9/11, the intelligence community had little good HUMINT on al-Qaeda.[25] A number of terrorism experts have argued that the CIA's inability to penetrate al-Qaeda with agents was the primary reason why the 9/11 attacks were not prevented. But the story of America's HUMINT before 9/11 is more complicated than that, and though it appears true the CIA did not have any agents inside bin Laden's inner circle, it did receive intelligence from a number of other human sources.

The Joint Inquiry reported that according to officials at the CIA Counterterrorist Center (CTC), the CIA had no penetrations of al-Qaeda leadership but it did have "numerous unilateral sources outside the leadership who were reporting on al-Qa'ida, and a larger number who were being developed for recruitment, prior to September 11. The best source was handled jointly by CIA and the FBI."[26] In addition to these unilateral sources, there were numerous human sources being handled by foreign intelligence services, as well as volunteer walk-ins. The Joint Inquiry stated that one of the walk-ins "was very good and provided information that was used to thwart attacks on US interests in Europe." But the report also noted that much of the information provided by volunteers "was considered bogus by CTC," and some volunteers were suspected of being sent by al-Qaeda.[27]

The intelligence community was making major efforts to improve its HUMINT on al-Qaeda several years before 9/11. George Tenet writes in his memoir that this effort was greatly increased after the 1998 East Africa embassy bombings, and by September of 1999 "we had more than one hundred recruited sources inside Afghanistan."[28] Tenet cannot be considered unbiased in describing the extensive efforts undertaken by the CIA, but his account appears to be broadly corroborated by Richard Clarke in his testimony to a closed session of the Joint Inquiry on June 11, 2002. Clarke was asked about "the state of US unilateral penetration" of al-Qaeda. He answered that the CTC had not been successful until 1999. Cofer Black was then put in charge, and "he was instructed by George Tenet to get human penetrations of al-Qa'ida, and over the course of the subsequent 3 years, they did go from [blanked out] penetrations of one sort or another, none of them very high level."[29]

Despite these advances, the intelligence community remained frustrated in its attempts to penetrate the al-Qaeda leadership, and it reported these limitations to senior intelligence and national security officials. A CTC presentation to CIA senior leadership in December 1999 noted that "while we need to disrupt operations, . . . we need to also recruit sources inside UBL's [i.e., Usama Bin Ladin's, as bin Laden's name was then spelled by the government] organization." And the same month the CTC briefed the National Security Council's "Small Group" of key officials, stating that "at this time, we have no penetrations inside UBL's leadership."[30]

THE STRATEGIC INTELLIGENCE AVAILABLE

As we have seen, the major official investigations and the conventional wisdom about 9/11 argue that one of the primary failings of the US intelligence community was at the strategic level, particularly in terms of strategic analysis. Senior intelligence officials have agreed that strategic analysis took second place, behind the needs of current intelligence and operations. For example, according to the Congressional Joint Inquiry, the CIA's inspector general examined the CTC in August 2001 and found that analysts were spending their time on crises and short-term demands, and "did not have the time to spot trends or to knit together the threads from the flood of information."[31]

But others have argued that the intelligence community actually did a very good job of providing strategic warning on the threat from al-Qaeda. Some of these are current or former intelligence officials who might be expected to present such a positive view. Tenet, for example, testified to the 9/11 Commission that from 1995 to the 9/11 attacks the CIA produced forty-six papers containing "significant strategic intelligence analysis on Bin Ladin, al-Qa'ida, and Islamic extremism."[32] Former senior CIA official Paul Pillar argues that in the years leading up to 9/11, the CIA provided strong strategic intelligence on the threat, both in classified assessments provided to policymakers and in public statements.[33]

How can these seemingly contradictory views be reconciled? Was strategic intelligence neglected, or did it accurately portray the threat? In order to judge the quality of strategic intelligence on bin Laden and terrorism, this section examines the intelligence that was available before the attacks.

Early Warnings about Bin Laden

The US intelligence community was slow to understand the seriousness of the threat posed by bin Laden and al-Qaeda. For example, although the first steps toward the formation of al-Qaeda were taken in 1988, the first reference to it in intelligence reporting appears to have been in late 1996, and the intelligence community did not provide an overall description of it until 1999.[34]

Intelligence reports on bin Laden himself date back to at least April 1993, when a CIA paper described him as "an independent actor [who] sometimes works with other individuals or governments," and concluded that bin Laden's group (apparently not named) "almost certainly played a role" in the December 1992 attack on a hotel in Aden, Yemen, housing US service members supporting the UN assistance operation in Somalia. An article that same month in the *National Intelligence Daily*, a top-level product provided to senior government officials, noted that hundreds of Islamic militants had received training the previous year in military camps in Afghanistan, and one camp was run by an Egyptian and funded by bin Laden.[35] A July 1993 CIA report noted that bin Laden had funded Egyptian terrorists in Sudan, and in that same year the State Department put bin Laden on its TIPOFF watch list of foreigners who were not allowed to enter the United States because of ties to terrorism or other illegal activity.[36] And then in August a State Department intelligence report identified him as a supporter of a new generation of militant Islamic fighters who was "particularly famous for his religious zeal and financial largess."[37]

A classified FBI report in 1995 described the emergence of "a new generation of Sunni Islamic terrorists," and mentioned bin Laden as the possible source for the funding of the 1993 World Trade Center attack.[38] As noted in chapter 5, the CIA bin Laden "virtual station" was formed in 1996.[39] But the station was initially located away from the central CIA headquarters, in an office building in Tysons Corner, in northern Virginia, and its personnel were relatively junior in grade, indicating its work was considered to be low priority. In addition, most of the bin Laden unit's staff were women, and some in the CIA called them "the Manson Family."[40]

In 1996, American officials received "a major breakthrough" in their understanding of al-Qaeda when the former al-Qaeda member named al-Fadl walked into the US embassy in Eritrea and became a long-time source of information.[41] But still, the consensus within the intelligence community was that he was a financier, not a director, of terrorist attacks.[42] The 9/11 Commission reported that "until 1996, hardly anyone in the US government understood that Usama Bin Ladin was an inspirer and organizer of the new terrorism."[43]

Bin Laden's Early Statements

Beginning at least as early as 1996, Osama bin Laden made it clear that he intended to do harm to the United States. In an interview published in July of that year in the London newspaper *The Independent*, he declared that the killing of Americans in the Khobar Towers bombing had marked "the beginning of war between Muslims and the United States."[44] In August 1996, he issued a "Declaration of Holy War on the Americans Occupying the Country of the Two Sacred Places," calling on Muslims worldwide to join in attacks against US forces to compel their withdrawal from the Arabian Peninsula.[45] In a second fatwa in February 1998, he called for the murder of any American as the "individual duty for every Muslim who can do it in any country in which it is possible to do it."[46] And as noted in chapter 5, he held several press conferences during which he made public threats against the West, including an interview with ABC-TV in May 1998 in which he said "it is far better for anyone to kill a single American soldier than to squander his efforts on other activities."[47]

Increasing Warnings about Bin Laden and Al-Qaeda

Intelligence reporting on the threat from bin Laden increased substantially in 1998. That spring the CIA learned from the Saudi government that it had disrupted bin Laden cells in its country planning to attack US forces with shoulder-fired missiles.[48] Then shortly after bin Laden's press conference in May, the intelligence community began to receive reporting that his organization was intending to strike within the United States. These reports were generally uncorroborated and their sources were often questionable, but they included a warning in June that bin Laden was considering attacks against Washington and New York, and that an attack in Washington would probably be against public places.[49]

By this time the US government had begun paying a great deal of attention to bin Laden. In May 1998 the CIA conducted a large-scale rehearsal of a plan to capture him (a plan that was never executed), and briefing papers that were prepared for the operation stated, "Sooner or later, Bin Ladin will attack US interests, perhaps using WMD [weapons of mass destruction]." Then in June a federal grand jury in New York City secretly indicted him on charges of conspiring to attack US defense installations.[50] Further reports came in that summer, including one in June 1998 with the title "Bin Ladin Threatening to Attack US Aircraft [with Antiaircraft Missiles]."[51]

Then in August 1998 came the attacks on the US embassies in Kenya and Tanzania, discussed in chapter 5. For many in the intelligence community, those attacks were a decisive moment in their understanding of the threat from al-Qaeda. The Congressional Joint Inquiry reported that "interviews of Intelligence Community personnel suggest that more than any other al-Qa'ida attack before September 11, the near-simultaneous bombing of the Embassies changed how the Intelligence Community perceived the threat of terrorism from that group."[52] Daniel Benjamin and Steven Simon write, "To those within the US government, including the present writers, who served at the time on the National Security Council staff, the attacks on the embassies in Nairobi and Dar es Salaam on August 7, 1998, were a turning point."[53]

In September 1998, the intelligence community prepared a memorandum detailing al-Qaeda's infrastructure in the United States, including its use of front organizations for terrorist activities.[54] The next month intelligence information indicated al-Qaeda was trying to establish a cell of operatives in the United States, and might be trying to recruit American Muslims and United States–based citizens from the Middle East and North Africa.[55] In November 1998, reporting indicated a bin Laden cell in the United Arab Emirates was attempting to recruit a group of five to seven men from the United States to travel to the Middle East for training in conjunction with a plan to strike US domestic targets. The report also said that bin Laden had affiliates in major US cities.[56] That same month the intelligence community learned that bin Laden had offered reward money for the assassination of four top US intelligence officers in response to an increase in reward money offered by the United States for information leading to the arrest of bin Laden.[57] And in the fall of 1998, several reports came in noting that bin Laden was considering a new attack method using biological toxins in food, water, or ventilation systems of US embassies.[58] A December 1, 1998, intelligence assessment of bin Laden read in part, "UBL is actively planning against US targets. . . . Multiple reports indicate UBL is keenly interested in striking the US on its own soil. . . . Al-Qa'ida is recruiting operatives for attacks in the US but has not yet identified potential targets."[59]

Then on December 4, 1998, DCI Tenet issued a directive to several CIA officials and his deputy for community management, stating: "We are at war. I want no resources or people spared in this effort, either inside CIA or the Community." His deputy faxed it to the heads of the other major intelligence agencies after removing sections dealing with covert action, but it appears that senior intelligence officials inside the CIA as well as elsewhere in the intelligence community did not clearly understand for whom the memo was intended. The 9/11 Commission writes that the director of the NSA thought the memo applied to the CIA, while senior CIA officials thought it applied to the rest of the intelligence community. Although the memo does appear to have been effective in mobilizing some parts of the community to increase collection efforts aimed at bin Laden, the 9/11 Commission noted, "The memorandum had little overall effect on mobilizing the CIA or the intelligence community."[60]

More threat warnings came in that suggested imminent attacks on US embassies abroad, and on December 18, 1998, Tenet sent what he describes as the first of eight letters to the president and "virtually the entire" national security community, laying out why he was concerned about the looming terrorist attacks. This letter was titled "Bin Ladin Ready to Attack," and in it he wrote, "I am greatly concerned by recent intelligence reporting indicating that Usama Bin Ladin is planning to conduct another attack against US personnel or facilities soon . . . possibly over the next few days. One of Bin Ladin's deputies has used code words we associated with terrorist operations to order colleagues in East Africa to complete their work."[61]

More reports of possible bin Laden attacks continued to come in to the intelligence system in 1999, including a threat to blow up the FBI building in Washington and a warning against a flight out of Los Angeles or New York. The *9/11 Commission Report* notes, "These warnings came amid dozens of others that flooded in."[62] Bin Laden also continued to make public threats; in January 1999 *Time* magazine ran an interview with him in which he declared "Hostility toward America is a religious duty."[63] In June 1999, the FBI put bin Laden on its "10 Most Wanted List."[64] In June 1999, testimony to the Senate intelligence committee, and in a July 1999 briefing to the House intelligence committee staff, the chief of the CTC described reports that bin Laden and his associates were planning attacks in the United States.[65]

In August 1999, the intelligence community learned that al-Qaeda had decided to target—which they believed meant to assassinate—the secretaries of state and defense, and the DCI.[66] In September 1999, and again later that year, intelligence officials learned that bin Laden and others were planning a terrorist act in the United States, possibly against specific landmarks in California and New York City.[67] According to former DCI Tenet, the intelligence community warned President Clinton before the millennium that bin Laden was planning "between five and fifteen attacks around the world; . . . some of these might be inside the United States."[68]

The Millennium Plot and Afterward

A number of plots uncovered around the millennium heightened the sense of danger. In early December 1999, the Jordanian authorities broke up a plot to attack hotels and tourist sites in Amman that had been planned by a Palestinian man working together with an American cab driver in Boston. Then on December 14, Ahmed Ressam was arrested while trying to cross into the United States at Port Angeles, Washington. The authorities later learned that he had planned to detonate a bomb at Los Angeles International Airport.[69] In late December Richard Clarke's staff warned in a memo, "Foreign terrorist sleeper cells are present in the US and attacks in the US are likely" (underlined in the original).[70]

There were several alarming reports in 2000, including one in February that bin Laden was making plans to assassinate US intelligence officials, and another in March that described the types of facilities that al-Qaeda might strike. Potential targets included the Statue of Liberty, along with skyscrapers, ports, airports, and nuclear power plants.[71]

Then on October 12, 2000, the USS *Cole* was attacked, killing seventeen crew members and wounding thirty-nine. US officials immediately suspected that al-Qaeda was responsible, and intelligence was acquired that linked al-Qaeda to the attack, but they were not able to prove that bin Laden was personally responsible until several key planners were captured after 9/11. In the course of the investigation into the *Cole* attack, US officials learned that there had been an earlier attempt, in January 2000, to attack the USS *The Sullivans*. That attempt had failed because the attack boat was overloaded and sank; but the boat was salvaged and used in the successful attack ten months later.[72]

Warnings about the Use of Aircraft

In addition to these general warnings about the threat from bin Laden and al-Qaeda, there had been a number of indications before 2001 that terrorists were interested in using aircraft in their attacks. There was a precedent for such an operation: In 1994 an Algerian group had hijacked an airliner, probably intending to blow it up over Paris but possibly trying to crash it into the Eiffel Tower. And in January 1995, a man named Murad, who had been involved in the "Bojinka" plot to blow up a dozen airliners over the Pacific, was arrested in Manila and told the Philippine authorities that he and Ramzi Yousef had also discussed crashing a plane into the CIA headquarters. Another indication of the potential threat came when a private airplane crashed onto the south lawn of the White House in 1994.[73]

In 1995, the CTC warned senior government officials, in the *President's Daily Brief* (*PDB*) as well as in briefings to the congressional intelligence oversight committees, of what it called "aerial terrorism" from a terrorist group filling an airplane with explosives and dive-bombing a target.[74] In January 1996, a report stated that individuals associated with the "blind Sheikh" Rahman planned to fly an aircraft from Afghanistan to the United States and attack the White House.[75] Then in October 1996, an intelligence report warned about an Iranian plot to hijack a Japanese plane over Israel and crash it into Tel Aviv.[76]

The White House Commission on Aviation Safety and Security, chaired by Vice President Al Gore, reported in February 1997 that "people and places in the United States have joined the list of targets" from terrorism.[77] In June 1998, the US embassy in Riyadh sent a cable to the State Department stating that a US official had met with Saudi officials to alert them to the threat from bin Laden, including against civilian aircraft.[78]

In 1998, there were a number of reports that terrorists might use aircraft filled with explosives. In August intelligence information came in that a group of unidentified Arabs hoped to fly an explosive-laden plane from Libya into the World Trade Center. The source was not believed credible, and it was not believed that Libyan aircraft had sufficient range to make such an attack possible.[79] In September reporting came in about a source who had walked into an American consulate in East Asia and talked about a possible plot to fly an explosives-laden aircraft into a US city. This report, too, could not be corroborated.[80] Then in November a report was received that an extremist Islamic Turkish group planned to crash an airplane packed with explosives into Ataturk's tomb during a government ceremony.[81]

On December 4, 1998, the *PDB* included an item received from a friendly government that reported al-Qaeda was preparing to hijack an aircraft in the United States in order to obtain the release of Sheikh Rahman and others. According to the source, the plan might be implemented before the start of Ramadan on December 20, and two members of the operational team had evaded security checks during a recent trial run at an unidentified New York airport. Later reports from the same source stated the planned hijacking had been stalled because two operatives had been arrested near either Washington or New York. US officials could not verify any such arrests or confirm the threat.[82]

Several years before the 9/11 attacks, FBI officials had expressed concern about suspicious individuals studying aviation in the United States. In May 1998, the FBI's chief pilot in Oklahoma City drafted a memo expressing concern about the number of Middle Eastern males studying at flight schools in Oklahoma. He was concerned that the men could be planning a terrorist attack, possibly to spread chemical or biological agents. His memo was put in the office's "Weapons of Mass Destruction" file, but there is no indication any action was requested or taken as a result of it.[83] Also in 1998, the FBI received reporting that a terrorist organization might be planning to bring students to the United States to study aviation. The FBI was aware that persons connected to this organization had performed surveillance and security tests at US airports already and had made comments suggesting an intention to target civil aviation.[84]

In mid-1999, the FBI received an intelligence report stating that a terrorist organization other than al-Qaeda wanted to send students for flight training, and that it planned to use students in the United States to gather intelligence on infrastructure facilities and public places frequented by Jews. The organization's leaders viewed it as "particularly important" that students obtain private pilot licenses. As a result, FBI headquarters sent a request to twenty-four field offices to investigate. Eventually the International Terrorism Analytic Unit at FBI headquarters assigned an analyst to search for information concerning one particular terrorist group that might be sending students to US flight schools. That analyst submitted a report in November 2000 stating that no information had been found concerning that group's recruitment of students studying aviation.[85]

In April 2000, a walk-in to the FBI's Newark office claimed he was part of a terrorist plot to hijack an aircraft. The man's name was Niaz Khan, and he said he had been to a training camp in Pakistan where he learned hijacking techniques. He had been sent to the United States, where he was to meet five or six others, including pilots. Their mission was to hijack a Boeing 747 plane and fly it to Afghanistan. After 9/11 he told his story to the media: He said that after arriving in the United States to meet a contact, he got cold feet. He took a bus to Atlantic City, where he gambled away the money he had been given. He then turned himself in to the FBI, which interrogated him for three weeks. They gave him two lie detector tests, which he passed, and even had him go back to Kennedy Airport wearing a recording device to try to locate other conspirators, but with no luck. So he was turned over to the British authorities, who reportedly let him go after a brief interview.[86]

Government Studies and Scenarios

In addition to intelligence reports, warnings about terrorists using airplanes also came in the form of studies, war games, and scenarios devised by and for government officials and agencies. What may be the first such warning came from the terrorism expert Brian Jenkins, who wrote in 1989 that "the nightmare of governments is that suicidal terrorists will hijack a commercial airliner and, by killing or replacing its crew, crash into a city or some vital facility."[87] In 1993, the Department of Defense sponsored a project known as Terror 2000, which was designed to look at the future of terrorism after the Cold War. Although much of the study focused on the threat of a weapon of mass destruction attack using chemical or biological weapons, participants discussed the possibility of a commercial airliner being crashed into a public building in Washington. Marvin

J. Cetron, one of the authors of the study, later recalled telling the group: "Coming down the Potomac, you could make a left turn at the Washington Monument and take out the White House, or you could make a right turn and take out the Pentagon."[88]

Richard Clarke chaired a 1998 exercise in which officials considered how to respond to a scenario involving a group of terrorists who took control of a Learjet in Atlanta, loaded it with explosives, and flew it toward a target in Washington. He later said he attributed his awareness of the threat posed by aircraft more to Tom Clancy novels than to intelligence warnings.[89] And in the spring of 1998, a three-person group that included the University of Pennsylvania terrorism specialist Stephen Gale presented Federal Aviation Administration (FAA) security officials with an analysis of the threat from airborne attacks. Gale later described the study as positing two scenarios: one in which terrorists crashed planes into nuclear power plants along the East Coast, and another in which they hijacked Federal Express cargo planes and crashed them into the World Trade Center, the Pentagon, the White House, the Capitol, the Sears Tower, and the Golden Gate Bridge. According to Gale, an FAA official told him the problem was too hard, and said, "You can't protect yourself from meteorites."[90]

In August 1999, the FAA's Civil Aviation Security intelligence office wrote a paper summarizing the bin Laden hijacking threat that identified several scenarios, including a suicide hijacking operation. The analysts thought such a scenario unlikely, as it would not allow for the hijackers to achieve their goal of freeing jailed extremists.[91] A September 1999 study for the Library of Congress warned of attacks using aircraft: "Suicide bomber(s) belonging to al-Qaida's Martyrdom Battalion could crash-land an aircraft packed with high explosives (C-4 and semtex) into the Pentagon, the headquarters of the Central Intelligence Agency (CIA), or the White House."[92]

In March 2000 a Justice Department attorney, apparently on his own initiative, wrote an analysis of the legal issues that would be involved in shooting down a US aircraft involved in such a plot.[93] And in April 2001 the North American Aerospace Defense Command considered including in an exercise a scenario in which a hijacked airliner coming from overseas crashes into the Pentagon. This was considered unrealistic, however, and a distraction from the main focus of the exercise (war in Korea), so the scenario was not included in the actual exercise.[94]

Top-Level Assessments about Terrorism

In 1995, when the intelligence community was still in the early stages of learning about this new threat, a National Intelligence Estimate was produced that portrayed the growing threat in broad but prophetic terms. The report was titled "The Foreign Terrorist Threat in the United States," and it warned: "Should terrorists launch new attacks, we believe their preferred targets will be US Government facilities and national symbols, financial and transportation infrastructure nodes, or public gathering places. Civil aviation remains a particularly attractive target in light of the fear and publicity that the downing of an airliner would evoke and the revelations last summer of the US air transport sector's vulnerabilities."[95]

Later assessments would be less prescient. In April 1997, the 1995 National Intelligence Estimate warnings were repeated—apparently largely word for word—in another intelligence community assessment. The 1997 report has not been made public, but the 9/11 Commission argued that it added little to the picture of the growing threat, and continued to refer to bin Laden as a "terrorist financier."[96] It was to be the last overall national-level intelligence assessment of the threat from terrorism produced until after the 9/11 attacks.

The FAA's Intelligence Office

Although the warnings about al-Qaeda and the terrorist threat against commercial aviation did not inspire high levels of concern within the intelligence community as a whole, one small, little-known intelligence office does appear to have taken the threat very seriously. This was the intelligence branch of the FAA. Although the FAA was not a formal member of the US intelligence community, it had a civil aviation intelligence division that operated 24 hours per day and had liaison personnel assigned at the FBI, the CIA, and the State Department.[97] The division dedicated as many as five analysts at a time to al-Qaeda, and in the words of the 9/11 Commission staff monograph on the FAA, "Numerous documents, reports and assessments produced by the FAA's intelligence division through the late 1990s and up to 9/11 reported on the growing threat posed by terrorists."[98]

The level of concern shown by the FAA's intelligence division is all the more remarkable because by most accounts before 9/11, the terrorist threat to commercial aviation had receded. By 2001, for example, it had been more than a decade since a US airliner had been hijacked or bombed.[99] But the case of the FAA's intelligence office is especially significant for this book because, despite its warnings about the terrorist threat, the office was unable to get much attention from senior officials at the FAA—an organization where one might expect warnings about terrorism directed at commercial aviation would be noticed. For that reason, the FAA serves as a valuable mini–case study of the failure of strategic warning before 9/11.

The FAA's intelligence office began producing reports in 1998 about the hijacking threat posed by al-Qaeda. For example, in December 1998 the FAA issued a security directive that said the 1993 attack on the World Trade Center had "dramatically demonstrated the capabilities and intent of international terrorists to operate in the United States." The directive mentioned bin Laden and radical Islamic terrorist groups in general and said, "Civil aviation has been a prominent target of these and other transnational terrorists. In the past several years, information has been received that individuals in the United States associated with loosely affiliated extremists have discussed targeting commercial aircraft and civil aviation facilities. Loosely affiliated extremists have also shown a particular interest in media reporting regarding airline and airport security."[100]

FAA warnings included the possibility that terrorists might try to crash a commercial jet into a US landmark. But the 9/11 Commission staff monograph on the FAA noted that in reports from 1998 and 1999 the intelligence office "viewed this possibility as 'unlikely' and a 'last resort.'"[101]

As noted earlier in this chapter, FAA officials were briefed on possible suicide hijacking scenarios in 1998, but there was no hard intelligence indicating that bin Laden or other terrorists were actually plotting to hijack commercial aircraft and use them as weapons.[102] A classified December 2000 report by the FBI and FAA—a report that had been mandated by Congress in 1996—stated that "FBI investigations confirm domestic and international terrorist groups operating within the US but do not suggest evidence of plans to target domestic civil aviation. . . . While international terrorists have conducted attacks on US soil, these acts represent anomalies in their traditional targeting which focuses on US interests overseas."[103]

Despite the lack of hard evidence of a threat, the FAA intelligence office continued to provide warnings. In the spring of 2001, FAA intelligence distributed an unclassified CD-ROM presentation to air carriers and airports that cited the possibility that terrorists might conduct suicide hijackings. The presentation stated "fortunately, we have no indication that any group is currently thinking in that direction."[104] Between March and May 2001, the intelligence office conducted a series of classified briefings for security officials at nineteen of the nation's largest airports, including Newark, Boston's Logan, and Dulles in Washington. The briefings covered the threat from bin Laden and the renewed interest in hijacking by terrorist groups. They noted that a domestic hijacking would be more difficult for terrorists to carry out than one overseas, but "if, however, the intent of the hijacker is not to exchange hostages for prisoners, but to commit suicide in a spectacular explosion, a domestic hijacking would probably be preferable."[105]

An FAA document published in the *Federal Register* on July 17, 2001, indicated that terrorist groups were active in the United States and were interested in targeting aviation. The notice stated that "terrorism can occur anytime, anywhere in the United States. Members of foreign terrorist groups, representatives from state sponsors of terrorism, and radical fundamentalist elements from many nations are present in the United States. . . . Thus, an increasing threat to civil aviation from both foreign sources and potential domestic ones exists and needs to be prevented and/or countered."[106]

The notice, which was in support of a proposed rule to improve airline security, included another section that reads today as very prescient. It noted that "civil aviation targets may be chosen by terrorists even if alternative, and (in their view) softer targets are available, especially since an attack on aviation seizes the public's imagination to a degree equaled by few other types of attack."[107]

The FAA's intelligence division also expressed its concern in the daily intelligence summaries it produced for the FAA leadership. Between April 1 and September 10, 2001, fifty-two summaries mentioned bin Laden, al-Qaeda, or both—mostly in the context of threats overseas. Five summaries mentioned hijacking as a capability for which al-Qaeda was training or possessed.[108]

These warnings do not appear to have made much of an impression on the leadership of the FAA. During the summer of 2001, for example, the FAA did not require any significant upgrade to security at domestic flight checkpoints.[109] In part, the lack of response to the intelligence division's warnings may have been a result of the fact that, as the 9/11 staff noted, the intelligence office "was not well connected to the agency's top policymakers."[110]

But the most important reason why the intelligence division's warnings had little impact appears to be that the warnings were chiefly based on unspecific, general, strategic-level threat reporting. In the absence of specific intelligence about threats within the United States, senior officials believed the primary threat was overseas. The FAA's senior security official, General Michael Canavan, testified to the 9/11 Commission that "there was no actionable intelligence that even hinted to me, or to anyone within my organization, that there was a threat to [domestic] aviation."[111] Jane F. Garvey, the former administrator of the FAA, testified to the 9/11 Commission that "prior to September 11, the intelligence provided to the FAA did not support a conclusion that there was any specific, credible threat of terrorists using aircraft as suicide weapons for attacks against the United States."[112] The 9/11 Commission's staff monograph found that "FAA policymakers required either a security incident or 'specific and credible' evidence of an 'actionable' threat before they would take urgent action to strengthen security."[113]

Warnings in 2001

The 9/11 Commission noted that "in the spring of 2001, the level of reporting on terrorist threats and planned attacks increased dramatically to its highest level since the millennium alert."[114] Threats included a source in March who claimed a group of bin Laden operatives were planning an unspecified attack in the United States in April, and a report in April that operatives in California and New York State were planning attacks that month.[115] In response to reports such as these, the intelligence community disseminated a warning at the end of March of a heightened threat of Sunni extremist terrorist attacks against US facilities, personnel, and other interests; and in late March and early April, the CIA "repeatedly issued warnings" that Abu Zubaydah was planning an operation in the near future. The warnings included calls from Tenet to Clarke, with Clarke relaying the reports to the national security adviser, Condoleezza Rice.[116]

On April 20, the interagency Counterterrorism Security Group (CSG) provided a briefing to senior officials that stated "Bin Ladin planning multiple operations."[117] A Deputies Committee meeting discussed al-Qaeda on April 30, 2001, and CIA briefing slides described al-Qaeda as the "most dangerous group we face." The briefing warned, "There will be more attacks."[118] Also in April, a source with terrorist connections speculated bin Laden would be interested in commercial pilots as potential terrorists. The source warned that terrorists sought "spectacular and traumatic" attacks, and that the first World Trade Center bombing would be the type of attack that would be appealing. No time frame for any attack was mentioned, and because the information was the source's speculation rather than hard information, the information was not disseminated within the intelligence community.[119]

In May, the 9/11 Commission reported, "the drumbeat of reporting grew louder." One report warned "Bin Ladin network's plans advancing," and a walk-in to the FBI claimed there was a plan to launch attacks on London, Boston, and New York. A phone call to a US embassy warned bin Laden supporters were planning an attack in the United States using high explosives.[120] A report stated that bin Laden supporters were planning to infiltrate into the United States from Canada in order to carry out an attack using high explosives, and in late May the Department of Defense reported that seven individuals associated with bin Laden had departed from various locations for Canada, the United Kingdom, and the United States.[121]

Between May and July the NSA reported at least thirty-three communications indicating a possible imminent terrorist attack, although none of the reports provided specific information on where, when, or how an attack might occur.[122] On May 23, 2001, the *Senior Executive Intelligence Brief* (*SEIB*, usually pronounced "seeb") reported a possible hostage plot against Americans abroad to force the release of prisoners including the "blind Sheikh" Rahman. The report, which noted that operatives might attempt to hijack an aircraft or storm a US embassy, led the FAA to distribute a circular to airlines noting the potential for an airline hijacking.[123] Still more reports came in about a planned attack in Israel, plots in Yemen and Italy, and an anonymous call about a cell in Canada that might be planning an attack against the United States. On May 29, Clarke wrote to Rice about the threat warnings: "When these attacks occur, as they likely will, we will wonder what more we could have done to stop them." Also in May, the CIA CTC chief Cofer Black told Rice that the current threat level was a 7 on a scale of 1 to 10, compared with an 8 during the millennium.[124]

In June and July threat reports reached "an even higher peak of urgency."[125] In June the CTC heard a report that some key al-Qaeda operatives were disappearing, while others were preparing for martyrdom.[126] A June 12 CIA report mentioned that Khalid Sheikh Mohammed (KSM), the man later identified as the planner of 9/11, was recruiting people to travel to the United States and conduct attacks.[127] On June 22 the CIA notified all station chiefs about a possible al-Qaeda suicide attack on a US target in the next few days, and asked that all US ambassadors be briefed.[128] That same day, the State Department notified all embassies of the terrorist threat and updated its worldwide public warning.[129]

A terrorist threat advisory in late June warned of near-term "spectacular" terrorist attacks, while other reports warned the "Bin Ladin Attacks May be Imminent," and "Bin Ladin and Associates Making Near-Term Threats." On June 21, the US Central Command raised its force protection level for US troops in six countries to the highest possible level, the US Fifth Fleet moved out of its port in Bahrain, and the US embassy in Yemen was closed. The CSG ordered foreign emergency response teams to be ready to deploy on four-hour notice.[130] The Italian authorities warned of the possibility of a suicide hijacking threat against the Group of Eight's summit in Genoa in July, and with American cooperation the site was guarded by surface-to-air missiles.[131]

On June 25, Richard Clarke warned Rice and Hadley in an email that six separate intelligence reports showed al-Qaeda personnel warning of a pending attack.[132] On June 28, President Bush was briefed on the state of the global terrorism threat. According to Tenet, NSA and CTC analysts had more than ten specific pieces of intelligence about impending attacks, and they had been seeing "never-before-seen efforts by Ayman al-Zawahiri to prepare terrorist operations." The briefing concluded with a PowerPoint slide saying, "Based on a review of all source reporting, we believe that Usama Bin Ladin will launch a significant terrorist attack against the United States and/or Israeli interests in the coming weeks."[133] At the end of June, a report on al-Qaeda noted that something "very, very, very, very" big was about to happen, and Clarke wrote to Rice that he and analysts at the major intelligence agencies were convinced attacks were likely in July. And the headline of a June 30 briefing to top officials said, "Bin Ladin Planning High-Profile Attacks."[134]

The summer of 2001 also saw warnings coming directly from bin Laden and al-Qaeda. In June bin Laden met with a reporter from the Middle East Broadcasting Center, and during the meeting his aides said there would be attacks against American and Israeli facilities within the next several weeks. The *Washington Post* reported the threats on July 8.[135] In addition, an al-Qaeda propaganda video was circulated in the Middle East during the summer of 2001. In the video, which was described at the time in the American press, al-Qaeda members boasted about the attack on the USS *Cole*, and bin Laden called for "blood, blood and destruction, destruction."[136]

The intelligence community presumably was aware of these public warnings, and it also heard similar reports from confidential sources: In July the CTC learned of an individual who had recently been in Afghanistan who reported that "everyone is talking about an impending attack."[137] But there may have been other clues from bin Laden that the intelligence community was not able to pick up. KSM later claimed to his interrogators that bin Laden had hinted at an upcoming attack a number of times during the summer of 2001, enough to generate rumors throughout the worldwide jihadist community. During a speech at one training camp, he urged trainees to pray for the success of a major operation involving twenty martyrs. KSM said he had been concerned about this lack of discretion and urged bin Laden not to make further comments about the plot.[138]

On July 2, 2001, the FBI issued a message to federal, state, and local law enforcement agencies summarizing the information regarding the bin Laden threats and indicating there was a potential for attacks against US targets abroad from groups "aligned or sympathetic to Usama Bin Laden." The message asked recipients to "exercise extreme vigilance," but stated, "The FBI has no information indicating a credible threat of terrorist attack in the United States."[139]

On July 10, 2001, an agent in the FBI's Phoenix field office sent a memo to FBI headquarters advising of the "possibility of a coordinated effort by Usama Bin Laden (UBL) to send students to the United States to attend civil aviation universities and colleges." He based his theory on the "inordinate number of individuals of investigative interest" attending such schools in Arizona.[140] He later explained to the Department of Justice's inspector general that he had "an investigative theory" or "hunch" that bin Laden might be sending students to attend civil aviation schools seeking ultimately to conduct terrorism against civil aviation targets, and he was seeking an analytical product or feedback in response to his theory. He said he was not contemplating that there was a plot to use airplanes as missiles, but terrorists could be attempting to develop expertise about where to put explosives or use other methods to cause an aircraft to crash.[141] The agent made four recommendations, but they were not acted on. No managers at the FBI saw the memo until after 9/11, and it was not shared outside the FBI.[142]

The warnings reached their peak in early July, when a briefing for senior government officials stated: "Based on a review of all-source reporting over the last five months, we believe that UBL will launch a significant terrorist attack against US and/or Israeli interests in the coming weeks. The attack will be spectacular and designed to inflict mass casualties against US facilities or interests. Attack preparations have been made. Attack will occur with little or no warning."[143]

This appears to be the intelligence that led to a no-notice briefing at the White House on July 10, 2001. Tenet writes that on that day Cofer Black and the CTC analysts had presented him with a "consolidated, strategic assessment." Tenet writes that "the briefing he gave me literally made my hair stand on end." He called Rice and told her he needed to see her immediately with an update on the al-Qaeda threat. Such a meeting was extremely unusual; Tenet writes, "I can recall no other time in my seven years as DCI that I sought such an urgent meeting at the White House."[144]

Tenet and Black, along with another CIA official named Rich, went to the White House. Rich began the briefing for Rice, Clarke, and Rice's deputy, Steve Hadley, by saying, "There will be a significant terrorist attack in the coming weeks or months!"[145] They could not pinpoint the day, but the briefing noted intelligence such as bin Laden's statement to trainees that there would be an attack in the near future. The attack will be "spectacular," Rich said, and multiple and simultaneous attacks were possible. They told Rice that the United States needed to go on a war footing immediately, and go on the offensive.[146]

Not all government officials were convinced by these reports. The 9/11 Commission noted that some believed the increased reporting might actually be deception by al-Qaeda. On June 30, an item in the SEIB appeared to attempt to counter such thinking, with the headline, "Bin Ladin Threats Are Real."[147] But by mid-July, reporting began to indicate that bin Laden's plans had been delayed. On July 13, the SEIB indicated that operations might have been delayed for as long as two months, but they had not been abandoned.[148] On July 27, Clarke informed Rice that the warnings about near-term attacks had decreased but he urged keeping readiness high during August, when many officials go on vacation.[149]

Despite the apparent decrease in the immediate threat, warnings continued to be issued in the late summer. On August 3, the CIA issued an advisory concluding that the threat of impending al-Qaeda attacks would likely continue indefinitely and suggesting that al-Qaeda was waiting for gaps in security before proceeding with planned attacks.[150] In August a SEIB noted that al-Qaeda members, including some US citizens, resided in or traveled to the United States and apparently maintained a support structure here.[151] And another report in August warned about a plot to either bomb the US embassy in Nairobi from an airplane, or crash an airplane into it. According to that report, two people who were acting on instructions from bin Laden had met in October 2000 to discuss this plot.[152]

The August 6 PDB

Perhaps the most famous warning from the summer of 2001 was the item in the PDB on August 6 titled "Bin Laden Determined to Strike in US." The item had been written after President Bush had asked his CIA briefers about whether any of the threats he was being warned about pointed to the United States as the target for attack. The item was a summary of what the intelligence community knew about such a threat, and two CIA analysts involved in preparing the item told the 9/11 Commission staff they believed it would communicate their view that the threat of a bin Laden attack in the United States was both current and dangerous.[153]

The *PDB* stated that "clandestine, foreign government, and media reports indicate Bin Ladin since 1997 has wanted to conduct terrorist attacks in the US." It warned that bin Laden apparently maintained a support structure in the United States, but said the intelligence community could not corroborate "some of the more sensational threat reporting," such as that bin Laden wanted to hijack a US aircraft to gain the release of the "blind Sheik" and other extremists. It stated that information from the FBI indicated "patterns of suspicious activity in this country consistent with preparations for hijackings or other types of attacks, including recent surveillance of federal buildings in New York." And it concluded by stating that the FBI was conducting "approximately 70 full field investigations" in the United States that were bin Laden related, and the CIA and FBI were investigating a threat phoned to the US embassy in the United Arab Emirates in May stating that a group of bin Laden supporters was in the United States planning attacks with explosives.[154] Most of the warnings in the *PDB* item were old, however, and the 9/11 Commission found that several of the most current pieces of information were either exaggerated or apparently not related to terrorism.[155]

The *Moussaoui* Case

On August 15, 2001, officials at a flight school near Minneapolis reported to the FBI that a man named Zacarias Moussaoui had raised their suspicions. He had enrolled in flight simulator training, but he had no aviation background, he had paid between $8,000 and $9,000 in cash for the course, and he said he only wanted to learn to take off and land.[156] Moussaoui was detained by the Immigration and Naturalization Service the next day, and the Minneapolis FBI office opened an investigation.

Over the next several weeks the Minneapolis field office had discussions and disputes with FBI Headquarters over whether or not sufficient grounds existed to obtain either a criminal or a Foreign Intelligence Surveillance Act warrant to search his belongings, which had been seized at the time of his arrest. At one point, a Minneapolis FBI supervisor told an agent at headquarters that "we want to make sure he doesn't get control of an airplane and crash it into the [World Trade Center] or something like that."[157] In late August, when FBI Headquarters concluded it could not obtain a warrant, the Minneapolis office began plans to deport Moussaoui to France, and to ask the French authorities to search his belongings once he was there. The 9/11 attacks occurred while these plans were being prepared.

Information about the Moussaoui case was shared with the rest of the intelligence community, and an August 23 briefing for the DCI included an item about Moussaoui titled "Islamic Extremist Learns to Fly." The briefing slides included a note that the subject had been arrested and "we are working the case with the FBI." It noted that the fundamentalist "wanted training on London–JFK flights."[158] Another item about the case was included in the DCI's August 30 briefing, and according to Tenet, on that same date a CIA officer expressed frustration about the case, writing, "If this guy is let go, two years from now he will be talking to a control tower while aiming a 747 at the White House."[159]

On September 4 the FBI sent a cable about the Moussaoui investigation to the CIA and other intelligence agencies, but it did not state that the agent working the case in Minneapolis suspected that Moussaoui had been training to hijack an aircraft.[160] Another update on Moussaoui was included in the September 10 briefing for the CIA's deputy director for operations, but it closely resembles the August 23 and 30 briefings, suggesting that little further information had come in since the earlier reports.[161]

The Views of other Government Agencies

It was not only the intelligence community that saw a growing risk from terrorism in the spring and summer of 2001; other government agencies and organizations also issued warnings about the threat. The State Department's annual publication *Patterns of Global Terrorism 2000* was released in April 2001. It mentioned bin Laden several times and said "al-Qaida has a worldwide reach, has cells in a number of countries, and is reinforced by its ties to Sunni extremist networks."[162] In the spring and summer of 2001 officials of the Federal Emergency Management Agency gave several public presentations at which they described the three most likely catastrophes to strike the United States as being a terrorist attack on New York, a hurricane hitting New Orleans, and a major earthquake in San Francisco.[163]

Immediately before the 9/11 attacks, two analytical organizations that are not part of the intelligence community had conducted separate investigations into the terrorist threat. The Congressional Research Service published a report on September 10 that stated, "Usama bin Ladin's network . . . poses an increasingly significant threat to US interests in the Near East and perhaps elsewhere." It added that allegations of past plots by bin Laden "suggest that the network wants to strike within the United States itself."[164]

The second study of the terrorist threat had been nearly completed before the 9/11 attacks, and was published shortly afterward. The General Accounting Office had been asked by Congress to examine the government's efforts to combat domestic terrorism, particularly involving weapons of mass destruction. Its report was published on September 20, 2001, and found that the government had made progress in developing its overall strategy and coordination for counterterrorism but that it needed to do more, including conducting a national threat and risk assessment and designating a single focal point for overall leadership and coordination of federal efforts against terrorism. It noted that according to the Department of Justice, the FBI was in the process of conducting a national-level threat assessment of the terrorist threat in the United States, and would publish a classified report in October 2001.[165]

Last-Minute Warnings

Several warnings came in immediately before the 9/11 attacks. According to press reports, the intelligence services of several US allies intercepted a phone call to bin Laden's wife, who was then in Syria, from either bin Laden himself or an associate. The call, which was passed on to the CIA, reportedly warned her to return to Afghanistan immediately.[166] George Tenet describes another warning received by the CIA on September 10: "A source we were jointly running with a Middle Eastern country went to see his foreign handler and basically told him that something big was about to go down. The handler dismissed him. Had we known it at the time, however, it would have sounded very much like all the other warnings we received in June, July, August, and early September—frightening but without specificity."[167]

Also on September 10, the NSA intercepted two messages from suspected al-Qaeda locations in Afghanistan: "the match begins tomorrow," and "tomorrow is zero hour." The messages were not translated until September 12, and a number of commentators have suggested this was a missed opportunity to detect the 9/11 plot.[168] Then–NSA director Michael Hayden testified before the Congressional Joint Inquiry that although these two messages did suggest "individuals with terrorist connections believed something significant would happen on September 11th," they did not contain any specific information about a possible attack.[169]

Even if these communications had referred to the 9/11 operation, and even if they had been translated and heard by intelligence analysts before the attacks took place, it seems unlikely that they could have stimulated any specific action that would have prevented the attacks. As Shultz and Vogt write, "These telephone comments are too cryptic to be actionable intelligence."[170] In any case, the 9/11 Commission staff later determined that these communications had probably referred not to the 9/11 attacks but to the opening of a Taliban and al-Qaeda military offensive in Afghanistan against the Northern Alliance following the September 9 assassination of the Northern Alliance's leader.[171]

THE TACTICAL INTELLIGENCE AVAILABLE

The strategic intelligence reviewed in the previous section was plentiful, but also frustratingly vague. In many cases it appears these reports were incorrect, the result of either misunderstanding by American intelligence agencies or deliberate falsification by informants or other sources. Even in those cases in which the intelligence warned about specific threats such as suicide airplane hijackings, these warnings did not point directly to the plot that unfolded on 9/11.

Precise, tactical-level warning—information about the plotters and what they were planning—was quite limited before the 9/11 attacks. No official study of the attacks has been able to find any one piece of intelligence on the operation that could have alerted the US intelligence community to the coming attacks but which was missed as the result of error or any other cause.[172] Neither of the two primary sources of American intelligence—HUMINT or SIGINT—was able to uncover what bin Laden referred to as the "planes operation." This does not mean, however, that specific, tactical-level intelligence on the 9/11 plot was completely unavailable. Two of the hijackers in particular—Nawaf al Hazmi and Khalid al Mihdhar—were tracked by American intelligence at many points before September 11, 2001, and those indications have often been cited as key warnings that were missed or not understood.[173] This section examines the information that was available to the American intelligence community before 9/11 on the plot itself.

Clues following the East Africa Embassy Bombings

One of the first pieces of intelligence leading to the 9/11 plot came from East Africa in the wake of the 1998 embassy bombings. One of the captured Nairobi plotters, Owhali, made a detailed confession to the FBI that included the telephone number of an al-Qaeda safe house in Yemen. The house belonged to a Yemeni bin Laden supporter named Ahmed al Hada, and when American intelligence began listening in on the phone number, they discovered that the house was an information clearing center for al-Qaeda. It would later be used to plan terrorist operations that included the attack on the USS *Cole*.[174]

Sometime early in 1999, the NSA intercepted communications from the house that referred to Hazmi and Mihdhar, but because they were then unknown and the information did not meet NSA reporting thresholds, the information was not disseminated in NSA reporting. Also in early 1999, another organization obtained the same or similar information, and the NSA received that report, but again it did not disseminate the information in regular intelligence channels.[175] The NSA continued to monitor communications from that location through 1999, and in December it learned that several suspected terrorists would be traveling to Kuala Lumpur for a meeting the next month. A CIA desk officer noticed links with al-Qaeda and with the 1998 embassy bombings and guessed that "something more nefarious [was] afoot."[176]

The Kuala Lumpur Meeting

At the request of US officials, the Malaysian security service kept watch on the men as they arrived in Kuala Lumpur. They were photographed as they traveled around the city and as they met at a condominium owned by a United States–educated microbiologist who was a supporter of bin Laden.[177] But then on January 8, Hazmi, Mihdhar, and another al-Qaeda operative named Khallad took a flight to Bangkok and disappeared. In early March 2000, the CIA station in Bangkok reported that Hazmi had left Thailand on January 15 on a United Airlines flight to Los Angeles; there was no information on Mihdhar, although it was later learned he had been on the same flight. No one outside the CTC was told about this. The CIA did not put their names on the State Department's TIPOFF watchlist, they did not tell the FBI, and nothing was done to track them.[178]

The Attackers in the United States

After arriving at Los Angeles International Airport on January 15, 2000, Hazmi and Mihdhar eventually settled in San Diego. They attempted to learn English and took flying lessons but proved poor at both. They lived openly under their true names, and Hazmi was even listed in the phone book.[179] In the early summer of 2000, the second group of hijackers, who had become associated with each other in Hamburg, arrived in the United States to start flight training. This group included Mohamed Atta, the tactical leader of the 9/11 operation. And then in April 2001, the "muscle" hijackers, who would storm the cockpits and subdue the passengers and crew, began arriving in the country.[180]

In the spring and summer of 2001, a CIA analyst assigned to the International Terrorism Operations Section at the FBI became interested in tracking down information about Mihdhar and his associates. He and several FBI analysts found that according to immigration records, Mihdhar had entered the country in January 2000, later left the United States in June 2000, and then returned on July 4, 2001. He was apparently still in the country, and at their urging the bin Laden unit placed a request for Mihdhar and Hazmi to be added to the State Department's TIPOFF watchlist; they were placed on the list on August 24.[181]

Meanwhile, in the summer of 2001, the intelligence community received several pieces of information concerning KSM. He had been indicted in 1996 for his role in the attempt to crash airliners over the Pacific, but before 9/11 his links to bin Laden were not understood. In April 2001, the CIA learned that someone known as "Mukhtar" was associated with al-Qaeda and might be planning terrorist attacks. In June, a report said that someone named "Khaled" was recruiting people to carry out terrorist attacks in the United States and elsewhere. The next month, a CIA source identified a photograph of KSM as being "Khaled." Then on August 28, the bin Laden unit received a report that KSM's nickname was Mukhtar. But no one connected these reports and understood the danger that KSM posed.[182]

Several FBI agents were still trying to locate Mihdhar, although there was no official push for them to do so. Because his original visa application had listed his destination as New York, on August 28 a message was sent to the FBI's New York field office asking it to search for him. An agent in New York was assigned to the case and began checking local databases and checked the hotel listed on

Mihdhar's US entry form. The agent noted that Mihdhar had entered the country through Los Angeles, and on September 11 he sent a request asking the Los Angeles field office to look for him.[183]

Evaluating the Warning before 9/11

How can we evaluate the quality of the warning that the US intelligence community provided before the 9/11 attacks? To some extent, as Jack Davis has pointed out, the question is largely a matter of where one decides to "put the goal-posts"—how much warning should be considered enough to constitute sufficient warning?[184] Davis argues that the numerous reports on the growing terrorist threat in the years before the attacks indicate the intelligence community had succeeded in providing policymakers with broad, strategic warning. This is also, not surprisingly, the view of the intelligence community; the CIA's in-house study of its work before 9/11 described what it called "a record of consistent efforts to warn policymakers of the seriousness of the al-Qa'ida threat."[185] A few outside observers have even argued that the quality of tactical warning was relatively high; Joshua Rovner and Austin Long write that "the intelligence community did a fairly good job at providing tactical warning before September 11," and cite examples such as the FAA's warnings about threats to commercial aviation.[186]

Many disagree with these positive assessments. Zegart, for example, believes Rovner and Long are setting the bar too low by accepting the intelligence community's reporting as representing a high-quality warning. She argues that because the ABC television network had been able to penetrate al-Qaeda and broadcast an interview with bin Laden in June 1998, "By that low standard, the premier US intelligence agency should be ABC News, not the CIA."[187] On tactical warning, in particular, most analysts believe the intelligence community did a poor job. Daniel Byman argues there was "a devastating failure of tactical warning. If policymakers listened to intelligence, they would know al-Qaeda was coming, but they would not know when, where, or how."[188]

As we saw in chapter 1, *strategic warning* consists of broad indications that an attack might occur, but without specifics as to where, when, or how the attack will take place. The many reports, briefings, and studies described in this chapter demonstrate that before 9/11, the US intelligence community had provided a great deal of such warning about the broad but growing threat from terrorism by al-Qaeda, and in particular about the threat to commercial air travel. Many of these warnings appeared to be quite specific, although they did not actually refer to the plot that came to fruition on September 11. These were strategic warnings, and although one can always argue there could have been more, or that warnings could have been presented in different ways, it was clearly available and plentiful.

The problem is that in order for intelligence to be useful in preventing attacks, strategic warning is not enough. This book argues that specific intelligence on the plot—*tactical warning*—is necessary, and here the American intelligence community was unsuccessful. Even the reporting on Mihdhar and Hazmi did not include the critical details about what kind of plot they were part of. The where, when, and how were not known.

RECEPTIVITY TOWARD WARNING

The limited amount of tactical intelligence available before 9/11 was not the only reason why intelligence failed to prevent the attacks. The quality of warning is only one of the two factors that determine whether intelligence is truly actionable. The second factor is receptivity: whether or not that warning was received and believed.[189] Here, too, a critical factor was absent.

Receptivity during the Clinton Administration

On the basis of public statements made by President Clinton and his top officials, it appears that they understood the growing threat from international terrorism. Amy Zegart notes that beginning in 1994, Clinton mentioned terrorism in every one of his State of the Union addresses, and in a 1998 address to the United Nations he said that terrorism ranked "at the top of the American agenda and should be at the top of the world's agenda."[190] Other senior government leaders appeared to agree; in July 1999, for example, Defense Secretary William Cohen wrote an op-ed in the *Washington Post* predicting a terrorist attack on US soil.[191]

The Clinton administration pursued a number of strategies against terrorism, including the large-scale capture plan in May 1998 mentioned earlier in this chapter that was never carried out. Although there were several other plans considered after the East Africa embassy bombings, the *9/11 Commission Report* notes that "no capture plan before 9/11 ever again attained the same level of detail and preparation."[192] Still, the fight against al-Qaeda appears to have had the attention of senior Clinton administration decision makers. Between 1998 and 2000, the "Small Group" of key principals met almost every week on terrorism, and the lower-level CSG met two or three times a week. Clinton sent the CIA at least four secret "memorandums of notification" authorizing it to kill or capture bin Laden and, later, other senior terrorists.[193]

But receptivity at the top is not necessarily enough, and other elements of the US government, including much of the CIA and the US military, do not appear to have been as enthusiastic about counterterrorism. Richard Clarke blames the failure against bin Laden in part on the CIA, which he argues was as an institution very reluctant to act against al-Qaeda in any major way, despite the aggressive posture taken by George Tenet and the officers within the CTC.[194]

Clarke and others have also criticized the US military for not being willing to use its special operations and other capabilities. Richard Shultz has described nine self-imposed restraints—which he calls "showstoppers"—that prevented special forces from ever being used before 9/11 to hunt down terrorists.[195] And an anecdote related by Clarke epitomizes the story of the military's pushing back against the president's desire for stronger action. In late August 1998, after the cruise missile retaliation for the embassy bombings, Clinton wanted to use US troops more directly. The president pulled aside Joint Chiefs of Staff chairman Hugh Shelton after a meeting and told him he thought that more effective than cruise missiles would be "the sight of US commandos, Ninja guys in black suits, jumping out of helicopters into their camps, spraying machine guns." But Clarke writes that "Shelton looked pained. He explained that the camps were a long way away from anywhere the United States could launch a helicopter raid. Nonetheless, America's top military officer agreed to 'look into it.'"[196]

Receptivity in the Bush Administration

President George W. Bush and his senior officials appear to have been less receptive than the Clinton team to intelligence about bin Laden and al-Qaeda. This was not for lack of warning, because as with all new presidents, Bush began receiving intelligence reports well before taking office. In September 2000, the acting deputy DCI, John McLaughlin, led a team to Bush's ranch in Crawford, Texas, for a four-hour review of sensitive intelligence, including an hour on terrorism. Ben Bonk, the deputy chief of the CTC, brought a mock-up suitcase to show how Aum Shinrikyo had spread sarin nerve agent in the Tokyo subway system in 1995, and Bonk told Bush that Americans would die from terrorism during the next four years.[197] The CIA established an office in Crawford to pass intelligence to Bush and his key advisers, and the briefings continued at Blair House in Washington during the transition. In addition to receiving intelligence reports, the new president was warned about terrorism by his predecessor: in December Bush and Clinton met for a two-hour discussion of national security and foreign policy, and Clinton recalls saying to Bush, "I think you will find that by far your biggest threat is Bin Ladin and the al-Qaeda."[198]

In early January 2001, Clarke briefed Rice on terrorism, and gave similar presentations to Cheney and Powell. One line in the briefing slides said that al-Qaeda had sleeper cells in more than forty countries, including the United States. Clarke describes Rice as having appeared skeptical as he briefed her, and later she downgraded his position of national coordinator for counterterrorism, no longer reporting directly to the top-level Principals Committee but instead reporting to the second-tier Deputies Committee.[199]

On January 25, 2001, Clarke submitted to Rice a memo that stated, "We *urgently* need. . . . a Principals level review on the *al Qida* network." Enclosed with the memo were two documents: a December 2000 paper, "Strategy for Eliminating the Threat from the Jihadist Networks of al Qida: Status and Prospects," and a copy of an earlier plan Clarke had written, called "Delenda."[200] But

Rice did not respond to the memo, and the Principals Committee meeting he called for did not take place until September 4. Instead, a Deputies Committee meeting was scheduled to discuss al-Qaeda, and even that meeting did not occur until April. When they did meet the deputies agreed to make bin Laden a top priority, but little concrete came from the meeting.[201]

President Bush did express concern about terrorism, and in the spring of 2001 he told his advisers that he was "tired of swatting at flies" and pushed them to do more about the problem.[202] At the end of May, Rice and Hadley asked Clarke and his staff for a new presidential directive that would set out a range of options for attacking al-Qaeda. A draft was circulated in early June that called for a multiyear effort involving diplomacy, covert action, economic measures, public diplomacy, law enforcement, and military action if necessary. But Clarke saw this as essentially the same as the proposals he had developed earlier, and in May or June he asked to be moved from counterterrorism to a portfolio dealing with cybersecurity.[203]

One of the most important warnings given to the White House before 9/11 may have been the no-notice meeting described above that Tenet and Black had with Rice on July 10. According to Bob Woodward, "it stood out in the minds of both Tenet and Cofer Black as the starkest warning they had given the White House on bin Laden and al-Qaeda." But the meeting does not appear to have made much of an impact; Woodward writes that both Tenet and Black felt they had not gotten through to Rice and she had given them the brush-off.[204]

When the Principals Committee had its first meeting on al-Qaeda on September 4, Clarke sent a note to Rice that criticized US counterterrorism efforts. He warned, "Decision makers should imagine themselves on a future day when the CSG has not succeeded in stopping al Qida attacks and hundreds of Americans lay dead in several countries, including the US." Clarke added, "That future day could happen at any time" (underlining in the original memo).[205] The principals approved a draft presidential directive authorizing a broad covert action program against al-Qaeda, but the meeting focused on the controversial topic of the development of an armed version of the Predator unmanned aerial vehicle. Clarke later described the meeting as "largely a nonevent."[206] On September 10 the deputies met to finalize a multiyear plan to topple the Taliban leadership in Afghanistan, and also on that day Hadley directed Tenet to have the CIA prepare new draft legal authorities for the covert action program envisioned by the draft presidential directive.[207]

Receptivity at the Tactical Level

There is one other level of government decision making at which receptivity toward intelligence warning before 9/11 should be considered: the tactical level, such as in New York City and at the World Trade Center itself. This level had little, if any, role to play in protecting against attacks such as the ones that were launched on September 11, 2001. For example, no single organization or individual had been given the responsibility of protecting the World Trade Center from aerial assault, and the local authorities did not have the power to implement the sort of increased airline security measures that might have headed off the attacks.[208]

But several important tactical-level organizations and decision makers were extremely concerned about the terrorist threat in their areas of responsibility, suggesting that receptivity toward threat warning was higher at the tactical than the strategic level. Richard Clarke, for example, testified before the Congressional Joint Inquiry that the FBI's New York field office was one of the few organizations that performed well before 9/11, and he praised the work of John O'Neill, the special agent in charge of that office: "He used the New York field office as a worldwide field office to go after bin Laden around the world."[209]

Evaluating Decision Makers' Receptivity

At one level, it can be argued that senior officials in both the Clinton and Bush administrations were highly receptive toward the intelligence they received about terrorism and al-Qaeda. After all, both presidents directed their staffs and the intelligence and national security communities to come up with better ways of attacking bin Laden and al-Qaeda. The military developed and practiced complex, dangerous operations to capture and kill terrorist leaders, while the CTC and other elements of the intelligence community searched for intelligence to support the plans being developed.

But in evaluating receptivity, as in judging the quality of warning, it matters where you put the goalposts. For intelligence to be truly actionable, it must be received by policymakers who believe in the seriousness of the threat, and who trust the intelligence agencies and officials working for them. Judged by this standard, receptivity was largely nonexistent before 9/11. Few senior officials appear to have believed that the threat from al-Qaeda was as serious as true believers such as Clarke and Tenet told them it was. And as the example of the FAA dramatically illustrates, even fewer paid attention when their intelligence staffs came to them with multiple warnings of a growing threat.

CONCLUSION

After reviewing the intelligence available before the 9/11 attacks and what was done with it, we can now go back to the basic puzzle of 9/11: How could the attacks have taken place, despite years of intelligence reports about the rising threat of terrorism and numerous warnings about just this sort of attack? Or to put the question another way, How much do you need to know before you can actually stop an enemy from attacking?

This chapter suggests that strategic intelligence—long-term, broad warnings about a threat—is not enough. Such warnings had been available for years, and had been repeatedly presented to presidents Clinton and Bush and their top advisers. And yet, as Jack Davis has written, these warnings failed to convince the nation's leaders to "generate appropriate, prudent, and affordable measures for increased preparedness."[210] The 9/11 attacks are an example of the paradox of strategic warning: Although senior officials say they want it and experts and blue ribbon commissions routinely argue that more is needed, strategic warning is actually not effective in preventing surprise attacks.

What was needed but unavailable was specific, tactical-level warning of the 9/11 plot, combined with decision makers willing to listen and respond to those warnings. To borrow imagery from the CIA's after-action report: Without tactical-level intelligence on the plot itself, policymakers were left with only warnings of smoke but no sightings of fire. To obtain such precise warning would have required a lengthy, focused intelligence effort not only against al-Qaeda's central network but also against its operatives in the United States and threats against commercial airliners. Such a focused collection effort was unlikely to have been undertaken in the absence of strong evidence that such a threat was realistic. But even if such intelligence had been available, it is not clear it would have been listened to and acted upon. Even if a human source or a communications intercept had revealed some specific aspect of the 9/11 plot, it might not have been believed. Many key decision makers were already unreceptive toward warnings about terrorism, and new threats about suicide aircraft hijacking might have been dismissed in the same way that earlier scenarios and speculations about such attacks had been dismissed.

Given the intelligence warning available and the lack of receptivity among policymakers, it is very unlikely that greater imagination among intelligence officials could have prevented the 9/11 attacks. Senior policymakers did not truly believe that terrorists might use commercial airliners as aerial bombs. The possibility had been imagined, and numerous government officials had been warned. But because no such attack had ever occurred before, these warnings were seen as little more than imaginative scenarios, and little action was taken against the threat.

CHAPTER 8

TESTING THE ARGUMENT

Why Do Terrorist Plots Fail?

A S WE SAW IN THE FIRST PART of this book, much of the difficulty in learning how to prevent conventional surprise attacks lies in the fact that in most of the cases we know about, the surprise attack was successful. Only in a very few cases, such as the Battle of Midway and the 1967 Six-Day War, is intelligence successful in both anticipating the coming attack and convincing policymakers to take action. Instead, the result is usually embarrassed intelligence agencies, surprised and angry decision makers, and a lack of lessons for how to prevent the problem from happening again the next time.

In the case of terrorist attacks the situation is different. Even here, the best-known cases are those in which the attack succeeds and terrorists are able to kill people and cause large-scale destruction. But the good news about terrorist attacks is that in many cases—more than most people probably are aware—the attack fails or the plot is foiled ahead of time. Although a few of these incidents become widely known, such as the Christmas Day 2009 airline bombing attempt, most of these *unsuccessful* terrorist attacks receive considerably less public attention. It is by studying these cases that we can find the most useful lessons for determining what works, and what does not, to prevent terrorist attacks.

This chapter examines a new data set of 227 terrorist plots against American targets that have been thwarted or otherwise failed during the past twenty-five years.[1] To the author's knowledge this is the most extensive database that has been developed of these "plots that failed." Government officials have occasionally in the past produced lists of thwarted attacks,[2] and scholars and terrorism analysts have published a few, mostly brief compilations and analyses of foiled plots.[3] Several useful works have examined the questions of why some terrorist attacks succeed while others fail, and why some terrorists quit or turn away from violence.[4] But no major study of the phenomenon of failed attacks has been published, and no attempt has been made—at least in the unclassified literature—to develop a comprehensive listing of, or analyze the lessons learned from, unsuccessful attacks and plots.[5]

The conventional wisdom about terrorist attacks—as with surprise attacks in general—is that in most cases the information needed to prevent an attack is already available, and the problem is not a lack of intelligence collection that prevents authorities from "connecting the dots" but rather a lack of effective analysis. This was the view following the September 11, 2001, terrorist attacks, and it was a finding of the White House review of the Christmas Day bombing attempt.[6] But the history of failed attacks shows that the conventional wisdom is wrong. Most terrorist plots are not disrupted when a highly skilled or imaginative analyst detects subtle clues that link otherwise insignificant bits of data. Nor are they often prevented through the use of exotic intelligence methods such as spy satellites and overseas agents. Instead, most are foiled when intelligence and law enforcement agencies obtain very precise information about individual plots being planned by specific groups. This precise warning becomes actionable when it is provided to receptive law enforcement authorities and policymakers, who take action to stop the plots.

The first section of this chapter considers the difficulties involved in studying failed terrorist plots and the question of whether or not such work can be useful or should even be undertaken. The second section reviews the major sources of data on failed plots and describes this chapter's data set and its limitations. The third section examines what these plots can tell us about why terrorist plots fail, and what types of intelligence appear to be most useful in thwarting attacks. The fourth section compares the intelligence available before two different unsuccessful terrorist attacks: the Christmas Day 2009 airline bombing attempt, which was widely considered an intelligence failure (even though the attack did not succeed); and the case of Najibullah Zazi, who was arrested in 2009 following a very successful intelligence and law enforcement investigation. This comparison demonstrates that the difference between intelligence failure and success against terrorist attacks is not a matter of better analysis or connecting the dots of subtle clues; instead, intelligence succeeds and plots are foiled mostly because the authorities are able to collect very specific, actionable intelligence.

THE DIFFICULTY OF STUDYING FAILED ATTACKS

Experts on terrorism and intelligence generally agree that it is difficult to study cases of failed terrorist attacks—or to look at it another way, that it is difficult to study intelligence success against terrorism. As the terrorism expert Brian Jenkins puts it, "We have thwarted a number of terrorist attacks; exactly how many is hard to say. It is difficult counting events that don't occur."[7] Senior intelligence community leaders make the same point. For example, Michael Hayden, then the director of the National Security Agency and later CIA director, testified to the Congressional Joint Inquiry into 9/11 that "while our successes are generally invisible to the American people, *everyone* knows when an adversary succeeds. NSA *has had* many successes, but these are even *more* difficult to discuss in open session" (emphasis in the original).[8]

There are several reasons why it might *not* be productive or useful to study these failed terrorist attacks. One reason often cited by intelligence and security officials is that information about how plots are foiled could prove useful to future attackers. Rohan Gunaratna acknowledges this argument: "Security and intelligence services and law enforcement agencies have thwarted over 100 low- and high-scale terrorist incidents since 9/11, the details of which are usually protected to secure convictions and protect intelligence sources."[9]

Another argument against focusing attention on failed plots and attacks is that such plots may provide an inaccurate measure of the threat, because terrorists tend to think about and "plan" more operations than they can ever hope to carry out. Brian Jenkins writes, "When not planning, they talk about operations—partly thinking about opportunities, partly fantasizing. Arrests and interrogations often reveal far more plots than officials knew about; knowing about them might have caused even greater alarm."[10] This tendency of terrorists to think big can be seen in the testimony of 9/11 planner Khalid Sheikh Mohammed (KSM) before a combatant status review tribunal at Guantánamo Bay, Cuba, in which he claimed to have played a part in at least thirty plots and plans, including assassination plots against former presidents Jimmy Carter and Bill Clinton as well as Pope John Paul II.[11]

Finally, it is possible that terrorists could use deception to suggest more plots than really exist in order to flood intelligence and law enforcement agencies with data. According to *The Economist*, "Some security officials suspect al-Qaeda may be deliberately flooding Britain with terrorist plots in hope of overwhelming its defences."[12] Compiling and analyzing such deceptive reports could, therefore, play into the terrorists' hands.

So why, if information on prevented terrorist attacks is difficult to obtain and could actually harm counterterrorist efforts, should anyone attempt to study such events? One reason is that examination of these events may have more to tell us about effective counterterrorism than does the more typical study of successful terrorist actions. Another reason for the study of failed plots is that even though we do not know very much about them, such events are already a part of the national discourse. Government officials and agencies frequently cite failed plots as evidence that the terrorist threat is real and counterterrorism policies are effective. For example, in his State of the Union Address in January 2007, President George W. Bush described several attacks that had been prevented and said that "our success in this war is often measured by the things that did not happen."[13] More recently the acting director of national intelligence, David Gompert, responding to a highly publicized series of articles in the *Washington*

Post, issued a statement that said "the men and women of the Intelligence Community have improved our operations, thwarted attacks, and are achieving untold successes every day."[14]

The most notable effort by US officials to claim credit for failed plots came in October 2005, when the White House released a list of ten "serious al-Qaida terrorist plots" that had been disrupted since September 11, 2001, and five additional efforts by al-Qaeda to case targets in the United States or infiltrate operatives into the country.[15] This list included some plots that are well known, such as the 2004 "British bomb plot" and the arrest in 2003 of a man who had wanted to destroy the Brooklyn Bridge. But still today, little is known about several other episodes described by the White House, such as a 2003 plot to attack a tourist site "outside the United States" and a plot to use commercial airplanes against targets on the East Coast in 2003.[16]

WHAT DO WE KNOW ABOUT FAILED ATTACKS?

Although some chronologies of terrorism incidents do include failed attacks, several of the most readily available public databases on terrorism exclude information on failed or otherwise unsuccessful terrorist attacks.[17] The website of the US National Counterterrorism Center Worldwide Incidents Tracking System, for example, states that "terrorists must have initiated and executed the attack for it to be included in the database; failed or foiled attacks, as well as hoaxes, are not included in the database."[18] The Global Terrorism Database, maintained by the National Consortium for the Study of Terrorism and Responses to Terrorism (known as START) at the University of Maryland, does include failed attacks, but not plots that were foiled before the attack was actually attempted.[19]

This chapter's data set is intended to include all unsuccessful terrorist plots or attacks against US persons or targets during the past twenty-five years. It was developed by the author, and it includes plots both within the United States and abroad, except that because of the difficulty of collection and because the circumstances are likely to be very different, attacks in Iraq or Afghanistan are excluded. It is based on only unclassified, openly available information—primarily press reports, government statements and reports, and court records.

This data set includes 227 attacks or plots against Americans that have been prevented or that were otherwise unsuccessful, dating back to 1987 and including data through December 2012. The list is shown in the appendix.[20] As shown in figure 8.1, the number of attacks and plots was at its peak in 2003, with 27 unsuccessful plots. Of the 227 total plots, 84 involved plots or attacks that occurred or were primarily planned outside the United States (labeled "overseas" in figure 8.1), whereas 143 plots were primarily planned or targeted within the United States (labeled "domestic"). Although a majority of these plots (169)

Figure 8.1 Unsuccessful Plots and Attacks against Americans, 1987–2012

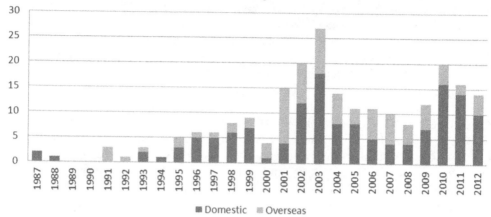

have taken place since the 9/11 attacks, a significant number of unsuccessful plots (58) took place before September 11, 2001.

Although 162 of these plots appear to have been inspired by radical Islamism (71 percent), 58 were attributed to domestic right-wing and antigovernment extremism (26 percent).[21] A total of 37 plots targeted US embassies, consulates, or other diplomatic facilities abroad, whereas American military bases, facilities, or personnel—both overseas and within the United States—were targeted in 50 plots.

Successful or Unsuccessful?

Determining whether a given terrorist event should be considered a success or failure is more difficult than it might seem. Even some attacks that result in significant damage or multiple deaths (e.g., the first World Trade Center bombing in 1993) might be considered a failure if seen from the point of view of the attacker's presumed intent to inflict even greater damage. Conversely, an attack that failed to kill anyone or do significant damage might nonetheless be logically coded as a success if it resulted in significant publicity for the attacker.

An attack is coded here as unsuccessful from the terrorists' point of view if it either (1) was not carried out for whatever reason or (2) was carried out but failed to kill or seriously injure anyone being targeted or to cause significant destruction. This coding method has the virtue of simplicity, although there is still ample room for debate over how individual cases should be coded. For example, the National Counterterrorism Center codes the Christmas Day 2009 airline bombing attempt as an attack, rather than as a near miss or a failed attack, because the attacker's improvised explosive device did detonate (although it failed to kill anyone).[22] It is coded here as a failed attack, because it did not kill anyone or cause significant damage.[23] This approach also does not allow for nuances—such as labeling an attack a partial success—and it does not allow for the consideration of other factors—such as whether an attack might in the long run prove to be beneficial or harmful to the cause of the attackers.[24]

Not included are incidents in which individuals or groups have been charged with providing support for terrorist organizations, unless there is evidence of directly aiding, facilitating, or planning violence or attacks.[25] Also excluded are incidents in which non-terrorist-related violence was prevented, such as thwarted episodes of workplace violence or prevented school shootings. In addition, several prominent terrorist plots have turned out to be either hoaxes or to have been unfounded, and these are not included.

Limitations of the Data

Because of the limitations of the information available, this data set cannot be considered comprehensive. There are undoubtedly more foiled plots about which nothing is publicly known. Even in cases for which a relatively large documentary record is available—such as those that have gone to trial—there may be little information available on the specific information used by the intelligence and law enforcement authorities to prevent the attack or foil the plot. But especially in the case of domestic plots and attacks, there is enough evidence available to derive at least initial conclusions about what methods and techniques appear to be successful in terrorism prevention.

Another limitation to this chapter's analysis should be noted. Because it only examines cases of unsuccessful plots and attacks, it is guilty of selecting cases on the dependent variable. By limiting the study to failed attacks, it is impossible to know whether the factors found to be involved—such as tips from the public and other forms of domestic human intelligence—are not also found in cases of successful attacks. It is certainly possible that police informants or undercover FBI agents (for example) have been involved in investigating terrorist cells that, nonetheless, were able to carry out successful attacks. This problem is difficult to overcome because few of these factors are tracked in standard terrorism databases, but future research comparing successful and unsuccessful plots could be useful here.

WHY DO TERRORIST PLOTS AND ATTACKS FAIL?

Determining exactly why any plot fails is difficult without having access to classified and law enforcement data. But in the great majority of these cases, the public record provides enough information for us to reach at least preliminary conclusions about what kinds of intelligence, counterterrorism, and law enforcement techniques were effective. The 227 cases have been divided into nine categories. Some were called off by the plotters, or were attempted but failed at the execution stage. Others were foiled through chance encounters with the police or as a by-product of other law enforcement investigations; or were prevented as a result of human intelligence, signals intelligence, detainee interrogation, intelligence from overseas, or public threats and announcements by the terrorists themselves. In 25 of these cases there is not enough information available in open sources—or in some cases those sources disagree significantly with each other—to assign a specific reason for the failure. The problem of "unknowns" is especially significant in the case of overseas plots; 17 of the 84 overseas plots are coded unknown. For domestic plots this problem is less acute, given that only 8 of 143 domestic plots have been coded as unknown.

Of note, these causal categories are not exclusive; that is, two or more factors or categories were involved in preventing some plots. The data are illustrated in figure 8.2, and the next paragraphs below discuss how these categories were coded and offer examples to illustrate how these factors have worked to prevent attacks from taking place.

A relatively rare category of plots—at least, it is rare that we know about them—is that attacks that are called off by the plotters themselves. The ten cases in this category include Saajid Badat, who had planned to carry out a second shoe bombing at the same time as Richard Reid, only to back out and later be arrested in Britain, and the al-Qaeda operative Iyman Faris, who considered and then rejected the possibility of destroying the Brooklyn Bridge.[26]

Figure 8.2   Reasons for Failure

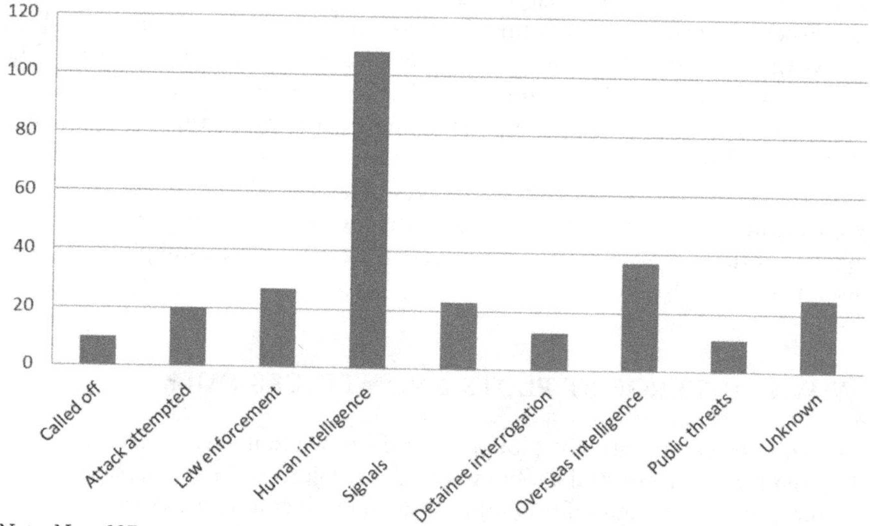

Note: N = 227.

Although failed plots that actually reach the stage of attempted execution are also relatively rare, several of the best-known recent plots—the Christmas Day 2009 airline bombing attempt, the May 2010 attempted car bombing in Times Square, and the October 2010 explosive packages plot—fall into this category. Only twenty cases reached this stage. Most of these took place overseas and involved attempted attacks on US embassies, consulates, and military facilities. A prominent example was the failed attempt in 2000 to attack the US Navy ship *The Sullivans* in Yemen before the successful attack on the USS *Cole*.[27]

Not all plots are foiled as a result of intelligence gathering or deliberate investigation by police and security officials. Twenty-seven failed when the plotters happened to encounter alert law enforcement officials through routine activity such as traffic stops, or when they were discovered by police officers investigating other crimes or complaints. Examples of chance encounters with law enforcement personnel include the December 1999 arrest of Ahmed Ressam, the would-be "Millennium bomber," when a customs agent became suspicious as he was attempting to cross into the United States at Port Angeles, Washington, and the 1988 arrest of a Japanese Red Army terrorist after a New Jersey state trooper noticed him acting suspiciously at a New Jersey Turnpike rest stop.[28] The "Bojinka" plot to blow up a dozen commercial airliners over the Pacific was uncovered in 1995 when the plotters started a fire in their Manila apartment that drew the attention of the Philippine authorities.[29] A domestic US example of a plot uncovered as a by-product of other police activity is that of a Los Angeles–area plot uncovered in 2005 after a gas station robbery led police to the suspects.[30]

Eleven plots were disrupted after the would-be terrorists announced their plans or in some other way made public threats. This appears to be a strictly domestic phenomenon—no overseas cases have been noted—and an example is James Kenneth Gluck, who was arrested in Florida in 1999 after sending a letter to judges in Colorado threatening to "wage biological warfare." When the police searched his home, they found the materials needed to make ricin.[31]

A large number of plots have been prevented as a result of intelligence or security operations overseas. Information on this category is particularly difficult to obtain, but cases have been coded as "overseas intelligence" if they have reportedly involved US intelligence operations abroad, intelligence from allies, or security and military operations carried out overseas. This category includes thirty-seven cases, most of them overseas plots. Examples include the announcement by the Tunisian authorities in January 2007 that they had killed or captured a number of Islamic extremists believed plotting to attack the American and British embassies in Tunis, and the 2012 plot by al-Qaeda operatives in Yemen to blow up an airliner.[32]

Signals intelligence (SIGINT)—including wiretapping, internet monitoring, and other forms of communications interception—is a mainstay of the US intelligence system, but publicly available information, at least, suggests that it may not be as useful as other methods in preventing terrorist attacks. Cases have been coded as SIGINT if they were foiled as a result of either telephone interception (wiretapping), or internet and email monitoring, or both. An example of a plotter detected through online activity is Hosam Majer Husein Smadi, who is charged with attempting to bomb a Dallas skyscraper. He came to the FBI's attention when he was discovered espousing terrorist attacks online.[33] Monitoring of internet chat room discussions was also reportedly involved in breaking up a plot in 2006 based in Beirut that aimed at blowing up the tunnels connecting Manhattan and New Jersey.[34] Intercepts of e-mails and telephone calls have reportedly helped foil other plots, such as one in Germany in 2007 targeting Ramstein Air Base.[35] But overall, only twenty-three attacks and plots appear to have been foiled as a result of some form of SIGINT.

Much of the debate over the use of intelligence in counterterrorism has focused on intelligence gained through interrogation, including the use of so-called enhanced techniques such as the waterboarding of detainees captured and held overseas. CIA reports released in August 2009 stated that information gained from detainees had been useful in thwarting a number of attacks, including a plot against the tallest building on the West Coast.[36] Because information on interrogations is typically both highly classified and controversial, it is difficult to judge the significance of such information in preventing attacks. Publicly available information—including claims by US intelligence and administration officials, which are difficult to verify—suggests that information gained from detainee interrogations has been a factor in thirteen cases.

Much more effective than either signals intelligence or detainee interrogation is human intelligence (HUMINT). This is not a surprise; it is commonly asserted that the most effective method of intelligence collection against terrorist targets is human intelligence, including in particular the difficult and lengthy task of penetrating terrorist groups. Brian Jenkins, for example, testified before the 9/11 Commission that "knowing what terrorists might do depends largely on human sources—undercover agents and informants. Penetrating small terrorist groups may take months, years."[37] More recently the former director of national intelligence Dennis C. Blair was quoted as telling reporters that the primary way US intelligence determines which terrorist organizations pose a direct threat is "to penetrate them and learn whether they're talking about making attacks against the United States."[38]

The record of foiled attacks suggests, however, that while human intelligence does indeed appear to be very useful in breaking up plots, this intelligence does not necessarily come from secret agents penetrating terrorist cells overseas. The information available indicates it is most often HUMINT of a rather prosaic kind at work: intelligence gathered through the use of informants, and from tips received from members of the public.[39] Cases were coded as involving HUMINT if they were prevented at least in part as a result of the work of undercover agents and informants, or tips from the public. Of the cases examined for this chapter, 108 involved at least one of these forms of human intelligence.

An example of a plot disrupted through the involvement of informants is that of four men charged with plotting to attack a Bronx, New York, synagogue and a National Guard base in Newburgh, New York, who were apparently discovered when they attempted to recruit an undercover informant who was operating out of a Newburgh mosque.[40] Another case involving an informant is the group of men who were arrested in 2007 on charges of plotting to blow up fuel tanks and fuel lines running beneath Kennedy International Airport in New York.[41]

In many cases an informant is placed among a group of plotters after the authorities first receive a tip from the public. This pattern was seen in the 2006 British airplane plot that led to tightened restrictions on carrying liquids on commercial aircraft and the aborted plan by a group of Miami men in 2006 to attack targets including the Sears Tower in Chicago and buildings in several other cities.[42] Another well-known example is the case of the group of men who plotted to attack the Fort Dix Army Base in New Jersey.[43]

These findings tend to confirm the argument of Stella Rimington, the former head of the British Security Service (MI5), that terrorism intelligence is not developed by spies overseas as often as one might expect. According to Rimington, "My own experience is that effective counter-terrorism frequently begins closer to home and may appear a lot more mundane."[44] In fact, one of the most significant findings of this chapter is that relatively mundane types of human intelligence—including informants, undercover operatives, and tips from the public—are the most effective counterterrorism tool, especially for breaking up domestic plots.

COMPARING FAILURE WITH SUCCESS

More broadly, this study of unsuccessful terrorist plots suggests that the type of intelligence available in these cases is significantly different from that available when intelligence fails. When intelligence is used to prevent a terrorist attack, we do not find that an analyst has been able to piece together a lot of little pieces of information, see the big picture, and convince a decision maker of the danger that is coming. The key factor is not the presence or absence of "imagination" or analytical skill. Instead, the critical factor is the collection of very precise, tactical-level intelligence that can be used to convince a decision maker to take the actions needed to prevent an attack.

To help make this point clearer, the next section of this chapter briefly compares the intelligence warning available before two attempted terrorist attacks. The first case is the Christmas Day 2009 bombing attempt, which—though foiled by passengers and crew onboard the plane—was widely seen as an intelligence failure. The second is the case of Najibullah Zazi, an Afghan immigrant who was arrested and prevented from carrying out an attack on the New York City subway system in September 2009.

The Christmas Day Bombing Attempt

The case of Umar Farouk Abdulmutallab, who attempted to blow up a Northwest Airlines flight on December 25, 2009, has become well known as an incident in which numerous warnings were missed by intelligence and national security officials. A White House review of the incident found that the US government had sufficient information about the attempted attack to have disrupted it, but the intelligence and counterterrorism communities failed to properly analyze and "connect the dots" of the available intelligence.[45] The then–director of national intelligence, Admiral Dennis Blair, testified to the Senate Homeland Security Committee that the failure in this case was not like the failure on 9/11, which had been a failure to collect or share intelligence; instead, the Christmas Day attempt represented a failure to connect, integrate, and understand the intelligence that already existed in the system.[46] In response to these failures, the White House directed the US intelligence community to implement a number of new policies and programs, many of which were directed at improving the process of intelligence analysis.[47] The goal has been to ensure that in the future, the dots of the available intelligence will be connected.

What was the intelligence that was missed? The warnings included:

➤ In May 2009 the British government rejected Abdulmutallab's application to renew a student visa and placed him on a watch list to prevent him from reentering Britain. It is not known whether the United States knew this.[48]

➤ In November 2009 Abdulmutallab's father, a Nigerian businessman, met with US officials (including CIA officers) at the US embassy in Abuja to express his concern that his son had fallen under the influence of religious extremists. He did not, however, say directly that his son was a terrorist or was planning an attack.[49]

➤ The day after the father's visit to the embassy in Abuja, the embassy sent a cable to the Department of State and other agencies in Washington informing them that Abdulmutallab could be involved with Yemeni-based extremists. Embassy officials misspelled his name, however, and as a result they did not realize that he held a valid US visa.[50]

➤ As a result of the embassy cable, Abdulmutallab's name was entered into the Terrorist Identities Datamart Environment (TIDE) database, which is a master list of information on people the federal government knows or suspects are involved in international terrorism.[51] But because the derogatory information about him did not meet the minimum standards that were used for watchlisting, he was not placed on the smaller no-fly watch list.[52] He was, however, placed on a list maintained by the State Department Consular Section called CLASS. US Customs and Border Protection officials noted that entry after the flight departed from Amsterdam, and as a result they had already planned to give Abdulmutallab additional screening once he arrived in Detroit.

> Other clues came from communications intercepts of al-Qaeda followers in Yemen that a man named "Umar Farouk" had volunteered for a coming operation. In addition, in December militants in Yemen were reportedly overheard discussing preparations for an event on Christmas Day.[53]

> It was considered suspicious that Abdulmutallab had paid for his round-trip ticket to Detroit with cash in Accra and that he did not have any checked luggage from the flight from Amsterdam to Detroit.

> On August 27, 2009, an assassination attempt was made on the Saudi assistant interior minister using a pentaerythritol tetranitrate (PETN)–based explosive device hidden in the underwear of the bomber, the same method used by the Christmas Day bomber. In September a UN expert on al-Qaeda gave a speech in Washington in which he warned that such a device could be brought onto an airplane.[54]

> On December 22, an al-Qaeda video released on Al Jazeera television warned that "we carry prayer beads, and with them we carry a bomb for the enemies of God."[55]

Seen in hindsight, these clues can appear to be clear warnings of the danger presented by Abdulmutallab. And because intelligence and homeland security officials were on the lookout for potential attacks—they were receptive toward warning—it can seem hard to understand why these warnings were missed. But in comparison with the next case, that of Najibullah Zazi, we can see that the intelligence available before the Christmas Day attempt was quite general and unspecific.

The Najibullah Zazi Plot

The case of Najibullah Zazi, who has pleaded guilty to plotting to conduct a coordinated, multiple-person attack on the New York City subway system, has been described by the authorities as one of the most serious in recent years.[56] Zazi, a permanent legal resident of the United States, was born in Afghanistan and raised in Pakistan, and he went to high school in Queens, New York. He admitted that he traveled to Pakistan in 2008 to fight for the Taliban against the United States, and while there he received training in bomb making. After returning to the United States, he moved to Colorado and found work as an airport shuttle driver, while at the same time beginning to assemble the materials needed to build a bomb. On September 8, 2009, he rented a car and began driving to New York, where he and two others planned to strap explosives to their bodies, board trains at the Grand Central and Times Square subway stations, and blow themselves up during rush hour.[57]

By this time, however, Zazi had been under surveillance by US officials for months in what was known as Operation High Rise.[58] The intelligence gathered on Zazi appears to have included the following:

> He reportedly first came to the attention of the US authorities as a result of intelligence gathered overseas. Some news reports indicate that the CIA initially learned about Zazi through sources in Pakistan and then notified the FBI.[59]

> Although the link with Pakistan is unconfirmed, it has become clear more recently that at least some early information on the case came from a tip from British intelligence.[60] In 2009, British officials had intercepted e-mails from a British citizen, Abid Naseer, to an account registered to a man named "Ahmad." Ahmad, whom officials describe as an al-Qaeda facilitator in Pakistan, had also been exchanging e-mail with Zazi. Shortly before Zazi left Colorado for New York, he sent an e-mail to Ahmad, stating that "the marriage is ready." This apparently signaled that the attack was imminent.[61]

> When Zazi suddenly began driving cross-country toward New York in September, FBI agents were following him.[62] To keep a close eye on him, local law enforcement agencies were reportedly enlisted to help by pulling him over several times for speeding.[63] As he approached New York City, Zazi's car was stopped and searched on the George Washington Bridge in an operation coordinated between the FBI and the New York Police Department (NYPD). He was told that it was a random drug search, and after nothing suspicious was found he was allowed to continue on his way. But later the authorities secretly broke into his car and searched his laptop, on which they discovered nine pages of handwritten bomb-making instructions.[64]

> Up to this point, law enforcement and intelligence officials had been able to combine national intelligence information with wiretaps, physical searches, and surveillance.[65] President Obama reportedly had begun receiving regular briefings on the case beginning in August, and was sometimes updated several times a day.[66]

> Then on September 10, the same day Zazi's car was stopped, officials from the NYPD's intelligence division approached a Queens imam in what was apparently an effort to gather more information about the case. The imam, Ahmad Wais Afzali, had provided information to NYPD officers in the past. Within hours of being interviewed, the imam spoke on the phone both with Zazi and with his father, tipping Zazi off that he was under investigation. Federal officials, who had not known about the intelligence division's actions, learned of the imam's involvement because they were monitoring Zazi's phone conversations. Believing their hand had been forced, they moved quickly to arrest Zazi and several accomplices.[67]

Success in the Zazi case did not come about because intelligence officials were able to piece together imprecise clues and warnings, such as those that had been available before the Christmas Day bombing attempt. Zazi's plot to attack the New York City subway system was foiled because investigators had precise information on what he was up to—information gathered through a wide variety of means, both within the United States and abroad. By comparison, it seems clear that the warnings available before the Christmas Day bombing attempt were much less specific, and it becomes easier to understand why they were not understood. The problem was not that the dots were not connected—it was that there was simply not enough specific intelligence information to enable the authorities to understand the threat and stop Abdulmutallab before he boarded his flight to Detroit.

CONCLUSION

This examination of unsuccessful terrorist plots and attacks strongly suggests that the conventional wisdom about intelligence failure and success is wrong. Attacks are not foiled when a sharp analyst puts together little bits of otherwise unrelated intelligence, realizes the danger ahead, and takes it all to a decision maker whose swift action averts catastrophe. Instead, most plots are foiled because officials have very precise, tactical-level intelligence, often from human sources, on what the plotters are up to. The intelligence picture is usually much clearer than it seems to have been before the Christmas Day attempt, suggesting that terrorist attacks are not prevented because intelligence officials connect the dots but because they collect and act on very precise warnings.

Precise, tactical-level intelligence is the first factor involved in making preventive action possible. The second factor is the presence of receptive policymakers, and in the case of thwarted terrorist attacks this factor has not been seen to play a very prominent role. This is in part because most of these plots and thwarted attacks were small scale, and handled primarily as law enforcement issues, with senior-level policymakers not necessarily becoming involved. As we have seen in earlier chapters on the East Africa embassy bombings and the 9/11 attacks, a lack of policymaker receptivity can certainly have a harmful effect on the ability to prevent more complex and dangerous attacks. But the main reason why receptivity has not been a factor is that in the case of terrorist plots and attacks, especially in the years since 9/11, intelligence officials have not needed to work very hard to convince decision makers of the seriousness of the threat; they were receptive already. As a result, the most critical factor in preventing terrorist attacks has been the availability of specific, tactical-level intelligence.

The analysis of this chapter reinforces a distinction that was noted earlier in this book between conventional surprise attacks and terrorist attacks. As we saw in chapter 4, in the case of conventional surprise attacks the most important factor is policymaker receptivity. Intelligence systems are often able to detect very specific indicators of an enemy preparing to launch a military attack, but solid evidence of the enemy's *intent* is usually not available. The decision to act on the warnings, then, depends largely on how receptive policymakers are to the assessments they receive from the intelligence concerning that intent.

In the case of surprise attacks from terrorists, however, the enemy's hostile intent is generally well understood, and policymakers—whether at the national level or the level of local law enforcement—are generally receptive to the warnings they receive. The key factor for decision makers is whether or not the intelligence and law enforcement authorities are able to provide specific enough warning to enable action.

CONCLUSION

Preventing Surprise Attacks Today

THIS BOOK CHALLENGES the conventional wisdom about why intelligence fails and how surprise attacks can be prevented. Studies dating back to Pearl Harbor have found that attacks happen because the important warning signals get lost amid the noise, and because intelligence analysts fail to connect the dots of widely scattered information in time to alert policymakers and foil a plot. But these studies have suffered from 20/20 hindsight, focusing only on cases in which intelligence fails and attacks succeed. They may help us understand some of the many reasons why intelligence fails, but they do little to explain how it can succeed.

This book turns the problem around. By comparing cases of intelligence success and intelligence failure, it asks: In cases of success in preventing attacks, what works? What is the difference between surprise attacks that kill people and even start wars, and those that are detected and stopped before they can be carried out? The answer is the combination of precise, tactical-level warning together with policymakers who are receptive to that warning.

The theory of preventive action proposed here is a limited one. I am not arguing that it provides the solution to the general problem of intelligence failure against any and all threats and challenges. Nor can this book claim to be a full test of the theory of preventive action against the problem of surprise attack, because such a test would require more extensive analysis across a wider number of cases than are currently available for study. It argues instead that the cases examined in this book provide strong evidence that in the relatively narrow problem of preventing surprise attacks—against both conventional and terrorist enemies—the two key factors are precise warning and decision maker receptivity. This chapter first reviews what these cases teach us about how intelligence can lead to preventive action, and then considers the contributions of this study for theory as well as policy. It concludes with a few observations about what this suggests for the future of surprise attacks, as well as for the broader problem of strategic surprise.

PREVENTIVE ACTION

This book has examined the puzzle of why the American intelligence community has often failed to prevent surprise attacks, even though post-attack investigations have almost invariably found that warnings had been available. To solve this puzzle, it proposed a *theory of preventive action*: If intelligence is to be most useful in preventing major surprise attacks, it must provide specific, tactical-level warning, and policymakers must be receptive to that warning. The cases reviewed here suggest that these two factors are, in fact, what separates intelligence failure from success. The difference between failure at Pearl Harbor and success at Midway, for example, was not that intelligence analysts were any more brilliant after Pearl Harbor or did a better job of piecing together subtle clues of what the Japanese were up to. The difference was that in early 1942 naval intelligence was able to break the Japanese Navy's operational code, providing precise warning to Admiral Nimitz and other leaders—who still required a lot of convincing before they became receptive to what intelligence was telling them.

The argument about preventive action may seem obvious, but it is contrary to the prevailing assumptions about how intelligence can best be used to prevent surprise attacks. The conventional wisdom, as seen in the *9/11 Commission Report*, argues that intelligence collection tends to work fairly well, but the system breaks down in the analysis of that data. In addition, the most critical intelligence is usually believed to be at the big-picture, strategic level. According to this standard view, the US intelligence community should not concentrate on acquiring tactical-level intelligence on potential attacks, because such precise warning is unlikely to be available.[1] Instead, according to this conventional thinking, more emphasis needs to be placed on developing broad, strategic-level intelligence on future threats.

This book argues that on the contrary, strategic intelligence does little to prevent surprise attacks. In many cases strategic warnings before attacks have been very imaginative, and analysts have often been able to forecast threat scenarios that proved to be extremely prescient. But these warnings have done little good, because they did not give the specific information about who, what, where, or when that was needed to create the sense of urgency that would have compelled decision makers to act and enable them to know what action to take. Conversely, when warning has been specific, and policymakers have been receptive, attacks have been successfully prevented.

Figure C.1 illustrates the relationship among these factors in several of the cases we have examined. The first factor in preventive action—precise, tactical-level warning—is critically important because surprise attacks—even major ones

Figure C.1 Theory of Preventive Action: Selected Cases

	Low policymaker receptivity	High policymaker receptivity
Strategic warning	Pearl Harbor 9/11 attacks	2009 Christmas Day bombing attempt
	(Attacks succeeded)	*(Intelligence failed, attack nearly succeeded)*
Specific warning	Tet Offensive East Africa embassy bombings	Battle of Midway Day of Terror plot Najibullah Zazi
	(Attacks succeeded)	*(Attacks prevented)*

such as Pearl Harbor and the September 11, 2001, terrorist attacks—are essentially tactical operations. Compared with broader conflicts such as wars and military campaigns, surprise attacks rely on individual actions by a relatively small number of people. Specific pieces of information and tactical-level actions by the authorities can be enough to prevent the attack. Tactical-level intelligence is also most useful for preventing attacks because decision makers are more likely to make use of it, even though conventional wisdom says they prefer big-picture, strategic-level intelligence. This is the *paradox of strategic warning*. Policymakers, especially at senior levels, typically say they want strategic intelligence; but this book demonstrates that they are actually less likely to respond to long-range, broad assessments than they are to specific, tactical-level warnings.

My argument about the importance of precise intelligence is not unique; Deborah Barger, for example, writes that "today, if the United States is to protect its citizens from a catastrophic terrorist attack, more precise 'tactical' warning—that a specific individual plans to strike at a specific place with a specific weapon at a specific time—is necessary. It is that level of precision that is likely to be the new threshold for intelligence 'success' in the future."[2]

The contribution of this study is to provide data to support this argument, and to suggest that such tactical-level intelligence is most likely to be useful when it is provided to policymakers and leaders who are receptive to it because they believe in the threat and they trust the intelligence they are given. Tactical-level warning is necessary (but not sufficient) to prevent surprise attacks because it can offer the defender a relative (but not absolute) decision advantage over the enemy. An attacker can pick and choose the time and place for action, whereas in the absence of a specific warning the defender must consider the possibility that an attack could come almost anywhere. This problem is even more pronounced when defending against terrorist attacks, which suggests the following logic. Strategic warning of a threat—such as warning about international terrorism before 9/11—can, if it is successful, lead to increased security, greater intelligence collection and analysis, and other actions both offensive and defensive. These actions might very well prevent a future attack. But it is much more likely that an attack will be foiled if more focused actions can be taken against specific enemies, or in defense of specific targets.[3] How much warning is enough? Here more work needs to be done, but the cases we have reviewed suggest that when decision makers are receptive, it does not take much to prevent an attack; but too much data, too much warning, are likely to be counterproductive.

The cases examined in this book demonstrate that the second factor in preventive action, policymaker receptivity, is a complex phenomenon. It is more than simply a matter of a leader's personality or that some decision makers believe in intelligence but others do not. Admiral Nimitz, for example, was very supportive of his intelligence staff, and as a result of Pearl Harbor he was certainly aware of the threat posed by the Japanese Navy. But in the spring of 1942 he was quite skeptical of the intelligence reporting with which he was being provided, and he was especially wary of the warnings coming from the new field of cryptology. Only after assigning two of his senior officers to closely examine the available intelligence, after intelligence had proved its value at the Battle of the Coral Sea, and after the ruse about Midway being short of water was Nimitz ready to put his trust—and the security of the fleet—in warnings that Midway was Japan's next target.

A policymaker is receptive toward warning when, through a combination of a *belief in the threat* and *trust in intelligence*, he or she is ready to act on that warning. Several factors appear to help increase receptivity, including geographical proximity to the threat. Before Midway, for example, intelligence personnel and military commanders in Hawaii were considerably more receptive to the possibility of a Japanese attack on Midway than were their counterparts in Washington. Similarly, US analysts and commanders in Vietnam during the period before the Tet Offensive were more receptive toward warnings of an impending enemy assault than were those in Washington. And in the case of the East Africa embassy bombings, Ambassador Bushnell in Nairobi was highly receptive toward intelligence and concerned about the threat to her post, but she did not have the authority to make the necessary security improvements or changes to the intelligence posture. The important decisions were made far away in Washington, where officials were not receptive.

In addition, threats that are more vivid and salient to the decision maker—such as warnings received at first hand or dangers experienced personally—are more likely to inspire receptivity than those received at second hand. Admiral Nimitz, for example, arrived at Pearl Harbor to assume command of the Pacific Fleet on Christmas Day 1941, and as he stepped out from his airplane he could smell oil, charred wood, and burned flesh; in the harbor small boats searched for the bodies of the dead, which were still rising to the surface.[4] He understood at first hand the damage that had been done. And as a result of the first World Trade Center bombing, the New York officials who worked together to prevent the 1993 Day of Terror plot had personal knowledge of the danger that such groups could pose to their city.

Other factors, however, operate on receptivity in a more complex manner. Intelligence failures such as at Pearl Harbor tend to increase a decision maker's belief in the threat but decrease his or her trust in intelligence. Intelligence successes, conversely, could have the opposite effect, decreasing the policymaker's concerns about the threat but increasing trust in intelligence. Here, too, is an avenue for further research.

THE VALUE OF STRATEGIC WARNING AND ANALYSIS

This study should not be seen as arguing that strategic intelligence is unimportant. The US intelligence community is putting more emphasis on strategic analysis today; for example, the Defense Intelligence Agency has announced that is "reinvigorating" its mission of strategic warning following its failure to properly understand and warn about the Arab Spring.[5] Such efforts should continue as long as they are not at the expense of tactical efforts. But the value of strategic intelligence has been misunderstood. As Jack Davis has pointed out, good strategic warning can ensure that appropriate resources are made available to detect and prevent threats—so strategic warning can improve the ability of intelligence analysts to provide tactical warning.[6] Strategic intelligence is also useful in its own right in the long-term fight against terrorism. Long-range, strategic intelligence will be needed to achieve long-range goals such as defeating al-Qaeda and its various offshoots.[7] But to achieve short-range goals such as preventing an attack next week, we need tactical intelligence.

The killing of Osama bin Laden by US Navy SEALs in May 2011 is perhaps the most prominent recent example of the successful use of intelligence for preventive action. The intelligence in this case was very precise—a particular house where bin Laden was suspected to live—but it could not be confirmed. The critical variable was that President Obama was ultimately receptive, and that he ordered the raid despite a fairly high degree of uncertainty among his senior advisers.[8]

Commentators today place too much importance on a few key strategic-level intelligence products such as National Intelligence Estimates and the *President's Daily Brief*. Many experts seem to believe that future surprises and attacks can be prevented if all the available information is assembled into such an intelligence product. But this book finds that even when such products are developed in response to specific questions from senior policymakers, those officials are not likely to take action unless they are independently convinced of the seriousness of the threat, and of the value of the intelligence.

Similarly, even though this study suggests that more attention needs to be placed on intelligence collection, this conclusion should not be taken to mean that the analytical part of the intelligence process should be neglected. The brilliant analytical skills of Joe Rochefort and Edwin Layton played a vital role in developing the intelligence needed to anticipate the Japanese attack on Midway. Today, there seems little doubt that it is good to have sharp, imaginative analysts in the intelligence and law enforcement communities who look carefully at every piece of information about future terrorist attacks and other threats.

But this study indicates that it is mistaken to believe that future attacks are likely to be prevented through imaginative analysis alone. The history of intelligence successes and failures strongly suggests that analytical assessments and estimates are not enough to convince decision makers to take seriously the warnings from intelligence. The Japanese "second attack on Pearl Harbor," Operation K, which Rochefort had predicted to no avail, provided a dramatic demonstration of that point. More recently, analytical tools such as scenario development and "red teaming," in which analysts seek to think like the enemy, have become popular. The history of surprise attacks provides little evidence that these can be helpful. As we have seen, before both Pearl Harbor and 9/11 many officials imagined what was to come—to little effect. This tends to confirm the comment by Schwartz and Randall that simply coming up with scenarios is not enough: "The point is that imagining things is the easy part. What is hard is imagining future scenarios that are sufficiently believable to spur one to act in advance and find ways to persuade others to act."[9] This book suggests that for a scenario to be sufficiently believable, it needs to be based not on imagination but on solid, tactical-level intelligence.

APPLES AND ORANGES

This book compares several different kinds of problems that are not normally discussed together in the scholarly literature on intelligence and surprise attack. One such apples-and-oranges comparison is that between surprise attacks that come at the beginning of a war and those that occur during war. Although most scholars have argued that the first situation holds much greater challenges for intelligence, the cases examined here have shown just how difficult it can be to avoid surprise attack *during war*. Before Midway, intelligence officials faced many of the same challenges as before Pearl Harbor, and only by directly comparing the two cases can we clearly understand what led to intelligence success in one case but not the other. Similarly, by comparing the surprises at the beginning of the Korean War and at the Chinese intervention, we see that the same factors, and the same failings, were at work.

Another potential apples-and-oranges problem for this book is that it explicitly compares the challenges posed by conventional surprise attacks with those posed by terrorist attacks. This speaks to the question posed earlier in this book: Is terrorism a truly new problem for intelligence, or are there more similarities than differences between surprise attacks of the past and those of today? I argue that there are indeed many important similarities between the two types of surprise attack, and that the history of conventional surprise attack holds lessons that can help us deal today with the problem of terrorist attacks and other types of new surprises. But the cases studied here—especially in chapters 4 and 8—show that the factors needed for preventive action do vary, depending on whether the challenge is a conventional attack or a terrorist surprise attack. In the case of conventional attacks, where modern intelligence systems are often able to gather a great deal of specific warning data, the most important factor is policymaker receptivity. But in the case of terrorist attacks, where policymakers are generally already willing to believe in the threat, the most important factor is the collection of specific, tactical-level intelligence on the developing plot or pending attack.

THE FUTURE OF SURPRISE

The history of surprise attacks tells us that even if we are watching for them, future surprises will look very different from anything we have seen before. Even if we have successfully anticipated what the target will be, such as was done in numerous war games and assessments before Pearl Harbor, an attack may still come from a new direction or in a new way, leaving intelligence officials flat-footed and defenders shocked. And even when an adversary strikes the same target twice, as we have seen with the World Trade Center, the result may still be surprise, intelligence failure, and disaster.

Such a future surprise could be relatively conventional, coming from a traditional, state-based adversary such as Iran or China. The example of Iraq's invasion of Kuwait in 1990 demonstrates that even when the most capable intelligence services in the world are focused on it, a conventional military force can still take actions that surprise policymakers. But surprise may also take a newer form, and one area where experts fear a surprise attack may be likely is that of cyberspace. The cases described in this book suggest that the danger may be even greater than many believe. Just as codebreaking before Pearl Harbor and Midway was a new and little-understood part of intelligence, our analysis and understanding of cyberthreats is still developing today. Admiral Nimitz and other American leaders were less inclined to listen to warnings about Japanese intentions because the information came from the obscure world of cryptology and codebreaking. There is a strong possibility that military and political leaders today may experience the same problem when it comes to warnings of cyberthreats. It does not seem to be an overstatement that today we are facing the same situation concerning cyberattack as the United States did before Pearl Harbor or

9/11: Strategic warnings of the threat are common, but specific, tactical-level intelligence on cyberthreats appears much less available.

When it comes to other kinds of threats and different types of intelligence assessments, the lessons of this book are even more pessimistic. Compared with many of the challenges facing intelligence and national security authorities, the problem of preventing surprise attacks is actually relatively simple. Even the most complex and dangerous plots involve only a finite number of conspirators and planners, and they typically go through a number of steps and stages that can be tracked and intercepted. In the terminology that is often used to describe intelligence challenges, surprise attacks are *secrets*—concrete problems that typically have solutions, such as concerning when and where an opponent is planning to strike. By comparison, many other kinds of threats and challenges can pose extremely complex problems for intelligence. This was the type of problem that American intelligence agencies, and the intelligence services of other nations, faced in attempting to determine whether or not Iraq was developing a weapons of mass destruction program before the United States–led invasion in 2003. Such a problem is a *mystery*, which Joseph Nye describes as "an abstract puzzle to which no one can be sure of the answer."[10]

Whether they are described as mysteries, strategic surprises, or black swans, it is clear that the challenges of the future will include many threats that are even more difficult to address than surprise attacks. But the study of surprise attacks does offer some useful lessons. As we saw in chapter 1, most of the literature on strategic surprise suggests that surprise is inevitable. This is not seen as the fault of intelligence agencies, but rather a function of how the world works. Nassim Nicholas Taleb and Mark Blyth made this point in examining why the Arab Spring revolutionary movement in the Middle East was almost completely unpredicted: "The final episode of the upheaval in Egypt was unpredictable for all observers, especially those involved. As such, blaming the CIA is as foolish as funding it to forecast such events."[11] For this reason, most experts argue, the best advice for governments, businesses, and individuals is to build the possibility of surprise into the planning process and to be ready to deal with the effects of surprise when it occurs.[12]

The cases examined in this book support the pessimistic prediction of these thinkers about the future of surprise; the history of surprise attacks certainly does teach us that surprise of some sort is inevitable. But the problem with much of this work is that it frequently leads to unhelpful advice—such as that in order to avoid being surprised, we should "expect the unexpected." This advice might be just the thing for a police officer walking a beat, or perhaps for a bouncer in a tough bar.[13] It is undoubtedly a good idea to try to prepare to meet the unexpected, and to develop plans to recover after failure and surprise. But the primary job of intelligence and national security officials is to foresee and prevent such surprises, and the cases examined here suggest that the theory of preventive action may be useful in understanding even this broader set of problems.

IMPLICATIONS FOR TODAY AND TOMORROW

The cases examined in this book offer several implications for American intelligence and national security today. First, they suggest that few of the reforms undertaken in the American intelligence community in recent years are likely to help prevent surprise attacks, because they are based on an incomplete understanding of what causes intelligence failure and what can produce intelligence success. Some of these intelligence reforms may be useful in other ways—such as by helping to centralize the sprawling American intelligence community and by bringing increased focus on key threats such as terrorism. But changes designed to improve analysis, increase the use of imagination, and connect the dots of available information are not likely to do much to help develop the precise intelligence that history shows is most often needed to prevent attacks.

Second, by challenging the conventional wisdom, this book provides support for those who believe that intelligence agencies and officials should be held accountable for major mistakes and disasters. If the signals-versus-noise problem is unsolvable—as Wohlstetter wrote about Pearl Harbor—then it certainly might be inappropriate to find blame with anyone for failing to prevent a surprise attack or other major intelligence failure. But if, as I argue, there are steps we can take to better our chances of improving intelligence and preventing surprise attacks, then it would be appropriate to demand a higher standard from our intelligence and national security officials.

Third, this book argues that more effort needs to be placed on intelligence collection, especially at the domestic and local level. Concerning the threat of terrorist attack, this study shows that the precise intelligence needed to prevent attacks is not usually developed through the use of strategic-level tactics that get much of the public's attention, such as spies who penetrate terrorist cells overseas or enhanced interrogations of captured suspects. These methods do occasionally produce results, but successes here are the exception rather than the rule. More typically, plots are disrupted as a result of tips from the public, informants working for local law enforcement, and long-term surveillance of suspects. That is the good news. The bad news is that actionable intelligence on terrorist threats is most often gathered through domestic intelligence and surveillance operations, which often have the potential for encroaching on civil liberties. More public discussion is needed in the United States and in other countries about where to strike the balance between security and liberty.

And finally, the findings of this book suggest that there may be more room for optimism than is usually found in the literature on intelligence and surprise attack. Additional research is needed to further test the theory of preventive action, and one direction for future research could be to expand the universe of surprise attack cases, especially to examine additional cases of intelligence success against surprise attack. Equally important would be to broaden the study beyond this book's focus on the American intelligence community. But even though we will never be able to eliminate the problem of intelligence failure—any more than we can eliminate failures in any other field of endeavor—the cases examined here suggest that we can at least learn to improve the work of intelligence, do a better job of understanding future threats, and help prevent surprise attacks.

CONCLUSION

The conclusions of this study are not those I expected to find when I began this work. I came to this project after spending twenty-one years as a naval intelligence officer, and my professional training had led me to believe that the key factor separating intelligence success from failure was *analysis*. I had been taught, and I believed, that all intelligence analysts had one primary goal: to connect the dots of widely scattered and indistinct information into timely warning that enabled senior leaders to take decisive action against a strategic threat. The model was, and largely remains, Edwin Layton's prediction to Admiral Nimitz of where and when the Japanese attack on Midway would come. But this study has convinced me that intelligence analysis alone—especially the big-picture, long-range analysis so often prized—will not prevent surprise attacks and head off intelligence failure.

Surprise attacks can be prevented in a number of ways, including by mistakes on the part of the plotters, through the use of defensive or preemptive offensive measures by the intended targets, or even by simple good luck. But this book argues that for intelligence to be most useful in preventing attacks, it needs to be precise, providing tactical-level intelligence warning to policymakers who are receptive to it. In the absence of precise tactical intelligence, threats may be imagined, but they are not likely to be believed. And unless decision makers are receptive to the intelligence they are given, they may be warned, but they are unlikely to listen. The task for the American intelligence community is to develop the capabilities to produce the necessary tactical-level intelligence, and to develop the needed linkages with decision makers, without having to wait for another surprise attack.

APPENDIX

Unsuccessful Plots and Attacks against American Targets, 1987–2012

Year	Name of Plot	Domestic	Overseas	Radical Islamist	Domestic Extremist	Other
2012	Alabama men arrested (Abukhdair, Wilson)	•		•		
	Florida brothers arrested in New York plot (Qazi)	•		•		
	California men arrested (Kabir)	•		•		
	Indonesia embassy plot		•	•		
	Amman attacks plot		•	•		
	New York Federal Reserve bomb plot (Nafis)	•		•		
	Chicago teen arrested (Daoud)	•		•		
	Fort Stewart, GA, plot	•			•	
	Al-Qaeda airline plot foiled		•	•		
	Ohio anarchists arrested	•			•	
	Minnesota supremacists (Johnson/Thomas)	•			•	
	US Capitol suicide bombing plot (Khalifi)	•		•		
	Algerian boat plot against US, European ships		•	•		
	Tampa bomb plot (Osmakac)	•		•		
2011	New York City bomb plot (Pimentel)	•		•		
	Georgia militia ricin plot	•			•	
	Azerbaijan embassy plot		•	•		
	Washington remote-controlled aircraft plot (Ferdaus)	•		•		
	Man arrested at JFK International Airport (Hasbajrami)	•		•		
	Fort Hood shooting plot (Abdo)	•		•		
	Turkish al-Qaeda plot		•	•		
	Obama assassination plot (Kodirov)	•		•		
	Seattle military recruiting center	•		•		
	Washington shooting suspect arrested (Melaku)	•		•		
	Iraqi nationals in Kentucky (Alwan, Hammadi)	•		•		
	New York synagogue plot (Ferhani, Mamdouh)	•		•		
	Alaska militia plot (Cox)	•			•	

Year	Name of Plot	Domestic	Overseas	Radical Islamist	Domestic Extremist	Other
2011	Saudi student plot (Aldawsari)	•		•		
	Pennsylvania man arrested (Begolly)	•		•		
	Spokane Martin Luther King Jr. parade bomb attempt	•			•	
2010	British bomb plot arrests (US embassy targeted)		•	•		
	Maryland military recruiting office (Martinez)	•		•		
	Washington subway plot (Younis/Facebook)	•		•		
	Portland Christmas tree lighting plot	•		•		
	Explosive packages intercepted		•	•		
	Washington subway plot (Ahmed)	•		•		
	Would-be terrorist arrested (Shehadeh)	•		•		
	Plot to bomb Wrigley Field in Chicago (Hassoun)	•			•	
	Chicago man plots to attack US troops (Masri)	•		•		
	Virginia man attempts to join Shabab (Chesser)	•		•		
	Alaska couple hit list (Rockwood)	•		•		
	New Jersey men arrested at JFK Airport (Alessa, Almonte)	•		•		
	Indonesia plot against foreigners		•	•		
	Texas man arrested (Bujol)	•		•		
	Times Square attempted car bombing	•		•		
	New York men charged with supporting al-Qaeda (Hanafi)	•		•		
	Connecticut white supremacists (Zrallack)	•			•	
	Chicago taxi driver arrested (Khan)	•		•		
	Hutaree militia arrests	•			•	
	British Airways employee arrested (Karim)		•	•		
2009	Christmas Day airline bombing attempt	•		•		
	Plot against US embassy in Yemen		•	•		
	Northern Virginia men arrested in Pakistan		•	•		
	Boston-area shopping mall plot (Mehanna)	•		•		
	Brooklyn man arrested in Kosovo (Kaziu)		•	•		
	Dallas skyscraper plot	•		•		
	Springfield, IL, courthouse plot	•		•		
	Najibullah Zazi plot	•		•		
	Kuwait arrests; plan to attack US Camp Arifjan		•	•		
	North Carolina arrests (Boyd)	•		•		
	Tunisian arrests (plan to kill US servicemen)		•	•		
	Newburgh, NY, bomb plot	•		•		

Year	Name of Plot	Domestic	Overseas	Radical Islamist	Domestic Extremist	Other
2008	Dirty bomb plot (Cummings)	•			•	
	Marine threat against Obama (Brittingham)	•			•	
	Long Island Rail Road possible plot (Vinas)	•		•		
	Obama assassination plot (Tennessee)	•			•	
	Attack on US consulate in Istanbul		•	•		
	Yemen mortar attack on housing complex (April)		•	•		
	Yemen embassy mortar attack (March)		•	•		
	Manila embassy plot		•	•		
2007	Ramstein Air Base plot		•	•		
	Goose Creek, SC, arrests (Ahmed Mohamed)	•		•		
	JFK Airport plot	•		•		
	Arms dealer Drug Enforcement Administration sting (Kassar)		•			•
	Fort Dix plot	•		•		
	Casablanca consulate bombing		•	•		
	Christopher Paul (Ohio man conspiring with al-Qaeda)		•	•		
	Ex-US sailor attack plot (Abujihaad; Paul R. Hall)	•		•		
	Al-Qaeda student visa plot		•	•		
	Tunis embassy targeted		•	•		
2006	Rockford shopping mall (Derrick Shareef)	•		•		
	Jordan plot against President Bush		•	•		
	Houston Taliban plot		•	•		
	Oslo men plotted against US and Israeli embassies		•	•		
	British airplane plot ("liquid bomb" plot)		•	•		
	New York tunnels plot (Hammoud)	•		•		
	Miami / Sears Tower	•		•		
	Amman airport attack plot		•	•		
	Atlanta casing plot (Ahmed, Sadequee)	•		•		
	SUV attack at University of North Carolina–Chapel Hill	•		•		
	Toledo, OH, conspiracy (Amawi, El-Hindi)		•	•		
2005	Gas refineries (Michael C. Reynolds)	•		•		
	American tourists in Jordan (cyanide plot)		•	•		
	Rocket attack on navy ships in Jordan		•	•		
	Los Angeles prison plot (JIS; Kevin James)	•		•		
	Would-be ricin maker arrested (Hughes)	•			•	
	Lodi, CA, plot	•		•		
	Neo-Nazi arrests (Carafa)	•			•	
	Support to al-Qaeda (Shah and Sabir)	•		•		
	Support to al-Qaeda (Grecula)	•			•	
	Plot against President Bush (Abu Ali)	•		•		
	Zarqawi tasked by bin Laden to plan attacks		•	•		

Year	Name of Plot	Domestic	Overseas	Radical Islamist	Domestic Extremist	Other
2004	Jeddah consulate attack		•	•		
	Tennessee extremist (Van Crocker)	•			•	
	Former National Guardsman arrested (Braden)	•			•	
	Financial institutions plot (New York Stock Exchange, International Monetary Fund Headquarters)	•		•		
	New York subway plot (Herald Square)	•		•		
	Albany sting (Aref/Araf, Hossain)	•		•		
	Chicago Federal Building (Nettles)	•			•	
	Islamabad embassy targeted		•	•		
	UK urban targets ("gas limos" plot)		•	•		
	NATO summit in Istanbul		•	•		
	Amman chemical bomb plot		•	•		
	British bomb plot (Operation Crevice)		•	•		
	Birmingham, AL, planned attacks (Hemphill)	•			•	
	Government and tourist sites tasking	•		•		
2003	Beirut embassy bombing attempt		•	•		
	Planned abortion clinic bombings (Jordi)	•			•	
	Columbus, OH, shopping mall (Abdi)	•		•		
	Michigan militia member arrested (Somerville)	•			•	
	NATO base plot (Trabelsi)		•	•		
	Antiaircraft missile sting (Lakhani)	•		•		
	Suicide bomber turned away (Banna)	•		•		
	East Coast airline plot	•		•		
	Brooklyn Bridge plot (Faris)	•		•		
	Virginia "paintball terrorists"	•		•		
	Planned attack on coast guard base (Revak)	•			•	
	Antigovernment extremist plot (Noster)	•			•	
	Nairobi embassy plot (truck bomb, plane)		•	•		
	Beirut embassy plot		•	•		
	Texas militia couple (Krar and Bruey)	•			•	
	Malike arrest in New York City	•		•		
	Camp Lemonier, Djibouti, truck bomb plot		•	•		
	Saudi Arabia housing compound plan		•	•		
	Karachi consulate explosives-laden aircraft plot		•	•		
	Mubtakkar gas plot	•		•		
	Planned abortion clinic bombings (Hull)	•			•	
	Washington state assassination plot (Brailey)	•			•	
	Ricin plot against US troops (Afghanistan and Kuwait)		•	•		
	Tourist sites tasking (White House list of five casings)	•		•		
	Gas station tasking (White House list; Majid Khan)	•		•		

Year	Name of Plot	Domestic	Overseas	Radical Islamist	Domestic Extremist	Other
2003	Southeast Asian cell (Hambali cell)	•		•		
	Tourist site outside United States (on White House list)		•	•		
2002	Milan cell planning attacks on US targets		•	•		
	Portland seven (Jeffrey Battle)	•		•		
	Lackawanna six	•		•		
	Drugs for Stingers ring (Ilyas Ali)		•	•		
	9/11 anniversary al-Qaeda plot against Southeast Asian embassies		•	•		
	Arabian Gulf shipping plot		•	•		
	Florida power station plot (Mandhai)	•		•		
	Florida Muslim center (Goldstein)	•			•	
	Seattle cell (Bly training camp; Ujaama)	•		•		
	North Carolina Klan leader (Barefoot)	•			•	
	Pennsylvania militia leader (Hertzog)	•			•	
	Jose Padilla ("dirty bomb"/apartment building plot)	•		•		
	Saudi air base attack (Sudanese man captured)		•	•		
	Strait of Gibraltar shipping plot		•	•		
	Sarajevo embassy bomb plot		•	•		
	Chicago cyanide arrest (Dr. Chaos/Konopka)	•			•	
	Montana militia (Project 7, Burgert)	•			•	
	Library Tower (West Coast airliner plot)	•		•		
	Neo-Nazi arrested in Nashville (Smith)	•			•	
	Strait of Hormuz plot (White House list)		•	•		
2001	Badat shoe bombing attempt	•		•		
	Richard Reid shoe bombing attempt	•		•		
	California mosque plot (Rubin and Krugel)	•			•	
	Singapore plot (Operation Jibril)		•	•		
	Eagle Base plot (Bosnia and Herzegovina)		•	•		
	Manila embassy		•	•		
	Al-Marri tasking (White House list of casings)	•		•		
	Paris embassy attack plot (Beghal)		•	•		
	New Delhi embassy attack plot		•	•		
	Plot against Group of Eight summit in Genoa and President Bush		•	•		
	Plot against US installations in Saudi Arabia		•	•		
	Plot against US embassy in Sanaa, Yemen		•	•		
	US ship in Indonesia planned suicide attack		•	•		
	Rome embassy attack called off		•	•		
	US ship in Malaysia (plot by Malaysian group)		•	•		

Year	Name of Plot	Domestic	Overseas	Radical Islamist	Domestic Extremist	Other
2000	Jakarta embassy car bomb plot		•	•		
	Houston federal building plot (McCool)	•			•	
	US ship in Malaysia attack planned		•	•		
	USS *The Sullivans* failed attack		•	•		
1999	Los Angeles Airport / Millennium plot (Ahmed Ressam)	•		•		
	Jordan al-Qaeda cell broken up		•	•		
	Florida militia leader arrested (Beauregard)	•			•	
	California propane storage facility plot	•			•	
	Ricin threat against judges (Gluck)	•			•	
	Alaskan oil pipeline plot (Reumayr)	•				•
	Colorado mosque targeted (Modig)	•			•	
	Aryan Nation bombing plot (Kelly)	•			•	
	Indian embassy, consulates targeted		•	•		
1998	East Coast airliner hijack plot to free blind sheik	•		•		
	Uganda embassy bombing thwarted		•	•		
	Washington bombing threat (Bazarte)	•			•	
	Republic of Texas militia arrests (Grebe, Wise)	•			•	
	Albania embassy bombing planned		•	•		
	Threatened chemical attack (Maltz)	•				•
	Michigan militia arrests (Carter)	•			•	
	White supremacist arrests (McGiffen)	•			•	
1997	New York City subway plot (Mezer, Khalil)	•		•		
	Fort Hood, TX, planned attack (Bradley Glover)	•			•	
	Planned Florida armored car plot (Orns)	•			•	
	Texas armored car plot ("Operation Sour Gas")	•			•	
	Kalamazoo, MI, arrest (Blasz)	•			•	
	Two plots against US embassies foiled		•	•		
1996	Phineas Priesthood arrests in Oregon	•			•	
	Mountaineer Militia plot disrupted (Looker)	•			•	
	Arizona militia arrests (Viper Team)	•			•	
	Washington State militia arrests (Pitner)	•			•	
	Georgia militia arrests (Starr, McCranie)	•			•	
	Singapore plot called off by al-Qaeda		•	•		
1995	Reno failed Internal Revenue Service building bombing (Bailie)	•			•	
	Oklahoma militia leader arrested (Lampley)	•			•	
	Antigovernment extremist arrested (Polk)	•			•	
	Bojinka plot against US airplanes (Manila)		•	•		
	Plot against US diplomats in Pakistan		•	•		

Year	Name of Plot	Domestic	Overseas	Radical Islamist	Domestic Extremist	Other
1994	Minnesota ricin plot (Minnesota Patriots Council)	•			•	
1993	Skinhead plot disrupted (Fisher and Boese)	•			•	
	Day of Terror (monuments) plot in New York City	•		•		
	Plot against President Bush in Kuwait		•	•		
1992	Bombing of Aden hotels housing US troops		•	•		
1991	Attack on US ambassador's residence in Jakarta		•			•
	Attempted bombing of cultural center in Manila		•			•
	Plot against US embassy in Zimbabwe		•			•
1988	Japanese Red Army terrorist arrested (Kikumura)	•				•
1987	Syrian terrorists attempt to enter Vermont	•		•		
	Militia leader arrested (F. Glenn Miller Jr.)	•			•	
	Totals	143	84	162	58	7

Note: This table has been updated from an earlier version published by Dahl, "Plots That Failed."

NOTES

INTRODUCTION

1. Wohlstetter, *Pearl Harbor*, 387.
2. Major studies of surprise attack that cite Wohlstetter include Betts, *Surprise Attack*; and Kam, *Surprise Attack*. More recent works building on Wohlstetter include Bar-Joseph and Levy, "Conscious Action."
3. Berkowitz, "Spying."
4. E.g., Byman, "Strategic Surprise," 147; and Parker and Stern, "Bolt from the Blue."
5. *9/11 Commission Report*, e.g., 277, 400.
6. Wirtz, "Responding to Surprise," 51.
7. Stern, "Review of Peter Bergen's 'The Longest War.'"
8. For example, the Markle Foundation warns that "today, we are still vulnerable to attack because—as on 9/11—we are still not able to connect the dots." Markle Foundation, *Nation At Risk*, 1.
9. "Remarks by the President on Strengthening Intelligence and Aviation Security," January 7, 2010, www.whitehouse.gov/the-press-office/remarks-president-strengthening-intelligence-and-aviation-security.
10. Central Intelligence Agency, *DCI Report*, 67.
11. Central Intelligence Agency, *DCI Task Force Report*, 2. For another example, a study by the House Permanent Select Committee on Intelligence in 1978 found that in every case of major intelligence failure since Pearl Harbor there had been sufficient information available for intelligence analysts to have issued actionable warning. This study was cited by John McCreary, a well-respected former senior defense intelligence analyst, in his *NightWatch* open source intelligence report examining the 2009 Christmas Day bombing attempt, dated January 8, 2010.
12. Jervis, "Response to James Lebovic's Review of *Why Intelligence Fails*," 1169.
13. One of the few works that does connect the literatures on surprise attack and terrorism is Morris, "Surprise and Terrorism."

CHAPTER 1

1. Van Riper, "Reinventing War," 32.
2. Kuhns, "Intelligence Failures," 80.

3. Betts, "Analysis, War, and Decision." A useful review of the literature on intelligence failure is given by Copeland, "Intelligence Failure Theory."

4. Lowenthal, "Burdensome Concept of Failure," 51.

5. Shulsky and Schmitt, *Silent Warfare*, 63.

6. US Congress, *Report of the Joint Committee on the Investigation of the Pearl Harbor Attack* (hereafter *Pearl Harbor Report*), 253.

7. *Pearl Harbor Report*, 253.

8. Wohlstetter, *Pearl Harbor*, 382.

9. Lieberman and Collins, "We Could Have Stopped the Terror at Fort Hood."

10. Diehl, "Obama Administration Ignored Clear Warnings on Egypt."

11. Wohlstetter, *Pearl Harbor*, 399.

12. See, e.g., Kent's best-known work, *Strategic Intelligence for American World Policy*.

13. Betts, "Analysis, War, and Decision," 88. For other traditional school analyses of intelligence failure, see Brady, "Intelligence Failures: Plus Ça Change"; Brody, "Limits of Warning"; Chan, "Intelligence of Stupidity"; and Stein, "'Intelligence' and 'Stupidity' Reconsidered."

14. Betts, *Surprise Attack*, 18.

15. Ibid., 4.

16. Handel, "Avoiding Political and Technological Surprise," 98. In addition, Mark M. Lowenthal argues that in nine out of the ten cases he examined, policymakers played a significant role in the failure; Lowenthal, "Burdensome Concept of Failure." Loch Johnson has written that the unwillingness of policymakers to accept the judgments of the intelligence community is a central problem in intelligence, and he has termed this phenomenon the "paradox of rejection." Johnson, "Analysis for a New Age," 663.

17. Betts, *Surprise Attack*.

18. Handel, "Avoiding Political and Technological Surprise," 103. Another useful discussion of psychological and other problems with intelligence is given by Michael I. Handel, "Strategic Surprise: The Politics of Intelligence and the Management of Uncertainty."

19. Heuer, *Psychology of Intelligence Analysis*.

20. Betts, "Analysis, War, and Decision," 83.

21. Knorr, "Failures in National Intelligence Estimates," 460. Robert Jervis put it slightly differently, arguing that we should expect the success rate of intelligence "to more closely approximate a batting average rather than a fielding percentage. Jervis, "What's Wrong with the Intelligence Process?" 28.

22. Jervis, "What's Wrong with the Intelligence Process?" 28.

23. Handel, "Yom Kippur War and the Inevitability of Surprise," 461. More recently, Stephen Marrin has reached a similar conclusion: "At the point, the conceptual and empirical study of surprise appears to have stalled. Though empirical studies have allowed researchers to derive the causes of failure, the conclusion that the causes are immutable prevents development of methods to counter future failures." Marrin, "Preventing Intelligence Failures," 661.

24. Examples include Betts, "How to Think about Terrorism"; Hedley, "Learning from Intelligence Failures"; Pillar, *Terrorism and US Foreign Policy*; and Heuer, "Limits of Intelligence Analysis."

25. Betts, "Fixing Intelligence," 44.

26. In a recent article Honig offers a useful description of what I call the reformist school, which he calls the revisionist school. In setting out the revisionist/reformist perspective, however, he cites several writers who I would argue are clearly in the traditionalist camp, e.g., Jervis. Honig, "New Direction for Theory-Building." See also Honig, "Surprise Attacks."

27. See, e.g., *9/11 Commission Report*, 408.

28. Wilensky, *Organizational Intelligence*, 179.

29. Cohen and Gooch, *Military Misfortunes*, 57.

30. Zegart, *Flawed by Design*, 185. For another example of this view, see Hastedt, "Organizational Foundations of Intelligence Failures."

31. For useful summaries, see Bansemer, "Intelligence Reform: A Question of Balance"; Best, "Proposals for Intelligence Reorganization, 1949–2004"; and Warner and McDonald, *US Intelligence Community Reform Studies since 1947*.

32. Zegart, "Empirical Analysis of Failed Intelligence Reforms," 35.

33. Hastedt, "Organizational Foundations of Intelligence Failures." Note, however, that the role of centralization in intelligence failure is a much-debated one, as many reformists over the years have argued that more centralized control would be better.

34. Wilensky, *Organizational Intelligence*, 42.

35. Cohen, "'No Fault' View of Intelligence," 72.

36. Zegart, "American Intelligence: Still Stupid."

37. Zegart has stated that "we had terrible strategic intelligence before 9/11." Zegart, KCET interview.

38. Kahn, "Intelligence Failure at Pearl Harbor," 147.

39. Levite, *Intelligence and Strategic Surprises*. Making a similar argument is Hybel, *Logic of Surprise*.

40. Levite, *Intelligence and Strategic Surprises*, 26.

41. Jenkins, "Prepared Statement for the 9/11 Commission."

42. "America Needs More Spies," *The Economist*. Gary Schmitt makes the same point: "The failure to forecast the specific attack that occurred on September 11, 2001, was hardly, or even principally, the fault of the US intelligence analytic community. With no CIA assets inside al-Qaeda's leadership to report on its activities and only a smattering of technical collection tidbits of overheard conversations, there were way too few 'dots' to connect." Schmitt, "Truth to Power? Rethinking Intelligence Analysis," 60.

43. For a classic discussion of the problem, see Fischhoff, "Hindsight Does Not Equal Foresight." For discussions of the dangers of hindsight bias for intelligence analysis, see Copeland, "Intelligence Failure Theory"; and Gladwell, "Connecting the Dots: The Paradoxes of Intelligence Reform."

44. *9/11 Commission Report*, 339.

45. McCarthy, "National Warning System," 15. See also Betts, "Surprise despite Warning," 557.

46. For useful overviews of the literature on strategic surprise, see Byman, "Strategic Surprise and the September 11 Attacks"; Parker and Stern, "Bolt from the Blue or Avoidable Failure?"; and Honig, "A New Direction for Theory-Building in Intelligence Studies."

47. This is an argument made by some American military officers and strategists who believe that the American military may be going too far in the pursuit of counterinsurgency capabilities and tactics and is neglecting the mission of conventional warfare. See,

e.g., Macgregor, "Remember the Blitzkrieg before It's Too Late." On Pentagon concerns about a threat from Iran, see Sanger and Shanker, "Gates Says US Lacks a Policy to Thwart Iran." On the more general threat from surprise attack today, see Wirtz, "Theory of Surprise"; and Arad, "Intelligence Management as Risk Management."

48. Daniel, "Panetta: Intelligence Community Needs to Predict Uprisings." See also Mulrine, "CIA Chief Leon Panetta: The Next Pearl Harbor Could be a Cyberattack."

49. For examples of studies comparing Pearl Harbor and 9/11, see Wirtz, "Déja Vu? Comparing Pearl Harbor and September 11"; Borch, "Comparing Pearl Harbor and '9/11'"; and Porch and Wirtz, "Surprise and Intelligence Failure." The *9/11 Commission Report* also compares the disasters (p. 339).

50. Betts, "How to Think about Terrorism," 46. For other examples of the view that the problems of 9/11 are similar to those that produced earlier failures, see Rovner and Long, "Perils of Shallow Theory"; and Pillar, "Adapting Intelligence to Changing Issues."

51. Berkowitz, "Spying."

52. McConnell, "Remarks."

53. Hayden, "Prepared Remarks at the Council on Foreign Relations."

54. Hoffman, "Intelligence and Terrorism," 219. To cite another example of this thinking in pre-9/11 literature, in 2000 the National Commission on Terrorism concluded that "no other single policy effort is more important for preventing, preempting, and responding to attacks" than intelligence. National Commission on Terrorism, *Countering the Changing Threat of International Terrorism*, 7.

55. Hayden, "Prepared Remarks at the Council on Foreign Relations."

56. Zegart, *Spying Blind*; Ranstorp, "Introduction: Mapping Terrorism Research." Other recent books examine the use of intelligence in the case of 9/11, but as part of broader reviews of American intelligence: Posner, *Preventing Surprise Attacks*; Russell, *Sharpening Strategic Intelligence*; and Betts, *Enemies of Intelligence*. For a review of the literature on the use of intelligence in counterterrorism, see Dahl, "Intelligence and Terrorism."

57. Part of the delay in the publication of *Pearl Harbor: Warning and Decision* was the result of classification review, although the book was based completely on unclassified sources. See her obituary: Sullivan, "Roberta M. Wohlstetter: Military Intelligence Expert."

58. George and Bennett, *Case Studies*, 78.

59. Byman, "Strategic Surprise and the September 11 Attacks." Parker and Stern define strategic surprise as "an abrupt revelation—often after being victimized by an attack or a sudden shift in the security environment—that one has been working with a faulty threat perception regarding an acute, imminent danger posed by a foreign threat to core national values." Parker and Stern, "Bolt from the Blue or Avoidable Failure," 303. A useful discussion of intelligence failure and strategic surprise is given by Copeland, "Intelligence Failure Theory."

60. Examples include Bracken, Bremmer, and Gordon, *Managing Strategic Surprise*; Cronin, *Impenetrable Fog of War*; and Nolan and MacEachin, *Discourse, Dissent, and Strategic Surprise*.

61. See, e.g., Taleb, *Black Swan*; and Bracken, Bremmer, and Gordon, *Managing Strategic Surprise*.

62. Schwartz, *Inevitable Surprises*, 3.

63. Clarke, *Worst Cases*, 96.

64. Bazerman and Watkins, *Predictable Surprises*. See also Bazerman and Watkins, "Airline Security, the Failure of 9/11, and Predictable Surprises." On predictable surprises, see also Irons, "Hurricane Katrina as a Predictable Surprise"; and Fukuyama, *Blindside*.

65. Taleb, "Learning to Expect the Unexpected."

66. Copeland, "Intelligence Failure Theory," 3816.

67. Richard Betts reached this conclusion decades ago, writing in his classic article on intelligence failure that "there is little evidence that either scholars or practitioners have succeeded in translating such knowledge into reforms that measurably reduce failure." Betts, "Analysis, War, and Decision," 62. For a more recent expression of this view, see Jervis, "Reports, Politics, and Intelligence Failures," 11.

68. Copeland, "Intelligence Failure Theory," 3807.

69. Cohen and Gooch, *Military Misfortunes*, 41.

70. Ibid. Another problem is that the information needed for such a study is likely to be classified. Stephen Marrin comments, "while such a study of successes might be promising, it would also be very difficult to accomplish from outside the intelligence community." Marrin, "Preventing Intelligence Failures by Learning from the Past," 661.

71. For a useful discussion of how difficult it can be to measure intelligence success, see Betts, *Enemies of Intelligence*, esp. 183–93.

72. A recent illustration of this view is given by Wilder, "An Educated Consumer Is Our Best Customer," an article that won an award from the Office of the Director of National Intelligence (DNI). The DNI has made official the view that intelligence is only useful in so far as it can support policy and decision making, in Intelligence Community Directive (ICD) 208, *Write for Maximum Utility* (cited by Jensen, "Intelligence Failures," 276).

73. For example, Jensen, "Intelligence Failures," 274–75. Marrin discusses the debate among intelligence professionals on this point in "Evaluating the Quality of Intelligence Analysis."

74. I am grateful to one of the anonymous reviewers of this book for providing comments that stimulated my thinking on this point.

75. "Bombing Suspect Provided 'Actionable Intelligence,' White House Says."

76. Kevin Derksen argues that in order for intelligence to be actionable in terms of counterterrorism, it needs to provide what he describes as the three "Ts": the type, timing, and target of an upcoming attack. Derksen, "Commentary," 255.

77. One version of this story is found in US House, *Intelligence Successes and Failures in Operations Desert Shield/Storm*, 22–23. I am grateful to an anonymous reviewer for making this point to me.

78. The quotation is attributed to Robert Bowie and is given by Haass, "Supporting US Foreign Policy in the Post–9/11 World."

79. Jones, "Intelligence and Command," 288.

80. Wirtz, "American Approach to Intelligence Studies," 34. Elsewhere Wirtz writes that "actionable intelligence was born" when Robert Gates, then the deputy director for analysis at the CIA, insisted that CIA analysts provide intelligence meeting the specific requirements of officials. Wirtz, "Intelligence–Policy Nexus," 142.

81. My definition of precision is similar to the way Mark Jensen describes specificity, as a subset of intelligence accuracy that "describes the precision or granularity of detail about a statement of fact or a judgment." Jensen, "Intelligence Failures," 271.

82. For a discussion of the differences between strategic, operational, and tactical intelligence in a military context, see Handel, "Intelligence and Military Operations," 27.

83. Wirtz describes such precise intelligence as "specific event prediction," and he notes that intelligence failures are considered inevitable because such prediction is rarely available. Wirtz, "Epilogue," 543.

84. Goodman, "America Is Safer since 9/11."

85. Pillar, "Great Expectations: Intelligence as Savior," 18. On the importance of strategic analysis against terrorism, see also Davis, "Strategic Warning."

86. My concept is different from the well-known "paradox of warning," which (as noted above) recognizes that if warnings are given of a potential attack, those warnings may inspire authorities to take countermeasures that may result in the enemy calling off the attack, leading to the impression that the warning was unnecessary.

87. Marrin, "Evaluating the Quality of Intelligence Analysis," 15.

88. In Stephen Van Evera's terminology, this is a "theory proposing" book, rather than one that tests an existing theory. Van Evera, Guide to Methods, 89.

89. On this point see, e.g., Hilsman, "Intelligence and Policy-Making in Foreign Affairs," 10; and Kuhns, "Intelligence Failures," 94–96. L. Keith Gardiner has noted that "policymakers dislike ambiguity and complexity because these qualities impede decision-making," while analysts tend to see the world as ambiguous and uncertain. Gardiner, "Dealing with Intelligence-Policy Disconnects," 345.

90. Paul Wolfowitz has made this observation, cited by Davis, "Paul Wolfowitz on Intelligence-Policy Relations." Longtime CIA official Harold P. Ford has written: "Estimates often do not rank high on the list of the types of intelligence digested by senior consumers. Time and time again, polls taken among decisionmakers over the years have yielded similar results: policymakers invariably value current intelligence reports the most, estimates less so." Ford, Estimative Intelligence, 176. Robert Jervis has written more generally that "policymakers say they need and want very good intelligence. They do indeed need it, but often do not want it." Jervis, "Politics and Psychology of Intelligence and Intelligence Reform," 1.

91. Ernest R. May makes this argument in his Strange Victory. See also Davis, "Improving CIA Analytic Performance."

92. This may explain how a decision maker such as then–national security adviser Condoleezza Rice may have received what Director of Central Intelligence George Tenet considered an urgent warning on July 10, 2001, and yet did not feel the information was enough to take action on, or even to remember. "Two Months before 9/11, an Urgent Warning to Rice."

93. On structured, focused comparisons, see George and Bennett, Case Studies, 67–72. On process tracing, see George and Bennett, Case Studies, 205–32; and Van Evera, Guide to Methods, 64–67.

CHAPTER 2

1. An earlier version of this chapter was presented at the American Political Science Association annual meeting in Seattle, September 2011.

2. Wohlstetter, Pearl Harbor.

3. Levy, "Qualitative Methods and Cross-Method Dialogue in Political Science," 201.

4. US Congress, *Report of the Joint Committee on the Investigation of the Pearl Harbor Attack*, 253. This is the one-volume final report by the Joint Committee on the Investigation of the Pearl Harbor Attack, and it is cited hereafter as *Pearl Harbor Report*. The thirty-nine volumes of hearings and documents were published separately as US Congress, *Hearings before the Joint Committee on the Investigation of the Pearl Harbor Attack* (Washington, DC: US Government Printing Office, 1946). This larger set of documents—which is much more useful for students of the attack—is cited hereafter as *Pearl Harbor Hearings*.

5. Some lists of the Pearl Harbor investigations also include a ninth study, a brief on-scene investigation by the navy secretary, Frank Knox, immediately after the attack. In addition, a later, tenth study was conducted by the undersecretary of defense, Edwin Dorn, in 1995–96 on the question of responsibility, to determine whether Admiral Kimmel and General Short, who had both been retired at their permanent two-star rank, should be posthumously advanced to the higher ranks they held at the time of the attack. A useful summary of the various Pearl Harbor investigations is given by Wirtz, "Responding to Surprise."

6. *Pearl Harbor Report*, 253.

7. Ibid., 238.

8. On the impact of Pearl Harbor on the formation of the CIA, see, e.g., Leary, *Central Intelligence Agency*, 19.

9. Wohlstetter, *Pearl Harbor*, 382.

10. Ibid., 48, 53.

11. Ibid., 229.

12. Ibid., 387.

13. For example, William F. Friedman, who was perhaps the most famous American cryptologist, argued after the war that with more imagination, intelligence analysts and government officials could have been able to "put the pieces of the jigsaw puzzle together" and figure out what the Japanese were doing. Friedman, *Special Research History (SRH) 125*, 63.

14. See, e.g., Stinnett, *Day of Deceit*. Most historians and Pearl Harbor scholars dismiss such claims. Thus, Marc Trachtenberg has termed "absurd and baseless" the charge that FDR knew of the Japanese plans and let the attack happen; see Trachtenberg, *Craft of International History*, 123. These works tend to rely on flimsy evidence or tenuous assumptions. A useful critique of the revisionist view is given by Zimmerman, "Pearl Harbor Revisionism." For a defense of the revisionists, see Villa and Wilford, "Signals Intelligence and Pearl Harbor."

15. Layton, "*And I Was There*," 217. See also Beach, *Scapegoats*.

16. This is the argument of Kirkpatrick, *Captains without Eyes*. Christopher Andrew takes a slightly different tack, arguing that the failure was largely due to FDR's preference for information from spies and other covert sources, rather than from signals intelligence, which turned out to be the key source of information. Andrew, *For the President's Eyes Only*, 3.

17. Cohen and Gooch, *Military Misfortunes*, 49.

18. Janis, *Groupthink*, 81–82.

19. Kahn, "United States Views," 500–501. Kahn also makes this argument in "Intelligence Failure at Pearl Harbor."

20. Levite, *Intelligence and Strategic Surprises*.

21. Hybel, *Logic of Surprise*, 95. See also Jacobsen, "Pearl Harbor: Who Deceived Whom?"

22. Richard Betts and James Wirtz both criticized Levite's methodology, especially his comparison of the use of intelligence at Pearl Harbor (an attack before war) and at the Battle of Midway (an attack conducted during wartime). See Betts, "Surprise, Scholasticism, and Strategy"; and Levite's response, "*Intelligence and Strategic Surprises* Revisited." See also Wirtz, "Review of Ariel Levite," In a more recent work, Betts describes Levite's argument as "thoroughly wrong"; see Betts, *Enemies of Intelligence*, 27.

23. Prange, *At Dawn We Slept*, 372. Magic was a key product of American codebreaking, and I will discuss it in the next section.

24. Ibid., 801.

25. This section focuses on intelligence concerning the Japanese naval threat. For a review of intelligence available on the Japanese Army, see Ford, "'Best-Equipped Army in Asia'?"

26. On the importance of COMINT, see Layton, "*And I Was There*," 55–56. On the preeminence of codebreaking over other sources of intelligence, see Kahn, "Pearl Harbor and the Inadequacy of Cryptanalysis," 35. *Cryptanalysis* means breaking codes and ciphers, while *cryptography* refers to encoding one's own messages. *Cryptology* is a term usually intended to include both cryptanalysis and cryptography; communications intelligence is a broader term including codebreaking, direction-finding, and traffic analysis; while signals intelligence is even broader, encompassing both communications intelligence and electronic intelligence (which deals mostly with radar). For a useful summary of these terms and more, see Kahn, *Codebreakers*, xiii–xvi.

27. Kahn, *Codebreakers*, 18.

28. Benson, *History of US Communications Intelligence during World War II*, 6–7. In addition to these three primary cryptanalysis centers, there were a number of subordinate radio intercept facilities and direction finder stations; in 1944, a classified study reported there were forty such stations. See National Security Agency, *Special Research History (SRH) 152*, 7. The picture of US radio intelligence in the Pacific in World War II is also complicated by the fact that a number of these centers changed names and even locations at different times; Cast, at Corregidor, for example, had earlier been located at Cavite Naval Base in Manila Bay; and later after the Japanese captured the Philippines, Cast was evacuated to Melbourne and became known as the Fleet Radio Unit, Melbourne, or FRUMEL, as well as by the code-name Belconnen. See also Carlson, *Joe Rochefort's War*, 107–8.

29. Elphick, *Far Eastern File*, 183.

30. Kahn, *Codebreakers*, 24.

31. Ibid., 24–25. Some Magic did reach Hawaii, occasionally relayed from other intelligence units such as Station Cast. E.g., see Layton, "*And I Was There*," 237.

32. Kahn, *Codebreakers*, 7.

33. In fact, the United States was never able to break the flag officers' code, and the Japanese themselves later abandoned it, possibly because of its slowness and complexity. Safford, *National Security Agency Special Research History (SRH) 149*, 15. One of the cryptologists at Hypo, Thomas Dyer, later said that they had felt the flag officers' code was

likely to hold more secret traffic than JN-25 but they had no luck with it: "I batted my head against a stone wall with very little to work on, I suppose, for about a year." Dyer, *Oral History of Captain Thomas H. Dyer*, 197.

34. *Pearl Harbor Hearings*, vol. 36, 61–62; Parker, *Pearl Harbor Revisited*; Layton, *"And I Was There,"* 78; Gish, "Cryptologic Analysis." Controversy has continued over how much of JN-25B had been broken before the attack on Pearl Harbor, but evidence from declassified files in the National Archives examined by intelligence scholars suggests that few JN-25B messages had been read and understood before December 7, 1941. Parker, *Pearl Harbor Revisited*; Budiansky, "Closing the Book on Pearl Harbor"; Budiansky, "Too Late for Pearl Harbor"; Jacobsen, "Foreknowledge of Pearl Harbor? No!" For a detailed argument supporting the revisionist view that at least some JN-25B traffic had been read before the attack, see Wilford, "Decoding Pearl Harbor."

35. Kahn, *Codebreakers*, 7–8. On the importance of traffic analysis in the early days of the war with Japan, see Whitlock, "Silent War against the Japanese Navy."

36. Captain Edwin T. Layton later testified that the most important sources of intelligence in the months prior to the attack on Pearl Harbor were attaché and observer reports, traffic analysis, and reports from the Office of Naval Intelligence in Washington. Layton testimony to the Hewitt inquiry, *Pearl Harbor Hearings*, 36, 112. On the intelligence produced by US naval attachés in Japan, see Mahnken, *Uncovering Ways of War*, 31–40.

37. The Office of Naval Intelligence had a section dedicated to monitoring domestic and foreign press reporting, and American military attachés in Japan routinely collected information from local newspapers. See Mahnken, "Gazing at the Sun," 426. But Kahn notes that press reporting on Japan was less useful for American leaders than press reporting on Germany. Kahn, "United States Views," 476–501.

38. For useful overviews of US intelligence sources in the Pacific War, see Spector, *Eagle against the Sun*, chap. 20; and Defalco, "Blind to the Sun."

39. Prange writes, "Defense against an attack on Pearl Harbor had been the basis of plans, maneuvers, blackouts, and reports for years." Prange, *At Dawn We Slept*, 253. In addition to the three documents described in this section, General Matthew Ridgway describes another episode in which a Pearl Harbor–type scenario was imagined before the war, but not believed. In his memoirs, Ridgway writes that in 1939, when he was stationed in San Francisco, he put on a command post exercise based on the assumption that the Pacific fleet had been neutralized or destroyed. But his scenario was loudly criticized, and he was told that such an assumption "was a possibility so improbable it did not constitute a proper basis for a maneuver." It appears that even he did not take such a threat very seriously; he notes that later when Pearl Harbor was attacked, he was stationed at the Army War Plans Division in Washington, and he and the rest of the division "were taken as much by surprise as were the officers and men of the ships that were attacked." Ridgway and Martin, *Soldier: The Memoirs of Matthew B. Ridgway*, 46–48.

40. Prange, *At Dawn We Slept*, 41.

41. Ibid., 45. The Joint Congressional Committee (*Pearl Harbor Report*, 76) cited this letter by Knox as a key warning neglected by the commanders in Hawaii.

42. "Joint Estimate Covering Joint Army and Navy Air Action in the Event of Sudden Hostile Action against Oahu or Fleet Units in the Hawaiian Area," *Pearl Harbor Hearings*, vol. 24, 349.

43. *Pearl Harbor Hearings*, vol. 14, 1024, 1026, 1031. This report is discussed by Prange, *At Dawn We Slept*, 185.

44. Wohlstetter, *Pearl Harbor*, 40–41; Kahn, *Codebreakers*, 39; Prange, *At Dawn We Slept*, 439–441; *Pearl Harbor Hearings*, vol. 10, 4680 (quoting Rochefort).

45. National Security Agency, *Special Research History (SRH) 147*, 38.

46. One of the continuing controversies about intelligence and Pearl Harbor concerns whether the Japanese fleet did in fact maintain radio silence up until December 7. Although revisionists argue there may have been radio traffic from the fleet (meaning the intercepts of those messages were covered up), most researchers have concluded that the fleet was silent. A recent review of the debate, critical of the revisionists, is given by Hanyok, "'Catching the Fox Unaware.'" Philip Jacobsen has written extensively on this question, including "Radio Silence and Radio Deception."

47. Prange, *At Dawn We Slept*, 353; Layton, *"And I Was There,"* 184–85.

48. National Security Agency, *Special Research History (SRH) 147*, 40.

49. Wohlstetter, *Pearl Harbor*, 51–52, 214–19; Prange, *At Dawn We Slept*, 360–61; *Pearl Harbor Hearings*, vol. 12, 154–55. The most extensive study of the issue is by Hanyok and Mowry, *West Wind Clear*.

50. Safford's testimony is in *Pearl Harbor Hearings*, vol. 8, 3579.

51. Wohlstetter, *Pearl Harbor*, 219. Layton discusses Safford's claim in a detailed author's note: Layton, *"And I Was There,"* 517–23. See also Prange, *Pearl Harbor: The Verdict of History*, 312–30; and Hanyok, "Pearl Harbor Warning That Never Was." A navy radio intercept operator, Ralph T. Briggs, later claimed that he intercepted the winds execute message on December 4, 1941, while on duty at the Navy Communications Station, Cheltenham, Maryland, but that the record of his report was later found to be missing from navy files. There are numerous discrepancies between the Safford and Briggs claims, however, and most who have studied the issue have concluded both men likely had mistakenly remembered events.

52. Wohlstetter, *Pearl Harbor*, 190.

53. Ibid., 49–50; Prange, *At Dawn We Slept*, 447–50.

54. Wohlstetter, *Pearl Harbor*, 221–26; Prange, *At Dawn We Slept*, 406.

55. *Pearl Harbor Hearings*, vol. 14, 1363; Wohlstetter, *Pearl Harbor*, 293.

56. *Pearl Harbor Hearings*, vol. 14, 1368; Wohlstetter, *Pearl Harbor*, 297.

57. *Pearl Harbor Hearings*, vol. 14, 1377–82; Wohlstetter, *Pearl Harbor*, 297–98. Wohlstetter does not see this memo as particularly alarming; she describes it as arguing primarily that Japan wanted to avoid a general war in the Pacific, but I take it to be much more ominous than that.

58. *Pearl Harbor Hearings*, vol. 15, 1783.

59. McCollum, *Oral History of Rear Admiral Arthur H. McCollum*, appendix.

60. On McCollum's meeting with Stark, see *Pearl Harbor Hearings*, vol. 8, 3384; and Wohlstetter, *Pearl Harbor*, 331.

61. *Pearl Harbor Hearings*, vol. 14, 1042.

62. Possible sources for the rumor have been reported to include a Japanese cook at the Peruvian embassy who had been reading a novel about an attack on Pearl Harbor, a drunken Japanese diplomat at a party, and the Peruvian minister's Japanese translator-secretary.

63. Prange offers the most complete discussion of this incident, but even his research could not determine the source with any confidence. Prange, *At Dawn We Slept*, 31–35.

64. Betts, *Surprise Attack*, 45.

65. Wohlstetter, *Pearl Harbor*, 211–13; Prange, *At Dawn We Slept*, 249.

66. The text of this message is in *Pearl Harbor Hearings*, vol. 12, 261.

67. Layton writes that if they had seen this information in Hawaii, they would have taken increased defensive precautions. He calls the failure to notify Hawaii "blind stupidity at the least, and gross neglect at best." Layton, *"And I Was There,"* 160, 167.

68. Prange, *At Dawn We Slept*, 484–85, 495–98. On the timing, Borch writes that the submarine was sunk at 6:40 a.m., but Prange reports that Outerbridge ordered the Ward to General Quarters at that time, which fits the rest of the timeline better. Borch, "Comparing Pearl Harbor and '9/11,'" 849.

69. Wohlstetter, *Pearl Harbor*, 6–12 (quoting Tyler on 12); Prange, *At Dawn We Slept*, 499–501.

70. Layton, *Oral History of Rear Admiral Edwin T. Layton*, 88. Layton also describes the story in *"And I Was There,"* 243–44.

71. *Pearl Harbor Hearings*, vol. 10, 4840.

72. Wohlstetter, *Pearl Harbor*, 43–44.

73. *Pearl Harbor Hearings*, vol. 10, 3196, 3198. This document was dated October 17, 1941.

74. Cohen and Gooch, *Military Misfortunes*, 52, citing *Papers of George Catlett Marshall*, vol. II, 413.

75. *Pearl Harbor Hearings*, vol. 14, 1044.

76. For example, in a memo to the president on November 5, Marshall and Stark said that the US Fleet was not ready for war with Japan. *Pearl Harbor Hearings*, vol. 14, 1061. See also Wohlstetter, *Pearl Harbor*, 246–47.

77. *Pearl Harbor Hearings*, vol. 14, 1083.

78. Wohlstetter, *Pearl Harbor*, 45.

79. Ibid., 44–46.

80. Coox, "Repulsing the Pearl Harbor Revisionists," 119–25.

81. Emmerson, "Principles versus Realities," 40.

82. Heinrichs, *Threshold of War*, 154.

83. Ronald Spector argues that FDR had failed to make his intentions clear, and US officials rejected license applications in the belief that was his intent; by the time he learned what had happened, it was too late to back down. Spector, *Eagle against the Sun*, 68. Scott Sagan finds it more likely that Dean Acheson, the official in charge of the interdepartmental Foreign Funds Committee that made such license decisions, made the decision on his own to block all exports, and that Roosevelt later decided not to overturn the policy either because he simply did not want to seem to be backing down, or because he did not believe Japan would actually go to war with the United States; Sagan, "From Deterrence to Coercion to War," 69–70. Waldo Heinrichs, conversely, argues the evidence suggests that FDR had indicated to acting secretary of state Sumner Welles that he wanted shipments stopped until he had discussed the issue with Churchill, and Welles passed along those instructions to Acheson. Heinrichs, "Russian Factor in Japanese–American Relations, 1941," 163–77.

84. Heinrichs, *Threshold of War*, 191.

85. Spector, *Eagle against the Sun*, 85.

86. Prange, *At Dawn We Slept*, 401.

87. Layton, *Oral History of Rear Admiral Edwin T. Layton*, 74. A slightly different version of this story is told by Prange, *At Dawn We Slept*, 471.

88. Wohlstetter, *Pearl Harbor*, 68.

89. Captain Theodore Wilkinson, the director of naval intelligence, later testified that he had expected an attack on either Siam or the Kra Peninsula of Thailand. But he added that Hawaii was possible, "in that the Japanese Navy's steaming radius and their capabilities, as the intelligence people say, and I am learning to say, and their probable capabilities indicated that they could come here. It was possible. So in fact was Seattle possible." *Pearl Harbor Hearings*, vol. 4, 1754.

90. Frederick Parker writes: "If the Japanese navy messages had enjoyed a higher priority and were assigned more analytic resources, could the US Navy have predicted the Japanese attack on Pearl Harbor from Japanese radio communications? Most emphatically yes!" Parker, "Unsolved Messages of Pearl Harbor," 312. See also Layton, *"And I Was There,"* 297–98.

91. The navy had originally planned for Pearl Harbor to begin working on JN-25 in July 1941, but instead Cavite was given the task after the British told their Singapore intelligence personnel to share what they had on JN-25 with Cavite. John Costello has described this as a "poisonous gift," because although it was well intended, the end result was that if Pearl Harbor had worked on it, with more expertise and more personnel available, they might well have been able to make more progress, and possibly could have anticipated the Japanese attack. Costello, "MacArthur, Magic, Black Jumbos and the Dogs That Didn't Bark," 235.

92. Parker, *Pearl Harbor Revisited*; Parker, "Unsolved Messages of Pearl Harbor," 295–313. A message dated October 28 from the chief of staff, First Air Fleet, referred to "near surface (?) torpedoes," while another from November 4 mentioned torpedoes to be fired "against anchored capital ships on the morning in question." The American communications intelligence system had even intercepted the message sent to the Japanese fleet on December 2 that established the attack date as December 8 (Japan time, indicated as 1208): A message intercepted on December 2, 1941, from CinC Combined Fleet read in part, "Climb NIITAKAYAMA 1208, repeat 1208." National Security Agency, *Special Research History (SRH) 406*, 63, 12, 114. See also *Pearl Harbor Hearings*, vol. 1, 185; and Prange, *At Dawn We Slept*, 445.

93. Prange, *At Dawn We Slept*, 736. Forrestal was endorsing the navy and Hewitt investigations into Pearl Harbor.

94. Parker, *Pearl Harbor Revisited*, 2.

CHAPTER 3

1. Mullen, "Why Midway Matters," 14–15; Fort, "Midway Is Our Trafalgar."

2. Some recent works have focused on operational failures on the US side, such as Falke, "What Went Wrong at Midway"; Linder, "Lost Letter of Midway"; and Kernan, *Unknown Battle of Midway*. Isom argues that mistakes were made on both sides, in "The Battle of Midway: Why the Japanese Lost," and in his *Midway Inquest*. In "Sheer Luck or Better Doctrine?" Wildenberg argues that it was better doctrine that won the battle for the Americans. Parshall and Tulley, in *Shattered Sword*, a detailed study based largely on

NOTES, CHAPTER 3 | 205

Japanese sources, argue that the Japanese defeat at Midway was the result of failings at all levels of the Japanese Navy.

3. An exception is the very useful new study by Carlson, *Joe Rochefort's War*. Two articles that do discuss the use of intelligence are Allen, "Midway: The Story That Never Ends," and Studeman, "Pacific Faces Crisis in Intel Analysis."

4. Lord, *Incredible Victory*; Prange, *Miracle at Midway*.

5. Potter and Nimitz, *Great Sea War*, 245, cited by Kahn, *Codebreakers*, 573.

6. Betts, "Surprise, Scholasticism, and Strategy," 332.

7. Levite, *Intelligence and Strategic Surprises*. Briefer comparisons between Pearl Harbor and Midway include those by Wirtz, "Theory of Surprise," 104–5; and Bracken, "How to Build a Warning System," 33–42.

8. Hulnick, *Keeping Us Safe*, 4.

9. Betts, "Surprise, Scholasticism, and Strategy," 336. Honig also sees the comparison of Pearl Harbor and Midway as inappropriate: "Surprise Attacks—Are They Inevitable?" 74.

10. Betts, "Surprise, Scholasticism, and Strategy," 338.

11. Ibid., 332.

12. Levite, "*Intelligence and Strategic Surprises* Revisited," 348.

13. Ibid., 29–33, 129.

14. Bar-Joseph, "Methodological Magic."

15. Van Evera, *Guide to Methods*, 57.

16. On case selection, see ibid., 84–87.

17. The starkest contrast in leadership is the change of senior officials in Hawaii from Admiral Kimmel and General Short before December 7, to Admiral Nimitz in the position of overall command prior to the Battle of Midway. But another difference in terms of the decision makers involved is that FDR and other senior officials in Washington were much less involved in the decision making for Midway than they had been concerning American policy in the Pacific before Pearl Harbor.

18. Prange, *Miracle at Midway*, 16, 21–24; Fuchida and Okumiya, *Midway: The Battle That Doomed Japan*, 60–61.

19. Fuchida and Okumiya, *Midway*, 71–72; Morison, *Coral Sea, Midway and Submarine Actions*, 75.

20. Prange, *Miracle at Midway*, 30–39; Morison, *Coral Sea, Midway and Submarine Actions*, 75–77.

21. Wirtz, "Responding to Surprise," 63.

22. See, e.g., US Navy, *Naval Doctrine Publication 2*, 21.

23. Studeman, "Pacific Faces Crisis in Intel Analysis." See also Elder, "Intelligence in War: It Can Be Decisive."

24. Kahn, *Codebreakers*, 573.

25. CinCPac message, June 28, 1942, cited by Connorton, *National Security Agency Special Research History (SRH) 012*, 323.

26. Prange, *Miracle at Midway*, 393. Prange agreed with Spruance, writing, "Of course, all of Hypo's information would have been useless had Nimitz not accepted Rochefort's estimate of the situation and acted upon it" (p. 384). In addition, Spruance later wrote: "Our success at the Battle of Midway was based primarily on the excellent intelligence which enabled Admiral Nimitz to exercise to the full his talent for bold, courageous and wise leadership." Foreword to Fuchida and Okumiya, *Midway*, vi.

27. Morison, *Coral Sea, Midway and Submarine Actions*, 80–81.

28. Keegan, *Intelligence in War*, 218.

29. Hanson, *Carnage and Culture*, 368.

30. Fuchida and Okumiya, *Midway*, 247. See also Morison, *Coral Sea, Midway and Submarine Actions*, 4. Fuchida was a senior aviator who led the air assault on Pearl Harbor and served aboard the aircraft carrier *Akagi*, flagship of the Nagumo force, during the Battle of Midway. Okumiya served as part of the Aleutians force during the Battle of Midway.

31. Fuchida and Okumiya, *Midway*, 247.

32. Parshall and Tully, *Shattered Sword*, 415.

33. Handel, "Intelligence and Military Operations," 38.

34. Prados, *Combined Fleet Decoded*, 317; Lord, *Incredible Victory*, 21. On Stimson, see Larew, "December 7, 1941: The Day No One Bombed Panama," 291.

35. Prange, *Miracle at Midway*, 32; Fuchida and Okumiya, *Midway*, 88. See also Horn, *Second Attack on Pearl Harbor*, 72–103; and Morison, *Coral Sea, Midway and Submarine Actions*, 69–70. This bombing took place in the early morning hours of March 4; some authors describe it as occurring on March 5, but this is probably because March 4 Hawaii time was March 5 in Japan.

36. Fuchida and Okumiya, *Midway*, 88. Morison writes: "Nimitz believed that they portended an offensive toward Hawaii, and he was right." Morison, *Coral Sea, Midway and Submarine Actions*, 70.

37. Horn, *Second Attack on Pearl Harbor*, 136–41; Parshall and Tully, *Shattered Sword*, 50. Carlson describes this shoot-down as taking place on the morning of March 11; *Joe Rochefort's War*, 251–52.

38. Parker, *Priceless Advantage*, 42; Prange, *Miracle at Midway*, 122–23; Parshall and Tully, *Shattered Sword*, 99.

39. Rochefort, *Oral History of Captain Joseph J. Rochefort*, 177. See also Layton, *"And I Was There,"* 383. Carlson discusses this request from King in *Joe Rochefort's War*, 284–89.

40. Rochefort, *Oral History of Captain Joseph J. Rochefort*, 173–75. This prediction is also described by Potter in "Admiral Nimitz and the Battle of Midway," 61.

41. Parker, *Priceless Advantage*.

42. Ibid. See also Carlson, *Joe Rochefort's War*, 226–30.

43. Kahn, *Codebreakers*, 563; Rochefort, *Oral History of Captain Joseph J. Rochefort*, 120.

44. Parker, "How OP-20-G Got Rid of Joe Rochefort," 219.

45. This change was evidently ordered by Captain Laurence Safford, head of the Navy's Communications Security Unit in Washington; see his memo in *Pearl Harbor Hearings*, vol. 18, 3336. See also Safford, *National Security Agency Special Research History (SRH) 149*, 15. (In this document, which was released in full by NSA in 2009, Safford refers to JN-25 as the "Numbers System.") Also see Rochefort, *Oral History of Captain Joseph J. Rochefort*, 120; Frederick D. Parker, *Pearl Harbor Revisited*, 49; and Kahn, *Codebreakers*, 562. For background on JN-25, see Budiansky, "Closing the Book on Pearl Harbor." Note that Winton says Hypo started working on JN-25 on December 17, but this appears to be incorrect; *Ultra in the Pacific*, 10.

46. Biard, "Breaking of Japanese Naval Codes," 152.

47. Rochefort, *Oral History of Captain Joseph J. Rochefort*, 143.

48. Parker, *Priceless Advantage*, 20; Layton, *"And I Was There,"* 376.

49. Elder, "Intelligence in War: It Can Be Decisive"; Porch and Wirtz, "Battle of Midway." Van Der Rhoer, who served in OP-20-G, also credits that organization without noting the contribution of Hypo; *Deadly Magic*.

50. Schorreck, *National Security Agency Special Research History (SRH) 23*. The intercepted message is also reproduced by Connorton, *National Security Agency Special Research History (SRH) 012*, 211.

51. Connorton, *National Security Agency Special Research History (SRH) 012*, 25–26.

52. Schorreck, *National Security Agency Special Research History (SRH) 230*, 7. For a general overview of the Battle of the Coral Sea and the role played by intelligence, see Spector, *Eagle against the Sun*, 156–63. For the largely contrary view of John Lundstrom, who argues that tactical intelligence support was poor during the Battle of the Coral Sea, see Lundstrom, *Black Shoe Carrier Admiral*, 157, and also his "A Failure of Radio Intelligence."

53. Connorton, *National Security Agency Special Research History (SRH) 012*, 262–63.

54. Layton, *"And I Was There,"* 376–77.

55. Whitlock, *Silent War against the Japanese Navy*, 49–50. See also Parker, *Priceless Advantage*, 43.

56. Schorreck, *National Security Agency Special Research History (SRH) 230*, 7; Connorton, *National Security Agency Special Research History (SRH) 012*, 263–64.

57. Schorreck, *National Security Agency Special Research History (SRH) 230*, 6. Also reprinted by Connorton, *National Security Agency Special Research History (SRH) 012*, 273.

58. Layton, *"And I Was There,"* 411.

59. Connorton, *National Security Agency Special Research History (SRH) 012*, 277; National Security Agency, *SRMN-005*, 233. The dash indicates a portion of the message that had not been recovered (decrypted).

60. Rochefort, *Oral History of Captain Joseph J. Rochefort*, 196.

61. Schorreck, *National Security Agency Special Research History (SRH) 230*, 7. On the change from AF to MI, see also National Security Agency, *SRMN-005*.

62. Schorreck, *National Security Agency Special Research History (SRH) 230*, 7.

63. Parker, *Priceless Advantage*, 50.

64. The story of the ruse is told in most accounts of Midway. Most useful are Prange, *Miracle at Midway*, 45–46; and Layton, *"And I Was There,"* 421–22. Less useful is the short piece by Weadon, *Battle of Midway: AF Is Short of Water*.

65. Rochefort, *Oral History of Captain Joseph J. Rochefort*, 198. See also Layton, *"And I Was There,"* 421.

66. Rochefort, *Oral History of Captain Joseph J. Rochefort*, 203, 211–12.

67. Kahn, *Codebreakers*, 569. Also crediting Rochefort for the idea are Prange, *Miracle at Midway*, 46; and Lord, *Incredible Victory*, 23.

68. Holmes, *Double-Edged Secrets*, 90. Layton confirms Holmes's role in the ruse, as does Donald M. Showers: Layton, *"And I Was There,"* 421; and *At the Interface: The WWII Recollections of Donald M. Showers*.

69. Schorreck, *National Security Agency Special Research History (SRH) 230*.

70. Lord, Prange, and Layton all indicate the message to Midway was sent around May 10, with the Japanese message sent in response about May 12.

71. Layton, *"And I Was There,"* 421. This cable is given by National Security Agency, *SRMN-005*, 235. This timing of the episode is supported by several authorities including Carlson, *Joe Rochefort's War*, and Parker, *Priceless Advantage*.

72. Dyer, *Oral History of Captain Thomas H. Dyer*, 242. As a result of the ruse, the Japanese added two fresh water tankers to the invasion fleet; see *At the Interface: The WWII Recollections of Donald M. Showers*.

73. Rochefort, *Oral History of Captain Joseph J. Rochefort*, 216.

74. Ibid.

75. Layton, *"And I Was There,"* 429. The precise timing of this intelligence break-through and Rochefort's appearance at Nimitz's staff meeting is not completely clear. Prange, Potter, and Lord suggest the meeting was on the morning of May 25, while Layton, Prados, and Budiansky describe it as occurring on the 27th. Schorreck describes the critical analysis as taking place on the 25th, beginning when a cryptanalyst in Melbourne pulled a message at random from a box of garbled traffic. He noted the message contained a code group for "Midway" and "attack," but he could make out nothing else. He immediately notified Hawaii and Washington, and after a brief period of concerted effort by all, the entire message was able to be understood. Schorreck, *National Security Agency Special Research History (SRH) 230*, 7–8. Symonds suggests that it may not have been any single Japanese message, but rather a series of decrypted messages, that provided the breakthrough; Symonds, *Battle of Midway*, 387–88.

76. Potter, *Nimitz*, 82–83.

77. On the operational plan, Kahn, *Codebreakers*, 570. On the changes to the Japanese codes, see Schorreck, *National Security Agency Special Research History (SRH) 230*; and Parker, *Priceless Advantage*, 54.

78. Layton, *Oral History of Rear Admiral Edwin T. Layton*, 30. Of note, in this account Layton says he gave the time as 0600 Midway time; in his book he says it would be 0700 local time; *"And I Was There,"* 430.

79. Layton, *Oral History*, 30; Layton, *"And I Was There,"* 438. See also the description of this incident in Prados, *Combined Fleet Decoded*, 324.

80. At least one account of this conversation suggests wrongly that Nimitz was talking to Rochefort, rather than Layton: Winton, *Ultra in the Pacific*, 2.

81. Layton, *"And I Was There,"* 429–30.

82. Potter does not make the timing clear, but appears to place it in late May. Potter, *Nimitz*, 83; Potter, "Admiral Nimitz and the Battle of Midway," 64. Studeman dates it as May 30.

83. Stephen Budiansky has pointed out that Prange states in a note that when he interviewed Layton in 1964, Layton said the encounter had taken place on the morning of June 4. Prange, however, noted that Potter, who had also interviewed Layton for his biography of Nimitz, placed it in late May, which Prange argued "seems more logical." But Budiansky credits John Lundstrom for pointing out to him that right up until June 3, messages from CinCPac (meaning Nimitz) continued to point to June 3 as the date of the expected attack—which is unlikely if Nimitz had been told by Layton to expect it on June 4. Although the initial contact and fighting between the two sides had taken place on June 3, the Japanese carriers were first located on June 4. Budiansky, *Battle of Wits*, 365n18; also see Lundstrom, *Black Shoe Carrier Admiral*, 240. See Prange, *Miracle at Midway*, 408n16. Budiansky attributes the apparent mistake about the date in Layton's

book to Layton's posthumous coauthors. Carlson, in his recent assessment of the evidence in *Joe Rochefort's War*, writes that although no specific date can be confirmed, he believes June 3 is most likely correct (523n25). It seems likely that we will never know for certain when this prediction—perhaps the most famous in American naval intelligence history—was made.

84. Levite, *Intelligence and Strategic Surprises*, 134.

85. Schorreck, *National Security Agency Special Research History (SRH) 230*, 4.

86. Rochefort, *Oral History of Captain Joseph J. Rochefort*, 205. Pete Azzole has written a series of articles based on Rochefort's oral history for *Cryptolog*, a journal of the US Naval Cryptologic Veterans Association, and these articles are available at www.usncva .org/clog/index.html. See also Layton, *"And I Was There,"* 373.

87. Potter, *Nimitz*, 21.

88. Layton, *Oral History of Rear Admiral Edwin T. Layton*, 79.

89. Layton, *"And I Was There,"* 356–57.

90. Prange, *Miracle at Midway*, 20.

91. Potter, *Nimitz*, 64.

92. Prange, *Miracle at Midway*, 37.

93. Heinl, *Marines at Midway*, 22.

94. Prange, *Miracle at Midway*, 29.

95. Potter, *Nimitz*, 78.

96. Layton, *"And I Was There,"* 409. It should be noted that Heinl cites information provided by a marine officer who had been on Midway at the time that does strongly indicate Nimitz was acting on advance intelligence. Lieutenant Colonel Robert C. McGlashan stated in a 1947 questionnaire from the Marine Corps Historical Section that he had seen a confidential letter from Nimitz to the navy and marine commanders on Midway after he returned to Hawaii from his inspection visit. The letter listed the enemy units that would soon be approaching Midway, and predicted D-Day would be about May 28. Then on May 25, Nimitz advised the defenders that the estimated attack date had been moved to the period of June 3–5. If that information could be confirmed, it would add significant details to the story of Midway and Nimitz's use of intelligence. See Heinl, *Marines at Midway*, 23.

97. Prange, *Miracle at Midway*, 37. Lord writes that at this time, Nimitz was "half convinced, but no more" that Midway was to be the next target. Lord, *Incredible Victory*, 22.

98. Layton, *Oral History of Rear Admiral Edwin T. Layton*, 122–23.

99. Lord, *Incredible Victory*, 22–23.

100. Lewin, *American Magic*, 91.

101. Layton, *"And I Was There,"* 405. Lewin calls the Battle of the Coral Sea a turning point for intelligence; Lewin, *American Magic*, 95–96.

102. Potter, *Nimitz*, 79; Lord, *Incredible Victory*, 24–25. Lord writes that Nimitz received Emmons's letter on May 16 or 17.

103. Layton, *"And I Was There,"* 413.

104. Lord, *Incredible Victory*, 25.

105. Parker, *Priceless Advantage*, 48.

106. Biard, "Breaking of Japanese Naval Codes," 156–57.

107. *At the Interface: The WWII Recollections of Donald M. Showers*. Showers later rose to the rank of rear admiral.

108. Parker, *Priceless Advantage*, 46.

109. Prados, *Combined Fleet Decoded*, 318.

110. Parker, *Priceless Advantage*, 47, 50. OP-20-G and the war plans staff could not themselves agree; they were engaged in a series of bitter disputes, including over Japanese intentions.

111. Andrew, *For the President's Eyes Only*, 126.

112. Kahn, "Roosevelt, Magic, and Ultra," 123–53.

113. Prange, *Miracle at Midway*, 155–59; Levite, *Intelligence and Strategic Surprises*, 121–22.

114. Layton, *Oral History of Rear Admiral Edwin T. Layton*, 48.

CHAPTER 4

1. Of the nine cases reviewed in this chapter, seven are examined by either Betts or Posner, or both, in their books on surprise attack. In *Surprise Attack*, Betts discusses the North Korean invasion of June 1950, the Chinese intervention later that year, the Israeli attack into Egypt in 1956, the 1967 Six-Day War, the 1968 invasion of Czechoslovakia, and the 1973 October War. In *Preventing Surprise Attacks*, Posner examines the Tet Offensive of 1968 and the 1973 October War. To these seven cases I have added two more recent prominent cases of surprise attack: the 1979 Soviet invasion of Afghanistan and the 1990 Iraqi invasion of Kuwait.

2. Johnson, "American Cryptology," 31. On the lack of intelligence focus at the start of the war, see also Finnegan, "Evolution of US Army HUMINT."

3. Betts, *Surprise Attack*, 53.

4. Rose, "Two Strategic Intelligence Mistakes."

5. Quoted by Aid, *Secret Sentry*, 25. See also Johnson, "American Cryptology"; and Johnson, *American Cryptology during the Cold War, 1945–1989, Book I.*

6. Laurie, "Korean War," 9.

7. Although most intelligence experts and historians describe the North Korean invasion as a failure of American intelligence, Thomas J. Patton defends the work done by the CIA at the time, arguing that analysts did well under the circumstances, and actually provided more warning in daily, low-level reports, than many later assessments recognize. See Patton, "Personal Perspective."

8. Mobley, "North Korea's Surprise Attack."

9. This is the view of one of the CIA's best-known writers on warning, Cynthia M. Grabo, in "Strategic Warning."

10. Mobley, "North Korea's Surprise Attack," 510.

11. Vanderpool, "COMINT," 1. As an example of the type of information gathered from communications intercepts, PRC civil communications in November revealed that an organization in Shanghai was sending a total of 30,000 maps of Korea to cities on the Sino-Korean border; the US Army G-2 estimated that this would be enough maps for ten divisions.

12. Rose, "Two Strategic Intelligence Mistakes."

13. Ibid.

14. National Intelligence Estimate 2/1, "Chinese Communist Intervention."

15. Grabo, "Strategic Warning," 86–87.

16. Betts, *Surprise Attack*, 56.

17. Bar-Joseph and Levy, "Conscious Action," 471–72; Budiansky, "What's the Use of Cryptologic History?" 772–73. For an interesting examination of why some officials were more receptive toward warning than others, see Ovodenko, "(Mis)interpreting Threats."

18. Although Operation Kadesh was the Israeli operation against the Sinai, the 1956 war also included a second attack against Egypt, a British-French operation to recapture the Suez Canal on October 31, known as Operation Musketeer. On the Israeli attack, see, e.g., Betts, *Surprise Attack*, 63–65; and Calhoun, "Musketeer's Cloak."

19. Director of Central Intelligence, Special National Intelligence Estimate Number 30-3-56, "Nasser and the Middle East Situation," iv–v.

20. US Department of State, *Foreign Relations of the United States, 1955–1957, Suez Crisis, July 26–December 31, 1956*, 787.

21. Ibid., 382.

22. This report was no. 325A, available in ibid., 798–99.

23. NIC #TS-6-372, ibid., 799.

24. The CIA report is quoted by Aid, *Secret Sentry*, 50.

25. Ibid.

26. Quoted by Calhoun, "Musketeer's Cloak," 51.

27. Office of the Director of National Intelligence, *Vision 2015*, 8.

28. Central Intelligence Agency, "CIA Statement on 'Legacy of Ashes.'" The CIA statement was made in response to a critical book on the CIA by Tim Weiner.

29. Kerr, "Track Record," 47.

30. Of note, Paul Pillar points out that even the successful predictions by US intelligence did not stop the war from happening or prevent it from causing long-lasting damage to the Middle East. Pillar, "Predictive Intelligence." For a contrarian view that the CIA's success was more a matter of luck than analytical skill, see Ginor and Remez, "Too Little, Too Late."

31. Robarge, "Getting It Right," 2.

32. Ibid., 4. See also Freshwater, "Policy and Intelligence," 4–5.

33. Freshwater, "Policy and Intelligence," 6; Robarge, "Getting It Right," 5. See also Hathaway and Smith, *Richard Helms*, 145.

34. The quotation is from Freshwater, "Policy and Intelligence," 7. The NSA information is from Aid, *Secret Sentry*, 136.

35. In fact, it was the other way around; as a result of the CIA's assessments in this case, Helms became a regular at Johnson's Tuesday lunches, and the intelligence–policy relationship became considerably closer.

36. Freshwater—the pen name for a CIA author who had been one of the analysts in this case—makes this point, arguing that the analytical success was a result of the previously established group of analysts who had already been able to reach judgments about the situation, which could then be quickly passed to decision makers.

37. Wirtz, *Tet Offensive*.

38. Ibid., 55–71.

39. Ibid., 253.

40. Ibid., 222.

41. Ford, *CIA*.

42. Director of Central Intelligence, "Intelligence Warning," 4.

43. Ovodenko, "Visions."

44. Betts, *Surprise Attack*, 83–84.

45. Johnson, *United States Cryptologic History, American Cryptology during the Cold War, 1945–1989, Book II*, 460. On the strategic warning available, see also MacEachin, "Analysis," 123.

46. Mark Kramer, director of the Cold War Studies Project at Harvard, quoted by Jim Vertuno, "CIA Monitored Soviet Forces before 'Prague Spring,'" Associated Press, April 16, 2010.

47. Memorandum for the Director of Central Intelligence, "Post Mortem on Czech Crisis."

48. Central Intelligence Agency Office of National Estimates, Memorandum for the Director, "The Czechoslovak Crisis," 7.

49. Central Intelligence Agency Intelligence Memorandum, "Military Developments in the Soviet-Czech Confrontation," 2.

50. Central Intelligence Agency, "The CIA and Strategic Warning: The 1968 Soviet-Led Invasion of Czechoslovakia," 7. This document cites Richelson, *Wizards of Langley*, for this information. The document is not dated and no author is identified, but the author is apparently Donald P. Steury, given that a slightly different, modified version of this article is available as a chapter in the book edited by Bischof, Karner, and Ruggenthaler, *Prague Spring*.

51. Aid, *Secret Sentry*, 144.

52. Central Intelligence Agency, "The CIA and Strategic Warning: The 1968 Soviet-Led Invasion of Czechoslovakia," 8.

53. At least one other senior intelligence official appears to have made the correct assessment and passed the warning on to a top decision maker: David McManis, an NSA officer who was deputy chief of the Situation Room at the White House, concluded on August 19 that an invasion appeared imminent, and passed his warning on to the national security adviser, Walt Rostow. Johnson, *United States Cryptologic History, Book II*, 458.

54. "Post-Mortem on Czech Crisis," 4.

55. Grabo, "Strategic Warning."

56. Betts, *Surprise Attack*, 78.

57. A recent book by the former head of the Research Branch of Israeli Military Intelligence notes that throughout the period leading up to the war, American intelligence assessments were even more positive than Israel's in believing that Egypt had no viable military option and thus was not likely to start a war. See Shalev, *Israel's Intelligence Assessment*.

58. Allen, "DHS Under Secretary for Intelligence and Analysis Charles E. Allen Address."

59. Ford, *Estimative Intelligence*, 245. Annex II of this book is a very useful study of the failure by US intelligence that was originally written for the US Defense Intelligence School in 1979.

60. Director of Central Intelligence, "Performance of the Intelligence Community," i.

61. Ibid., 4.

62. Mary McCarthy writes that "the failure to warn of the Arab attack on Israel in October 1973 is one of the clearest examples of an intelligence disaster resulting from the

assumption that foreign leaders will temper their intentions with a rational analysis of capabilities." McCarthy, "National Warning System," 12.

63. "Transcript of Secretary Kissinger's Staff Meeting," 22.

64. Director of Central Intelligence, "Soviet Invasion," 15; MacEachin, *Predicting the Soviet Invasion*, 15–20.

65. Director of Central Intelligence, "Soviet Invasion," 35.

66. MacEachin, *Predicting the Soviet Invasion*, 33. On NSA's predictions, see also Aid, *Secret Sentry*, 168–69.

67. On President Carter's surprise, see Georgetown University, "Soviet Invasion," 7.

68. Director of Central Intelligence, "Soviet Invasion," 38. See also MacEachin, who notes that CIA officers later joked that their analysts got it right, while the Soviets got it wrong; MacEachin, *Predicting the Soviet Invasion*, 46.

69. Armstrong et al., "Hazards," 254. See also a study by the Georgetown University Institute for the Study of Diplomacy, "Soviet Invasion."

70. Director of Central Intelligence, "Soviet Invasion," 4.

71. Johnson, *United States Cryptologic History, Book III*, 254. John Diamond offers a more balanced discussion of whether this case marks an intelligence failure or not, noting that even within the intelligence community there has been uncertainty about how to categorize it; Diamond, *CIA*, 71–72.

72. "CIA Statement on 'Legacy of Ashes.'"

73. For background see, e.g., Karabell and Zelikow, "Iraq, 1988–1990." Also useful is Diamond, *CIA*, 107–40.

74. Allen, "Warning," 38; US Central Command, *Operation Desert Shield*, 2.

75. Allen, "Warning," 40.

76. Ibid., 41–42.

77. Ibid., 43.

78. Russell, "CIA's Strategic Intelligence," 194.

79. Shellum, *Chronology*, 7.

80. Russell, "CIA's Strategic Intelligence," 194. Allen notes that during an intelligence community teleconference on July 31, the view of most analysts was that no major military action was likely; Allen, "Warning," 41.

81. Karabell and Zelikow, "Iraq," 199.

82. Russell, "CIA's Strategic Intelligence," 196.

83. Allen, "Intelligence," 5.

84. McCarthy, "National Warning System," 7.

85. Quoted by McManis, "Technology," 20.

86. Chan, "Intelligence," 179.

CHAPTER 5

1. The principal source of information for this chapter is the transcript and other material resulting from the 2001 federal trial conducted in US District Court in New York City, *United States v. Bin Laden*, in which four defendants were convicted on a variety of charges related to the embassy bombings. The official investigation into the bombings is the Crowe Commission Report, formally known as *Report of the Accountability Review Boards on the Embassy Bombings in Nairobi and Dar Es Salaam on August 7, 1998*. The

9/11 Commission Report is another key source concerning intelligence reporting on the embassy attacks. Especially useful secondary sources are Nolan and MacEachin, *Discourse, Dissent, and Strategic Surprise*; Miller, Stone, and Mitchell, *The Cell*; and Ridgway Center, "Anatomy of a Terrorist Attack."

2. *9/11 Commission Report*, 61, 68. See also trial testimony of al-Fadl, February 6, 2001, 290; *United States v. Ali Mohamed* Plea Agreement, S(7) 98 Cr. 1023 (LBS) (SDNY 2000), 30; Gunaratna, *Inside Al-Qaeda*, 195. For arguments supporting the existence of a link between Iran and the embassy bombings, see the ruling by federal judge John D. Bates in the case of *James Owens et al. v. Republic of Sudan et al.*, issued November 28, 2011.

3. *9/11 Commission Report*, 67.

4. Ibid., 60. The US federal indictment of bin Laden in 1998 included charges of assisting in anti–United States efforts in Somalia; see *United States v. bin Laden*, S(9) 98 Cr. 1023, 16–17.

5. For background on Mohamed, see Weiser and Risen, "The Masking of a Militant"; Waldman, "Lapses in Handling Sergeant"; Emerson, *American Jihad*, 55–60.

6. Quinn-Judge and Sennott, "Figure Cited in Terrorism Case Said to Enter US with CIA Help." CIA officials later denied they had helped him; Risen, "CIA Said to Reject Bomb Suspect's Bid to Be Spy." Other reports indicate Mohamed arrived in the United States despite the efforts of CIA officials to put him on the State Department watch list; see Weiser and Risen, "Masking of a Militant."

7. Wright, *Looming Tower*, 180–81.

8. Weiser and Risen, "Masking of a Militant."

9. I discuss Nosair in chapter 6.

10. Emerson, *American Jihad*, 57; Weiser and Risen, "Masking of a Militant."

11. On the San Jose interview, see Wright, *Looming Tower*, 181–82. Wright argues that this was a very big missed opportunity, because although an FBI agent filed a report about his statements, nothing was done to try to enlist him as a double agent.

12. An al-Qaeda presence appears to have been first established in Nairobi by a man name Khalid al Fawwaz, who was sent there some time in 1993 to establish businesses and acquire residences. Indictment S(10), 18.

13. *9/11 Commission Report*, 68; *United States v. Ali Mohamed* Plea Agreement; Wright, *Looming Tower*, 198; Bergen, *Holy War, Inc.*, 135. On Kherchtou, who later became a US government informant, see trial testimony February 21, 2001; Feuer, "Witness in Bombing Case Describes Scouting Mission"; Benjamin and Simon, *Age of Sacred Terror*, 124–27.

14. *United States v. Ali Mohamed* Plea Agreement, 27; Wright, *Looming Tower*, 198.

15. Wright, *Looming Tower*, 198; *9/11 Commission Report*, 68.

16. Bin Laden interview by Al-Jazeera Television, June 1999, cited by Bergen, *Holy War, Inc.*, 89.

17. *United States v. Ali Mohamed* Plea Agreement.

18. This cell member was Owhali; testimony by FBI special agent Stephen Gaudin, March 7, 2001, 2020–21.

19. Wright, *Looming Tower*, 272.

20. He is also known as Mohamed Saddiq Howaida.

21. McKinley, "In-Laws Say Bomb Suspect Led Quiet Life"; trial testimony of FBI agent Anticev, February 28, 2001, 1649; indictment S(10), 18. Also see the website for the

PBS *Frontline* television episode "Hunting Bin Laden," which provides a translation of the original interrogation notes made by Pakistani officials after questioning Odeh; www .pbs.org/wgbh/pages/frontline/shows/binladen/bombings/interrogation.html.

22. Watson et al., "Our Target Was Terror"; Hamm, *Terrorism as Crime*, 55.

23. Indictment S(10), 19. See also Shultz and Beitler, "Tactical Deception and Strategic Surprise."

24. *9/11 Commission Report*, 63.

25. On Banshiri's death, see ibid., 65–69. Also see the trial testimony of Ashif Juma, who was with Banshiri when he died, February 14, 2001, transcript, 626–27; and the testimony of Kherchtou, February 22, 2001, 1264–67; Bergen, *Holy War, Inc.*, 109; and indictment S(9), 22, also found in indictment S(10), on 24.

26. *9/11 Commission Report*, 68; Hugh Davies, "Saudis Detain Member of anti-American Terror Group," *Daily Telegraph*, August 2, 1997. Miller and Stone write that Tayyib had agreed to share secrets with the Saudis in exchange for asylum, but only on the condition that none of his information would be passed to the Americans; the Saudis, they report, kept their end of the bargain. Miller, Stone, and Mitchell, *Cell*, 200. Tayyib was apparently arrested some time before August; a classified CIA report dated May 7, 1997, reported that Tayyib was at that time "under arrest in an unspecified country." A portion of this report is reprinted in Gertz, *Breakdown*, 178.

27. Miller, Stone, and Mitchell, *Cell*, 200. The concern felt among the cell members is discussed in trial transcript closing arguments, May 1, 5340–45.

28. *9/11 Commission Report*, 68–69. The fax was presented into evidence as government exhibit 300A-T on May 1, transcript, beginning on 5347; the quotation about "hit the Americans in Somalia" is on 5349. The information gained from the search of el Hage's house is discussed later in this chapter.

29. *9/11 Commission Report*, 69. John Miller describes his May 1998 interview in "Greetings, America. My Name Is Osama Bin Laden." PBS *Frontline*, www.pbs.org/wgbh/ pages/frontline/shows/binladen/who/miller.html.

30. Hamm, *Terrorism as Crime*, 65.

31. *United States v. Bin Laden* Indictment, S(10) 98 Cr. 1023 (LBS) (SDNY 2001), 36. According to unconfirmed reports, the explosives used in the bombings were brought to Kenya by ship. See Mintz, "15 Freighters Believed to Be Linked to Al-Qaeda"; and John Mintz, "On the Waterfront," CBSNews.com, August 3, 2003.

32. Trial testimony of FBI agent Gaudin, March 7, 2001, 2007. See also Hamm, *Terrorism as Crime*, 110.

33. On Saleh, see trial testimony by FBI agent Anticev, February 28, 2001, 1652–53; Schmidt and Farah, "Al-Qaeda's New Leaders"; and Hamm, *Terrorism as Crime*, 59–60.

34. Trial testimony March 7, 2001; *9/11 Commission Report*, 69; Vick, "Assault on a US Embassy"; Bergen, *Holy War, Inc.*, 110–11. Some sources state that Owhali arrived in Nairobi on August 1, but his own statements, as discussed in the trial testimony, convincingly indicate that it was August 2.

35. Post, "New Face of Terrorism," 456. In this article Post describes interviewing an unnamed suspect in the Tanzania bombing, and from the description of the suspect it is clearly KK Mohamed; in addition, Post later testified in 2001 for Mohamed's defense. See Weiser, "Defense Psychiatrist Tells Jury of Embassy Bomber's Remorse." See also Bergen, *Holy War, Inc.*, 113–14; and Hamm, *Terrorism as Crime*, 61.

36. Trial testimony February 28, March 7, and March 19, 2001; Bergen, *Holy War, Inc.*, 115.

37. Trial testimony May 1, 2001, 5376; April 4, 2001, 3894; see also Bergen, *Holy War, Inc.*, 108. These code names were used in al-Qaeda's claims of responsibility after the bombings, but it is not clear whether they were used in internal planning prior to the attacks.

38. For the attack itself, see the Crowe Commission Report. Ambassador Bushnell testified about her experience that day on March 1, 2001, 1858–63. Another detailed description of the attack is included in the US government's closing argument during the trial, May 2, 2001, 5440–47.

39. John Lange, the deputy chief of mission in Dar es Salaam, was in charge of the embassy because there had been no ambassador assigned. He testified about the attack on March 13, 2001, 2501; he described the bombing as taking place at 10:39 a.m.

40. "The War on Terrorism: Remembering the Losses of KENBOM/TANBOM," Federal Bureau of Investigation press release August 6, 2003, www.fbi.gov/page2/aug03/kenbom080603.htm.

41. Useful information on the FBI investigation is given by Kaplan, "On Terrorism's Trail."

42. *9/11 Commission Report*, 115–16.

43. Aid, "All Glory Is Fleeting," 87. See also Vistica and Klaidman, "Tracking Terror."

44. *9/11 Commission Report*, 69–70.

45. Lamberth later stated that the information produced by these wiretaps proved very useful in prosecuting the case in the 2001 trial. Pincus, "Judge Discusses Details."

46. Kaplan, "On Terrorism's Trail." On the Nissan identification, see also trial testimony March 13, 2001, 2554.

47. Trial testimony March 12, 2001, 2242.

48. Odeh has been described as being so unimportant to al-Qaeda that he was only given a poorly forged passport. Bergen, "Bin Laden Trial," 432. But it appears instead that through his own incompetence he was unable to get his own passport renewed, and finally Saleh in exasperation gave him the Yemeni fake. See Hamm, *Terrorism as Crime*, 69–70. On Odeh's arrival in Pakistan, see testimony by Pakistani immigration officials in the trial transcript, April 2 and April 3, 2001. Bernsten describes Odeh as arriving in Karachi on August 8 (*Jawbreaker*, 25), but the trial testimony indicates it was August 7.

49. Watson et al., "Our Target Was Terror"; Kaplan, "On Terrorism's Trail."

50. Trial testimony March 7, 2001, 2030. See also Bergen, *Holy War, Inc.*, 120–21. One of the pieces of information Owhali revealed to investigators concerned an al-Qaeda safe house and associated phone number, which would later become the first clue leading the intelligence community to several of the future 9/11 hijackers. This information is discussed in chapter 7.

51. Trial testimony March 19, 2001.

52. *Report of the Accountability Review Boards on the Embassy Bombings in Nairobi and Dar Es Salaam* [Crowe Commission Report].

53. Ibid., cover letter.

54. Admiral William J. Crowe, "Press Briefing," Washington, January 8, 1999, www.state.gov/www/policy_remarks/1999/990108_emb_rpt.html.

55. Crowe Commission Report, "Executive Overview."

56. According to a report in the *New York Times*, the full, classified version of the Crowe Report included intelligence reports that showed that the intelligence community "had growing evidence that the embassy was a target of terrorist plots, and that terrorists hostile to American interests were active in Kenya." But even the full report did not include any warnings of an attack on a specific day. Risen and Weiser, "Before Bombings, Omens and Fears."

57. For example, see McKinley, "Security Flaws Left Embassy in Nairobi Open to Attack." But not everyone agrees that physical security had been an obvious and neglected problem: Smith Hempstone, the US ambassador to Kenya from 1989 to 1993, wrote after the attacks that he had felt the security posture was "reasonable, if not in retrospect adequate." Hempstone, "Embassies at Risk."

58. Not everyone who has studied the intelligence community's actions before the embassy bombings believes the IC was negligent. Paul Pillar, who had served as a senior intelligence official during that period, claims the IC had been doing a good job of producing strategic intelligence on the threat of radical Islamist terrorism and bin Laden, and had imparted the seriousness of that threat to policymakers, before the embassy attacks of 1998. See Pillar, "Adapting Intelligence to Changing Issues," 160–61.

59. Nolan and MacEachin, *Discourse, Dissent, and Strategic Surprise*.

60. Ibid., 36.

61. Other useful examinations of the embassy bombings include Vadlamudi, "The US Embassy Bombings in Kenya and Tanzania," 106–8; Hamm, *Terrorism as Crime*, chap. 2; and Copeland, "Surprise, Intelligence Failure, and Mass Casualty Terrorism."

62. *9/11 Commission Report*, 118.

63. Bamford, *Pretext for War*, 208.

64. Gladwell, "Connecting the Dots." Gladwell is actually attributing this belief to John Miller, Michael Stone, and Chris Mitchell, the authors of the book *The Cell*.

65. Miller, Stone, and Mitchell, *Cell*, 194.

66. Ibid., 341.

67. *Report of the Secretary of State's Advisory Panel on Overseas Security* (Inman Report).

68. The embassy building in Nairobi, built in the early 1980s, was located at the intersection of two of the city's busiest streets. Nairobi was designated as a "medium" threat post, and the embassy met State Department physical security standards except for the 100-foot setback. The embassy in Dar es Salaam was the former Israeli Embassy compound, and because the post was rated a "low" threat, the setback was considered adequate, even though it did not meet the Inman standard of 100 feet. Crowe Commission Report, sections on Nairobi and Dar es Salaam "Discussion and Findings."

69. Aid, *All Glory Is Fleeting*, 83. Aid cites a confidential interview as the source about NSA monitoring.

70. *9/11 Commission Report*, 109.

71. On the bin Laden unit comments, see "9/11 Commission Staff Statement Number 7," 4.

72. *9/11 Commission Report*, 60; Benjamin and Simon, *Age of Sacred Terror*, 132.

73. *9/11 Commission Report*, 60; "9/11 Commission Staff Statement Number 5," 4–5; Benjamin and Simon, *Age of Sacred Terror*, 224–25.

74. Weiner and Risen, "Decision to Strike Factory"; Gellman, "US Was Foiled Multiple Times." See also Hendrickson, *Clinton Administration's Strikes on Usama Bin Laden*, 196–216.

75. Gellman, "US Was Foiled Multiple Times."

76. Tenet and Harlow, *At the Center of the Storm*, 102.

77. *9/11 Commission Report*, 110.

78. Aid, "All Glory Is Fleeting," 86.

79. Ibid., 87. On the satellite phone, see also the testimony by the agent who sold it to the al-Qaeda operative in 2001, in trial testimony March 20; the phone is also discussed in the government's closing arguments on May 1. Bin Laden stopped using that telephone after the US missile strikes that were launched in August 1998 in response to the embassy bombings, and the 9/11 Commission reported that this was the result of an article in the *Washington Times* newspaper about his use of satellite phones. But it appears that this story is a myth; Kessler, "File the Bin Laden Phone Leak under 'Urban Myths.'" Another useful analysis that reaches essentially the same conclusion is by Shafer, "Don't Blame the *Washington Times*."

80. US Department of State, "Terrorism / Usama Bin Ladin: Who's Chasing Whom?" See also Lichtblau, "State Dept. Says It Warned about bin Laden."

81. Central Intelligence Agency, *Annual Report on Intelligence Community Activities*.

82. On al-Fadl, see Miller, Stone, and Mitchell, *Cell*, 154–65; and Mayer, "Junior." See al-Fadl's trial testimony on February 7, 2001, 382–91, in which he describes how he became a US informant and went into the witness protection program; and the *9/11 Commission Report*, 62, 109. In his testimony and in the *9/11 Commission Report* the country in which he turned himself in is not identified, but other accounts describe it as Eritrea. The 9/11 Commission staff report, *Monograph on Terrorist Financing*, appears to confirm this fact, stating that much of the intelligence community's early reporting on al-Qaeda "came from a single source, a former al-Qaeda operative, who walked into the US Embassy in Eritrea in 1996" (p. 35).

83. Mayer, "Junior."

84. *9/11 Commission Report*, 109.

85. "The Foreign Terrorist Threat in the US: Revisiting Our 1995 Estimate," ICB 97–8, April 1997, cited in *9/11 Commission Report*, 342.

86. *9/11 Commission Report*, 342.

87. Benjamin and Simon, *Age of Sacred Terror*, 147. Bergen writes that although this interview was conducted on March 22, 1997, it was not aired on CNN until May 10. Bergen, *Osama Bin Laden I Know*, 450n15.

88. Bergen, *Holy War, Inc.*, 190, 103. This news conference, held on May 26, 1998, did not receive much publicity at the time. See Nic Robertson, "Previously Unseen Tape Shows bin Laden's Declaration of War," CNN.com, August 20, 2002, and Gutman, "Examining Closely Why an Important Story Is Not Widely Told." Also Bergen, *Osama Bin Laden I Know*, 202.

89. The State Department warning was evidently sparked primarily by the interview bin Laden gave to John Miller of ABC; see "US Increases Security Following 'Serious' Threats of Terrorist Attack," Agence France-Presse, in English, June 13, 1998. For the citation to this Agence France-Presse article I am indebted to Vadlamudi, "US Embassy Bombings in Kenya and Tanzania," 108. Bergen writes that the warning was issued as a result of the May 26 bin Laden press conference, but news accounts of the warning suggest the trigger event was the ABC interview. Bergen, *Holy War, Inc.*, 110.

90. *Crowe Commission Report*, "Nairobi: Discussion and Findings."

91. *9/11 Commission Report*, 127, 484n103; Kifner, "U.S Fury on 2 Continents"; Anonymous, *Through our Enemies' Eyes*, 213. Some reports suggest that this operation took place after the East Africa bombings; see Gellman, "Broad Effort Launched after '98 Attacks." But the *9/11 Commission Report* notes cite CIA reports on the operation from July, clearly indicating the timing for at least part of the Albania operation was earlier, and thus could at least in theory have contributed to the intelligence picture before August. See also a detailed description of the Albanian operation *prior* to the East Africa embassy bombings given by Higgins and Cooper, "CIA-Backed Team Used Brutal Means."

92. *Joint Congressional Inquiry*, Appendix on "Evolution of the Terrorist Threat and the US Response 1983–2001," 20; Coll, *Ghost Wars*, 404.

93. *United States v. Ali Mohamed* Plea Agreement, 26.

94. Trial testimony by FBI agent Anticev, February 28, 1663.

95. For an overview of al-Qaeda's deception tactics, see Shultz and Beitler, "Tactical Deception and Strategic Surprise."

96. Aid, "All Glory Is Fleeting," 88.

97. This episode is described earlier in this chapter, and by Miller, Stone, and Mitchell, *Cell*, 200; *9/11 Commission Report*, 68.

98. Government prosecutors testified on February 27, 2001, that several phone numbers had been wiretapped between July 1996 and September 1997; trial transcript, 1575. On the "something bad" quotation, see Vistica and Klaidman, "Tracking Terror"; and Aid, "All Glory Is Fleeting," 88

99. Risen and Weiser, "Before Bombings, Omens and Fears."

100. Waller, "Inside the Hunt for Osama." Hamm identifies the September 1997 walk-in as al-Fadl, but this is not consistent with other reporting on al-Fadl. *Terrorism as Crime*, 63. The Crowe Commission states that a year before the bombings, there had been a report alleging that the embassy in Dar es Salaam would "have to be attacked" after the Nairobi embassy was bombed; this threat is not further identified, but it could be related to the al-Haraiman group. The *Crowe Commission Report* found that this report was fully disseminated but its source was not deemed credible; see section on "Dar es Salaam: Discussion and Findings."

101. Risen and Weiser, "Before Bombings, Omens and Fears." Risen and Weiser reported that the CIA inspector general was investigating the case, but to my knowledge nothing official has been released about that investigation. Gary Berntsen is also critical of the CIA station chief in Nairobi, arguing that a station chief from the Directorate of Operations might have been more effective in preventing the attacks. He writes that at the time of the attacks, the station chief was on leave in the United States; see Berntsen, *Jawbreaker*, 8. For further information about the Al-Haramain Islamic Foundation and its suspected connection with terrorist groups, see the 9/11 Commission Monograph on Terrorist Financing, 114–30.

102. On el Hage's background, see Miller, Stone, and Mitchell, *Cell*, 196–97; Bonner, "Public Face of Terror Suspect"; and Cloud, "Can a Tire Repairman in Texas Be the Key?"

103. Miller, Stone, and Mitchell, *Cell*, 199–200.

104. Ibid., 200–201.

105. His grand jury testimony of September 24, 1997, was later introduced in the 2001 trial, on February 15, transcript, 721–887. After the embassy bombings he was again

brought before a grand jury, and that testimony was read into the record on March 22, 2001.

106. The search is described in a ruling by federal judge Leonard B. Sand, 126 F. Supp 2d 264; 2000 US Dist. LEXIS 18228, issued December 19, 2000, after el Hage requested that the evidence from this search be suppressed because the US officials did not have a search warrant. Judge Sand ruled that a warrant was not required for such a case of foreign intelligence surveillance.

107. This letter was discussed during the trial on May 1, 2001, 5347–58. FBI special agent Daniel Coleman testified about finding the computer, testimony February 21, 1078–88. A translation of the letter is available at the PBS *Frontline* site, www.pbs.org/wgbh/pages/frontline/shows/binladen/upclose/computer.html. The quotations from the letter cited in this paragraph come from the *Frontline* translation.

108. Wright, *Looming Tower*, 244.

109. Nolan and MacEachin, *Discourse, Dissent, and Strategic Surprise*, 38. This CIA official's testimony to the Crowe Commission does not appear to have been publicly released, and this incident is not described in the *Crowe Commission Report*.

110. Nolan and MacEachin, *Discourse, Dissent, and Strategic Surprise*, 38. There is no indication that these documents held clues to the plot against the embassies. The analyst's draft report is discussed in one of the 9/11 Commission's staff statements, which reports that after the analyst wrote a lengthy, comprehensive paper, her supervisor decided not to publish it, and instead assigned four separate analysts to work on different parts of the topic. "As an indicator of the scarcity of analysts and the press of current intelligence reporting work, it took more than two years for two of these papers to be published at all. The other two were not finished until after 9/11." "9/11 Commission Staff Statement Number 11," 4–5.

111. Risen and Weiser, "Before Bombings, Omens and Fears"; Bonner and Risen, "Nairobi Embassy Received Warning of Coming Attack."

112. The Georgetown study quotes the *Crowe Commission Report* as stating, on 393, that Israeli intelligence identified Ahmed as a fraud; this does not appear in the publicly released version of the Crowe Report; it may be in the classified version, which has not been released. In the unclassified version, the Crowe Report does not specifically address the Ahmed warning, but states that warning intelligence had been received in 1997 about vehicle bomb attacks or assassination, "but by early 1998 these alleged threats had been discredited or found moot" (section on "Nairobi: Discussion and Findings").

113. "Charges Dropped in an Embassy Bombing," *New York Times*, March 20, 2000.

114. Berntsen, *Jawbreaker*, 22–23. Another former CIA officer, Melissa Boyle Mahle, has described a source that might be Ahmed: She writes that in early 1998 a walk-in told CIA officers in Africa about a plot to blow up the embassy in Nairobi; he was judged a fabricator, and "the walk-in would rejoin his al-Qa'ida cell and take his revenge upon the Americans." Mahle, *Denial and Deception*, 273.

115. Risen and Weiser, "Before Bombings, Omens and Fears."

116. Nolan and MacEachin, *Discourse, Dissent, and Strategic Surprise*, 48.

117. Risen and Weiser, "Before Bombings, Omens and Fears."

118. Ibid. See also the *Crowe Commission Report*.

119. Risen and Weiser, "Before Bombings, Omens and Fears."

120. Ibid.; *Crowe Commission Report*.

121. Risen and Weiser, "Before Bombings, Omens and Fears."

122. Ibid.; *Crowe Commission Report*. The Regional Security Officer in Nairobi said later about the problem of crime and violence, "This [crime] was the major threat to the community inside the embassy. Terrorism really wasn't the primary threat." Katz, *Relentless Pursuit*, 238.

123. Katz, *Relentless Pursuit*, 241.

124. Nolan and MacEachin, *Discourse, Dissent, and Strategic Surprise*, 48. Of note, Bushnell served as an adviser to the Nolan and MacEachin study.

125. *Crowe Commission Report*, "Dar es Salaam: Discussion and Findings." On the security measures implemented by the new regional security officer in Dar es Salaam, see also Katz, *Relentless Pursuit*, 247–51. Katz writes that three drills were actually scheduled for that morning: for a fire, a bomb threat, and a "full-blown terrorist assault."

126. *9/11 Commission Report*, 111.

127. According to the 9/11 Commission staff, "In 1996, the CTC [the CIA Counterterrorism Center] devised an innovative strategy combining intelligence and law enforcement tools to disrupt terrorist activity around the world." *9/11 Commission Staff Statement Number 7*, 3.

128. Waller, "Inside the Hunt for Osama." It is not clear where within the CIA decisions concerning security in Nairobi were made, but in at least one instance—the Al-Haramain case—it appears that CIA officials in Washington were more aggressive than the Nairobi station chief in wanting to act on threat warnings. There have been unconfirmed reports that several of the plotters were seen conducting surveillance of the embassy in Nairobi, suggesting that an increased local alert posture might have detected the plotters. Subiri writes: "Four days earlier, three Arab males were spotted filming the embassy building. Alerted of the incident by passers-by, the guards, thinking the intruders were tourists, ignored the warning." Subiri, *Bombs That Shook Nairobi and Dar*, 40.

CHAPTER 6

1. *US v. Omar Ahmad Ali Abdel Rahman, et al.*, indictment S5 93 Cr. 181 (MBM) (SDNY 1994), 6.

2. Fried, "Sheik Sentenced."

3. The case is sometimes referred to as the "landmarks" or the "monuments" plot. Others who have examined the case include Gleis, "Connecting the Dots"; Smith, Damphousse, and Roberts, "Pre-Incident Indicators"; and Center for Terrorism and Intelligence Studies, "Jericho Option." See also the book by the government attorney who led the prosecution of the case, Andrew C. McCarthy, *Willful Blindness*; and McCarthy, "Testimony before the US Senate Judiciary Committee." The primary sources of information for this chapter are the records and transcripts resulting from the initial trial of the plotters, *US v. Omar Ahmad Ali Abdel Rahman, et al.*, US District Court, Southern District of New York, held in 1995; and the appeal made by the defendants to the Second US Circuit Court of Appeals, with a decision handed down in August 1999, 189 F. 3rd 88 (2nd Cir. 1999). Other useful sources of information on the case include Miller, Stone, and Mitchell, *Cell*; and Lance, *1000 Years for Revenge*.

4. *US v. Rahman* indictment S5 93 Cr. 181, 8.

5. *US v. Rahman*, 189 F. 3rd 88 (2nd Cir. 1999). Also Bernstein, "FBI Has Kept 2 in Bomb Trial under Surveillance"; and Miller, Stone, and Mitchell, *Cell*, 51.

6. Miller, Stone, and Mitchell, *Cell*, 51; McCarthy, "Testimony before the US Senate Judiciary Committee," 4.

7. *US v. Rahman* indictment S5 93 Cr. 181, 8; *US v. Rahman*, 189 F. 3rd 88 (2nd Cir. 1999).

8. Emerson, *American Jihad*, 50. The 9/11 Commission found that Abdel Rahman had been able to enter and remain in the United States "owing to a series of exceptional failures in the border security system, some with eerie parallels to the 9/11 hijackers." Eldridge, *9/11 and Terrorist Travel*, 49. See also Camarota, "Open Door."

9. On the Kahane assassination, see Miller, Stone, and Mitchell, *Cell*, 38–40.

10. Ibid., 45.

11. Blumenthal, "Clues Hinting at Terror Ring Were Ignored." See also Miller, Stone, and Mitchell, *Cell*, 45–46.

12. Although the Kahane killing took place in a crowded hotel ballroom, no witness testified to actually seeing Nosair fire the fatal shots. On the trial outcome, see McFadden, "For Jurors, Evidence in Kahane Case Was Riddled with Gaps." During the Day of Terror trial in 1995, Nosair was again charged with the Kahane murder, under a federal provision that does not constitute double jeopardy. He was convicted of the killing, along with other charges related to the Day of Terror plot itself.

13. *US v. Rahman*, 189 F. 3rd 88 (SDNY 1999).

14. *US v. Rahman*, Salem trial testimony March 13, 4917–23. See also McKinley, "Trade Center Defendants Plotted," *New York Times*, March 14, 1995.

15. For basic information on Yousef, see Ackerman and Vadlamudi, "Case of Ramzi Yousef." On questions concerning Yousef's identify, see Reeve, *New Jackals*, 250–51.

16. On Yousef's background, see Reeve, *New Jackals*, 112–34; and Lance, *1000 Years for Revenge*, 22–25.

17. Miller, Stone, and Mitchell, *Cell*, 86.

18. *US v. Rahman* indictment, 13; Miller, Stone, and Mitchell, *Cell*, 90.

19. For background on the World Trade Center attack, see *US v. Rahman*, 189 F. 3rd 88 (2nd Cir. 1999) and Dwyer, *Two Seconds*.

20. Miller, Stone, and Mitchell, *Cell*, 103–5; Dwyer, *Two Seconds*, 91–100.

21. McCarthy, "Testimony before the US Senate Judiciary Committee," 8. On Ali Mohamed, see Waldman, "Lapses in Handling Sergeant Mirror Larger Failings." I discuss Ali Mohamed in more detail in chapter 5.

22. McCarthy, "Testimony before the US Senate Judiciary Committee"; Miller, Stone, and Mitchell, *Cell*, 113.

23. *US v. Rahman*, 189 F. 3rd 88 (2nd Cir. 1999). On Haggag, see also Miller, Stone, and Mitchell, *Cell*, 112.

24. McKinley, "Trial Details the Selecting of Bomb Targets."

25. Ibid.; *US v. Rahman*, 189 F. 3rd 88 (2nd Cir. 1999); *US v. Rahman* Trial Testimony, 5360–62.

26. *US v. Rahman*, 189 F. 3rd 88 (2nd Cir. 1999); Dwyer, *Two Seconds*, 210–11.

27. Miller, Stone, and Mitchell, *Cell*, 115.

28. Salem secretly taped this conversation, and the transcript of the recording was introduced as evidence in the 1995 trial as government exhibit 311T; these quotations are

from pp. 6 and 7 of the transcript. The conversation is also described by McKinley, "Many Faces of Witness." See also *US v. Rahman* indictment and *US v. Rahman*, 189 F. 3rd 88 (2nd Cir. 1999).

29. *US v. Rahman*, 189 F. 3rd 88 (2nd Cir. 1999). *US v. Rahman* trial exhibit 323T, tape recording of May 29–30, 7.

30. Trial exhibit 323T, 8–9.

31. Salem trial testimony March 22, 5615; *US v. Rahman* indictment; *US v. Rahman*, 189 F. 3rd 88 (2nd Cir. 1999).

32. Fried, "'Stalled' Cars Were to Destroy Tunnels."

33. *US v. Rahman* trial exhibit 362T, 9.

34. Ibid.

35. This videotape was shown in court on March 22. See trial testimony March 22, 5637–47 and exhibit 383T (the transcript of the recording made June 23–24). Also see McKinley, "Lawyer Forces Bomb-Trial Witness."

36. *US v. Rahman*, 189 F. 3rd 88 (2nd Cir. 1999).

37. White, "Statement before the Joint Congressional Inquiry," 8.

38. Church, "Terror Within."

39. Ibid.

40. US Department of State, *Patterns of Global Terrorism*, 1991, 1–2.

41. Gates, "Statement of the Director of Central Intelligence before the Senate Armed Services Committee."

42. Federal Bureau of Investigation, *Terrorism in the United States 1982–1992*, 13.

43. Ibid., 18–19.

44. Ibid., 13.

45. Ibid., 12.

46. US Department of State, *Patterns of Global Terrorism 1992*, iii.

47. MacFarquhar, "In Bombing Trial, a Deluge of Details."

48. Dwyer, *Two Seconds*, 183.

49. Mitchell, "Official Recalls Delay"; Blumenthal, "Tapes in Bombing Plot." Some accounts say he first arrived in the United States in 1988, but most accounts agree it was 1987.

50. Blumenthal, "Informer"; Blumenthal, "Tapes in Bombing Plot."

51. *US v. Rahman* trial testimony March 7, 4584–85; Blumenthal, "Tapes in Bombing Plot"; Blumenthal, "Informer"; Mitchell, "Official Recalls Delay." On his admission of lying about his background, see his trial testimony of March 7, 1995, 4575, and McKinley, "Key Witness."

52. Blumenthal, "Informer."

53. Lance, *1000 Years for Revenge*, 53. Salem testified at the trial that Floyd first came to the hotel in the spring of 1991 (not August), but he also said he was not very good at remembering dates; testimony of March 7, 4588–4609. He explained to his wife that his connection with the FBI began when the Bureau sought him out because he was a well-connected Egyptian who made repeated trips abroad, which made him of interest to the FBI following the Iraqi invasion of Kuwait. The truth appears to be more mundane and coincidental. Blumenthal, "Informer."

54. On the New York JTTF, see *9/11 Commission Report*, 81–82; and White, "Prosecuting Terrorism."

55. Blumenthal, "Informer."

56. Trial transcript, 4609; McKinley, "Key Witness."

57. Lance, *1000 Years for Revenge*, 58–59.

58. Ibid., 60. See also Salem's trial testimony March 7, 1995, 4609–11.

59. *US v. Rahman*, 189 F. 3rd 88 (2nd Cir. 1999). Also trial transcript March 7, 1995, 4713–15.

60. This period is discussed in trial transcript, 4611–22; 4874–85; 6094–95. See also Miller, Stone, and Mitchell, *Cell*, 70; and *US v. Rahman* indictment, 9.

61. Trial transcript, 4710–13.

62. *US v. Rahman*, 189 F. 3rd 88 (2nd Cir. 1999); Lance, *1000 Years for Revenge*, 66–67.

63. *US v. Rahman*, 189 F. 3rd 88 (2nd Cir. 1999); Miller, Stone, and Mitchell, *Cell*, 73.

64. McKinley, "Witness in Bombing Plot Once Failed Lie-Detector Tests."

65. Trial testimony March 13, 4939–44; Miller, Stone, and Mitchell, *Cell*, 74–75, 85–93.

66. *US v. Rahman*, 189 F. 3rd 88 (2nd Cir. 1999).

67. Lance, *1000 Years for Revenge*, 102–3.

68. Ibid., 103–4.

69. Ibid., 104.

70. Salem testimony March 13, 1995, 4998–5004; Lance, *1000 Years for Revenge*, 134–36.

71. Lance, *1000 Years for Revenge*, 136. This episode is also described in a 9/11 Commission *Memorandum for the Record* of its staff interview with NYPD detective Louis Napoli, September 4, 2003.

72. Lance, *1000 Years for Revenge*, 151–52; Miller, Stone, and Mitchell, *Cell*, 113.

73. Lance, *1000 Years for Revenge*, 152; Miller, Stone, and Mitchell, *Cell*, 114.

74. Miller, Stone, and Mitchell, *Cell*, 115–16; Dwyer, *Two Seconds*, 217–18.

75. Blumenthal, "Informer."

76. Trial testimony March 7, 1995, 4579–80; MacFarquhar, "In Bombing Trial, a Deluge of Details." The *Times* story reported that the $7,000 monthly payments were installments on the overall figure, but testimony at the trial indicated the $7,000 payments were separate from the $1,056,200 figure he received.

77. Miller, Stone, and Mitchell, *Cell*, 81. Wilson's role is also described in *US v. Rahman*, 189 F. 3rd 88 (2nd Cir. 1999).

78. *US v. Rahman*, 189 F. 3rd 88 (2nd Cir. 1999); Dwyer, *Two Seconds*, 281.

79. Weiser, "Remorseful Terror Conspirator Gets an 11-Year Sentence." The government's letter describing his assistance has not been made public.

80. Blumenthal, "Tapes in Bombing Plot." Salem discussed his decision to make tape recordings in his testimony on March 13.

81. Ibid.; Blumenthal, "Informer."

82. The August 1993 indictment is the S3 version of the indictment, S3 93-CR-181. See also Tabor, "US Indicts Egyptian Cleric."

83. Miller, Stone, and Mitchell, *Cell*, 84.

84. A more recent foiled plot that fits this pattern is the attempted attack on Fort Dix, New Jersey, in 2007; e.g., see Ripley, "Fort Dix Conspiracy." For other attempts to analyze

the typical stages of a terrorist plot, see Pluchinsky, "Typology and Anatomy"; and Jackson, *Breaching the Fortress Wall.*

CHAPTER 7

1. Wirtz, "Responding to Surprise," 56.
2. *9/11 Commission Report.*
3. Rovner and Long make a similar comparison of strategic and tactical warning; see Rovner, Long, and Zegart, "Correspondence: How Intelligent Is Intelligence Reform?"
4. US Congress, *Joint Inquiry Report.*
5. Ibid., 60.
6. On the limitations of the *Joint Inquiry Report,* see Falkenrath, "The 9/11 Commission Report: A Review Essay," 172.
7. *9/11 Commission Report,* 342. The 9/11 Commission staff believed that the demands of providing short-term "current" intelligence drained resources away from long-term, strategic analysis, and provided the following definitions: "Tactical analysis studies a particular case involving an individual or group as a guide to specific operations. Strategic analysis looks beyond the particular in order to see patterns, notice gaps, or assemble a larger picture on a wider timeframe to guide the development of national policy." *9/11 Commission Staff Statement Number 11,* 3.
8. It appears that two such comprehensive products were under way but not available in time. The CIA inspector general's report noted that a CIA-produced comprehensive assessment of the terrorist threat to the United States was being edited as of 9/11; Central Intelligence Agency, *OIG Report on CIA Accountability with Respect to the 9/11 Attacks,* xviii. The FBI was also conducting a comprehensive assessment of the risk of the terrorist threat to the United States, and in September 2001 it had completed a draft of a report titled "FBI Report on the Terrorist Threat to the United States and a Strategy for Prevention and Response." See US Department of Justice, *Review of the Federal Bureau of Investigation's Counterterrorism Program.*
9. *9/11 Commission Report,* 343.
10. Presumably other intelligence agencies conducted after-action reviews following 9/11, but they have not been made public.
11. US Department of Justice, *Review of the FBI's Handling of Intelligence Information related to the September 11 Attacks.* The full 421-page report remains classified.
12. Ibid., 84n84.
13. Central Intelligence Agency, *OIG Report on CIA Accountability with Respect to the 9/11 Attacks.*
14. Ibid., vii.
15. Ibid., xviii.
16. Central Intelligence Agency, *DCI Report: The Rise of UBL and Al-Qa'ida,* 67. Another survey of what the intelligence community knew about al-Qaeda before 9/11 is Fenner, Stout, and Goldings, *Ten Years Later,* especially the chapters by Stout and Storer.
17. Tenet, "Testimony before the Senate Select Committee on Intelligence," 136. On the views of other members of the CIA leadership after 9/11, see Powers, "Trouble with the CIA."
18. Rovner, "Why Intelligence Isn't to Blame for 9/11," 3.

19. Clarke, *Against All Enemies*, xxiv.

20. There is a large conspiracy theory literature surrounding 9/11, little of it useful. For a discussion of this literature see Goldberg, "Who Profited from the Crime?" See also Sunstein and Vermeule, "Conspiracy Theories: Causes and Cures."

21. Much of the material for this section is derived from the 9/11 Commission Staff Statement 11, "The Performance of the Intelligence Community."

22. One unnamed intelligence official was quoted as saying about imagery: "We had amazing satellite pictures of them having graduation ceremonies at the camps, but we never had a clue what they planned to do when they left Afghanistan." Johnston, "Lack of Pre-9/11 Sources."

23. Clarke is quoted by Senator Bob Graham, the cochair of the Joint Inquiry, in his book *Intelligence Matters*, p. 128, citing Clarke's testimony of June 11, 2002. In the transcript of that session that was later publicly released, a comment was made to Clarke that he had told the Inquiry staff that 90 percent of the high-quality work on al-Qaeda came from NSA; Clarke's response was blacked out, suggesting that the quote cited by Graham was made at that point. See Clarke, "Testimony before the Joint Congressional Inquiry," 20.

24. Aid, "All Glory Is Fleeting," 95. Aid's article is a useful survey of the contributions of SIGINT in the fight against terrorism. See also Aid, *Secret Sentry*.

25. The *New York Times*, for example, reported that "American intelligence agencies failed to obtain reliable human sources inside the Afghanistan training camps run by Al-Qaeda before September 2001." Johnston, "Lack of Pre-9/11 Sources." In addition, Bill Gertz quotes a July 1, 1996, CIA classified report that stated, "We have no unilateral sources close to bin Laden, nor any reliable way of intercepting his communications." Gertz, *Breakdown*, 10.

26. *Joint Inquiry Report*, 91.

27. *Joint Inquiry Report*, 92. The Joint Inquiry also noted that the Defense Humint Service, run by DIA, "had some success against the Taliban, but little against al-Qa'ida" (p. 386).

28. Tenet and Harlow, *At the Center of the Storm*, 120.

29. A redacted version of the transcript of this session was later released. Clarke, "Testimony before the Joint Congressional Inquiry," 16. In a similar account, Steve Coll writes that although the CIA had not been able to recruit any agents inside the core of the al-Qaeda leadership, it had had success recruiting unilateral agents who could operate in Afghanistan. "In 1999, for the first time, the CIA generated more unilateral reports about bin Laden from its own agents than reports from liaisons with other intelligence agencies." Coll, *Ghost Wars*, 492.

30. *Joint Inquiry Report*, 387–88.

31. Ibid., 61, 336–39.

32. Tenet, "Written Statement for the Record of the Director of Central Intelligence before the National Commission on Terrorist Attacks upon the United States," 8.

33. Pillar, "Good Literature and Bad History," 1025. See also Pillar's book, *Intelligence and US Foreign Policy*, 250–51.

34. The *Joint Inquiry Report* states that the first reference to al-Qaeda was in late 1996 (appendix 1, "Evolution of the Terrorist Threat," p. 13). The 9/11 Commission reported that the first description of al-Qaeda it could find in intelligence documents was in 1999; *9/11 Commission Report*, 341.

35. *Joint Inquiry Report*, 194, and table in appendix 1 titled "Evolution of the Terrorist Threat and US Response, 1983–2001," p. 5.

36. *9/11 Commission Report*, 108–9, and 479n1.

37. US Department of State, "The Wandering Mujahidin: Armed and Dangerous," 2.

38. The FBI report is described by Pincus, "Mueller Outlines Origin, Funding of Sept. 11 Plot"; and in more detail by Coll, *Ghost Wars*, 278–79.

39. The FBI had established its Radical Fundamentalist Unit in 1994, its Counterterrorism Center in 1996, and its Bin Ladin Unit in 1999. For background on the FBI's counterterrorism efforts, see chapter 2 of US Department of Justice, *A Review of the FBI's Handling of Intelligence Information Related to the September 11 Attacks*.

40. Zeman et al., "Path to 9/11." Coll writes that members of the Bin Laden Unit called themselves "the Manson Family" because they had gotten a reputation as crazed alarmists about al-Qaeda; Coll, *Ghost Wars*, 454.

41. *9/11 Commission Report*, 109; I discuss al-Fadl in depth in chapter 5.

42. Central Intelligence Agency, *Usama Bin Laden: Islamic Extremist Financier*.

43. *9/11 Commission Report*, 108. A CIA internal study put the situation in a more positive light, reporting that as of 1996 "our awareness of the threat represented by Bin Ladin had grown significantly." Central Intelligence Agency, *DCI Report: The Rise of UBL and Al-Qa'ida*, 5.

44. Robert Fisk, "Arab Rebel Leader Warns the British: 'Get Out of the Gulf,'" *The Independent*, July 10, 1996.

45. *9/11 Commission Report*, 48. This 60-page fatwa has been called the "Ladenese Epistle." See Emerson, *American Jihad*, 148.

46. *9/11 Commission Report*, 47.

47. Ibid., 47.

48. Ibid., 115.

49. *Joint Inquiry Report*, 198; Joint Inquiry appendix 1, "Evolution of the Terrorist Threat," 19. Hill, "Joint Inquiry Staff Statement, Part I," 15. According to the Joint Inquiry report, this threat information was provided to senior US officials in July 1998.

50. On the capture plan, see the *9/11 Commission Report*, 112–14; the quotation is on p. 112. As described in chapter 5, the federal indictment was revised and publicly released in November 1998.

51. *9/11 Commission Report*, 342.

52. Hill, "Joint Inquiry Staff Statement, Hearing on the Intelligence Community's Response to Past Terrorist Attacks against the United States from February 1993 to September 2001," 4. The staff received similar comments from officials on the National Security Council staff and in the Counterterrorism Center; see Hill, "Joint Inquiry Staff Statement, Part I," 17.

53. Benjamin and Simon, "A Failure of Intelligence?"

54. Hill, "Joint Inquiry Staff Statement, Part I," 15.

55. Ibid.; *Joint Inquiry Report*, 125.

56. *Joint Inquiry Report*, 200. Also Joint Inquiry appendix 1, "Evolution of the Terrorist Threat," p. 22.

57. Hill, "Joint Inquiry Staff Statement, Part I," 15–16.

58. *Joint Inquiry Report* appendix 1, "Evolution of the Terrorist Threat," 23.

59. *Joint Inquiry Report*, 17.

60. *9/11 Commission Report*, 357. In his memoirs Tenet argues that the most important effect of the memo was to direct Charlie Allen, his deputy for intelligence collection, to make bin Laden and al-Qaeda a top priority, and as a result the intelligence community put together a worldwide effort including HUMINT and other sources. Tenet and Harlow, *At the Center of the Storm*, 119–20.

61. *9/11 Commission Report*, 130, 485n114; the quotation is from Tenet and Harlow, *At the Center of the Storm*, 122.

62. *9/11 Commission Report*, 141.

63. Rahimulla Yusufzai, "Conversation with Terror," *Time*, January 11, 1999.

64. Joint Inquiry appendix 1, "Evolution of the Terrorist Threat," 24.

65. Hill, "Joint Inquiry Staff Statement, Part I," 18. In addition, a nearly 400-page study published in 1999 by Sandia National Laboratory, based on open-source information, concluded that bin Laden posed a significant threat to the US; Sandia National Laboratories, "Osama Bin Laden: A Case Study."

66. Hill, "Joint Inquiry Staff Statement, Part I," 16; *Joint Inquiry Report*, 200.

67. Hill, "Joint Inquiry Staff Statement, Part I," 16; *Joint Inquiry Report*, 125.

68. Tenet and Harlow, *At the Center of the Storm*, 125.

69. On these plots, see, e.g., *9/11 Commission Report*, 174–79.

70. Ibid., 179, as noted in 501n34.

71. Hill, "Joint Inquiry Staff Statement, Part I," 16; *Joint Inquiry Report*, 200.

72. *9/11 Commission Report*, 195. Information gathered from Yemeni interrogations of several *Cole* suspects revealed that one of the individuals who had provided the attackers with directions was named Khallad. An FBI agent recognized this name, which had come up in debriefings from "an important al-Qaeda source" who had been meeting with FBI and CIA officers. (Although not identified, this source was presumably Fadl.) The source was shown a copy of a photo of Khallad received from the Yemenis, and the source identified him as being a "run boy" for bin Laden. 9/11 Commission Report, 192. Only after Khallad and another Cole planner named Nashiri were captured following 9/11 could bin Laden's complicity be proved; see *9/11 Commission Staff Statement Number 15*, 8–9. For background on the Cole bombing, see *9/11 Commission Staff Statement Number 6*.

73. On these incidents, see the *9/11 Commission Report*, 345.

74. Johnson, "Feature Review," 329; Johnson, "Shock Theory," 353.

75. *Joint Inquiry Report*, 210; Hill, "Joint Inquiry Staff Statement, Part I," 26.

76. Hill, "Joint Inquiry Staff Statement, Part I," 26; *9/11 Commission Staff Statement Number 11*, 6. Also see *Joint Inquiry Report*, 210.

77. White House Commission on Aviation Safety and Security (Gore Commission), 25. As the 9/11 Commission noted, the Gore Commission did not mention suicide hijackings or the use of aircraft as weapons; *9/11 Commission Report*, 344.

78. US Department of State, "Saudi Arabia: Meeting with ———— Re Bin Laden Threat."

79. This report is described in different ways in several of the official investigations into 9/11, but the most complete description appears to be in the US Department of Justice, *Review of the FBI's Handling of Intelligence Information Related to the September 11 Attack*, 97–98. See also *9/11 Commission Report*, 345, 561n14; Joint Inquiry Staff Statement, September 18, 27; and *Joint Inquiry Report*, 199.

80. *9/11 Commission Report*, 344. This appears to be the same report described in the Joint Inquiry staff Statement, September 18, 2002, 15; and in the *Joint Inquiry Report*, 199.

81. Joint Inquiry Staff Statement, September 18, 2002, 27.

82. The declassified version of this item is in the *9/11 Commission Report*, 128–30, and discussed on 344. The item is also available on the CIA Freedom of Information Act website, www.foia.cia.gov. According to the 9/11 Staff Statement 11 (p. 6), this 1998 report was the source of the allusion to hijacking in the better-known August 2001 *PDB*.

83. Hill, "Joint Inquiry Staff Statement, the FBI's Handling of the Phoenix Electronic Communication and Investigation of Zacaria Moussaoui Prior to September 11, 2001," 3, 12. Also *Joint Inquiry Report*, 333–34; US Department of Justice, *A Review of the FBI's Handling of Intelligence Information Related to the September 11 Attacks*, 98.

84. Joint Inquiry Staff Statement September 24, 2002, 12. The staff report notes that there was no information to indicate this group followed through with their plans.

85. Joint Inquiry Staff Statement September 24, 2002, 3, 12–13; *Joint Inquiry Report*, 334; US Department of Justice, *A Review of the FBI's Handling of Intelligence Information Related to the September 11 Attacks*, 97. The Department of Justice's inspector general noted that in 2002 the FBI researched this report and concluded the information had likely been a fabrication. The 9/11 Commission monograph on the FAA states that "in 1998 the FBI tasked its field offices to examine whether Islamist extremists in their area were taking flying lessons." Despite the discrepancy in the date, this could refer to the same incident. 9/11 Commission, *Monograph on Four Flights and Civil Aviation Security*, 64.

86. Lisa Myers, "Did Al-Qaida Trainee Warn FBI before 9/11?" NBC News, July 26, 2004, www.msnbc.msn.com/id/5131524/. The episode is also described in the Joint Inquiry staff statement September 18, 2002, 28, and the *Joint Inquiry Report*, 211.

87. Jenkins, "Terrorist Threat to Commercial Aviation," 10.

88. Warrick and Stephens, "Before Attack, US Expected Different Hit"; Cetron and Probst, *Terror 2000*.

89. *9/11 Commission Report*, 345, 347, 457–58n98. In Clancy's 1994 book *Debt of Honor*, a terrorist hijacks an airliner and flies it into the Capitol building in Washington.

90. Fainaru, "Clues Pointed to Changing Terrorist Tactics."

91. *9/11 Commission Report*, 345. I describe this and other FAA intelligence products in more detail below.

92. Hudson, *Sociology and Psychology of Terrorism*.

93. *9/11 Commission Report*, 346, 561n21.

94. Ibid., 346. This exercise was called "Positive Force." See also Graham, "Pentagon Crash Scenario Was Rejected."

95. Quoted in 9/11 Commission, *Monograph on Four Flights and Civil Aviation Security*, 54. This National Intelligence Estimate, number 95–13, July 1995, has not been publicly released, but it is also described in George Tenet's prepared statement before the Joint Inquiry, October 17, 2002, 20, and again by Tenet in *At the Center of the Storm*, 104.

96. *9/11 Commission Report*, 341–42. Tenet quotes the 1997 assessment in his October 17, 2002, testimony, with wording very similar to that of the 1995 National Intelligence Estimate—which is not surprising, as the 1997 report is described as an update to the earlier one. The 1997 report is also quoted in the *Joint Inquiry Report*, 213.

97. *9/11 Commission Staff Statement Number 3*, 3.

98. On five analysts: *Joint Inquiry Report*, 60. The quotation is from 9/11 Commission, *Monograph on Four Flights and Civil Aviation Security*, 54.

99. *Monograph on Four Flights*, 53.

100. Ibid., 63. The monograph also cites a similar FAA warning from May 1998.

101. Ibid., 53.

102. *9/11 Commission Staff Statement Number 3*, 4.

103. Joint Inquiry Staff Statement Part I, 29; *Joint Inquiry Report*, 213–14.

104. 9/11 Commission, *National Commission on Terrorist Attacks upon the United States Monograph on Four Flights and Civil Aviation Security*, 53. This presentation is also cited in 9/11 Commission, *9/11 Commission Staff Statement Number 3*, 4.

105. 9/11 Commission, *Monograph on Four Flights and Civil Aviation Security*, 54–55, 59; the quotation is on 59.

106. "Part II, Department of Transportation, Federal Aviation Administration, 14 CFR Parts 107 and 139, Airport Security: Final Rule," *Federal Register* 66, no. 137 (July 17, 2001): 37313. This quotation is also cited by 9/11 Commission, *Monograph on Four Flights and Civil Aviation Security*, 63.

107. "Part III, Department of Transportation, Federal Aviation Administration, 14 CFR Part 108," 37331. This passage is also reprinted in the prepared statement by Mary Schiavo before the 9/11 Commission on May 23, 2003.

108. 9/11 Commission, *Monograph on Four Flights and Civil Aviation Security*, 55.

109. Ibid., 56.

110. Ibid., 62.

111. Canavan, "Testimony before the 9/11 Commission," 85. A portion of Canavan's testimony is included in the FAA monograph, but his quotation is partially blacked out. His unredacted comments are included in the transcript of the May 23 session available on the 9/11 Commission website, http://govinfo.library.unt.edu/911/archive/hearing2/index.htm. Canavan was invited to attend a meeting of the National Security Council's Counterterrorism Security Group in early July 2001, and he stated later that the primary concern among those at the meeting was that a threat would be overseas; 9/11 Commission, *Monograph on Four Flights and Civil Aviation Security*, 55–56.

112. Garvey, "Statement to the 9/11 Commission."

113. 9/11 Commission, *Monograph on Four Flights and Civil Aviation Security*, 62.

114. *9/11 Commission Report*, 255.

115. Joint Inquiry Staff Statement Part I, 20. Also, in January 2001 French intelligence officials gave the CIA a vague warning that al-Qaeda was plotting an airline hijacking that could possibly involve American air carriers. Angela Doland, "France Warned CIA of Hijack Plot in 2001," Associated Press, April 16, 2007.

116. *9/11 Commission Report*, 255. Early 2001 also saw two important terrorism trials, of the East Africa embassy bombers and of Ahmed Ressam, which highlighted the threat.

117. *9/11 Commission Report*, 255.

118. Ibid., 203.

119. Joint Inquiry Staff Statement Part I, September 18, 2002, 16–17; *Joint Inquiry Report*, 200.

120. *9/11 Commission Report*, 255–56.

121. Joint Inquiry Staff Statement, September 18, 2002, 20.

122. Ibid.; *Joint Inquiry Report*, 203–4.

123. This article was titled "Terrorist Groups Said Cooperating on US Hostage Plot"; *9/11 Commission Report*, 533n10. This report is also described in the *Moussaoui* trial Government Exhibit ST00003 (which is a stipulation concerning intelligence reporting).

124. *9/11 Commission Report*, 256.

125. Ibid.

126. Joint Inquiry Staff Statement, September 18, 2002, 20.

127. *9/11 Commission Report*, 256; *Joint Inquiry Report*, 30–31.

128. *9/11 Commission Report*, 256.

129. *United States v. Zacarias Moussaoui* Government Exhibit ST00003 (Stipulation Concerning Intelligence), Cr. No. 01–455 (Eastern Dist. Va. 2006), 3.

130. *9/11 Commission Report*, 257.

131. Isikoff and Hirsh, "What Went Wrong"; Fainaru, "Clues Pointed to Changing Terrorist Tactics."

132. *9/11 Commission Report*, 257.

133. Tenet and Harlow, *At the Center of the Storm*, 149.

134. *9/11 Commission Report*, 257.

135. Constable, "In Bin Laden's Lair, Small Talk and a Warning." The interview is also described by Coll, *Ghost Wars*, 560; *9/11 Commission Report*, 257; and the *United States v. Moussaoui* stipulation on intelligence reporting, 3.

136. Diana Elias, "Laden's Group Boasts of Cole Attack," Associated Press, June 19, 2001; see also Coll, *Ghost Wars*, 560. The tape is also described by Burns, "America the Vulnerable Meets a Ruthless Enemy."

137. Joint Inquiry Staff Statement, September 18, 2002, 20.

138. *United States v. Zacarias Moussaoui*, "Substitution for the Testimony of Khalid Sheikh Mohammed," Cr. No. 01–455 (2006), 31.

139. *9/11 Commission Report*, 258.

140. Kenneth J. Williams memorandum, "Zakaria Mustapha Soubra," July 10, 2001, 1. This "Phoenix memo" is available in redacted form in the reports of several official investigations, including as an appendix to the Department of Justice's inspector general's report, and in appendix 2 to the Joint Inquiry report. But a version with fewer deletions was introduced in the *Moussaoui* trial as Defendant's Exhibit 129, and that is the version used here.

141. US Department of Justice, *A Review of the FBI's Handling of Intelligence Information Related to the September 11 Attacks*, 66–67.

142. *9/11 Commission Report*, 272; US Department of Justice, *A Review of the FBI's Handling of Intelligence Information Related to the September 11 Attacks*, 88; *9/11 Commission Staff Statement Number 10*, 9. Of note, it was later concluded that none of the individuals that agent Williams mentioned in his memo were involved in the 9/11 plot; US Department of Justice, *A Review of the FBI's Handling of Intelligence Information Related to the September 11 Attacks*, 80.

143. Joint Inquiry Staff Statement, September 18, 23. The *Joint Inquiry Report*, appendix 1, "Evolution of the Terrorist Threat" (p. 43), dates this as June 28; Coll, however, cites the same quote and says this was from a briefing paper prepared July 10; Coll, *Ghost Wars*, 561.

144. Tenet and Harlow, *At the Center of the Storm*, 151.

145. Ibid. This meeting is also described by Bob Woodward, evidently based largely on interviews with Tenet; see Woodward, *State of Denial*, 51–52. Woodward writes that at the meeting "Black emphasized that this amounted to strategic warning, meaning the problem was so serious that it required an overall plan and strategy" (p. 51).

146. Tenet and Harlow, *At the Center of the Storm*, 152.

147. *9/11 Commission Report*, 259.

148. Ibid.

149. Ibid., 260.

150. Ibid.

151. *Joint Inquiry Report*, 171. This appears to be the same information reported in the August 6, 2001, *PDB*, discussed in the next section.

152. Joint Inquiry Staff Statement September 18, 2002, 28; *Joint Inquiry Report*, 212.

153. *9/11 Commission Report*, 260.

154. The *PDB* (with redactions) is reprinted in the *9/11 Commission Report*, 261–62.

155. The report about surveillance of federal buildings in New York referred to two individuals who had been stopped after being seen taking pictures of buildings containing FBI offices; after an extensive investigation, the FBI could not connect the men's actions to terrorism. The commission also concluded that the "70 full field investigations" number was "generous," and included a number of investigations that should not have been included, including one that related to a dead person. *9/11 Commission Report*, 535n37.

156. The Department of Justice review found that media reports wrongly stated he did *not* want to learn to take off or land the plane; according to the FBI, the flight school manager said he *only* wanted to learn to take off and land. US Department of Justice, *A Review of the FBI's Handling of Intelligence Information Related to the September 11 Attacks*, 105n94.

157. US Department of Justice, *A Review of the FBI's Handling of Intelligence Information Related to the September 11 Attacks*, 153. This comment is noted in the Minneapolis agent's notes of his conversation. The headquarters agent on the other end of the phone call, however, told the inspector general's investigators he did not recall the Minneapolis agent making such as comment. The *9/11 Commission Report* cites a slightly different version of the Minneapolis agent's statement, p. 275. The agent who made the statement was evidently speculating without specific evidence about a threat to the World Trade Center. During the trial of Zacarias Moussaoui, the FBI agent who arrested Moussaoui testified that he had heard agent Greg Jones make the statement about the World Trade Center. He said that after 9/11 he asked Jones about the statement, and Jones told him it had been a hypothetical scenario designed to try to get Washington moving. See Richard A. Serrano, "Agent Faults FBI on 9/11," *Los Angeles Times*, March 21, 2006.

158. DCI Update, Terrorist Threat Review, August 23, 2001 (orig. "Top Secret"); Defendant's Exhibit 660 in *Moussaoui* trial. This briefing is also described in the *9/11 Commission Report*, 275.

159. Tenet and Harlow, *At the Center of the Storm*, 203.

160. *9/11 Commission Report*, 274; Joint Inquiry Staff Statement, September 18, 2002, 20.

161. These briefing slides are included as exhibits 672 and 674 in the trial *United States v. Moussaoui*.

162. US Department of State, *Patterns of Global Terrorism 2000*, appendix B.

163. Although the Federal Emergency Management Agency (FEMA) scenarios do not appear to have been presented in any formal documents, several separate press accounts relate FEMA officials presenting such a list at meetings and conferences in April and August 2001. See Berger, "New Orleans Faces Doomsday Scenario"; Krugman referred to this article in "Can't-Do Government." I first became aware of these scenarios from Betts, *Enemies of Intelligence*, 111.

164. Katzman, *Terrorism: Near Eastern Groups and State Sponsors, 2001*, summary page.

165. US General Accounting Office, *Combating Terrorism: Selected Challenges and Related Recommendations*, 47.

166. Powers, "Trouble with the CIA"; Aid, All Glory Is Fleeting," 93.

167. Tenet and Harlow, *At the Center of the Storm*, 160.

168. See, e.g., Gertz, *Breakdown*, 129–30; Bamford, *Pretext for War*, 249; and Bobbitt, "Why We Listen."

169. Hayden, "Statement for the Record by Lieutenant General Michael V. Hayden, USAF, Director, National Security Agency, before the Joint Congressional Inquiry," 4.

170. Shultz and Vogt, "It's War!" 21.

171. *9/11 Commission Staff Statement Number 11*, 9. For references to news accounts about the controversy over these communications, see Aid, "All Glory Is Fleeting," 93, 116n114.

172. For example, the *Joint Inquiry Report* found that "while the Intelligence Community had amassed a great deal of valuable intelligence regarding Usama Bin Ladin and his terrorist activities, none of it identified the time, place, and specific nature of the attacks that were planned for September 11, 2001." Part 1, 7.

173. For example, the 9/11 Commission identified ten "operational opportunities" that were missed by the CIA and FBI, and eight of them deal with Hazmi and Mihdhar or the Kuala Lumpur meeting. (The other two are the failure of the FBI to recognize the importance of Moussaoui, and the CIA's failure to properly handle information it received in August 2001 about KSM.) *9/11 Commission Report*, 355–56.

174. Aid, "All Glory Is Fleeting," 90; Aid, *Secret Sentry*, 209–12; Isikoff and Klaidman, "Hijackers We Let Escape."

175. *Joint Inquiry Report*, 155. The *Joint Inquiry Report* does not identify the location of these communications other than referring to it as "a suspected terrorist facility in the Middle East," but it appears to clearly refer to the house in Yemen described in the *Newsweek* article of June 10, 2002. George Tenet uses the same phrase in *At the Center of the Storm*, writing that during the investigation of the East Africa Embassy bombings, FBI agents found a telephone number "of a suspected terrorist facility in the Middle East" (p. 194). Bob Graham, who served as cochair of the Joint Inquiry, writes that the information provided by Owhali after the embassy bombings included the location of an al-Qaeda safe house and its phone number, although he does not state that the house was in Yemen: "It quickly became clear that the place was more than a safe house: it was an al-Qaeda logistics center. Information flowed in from operatives around the world, where it was then relayed to Osama bin Laden at his Afghanistan hideout." Graham, *Intelligence Matters*, 5.

176. *9/11 Commission Report*, 181; *Joint Inquiry Report*, 155–56; Tenet and Harlow, *At the Center of the Storm*, 194; Bob Graham, *Intelligence Matters*, 5.

177. Isikoff and Klaidman, "Hijackers We Let Escape."

178. *9/11 Commission Report*, 181–82, 353–54.

179. Ibid., 221. After 9/11, the FBI learned that a longtime FBI counterterrorism informant had numerous contacts with Hazmi and Mihdhar. The informant cooperated with the FBI after the attacks, and he is not believed to have been involved in the plot. *Joint Inquiry Report*, 158, 163.

180. *9/11 Commission Report*, 223–37. The *9/11 Commission Report* (p. 231) notes that the so-called muscle hijackers were not actually physically imposing, most being between 5 feet 5 inches and 5 feet 7 inches in height.

181. Ibid., 270.

182. Ibid., 276–77.

183. Ibid., 267–72.

184. Davis, "Strategic Warning: Intelligence Support."

185. Central Intelligence Agency, *DCI Report: The Rise of UBL and Al-Qa'ida*, 1.

186. Rovner, Long, and Zegart, "Correspondence: How Intelligent Is Intelligence Reform?" 201.

187. Ibid., 207.

188. Byman, "Strategic Surprise and the September 11 Attacks," 152. A similar argument is made by Derksen, that in order to prevent the attacks officials needed, but did not have, what he calls the "three Ts of tactical intelligence": the type, timing, and target of the upcoming attack. Derksen, "Commentary: The Logistics of Actionable Intelligence Leading to 9/11," 255.

189. A possibly apocryphal story about Henry Kissinger expresses how important it is for warnings to be believed. While secretary of state, the story goes, Kissinger once complained about an intelligence failure. An intelligence official interjected, "but we warned you, sir," to which Kissinger replied, "Yes, but you didn't persuade me." This story is told by Naftali, *Blind Spot*, 322–23.

190. Zegart, "September 11 and the Adaptation Failure of US Intelligence Agencies," 84–85.

191. Cohen, "Preparing for a Grave New World." This article was a strongly worded warning, stating that "the race is on between our preparations and those of our adversaries," although it focused on the threat of a chemical or biological attack.

192. *9/11 Commission Report*, 114.

193. Miller, "Planning for Terror but Failing to Act."

194. Clarke, *Against All Enemies*, 210.

195. Shultz, "Showstoppers."

196. Clarke, *Against All Enemies*, 190. The incident is also described by Benjamin and Simon, *Age of Sacred Terror*, 318, and in the *9/11 Commission Report*, 189.

197. *9/11 Commission Report*, 198. In his memoir, Tenet recounts an anecdote that suggests president-elect Bush was not impressed by the intelligence he was receiving in the briefings in Texas. One morning after his briefing he said, "Well, I assume I will start seeing the good stuff when I become president." But he was already seeing "the good stuff," Tenet says. *At the Center of the Storm*, 136.

198. *9/11 Commission Report*, 198–99. Bush told the 9/11 Commission he remembered that Clinton had emphasized other issues such as North Korea and the Mideast peace process.

199. *9/11 Commission Report*, 199; Clarke, *Against All Enemies*, 229–30.

200. *9/11 Commission Report*, 201. The memo and the December 2000 paper (but not the Delenda plan) have been released publicly and are available on the website of the National Security Archive: Richard A. Clarke, "Presidential Policy Initiative/Review: The Al-Qida Network," memorandum, January 25, 2001, www.gwu.edu/~nsarchiv/NSAEBB/NSAEBB147/index.htm.

201. Clarke, *Against All Enemies*, 230–32. Coll writes that the January 25 memo "went nowhere" (*Ghost Wars*, 543). On Rice's reaction to Clarke's memo, see Bumiller, *Condoleezza Rice: An American Life*, 142. On the deputies meeting, see also Coll, *Ghost Wars*, 558–59.

202. *9/11 Commission Staff Statement Number 8*, 10. Also see *9/11 Commission Report*, 202, 510n185. Rice recalled this comment as being made in May 2001, while Clarke said it was in March.

203. *9/11 Commission Report*, 204 5.

204. Woodward, *State of Denial*, 51–52. Rice later recalled that the information in the July 10 briefing was not very specific and mostly pointed to threats overseas. Bumiller, *Condoleezza Rice*, 156–58.

205. *9/11 Commission Report*, 212.

206. Clarke, *Against All Enemies*, 237; Benjamin and Simon, *Age of Sacred Terror*, 345–46; *9/11 Commission Report*, 212–14.

207. *9/11 Commission Report*, 214.

208. Fred Borch writes, "no military commander had the mission of protecting the World Trade Center or the Pentagon." Borch, "Comparing Pearl Harbor and '9/11,'" 859.

209. Clarke, *Testimony before the Joint Congressional Inquiry*, 25. This testimony was later released in redacted form. His comments about the FBI are also cited by Graham, *Intelligence Matters*, 137. O'Neill resigned from the FBI to become the chief of security for the World Trade Center, and died on 9/11. On O'Neill, see Wright, "Counter-Terrorist"; and Wright, *Looming Tower*. Also useful are the transcript and other materials available from the PBS *Frontline* broadcast "The Man Who Knew," www.pbs.org/wgbh/pages/frontline/shows/knew/.

210. Davis, "Strategic Warning: Intelligence Support," 177.

CHAPTER 8

1. This chapter draws on and updates my article "The Plots That Failed."

2. The best known of these may be a list released by the White House in 2005 of ten plots that had been disrupted since the 9/11 attacks, discussed later in this chapter.

3. Brian Jenkins provides a list of some forty-six failed plots, but he provides few details and no citations, in *Unconquerable Nation*, 185–91. Useful recent listings are Carafano, Bucci, and Zuckerman, "Fifty Terror Plots Foiled"; and Beutel, "Data on Post-9/11 Terrorism."

4. Homeland Security Institute, *Underlying Reasons for Success and Failure of Terrorist Attacks*; Jackson and Frelinger, *Understanding Why Terrorist Operations Succeed or Fail*; Jacobson, "Terrorist Dropouts."

5. Exceptions include a study that examines thirty-two attacks thwarted since 9/11: Difo, "Ordinary Measures, Extraordinary Results," and Strom et al., *Building on Clues*, which examines eighty-six foiled and executed terrorist plots against US targets. Another useful study that includes failed plots, but which is limited to post-9/11 radical Islamist attacks, is Bjelopera, *American Jihadist Terrorism*. Also valuable, but with a more limited scope than this study, are New America Foundation, "Homegrown Terrorism Cases"; and Kurzman, *Muslim-American Terrorism*.

6. White House, "Summary of the White House Review."

7. Jenkins, "Lessons for Intelligence."

8. Hayden, "Statement for the Record before the Joint Inquiry."

9. Gunaratna, "Combating the Al-Qaida Associated Groups," 190.

10. Jenkins, "Intelligence and Homeland Security," 127.

11. Liptak, "Suspected Leader of 9/11 Attacks Is Said to Confess." A CIA study of the results of detainee interrogation found that detainees "often try [to] pass incomplete or intentionally misleading information, perhaps hoping that the volume of the reporting will make it difficult to sort out the truth." Central Intelligence Agency, *Detainee Reporting Pivotal*, 6. In a separate report—completed before KSM's Guantánamo testimony—the CIA argued that information obtained from his debriefing led to disruption of several plots against the United States: Central Intelligence Agency, "Khalid Shaykh Muhammad."

12. "Waiting for Al-Qaeda's Next Bomb," 30.

13. State of the Union Address, January 23, 2007.

14. Gompert, "Reaction to the *Washington Post* series." Of note, the principal reporter for the *Washington Post* series, Dana Priest, said in an interview that she had asked intelligence officials for examples of intelligence successes but she was not provided with any: "We asked them to share with us anything they could, plots that were foiled that we could put in the paper because we didn't have many examples. We said give us things, just in generalities . . . and we didn't receive anything back." NPR, *Talk of the Nation*, July 19, 2010; transcript at www.npr.org/templates/story/story.php?storyId=128624199.

15. White House, "Fact Sheet: Plots, Casings, and Infiltrations."

16. For an examination of what is known about the incidents on the White House list, see "Thwarted Terrorist Attacks," *NYU Review of Law and Security*; and Goo, "List of Foiled Plots."

17. A prominent database that does include failed attacks is the International Terrorism: Attributes of Terrorist Events (ITERATE) database maintained by Edward F. Mickolus. The ITERATE database, however, only tracks international terrorism, so it does not capture purely domestic plots and attacks. On ITERATE, see Flemming, Mickolus, and Sandler, "Research Note: Using the ITERATE and DOTS Databases." Published listings of terrorist activities that do cover failed attacks include Hewitt, *Political Violence and Terrorism*; and Gartenstein-Ross, Goodman, and Grossman, *Terrorism in the West 2008*.

18. National Counterterrorism Center Worldwide Incidents Tracking System, "Methodology," www.nctc.gov/witsbanner/wits_subpage_criteria.html.

19. See the Global Terrorism Database, www.start.umd.edu/gtd/faq/. A recent study sponsored by the Department of Defense found that it was difficult to find good-quality, openly available data on terrorism events in general, whether successful or unsuccessful; MITRE Corporation, *Rare Events*, 44–45.

20. The full data set, including criteria for the coding of intelligence and other factors, is available from the author.

21. Seven plots are attributed to "other," neither radical Islamism nor domestic extremism. The causes in these cases vary and are not always clear, e.g., in the case of a man who wanted to bomb the Alaskan oil pipeline during the millennium celebrations in order to manipulate the oil futures market and cause financial panic. "Canadian Man Pleads Guilty to Plot to Blow Up Trans-Alaska Oil Pipeline," Associated Press, March 13, 2008.

22. National Counterterrorism Center, *2009 Report on Terrorism*, 5.

23. I have not attempted to define "significant" damage or destruction, but further research would be useful in helping to determine a threshold; at what point does a certain level of destruction in an attack suggest that it was "successful"?

24. A fuller discussion of the various factors involved in determining whether to define attacks as successful or unsuccessful is given by Jackson and Frelinger, *Understanding Why Terrorist Operations Succeed or Fail*, 2–3.

25. A prominent example of this sort of case not counted as a failed plot is that of the Holy Land Foundation for Relief and Development, a Texas-based Muslim charity accused by the US government of providing support to Hamas. Five of its leaders were convicted on a variety of counts, including support of terrorism, in 2008, but the group was not accused of directly financing terrorist bombings or attacks. Kovach, "Five Convicted in Terrorism Financing Trial."

26. For Saajid Badat, see Jacobson, "They Trained, They Plotted, Then They Bailed." For Iyman Faris, see *KSM's Brooklyn Bridge Plot*, NEFA Foundation, August 2007, www.nefafoundation.org.

27. In several cases plotters have thought they were carrying out attacks, only to find that law enforcement officials had supplied them with nonfunctioning weapons or explosives. These are not counted as actual attempted attacks but as cases stopped at an earlier stage for some other reason (e.g., an informant was involved and provided the fake weapons).

28. For Ahmed Ressam, see *9/11 Commission Report*, 176–79. For the Japanese Red Army terrorist, see Hanley, "Suspected Terrorist Convicted."

29. See, e.g., Homeland Security Institute, *Underlying Reasons for Success and Failure*, 61–65.

30. Krikorian, "Plot Posed a Real, Immediate Threat."

31. Southern Poverty Law Center, "Second Wave," 18.

32. Smith, "North Africa Feared as Staging Ground for Terror"; Shane and Schmitt, "Qaeda Plot to Attack Plane Foiled."

33. *USA v. Hosam Maher Husein Smadi*, Criminal Complaint, September 24, 2009.

34. Baker and Rashbaum, "3 Held Overseas."

35. Whitlock, "Trial Opens."

36. Central Intelligence Agency, *Detainee Reporting Pivotal*. Large sections of this report remain blacked out in the redacted version that has been publicly released, suggesting that additional plots and attacks may have been prevented but are too sensitive to make public.

37. Brian M. Jenkins, "Prepared Statement for the 9/11 Commission."

38. DeYoung and Pincus, "Success against Al-Qaeda Cited."

39. This is not a new finding. A RAND Corporation study on terrorism in the 1970s found that informants and undercover sources were more often useful than wiretaps or other sources. Wildhorn, Jenkins, and Lavin, *Intelligence Constraints*, xi. The importance of human intelligence in preventing terrorist attacks has also been seen in France; a French antiterrorism official recently claimed that fifteen plots thwarted in recent years were all stopped as a result of information received from human sources. See Cody, "Europe's Antiterrorism Agencies Favor Human Intelligence."

40. Rashbaum and Fahim, "Informer's Role in Bombing Plot."

41. Buckley and Rashbaum, "4 Accused of Plot."

42. On the British case, see, e.g., Van Natta, Sciolino, and Grey, "Details Emerge." On the Miami case, see "The Miami Plot to Bomb Federal Buildings and the Sears Tower," NEFA Foundation, January 2008, available at www.nefafoundation.org.

43. I examine the Fort Dix case in "Plots That Failed," 632–33.

44. Rimington, "'Humint' Begins at Home." The study by Strom and others, *Building on Clues*, reached similar findings, noting that routine law enforcement activities and public vigilance are key factors in preventing terrorist attacks.

45. "Summary of the White House Review of the December 25, 2009, Attempted Terrorist Attack."

46. Blair, "Statement for the Record before the Senate Homeland Security and Governmental Affairs Committee," 2.

47. White House, "Attempted Terrorist Attack on December 25, 2009: Intelligence, Screening, and Watchlisting System Corrective Actions."

48. Lipton, Schmitt, and Mazzetti, "Review of Jet Bomb Plot."

49. "Summary of the White House Review of the December 25, 2009, Attempted Terrorist Attack," 3; Mazzetti and Lipton, "Spy Agencies Failed."

50. Jacobs, "Written Statement of Janice L. Jacobs," 3.

51. Travers, "Statement for the Record"; Mazzetti and Lipton, "Spy Agencies Failed."

52. The Senate Select Committee on Intelligence criticized the decision not to place him on the no-fly list; see US Senate, "Unclassified Executive Summary."

53. Lipton, Schmitt, and Mazzetti, "Review of Jet Bomb Plot."

54. Ibid.

55. Ibid.

56. I discuss the Zazi case in more detail in "Plots That Failed."

57. Sulzberger and Rashbaum, "NY Terror Suspect Admits Guilt and Cooperates"; Marzulli, "Zazi, Al-Qaeda Pals Planned Rush-Hour Attack on Grand Central, Times Square Subway Stations."

58. Miller, "Bullet Dodged."

59. On the CIA in Pakistan, see Brian Ross, Richard Esposito, and Clayton Sandell, "FBI Arrests Three Men in Terror Plot That Targeted New York," ABC News, September 20, 2009, http://abcnews.go.com/Blotter/men-arrested-fbi-nyc-terror-plot/story?id = 8618 732; and Lolita Baldor, "NY Suspect Had Senior Al-Qaida Contact," Associated Press, October 6, 2009.

60. "British Spies Help Prevent al-Qaeda-Inspired Attack on New York Subway," *The Telegraph* (London), November 9, 2009; Dina Temple-Raston, "Feds: NY Subway Bomb Plot Included UK Targets," NPR, July 8, 2010, www.npr.org/templates/story/story .php?storyId = 128368594.

61. US Department of Justice, "Charges Unsealed Against Five Alleged Members of Al-Qaeda Plot to Attack the United States and United Kingdom," press release, July 7, 2010, www.justice.gov/opa/pr/2010/July/10-nsd-781.html; Love, "Alleged Al-Qaeda Operatives Indicted"; Pantucci, "Manchester, New York and Oslo," 10–13.

62. Temple-Raston, "Terrorism Case Shows Range."

63. Ibid.

64. *US v. Najibullah Zazi* criminal complaint, September 19, 2009, 6.

65. Temple-Raston, "Terrorism Case Shows Range."

66. Baldor, "NY Suspect Had Senior Al-Qaida Contact."

67. Rashbaum and Baker, "How Using Imam in Terror Inquiry Backfired on Police."

CHAPTER 9

1. See, e.g., Grabo, "Strategic Warning," 89.

2. Barger, "It Is Time," 26.

3. I am grateful to an anonymous reviewer for stimulating my thinking here.

4. Potter, *Nimitz*, 16.

5. Pellerin, "DIA Five-Year Plan." Robert Haddick discusses this DIA document and argues, much as I do, that "strategic intelligence and warning, while vital, should not come at the expense of tactical warning." Haddick, "Strategic Error."

6. Davis, "Strategic Warning," 176.

7. Edward Marks makes an argument similar to mine, that whereas most counterterrorism activities are tactical in nature, "solving" the problem of terrorism is a strategic question that requires strategic-level thinking and action. Marks, "Terrorism."

8. Allison, "How It Went Down."

9. Schwartz and Randall, "Ahead of the Curve," 94.

10. Nye, "Peering into the Future." For a more recent discussion of riddles and mysteries, see Treverton, "Risks and Riddles."

11. Taleb and Blyth, "Black Swan."

12. Crocker, "Reflections," 183; Fukuyama, *Blindside*.

13. In the 1989 movie *Roadhouse*, "expect the unexpected" was a key piece of advice from Dalton, the rugged bouncer played by Patrick Swayze; see www.imdb.com/title/tt0098206/quotes.

BIBLIOGRAPHY

9/11 Commission. *The 9/11 Commission Report: Final Report of the National Commission on Terrorism Attacks upon the United States*, authorized ed. New York: W. W. Norton, 2004.

———. *9/11 Commission Staff Statement Number 3: The Aviation Security System and the 9/11 Attacks*. Washington, DC, 2004.

———. *9/11 Commission Staff Statement Number 5: Diplomacy*. Washington, DC: 9/11 Commission, 2004.

———. *9/11 Commission Staff Statement Number 6: The Military*. Washington, DC: 9/11 Commission, 2004.

———. *9/11 Commission Staff Statement Number 7: Intelligence Policy*. Washington, DC: 9/11 Commission, 2004.

———. *9/11 Commission Staff Statement Number 8: National Policy Coordination*. Washington, DC: 9/11 Commission, 2004.

———, *9/11 Commission Staff Statement Number 10: Threats and Responses in 2001*. Washington, DC: 9/11 Commission, 2004.

———. *9/11 Commission Staff Statement Number 11: The Performance of the Intelligence Community*. Washington, DC: 9/11 Commission, 2004.

———. *9/11 Commission Staff Statement Number 15: Overview of the Enemy*. Washington, DC: 9/11 Commission, 2004.

———. *Memorandum for the Record* of staff interview with NYPD Detective Louis Napoli, September 4, 2003. www.archives.gov/legislative/research/9-11/commission-memoranda.html.

———. *National Commission on Terrorist Attacks upon the United States Monograph on Four Flights and Civil Aviation Security*. Washington, DC: 9/11 Commission, 2004.

Ackerman, Gary A., and Sundara Vadlamudi. "The Case of Ramzi Yousef." In *Countering Terrorism and Insurgency in the 21st Century, International Perspectives*, vol. 3, *Lessons from the Fight against Terrorism*, edited by James J. F. Forest. Westport, CT: Praeger, 2007.

Aid, Matthew M. "All Glory Is Fleeting: Sigint and the Fight against International Terrorism." *Intelligence and National Security* 18, no. 4 (Winter 2003): 72–120.

———. *The Secret Sentry: The Untold History of the National Security Agency*. New York: Bloomsbury Press, 2009.

Allen, Charles E. "DHS Under Secretary for Intelligence and Analysis Charles E. Allen Address to the Washington Institute for Near East Policy." May 6, 2008. www.dhs.gov/xnews/speeches/sp_1210107524856.shtm.

———. "Intelligence: Cult, Craft, or Business?" Incidental Paper, Seminar on Intelligence, Command, and Control, Harvard University Program on Information Resources Policy, July 2001.

———. "Warning and Iraq's Invasion of Kuwait: A Retrospective Look." *Defense Intelligence Journal* 7, no. 2 (Fall 1998): 33–44.

Allen, Thomas B. "Midway: The Story That Never Ends." *US Naval Institute Proceedings*, June 2007, 62–67.

Allison, Graham. "How It Went Down." *Time*, May 7, 2012. www.time.com/time/magazine/article/0,9171,2113156,00.html.

"America Needs More Spies." *The Economist*, July 10, 2003.

Andrew, Christopher. *For the President's Eyes Only: Secret Intelligence and the American Presidency from Washington to Bush.* New York: HarperCollins, 1995.

Anonymous [Michael Scheuer]. *Through Our Enemies' Eyes: Osama Bin Laden, Radical Islam, and the Future of America.* Washington, DC: Brassey's, 2002.

Arad, Uzi. "Intelligence Management as Risk Management: The Case of Surprise Attack." In *Managing Strategic Surprise: Lessons from Risk Management and Risk Assessment*, edited by Paul Bracken, Ian Bremmer, and David Gordon. New York: Cambridge University Press, 2008.

Armstrong, Willis C., William Leonhart, William J. McCaffrey, and Herbert C. Rothenberg. "The Hazards of Single-Outcome Forecasting." In *Inside CIA's Private World: Declassified Articles from the Agency's Internal Journal*, edited by H. Bradford Westerfield, 238–254. New Haven, CT: Yale University Press, 1995.

At the Interface: The WWII Recollections of Donald M. Showers. DVD produced by Shoestring Educational Productions, Inc., 2007.

Baker, Al, and William K. Rashbaum. "3 Held Overseas in Plan to Bomb New York Target." *New York Times*, July 8, 2006.

Bamford, James. *A Pretext for War: 9/11, Iraq, and the Abuse of America's Intelligence Agencies, with a New Afterward.* New York: Anchor Books, 2005.

Bansemer, John D. "Intelligence Reform: A Question of Balance." Paper for Harvard Program on Information Resources Policy, October 2005.

Barger, Deborah G. "It Is Time to Transform, Not Reform, US Intelligence." *SAIS Review* 24, no. 1 (Winter–Spring 2004): 23–31.

Bar-Joseph, Uri. "Methodological Magic." *Intelligence and National Security* 3, no. 4 (October 1988): 134–55.

Bar-Joseph, Uri, and Jack S. Levy. "Conscious Action and Intelligence Failure." *Political Science Quarterly* 124, no. 3 (2009): 461–88.

Bazerman, Max H., and Michael D. Watkins. "Airline Security, the Failure of 9/11, and Predictable Surprises." *International Public Management Journal* 8, no. 3 (2005): 365–77.

———. *Predictable Surprises: The Disasters You Should Have Seen Coming, and How to Prevent Them.* Boston: Harvard Business School Press, 2004.

Beach, Edward L. *Scapegoats: A Defense of Kimmel and Short at Pearl Harbor.* Annapolis, MD: Naval Institute Press, 1995.

Benjamin, Daniel, and Steven Simon. *The Age of Sacred Terror.* New York: Random House, 2002.

———. "A Failure of Intelligence?" *New York Review of Books*, December 20, 2001.

———. *The Next Attack: The Failure of the War on Terror and a Strategy for Getting It Right*. New York: Times Books, 2005.

Benson, Robert Louis. *A History of US Communications Intelligence during World War II: Policy and Administration (CCH-S54–97–01)*. US Cryptologic History, series IV: World War II, vol. 8. Washington, DC: Center for Cryptologic History, National Security Agency, 1997.

Bergen, Peter L. "The Bin Laden Trial: What Did We Learn?" *Studies in Conflict and Terrorism* 24, no. 6 (November 2001): 429–34.

———. *Holy War, Inc.: Inside the Secret World of Osama Bin Laden*, updated ed. New York: Touchstone, 2002.

———. *The Osama Bin Laden I Know: An Oral History of Al-Qaeda's Leader*. New York: Free Press, 2006.

Berger, Eric. "New Orleans Faces Doomsday Scenario." *Houston Chronicle*, December 1, 2001.

Berkowitz, Bruce. "Spying in the Post–September 11 World." *Hoover Digest* 2003, no. 4. www.hoover.org/publications/hoover-digest/article/6728.

Bernstein, Richard. "FBI Has Kept 2 in Bomb Trial under Surveillance since 1989." *York Times*, February 8, 1995.

Berntsen, Gary. *Jawbreaker: The Attack on Bin Laden and Al-Qaeda: A Personal Account by the CIA's Key Field Commander*. New York: Crown, 2005.

Best, Richard A., Jr. "Proposals for Intelligence Reorganization, 1949–2004." CRS Report for Congress, September 24, 2004.

Betts, Richard K. "Analysis, War, and Decision: Why Intelligence Failures Are Inevitable." *World Politics* 31, no. 1 (October 1978): 61–89.

———. *Enemies of Intelligence: Knowledge and Power in American National Security*. New York: Columbia University Press, 2007.

———. "Fixing Intelligence." *Foreign Affairs*, January–February 2002.

———. "How to Think about Terrorism." *Wilson Quarterly*, Winter 2006, 44–49.

———. *Surprise Attack: Lessons for Defense Planning*. Washington, DC: Brookings Institution Press, 1982.

———. "Surprise, Scholasticism, and Strategy: A Review of Ariel Levite's Intelligence and Strategic Surprises." *International Studies Quarterly* 33, no. 3 (September 1989): 329–43.

Betts, Richard K., and Thomas G. Mahnken, eds. *Paradoxes of Strategic Intelligence: Essays in Honor of Michael I. Handel*. London: Frank Cass, 2003.

Beutel, Alejandro J. "Data on Post-9/11 Terrorism in the United States." Muslim Public Affairs Council Policy, January 2012.

Biard, Forrest R. "Breaking of Japanese Naval Codes: Pre-Pearl Harbor to Midway." *Cryptologia* 30, no. 2 (April 2006): 151–58.

Bischof, Gunter, Stefan Karner, and Peter Ruggenthaler, eds. *The Prague Spring and the Warsaw Pact Invasion of Czechoslovakia in 1968*. Lanham, MD: Lexington Books, 2010.

Bjelopera, Jerome P. *American Jihadist Terrorism: Combating a Complex Threat*. Washington, DC: Congressional Research Service, 2011.

Blair, Dennis C. "Statement for the Record before the Senate Homeland Security and Governmental Affairs Committee." January 20, 2010.

Blumenthal, Ralph. "Clues Hinting at Terror Ring Were Ignored, Officials Say." *New York Times*, August 27, 1993.

———. "The Informer: Tangled Ties and Tales of F.B.I. Messenger." *New York Times*, January 9, 1994.

———. "Tapes in Bombing Plot Show Informer and FBI at Odds." *New York Times*, October 27, 1993.

Bobbitt, Philip. "Why We Listen." *New York Times*, January 30, 2006.

"Bombing Suspect Provided 'Actionable Intelligence,' White House Says." CNN.com, January 5, 2010.

Bonner, Raymond. "Public Face of Terror Suspect: Low-Key Family Man." *New York Times*, September 27, 1998.

Bonner, Raymond, and James Risen. "Nairobi Embassy Received Warning of Coming Attack." *New York Times*, October 23, 1998.

Borch, Fred L. "Comparing Pearl Harbor and '9/11': Intelligence Failure? American Unpreparedness? Military Responsibility?" *Journal of Military History* 67, no. 3 (July 2003): 845–60.

Bracken, Paul. "How to Build a Warning System." In *Managing Strategic Surprise: Lessons from Risk Management and Risk Assessment*, edited by Paul Bracken, Ian Bremmer, and David Gordon. Cambridge: Cambridge University Press, 2008.

Bracken, Paul, Ian Bremmer, and David Gordon, eds. *Managing Strategic Surprise: Lessons from Risk Management and Risk Assessment*. Cambridge: Cambridge University Press, 2008.

Brady, Christopher. "Intelligence Failures: Plus Ça Change . . ." *Intelligence and National Security* 8, no. 4 (October 1993): 86–96.

Brody, Richard. "The Limits of Warning." *Washington Quarterly* 6, no. 3 (Summer 1983): 40–48.

Buckley, Cara, and William K. Rashbaum. "4 Accused of Plot to Blow Up Facilities at Kennedy Airport." *New York Times*, June 3, 2007.

Budiansky, Stephen. *Battle of Wits: The Complete Story of Codebreaking in World War II*. New York: Touchstone, 2000.

———. "Closing the Book on Pearl Harbor." *Cryptologia* 24, no. 2 (April 2000): 119–30.

———. "Too Late for Pearl Harbor." *US Naval Institute Proceedings*, December 1999, 47–51.

———. "What's the Use of Cryptologic History?" *Intelligence and National Security* 25 no. 6 (December 2010): 772–73.

Bumiller, Elisabeth. *Condoleezza Rice: An American Life: A Biography*. New York: Random House, 2007.

Burns, John F. "America the Vulnerable Meets a Ruthless Enemy." *New York Times*, September 12, 2001.

Bush, George W. *State of the Union Address*, January 23, 2007. Transcript, *New York Times*, January 24, 2007. www.nytimes.com/2007/01/23/washington/23bush-transcript.html.

Byman, Daniel. "Strategic Surprise and the September 11 Attacks." *Annual Review of Political Science* 8, no. 1 (2005): 145–70.

Calhoun, Ricky-Dale. "The Musketeer's Cloak: Strategic Deception during the Suez Crisis of 1956." *Studies in Intelligence* 51, no. 2 (2007): 47–58.

Camarota, Steven A. *The Open Door: How Militant Islamic Terrorists Entered and Remained in the United States*. CIS Paper 21. Washington, DC: Center for Immigration Studies, 2002.

Canavan, Michael A. "Testimony before the 9/11 Commission." Washington, DC, May 23, 2003. http://govinfo.library.unt.edu/911/archive/hearing2/index.htm.

Carafano, James Jay, Steve Bucci, and Jessica Zuckerman. "Fifty Terror Plots Foiled since 9/11: The Homegrown Threat and the Long War on Terrorism." *Heritage Foundation Backgrounder* 2682, April 2012.

Carlson, Elliot. *Joe Rochefort's War: The Odyssey of the Codebreaker Who Outwitted Yamamoto at Midway.* Annapolis, MD: Naval Institute Press, 2011.

Center for Terrorism and Intelligence Studies. "The Jericho Option: Al-Qa'ida and Attacks on Critical Infrastructure." Report UCRL-SR-224072, June 8, 2006. https://e-reports-ext.llnl.gov/pdf/337776.pdf.

Central Intelligence Agency. *Annual Report on Intelligence Community Activities.* January, 1997. Available at the CIA's Freedom of Information Act website, www.foia.cia.gov.

———. "CIA Statement on 'Legacy of Ashes.'" August 6, 2007. www.cia.gov/news-infor mation/press-releases-statements/press-release-archive-2007/legacy-of-ashes.html.

———. "The CIA and Strategic Warning: The 1968 Soviet-Led Invasion of Czechoslovakia." N.d. www.foia.cia.gov/CzechInvasion/8-StrategicWarning/2009-09-01.pdf.

———. *DCI Report: The Rise of UBL and Al-Qa'ida and the Intelligence Community Response.* Draft, Director's Review Group, March 19, 2004. www.gwu.edu/~nsarchiv/NSAEBB/NSAEBB381/.

———. *DCI Task Force Report: Improving Intelligence Warning.* May 29, 1992. www.gwu.edu/~nsarchiv/NSAEBB/NSAEBB381/.

———. *Detainee Reporting Pivotal for the War against Al-Qa'ida.* June 3, 2005.

———. "Khalid Shaykh Muhammad: Preeminent Source on Al-Qa'ida." July 13, 2004.

———. "Military Developments in the Soviet-Czech Confrontation." Intelligence Memorandum, August 2, 1968.

———. "Office of National Estimates Memorandum for the Director—The Czechoslovak Crisis." July 17, 1968.

———. *OIG Report on CIA Accountability with Respect to the 9/11 Attacks (Unclassified Version Released August 2007).* Washington, DC: CIA Office of the Inspector General, 2005.

———. *Usama Bin Laden: Islamic Extremist Financier.* 1996. Report released by the US Department of State, August 1996. http://www2.gwu.edu/~nsarchiv/NSAEBB/NSAEBB55/ciaubl.pdf.

Cetron, Marvin J., and Peter S. Probst. *Terror 2000: The Future Face of Terrorism.* Washington, DC: US Department of Defense, 1994. The study was not officially published, but it is available on the Department of Defense Freedom of Information Act website, www.dod.mil/pubs/foi/terrorism/.

Chan, Steve. "The Intelligence of Stupidity: Understanding Failures in Strategic Warning." *American Political Science Review* 73, no. 1 (March 1979): 171–80.

Church, George J. "The Terror Within." *Time,* July 5, 1993.

Clarke, Lee. *Worst Cases: Terror and Catastrophe in the Popular Imagination.* Chicago: University of Chicago Press, 2006.

Clarke, Richard A. *Against All Enemies: Inside America's War on Terror,* paperback ed. New York: Free Press, 2004.

———. "Testimony before the Joint Congressional Inquiry." Washington, DC, June 11, 2002. www.fas.org/irp/congress/2002_hr/061102clarke.pdf.

Cloud, David S. "Can a Tire Repairman in Texas Be the Key to Solving Terror Plot?" *Wall Street Journal*, October 29, 1998.

Cody, Edward. "Europe's Antiterrorism Agencies Favor Human Intelligence over Technology." *Washington Post*, May 12, 2010.

Cohen, Eliot A. "The 'No Fault' View of Intelligence." In *Intelligence Requirements for the 1990s: Collection, Analysis, Counterintelligence, and Covert Action*, edited by Roy Godson. Lexington, MA: Lexington Books, 1989.

Cohen, Eliot A., and John Gooch. *Military Misfortunes: The Anatomy of Failure in War.* New York: Vintage Books, 1991.

Cohen, William S. "Preparing for a Grave New World." *Washington Post*, July 26, 1999.

Coll, Steve. *Ghost Wars: The Secret History of the CIA, Afghanistan, and Bin Laden, from the Soviet Invasion to September 10, 2001.* New York: Penguin, 2004.

Connorton, John V. *National Security Agency Special Research History (SRH) 012, the Role of Radio Intelligence in the American—Japanese Naval War (August, 1941–June, 1942), Vol. I.* Washington, DC: National Security Agency, 1942.

Constable, Pamela. "In Bin Laden's Lair, Small Talk and a Warning." *Washington Post*, July 8, 2001.

Coox, Alvin D. "Repulsing the Pearl Harbor Revisionists: The State of Present Literature on the Debacle." In *Pearl Harbor Reexamined: Prologue to the Pacific War*, edited by Hilary Conroy and Harry Wray. Honolulu: University of Hawaii Press, 1990.

Copeland, Thomas E. "Intelligence Failure Theory." In *The International Studies Encyclopedia*, edited by Robert A. Denemark. Oxford: Blackwell 2010.

———. "Surprise, Intelligence Failure, and Mass Casualty Terrorism." PhD diss., Graduate School of Public and International Affairs, University of Pittsburgh, 2006.

Costello, John E. "MacArthur, Magic, Black Jumbos and the Dogs That Didn't Bark: New Intelligence on the Pearl Harbor Attack." In *In the Name of Intelligence: Essays in Honor of Walter Pforzheimer*, edited by Hayden B. Peake and Samuel Halpern. Washington, DC: NIBC Press, 1994.

Crocker, Chester A. "Reflections on Strategic Surprise." In *The Impenetrable Fog of War: Reflections on Modern Warfare and Strategic Surprise*, edited by Patrick M. Cronin. Westport, CT: Praeger, 2008.

Cronin, Patrick M., ed. *The Impenetrable Fog of War: Reflections on Modern Warfare and Strategic Surprise.* Westport, CT: Praeger, 2008.

Dahl, Erik J. "Intelligence and Terrorism." In *The International Studies Encyclopedia*, edited by Robert A. Denemark. Oxford: Blackwell 2010.

———. "The Plots That Failed: Intelligence Lessons Learned from Unsuccessful Terrorist Attacks against the United States." *Studies in Conflict and Terrorism* 34, no. 8 (August 2011): 621–48.

Daniel, Lisa. "Panetta: Intelligence Community Needs to Predict Uprisings." American Forces Press Service, February 11, 2011.

Davis, Jack. "Improving CIA Analytic Performance: Analysts and the Policymaking Process." *Sherman Kent Center for Intelligence Analysis Occasional Papers* 1, no. 2 (September 2002).

———. "Paul Wolfowitz on Intelligence-Policy Relations." *Studies in Intelligence* 39, no. 5 (1996).

———. "Strategic Warning: Intelligence Support in a World of Uncertainty and Surprise." In *Handbook of Intelligence Studies*, edited by Loch K. Johnson. London: Routledge, 2007.

Defalco, Ralph Lee III. "Blind to the Sun: US Intelligence Failures before the War with Japan." *International Journal of Intelligence and CounterIntelligence* 16, no. 1 (Spring 2003): 95–107.

Derksen, Kevin Michael. "Commentary: The Logistics of Actionable Intelligence Leading to 9/11." *Studies in Conflict and Terrorism* 28, no. 3 (May–June 2005): 253–68.

DeYoung, Karen, and Walter Pincus. "Success against Al-Qaeda Cited." *Washington Post*, September 30, 2009.

Diamond, John. *The CIA and the Culture of Failure: US Intelligence from the End of the Cold War to the Invasion of Iraq.* Stanford, CA: Stanford University Press, 2008.

Diehl, Jackson. "Obama Administration Ignored Clear Warnings on Egypt." *Washington Post*, February 9, 2011.

Difo, Germain. "Ordinary Measures, Extraordinary Results: An Assessment of Foiled Plots since 9/11." American Security Project Report, May 2010.

Director of Central Intelligence. "Intelligence Warning of the Tet Offensive in South Vietnam (Interim Report)." April 1968.

———. "The Performance of the Intelligence Community before the Arab-Israeli War of October 1973: A Preliminary Post-Mortem Report." December 1973. A redacted version of this report was made public in 2009, and the most useful version is available from the National Security Archive, www.gwu.edu/~nsarchiv/NSAEBB/NSAEBB276/doc04.pdf.

———. "The Soviet Invasion of Afghanistan: Implications for Warning." Interagency Intelligence Memorandum, October 1980. www.cia.gov/library/center-for-the-study-of-intelligence/csi-publications/books-and-monographs/index.html.

———. "Special National Intelligence Estimate Number 30-3-56: Nasser and the Middle East Situation." July 31, 1956. www.foia.cia.gov/docs/DOC_0000011513/DOC_000 0011513.pdf.

Drea, Edward J. *In the Service of the Emperor: Essays on the Imperial Japanese Army.* Lincoln: University of Nebraska Press, 1998.

Dwyer, Jim. *Two Seconds under the World: Terror Comes to America—The Conspiracy behind the World Trade Center Bombing.* New York: Crown, 1994.

Dyer, Thomas H. *Oral History of Captain Thomas H. Dyer.* Annapolis, MD: US Naval Institute Press, 1986.

Elder, Gregory. "Intelligence in War: It Can Be Decisive." *Studies in Intelligence* 50, no. 2 (2006).

Eldridge, Thomas R. *9/11 and Terrorist Travel: Staff Report of the National Commission on Terrorist Attacks upon the United States.* Washington, DC: National Commission on Terrorist Attacks upon the United States, 2004.

Elphick, Peter. *Far Eastern File: The Intelligence War in the Far East, 1930–1945.* London: Hodder and Stoughton, 1997.

Emerson, Steven. *American Jihad: The Terrorists Living among Us*, paperback ed. New York: Free Press, 2003.

Emmerson, John K. "Principles versus Realities: US Prewar Foreign Policy toward Japan." In *Pearl Harbor Reexamined: Prologue to the Pacific War*, edited by Hilary Conroy and Harry Wray5. Honolulu: University of Hawaii Press, 1990.

Fainaru, Steve. "Clues Pointed to Changing Terrorist Tactics." *Washington Post*, May 19, 2002.

Falke, Brian. "What Went Wrong at Midway." *US Naval Institute Proceedings*, June 2002, 64.

Falkenrath, Richard A. "The 9/11 Commission Report: A Review Essay." *International Security* 29, no. 3 (Winter 2004–5): 170–90.

Federal Bureau of Investigation. *Terrorism in the United States 1982–1992*. Washington, DC: Federal Bureau of Investigation, 1993.

Fenner, Lorry M., Mark E. Stout, and Jessica L. Goldings, eds. *Ten Years Later: Insights on al-Qaeda's Past & Future through Captured Records*. Washington, DC: National Defense University, 2012.

Feuer, Alan. "Witness in Bombing Case Describes Scouting Mission by 3 Men Near Embassy." *New York Times*, February 22, 2001.

Finnegan, John P. "The Evolution of US Army HUMINT: Intelligence Operations in the Korean War." *Studies in Intelligence* 55, no. 2 (June 2011). Orig. pub. in classified form in 2000.

Fischhoff, B. "Hindsight Does Not Equal Foresight: The Effect of Outcome Knowledge on Judgment under Uncertainty." *Journal of Experimental Psychology: Human Perception and Performance* 1 (1975): 288–99.

Flemming, Peter A., Edward Mickolus, and Todd Sandler. "Research Note: Using the ITERATE and DOTS Databases." *Journal of Strategic Security* 1, no. 1 (November 2008): 57–76.

Ford, Douglas. "'The Best-Equipped Army in Asia'? US Military Intelligence and the Imperial Japanese Army before the Pacific War, 1919–1941." *International Journal of Intelligence and CounterIntelligence* 21, no. 1 (2008): 86–121.

Ford, Harold P. *CIA and the Vietnam Policymakers: Three Episodes 1962–1968*. CIA Center for the Study of Intelligence, 1998. www.cia.gov/library/center-for-the-study-of-intelligence/csi-publications/books-and-monographs/cia-and-the-vietnam-policymakers-three-episodes-1962–1968/index.html.

———. *Estimative Intelligence: The Purposes and Problems of National Intelligence Estimating*, rev. ed. Lanham, MD: University Press of America, 1993.

Fort, Brian. "Midway Is Our Trafalgar." *US Naval Institute Proceedings* 132, no. 6 (June 2006): 62–66.

Freshwater, J. L. [pseudonym]. "Policy and Intelligence: The Arab-Israeli War." *Studies in Intelligence* 13, no. 1 (Winter 1969): 1–8.

Fried, Joseph B. "Sheik Sentenced to Life in Prison." *New York Times*, January 18, 1996.

———. "'Stalled' Cars Were to Destroy Tunnels, Tapes Indicate." *New York Times*, June 18, 1995.

Friedman, William F. *Special Research History (SRH) 125, Certain Aspects of "Magic" in the Cryptological Background of the Various Official Investigations into the Pearl Harbor Attack*. Washington, DC: National Security Agency, 1956.

Fuchida, Mitsuo, and Masatake Okumiya. *Midway: The Battle That Doomed Japan*. Annapolis, MD: Naval Institute Press, 1955.

Fukuyama, Francis, ed. *Blindside: How to Anticipate Forcing Events and Wild Cards in Global Politics*. Washington, DC: Brookings Institution Press, 2007.

Gardiner, L. Keith. "Dealing with Intelligence-Policy Disconnects." In *Inside CIA's Private World: Declassified Articles from the Agency's Internal Journal, 1955–1992*, edited by H. Bradford Westerfield. New Haven, CT: Yale University Press, 1995.

Gartenstein-Ross, Daveed, Joshua D. Goodman, and Laura Grossman. *Terrorism in the West 2008: A Guide to Terrorism Events and Landmark Cases*. Washington: FDD Press, 2009.

Garvey, Jane F. "Statement to the 9/11 Commission." Washington, DC, January 27, 2004. http://govinfo.library.unt.edu/911/hearings/hearing7/witness_garvey.htm.

Gates, Robert M. "Statement of the Director of Central Intelligence before the Senate Armed Services Committee." Washington, DC, January 22, 1992. Available at www.foia.cia.gov.

Gellman, Barton. "Broad Effort Launched after '98 Attacks." *Washington Post*, December 19, 2001.

———. "US Was Foiled Multiple Times in Efforts to Capture Bin Laden or Have Him Killed." *Washington Post*, October 3, 2001.

George, Alexander L., and Andrew Bennett. *Case Studies and Theory Development in the Social Sciences*. Cambridge, MA: MIT Press, 2005.

Georgetown University Institute for the Study of Diplomacy. "The Soviet Invasion of Afghanistan in 1979: Failure of Intelligence or of the Policy Process?" Working Group Report 111, September 26, 2005.

Gerecht, Reuel Marc. *Not Worth a Blue Ribbon*. Washington, DC: American Enterprise Institute, 2004.

Gertz, Bill. *Breakdown: How America's Intelligence Failures Led to September 11*. Washington, DC: Regnery, 2002.

Ginor, Isabella, and Gideon Remez. "Too Little, Too Late: The CIA and US Counteraction of the Soviet Initiative in the Six-Day War, 1967." *Intelligence and National Security* 26, nos. 2–3 (April–June 2011): 291–312.

Gish, Donald M. "A Cryptologic Analysis." *International Journal of Intelligence and CounterIntelligence* 6, no. 3 (Fall 1993): 363–88.

Gladwell, Malcolm. "Connecting the Dots: The Paradoxes of Intelligence Reform." *New Yorker*, March 10, 2003. Available at www.newyorker.com.

Gleis, Joshua L. "Connecting the Dots: Osama Bin Laden and Al-Qaeda Involvement in Terrorism Prior to 9/11." *Praeger Security International Online*, November 30, 2006.

Goldberg, Robert Alan. "Who Profited from the Crime? Intelligence Failure, Conspiracy Theories and the Case of September 11." *Intelligence and National Security* 19, no. 2 (Summer 2004): 249–61.

Gompert, David C. "Reaction to the *Washington Post* Series." Director of National Intelligence press release, July 19, 2010. www.dni.gov/press_releases/20100719_release.pdf.

Goo, Sara Kehaulani. "List of Foiled Plots Puzzling to Some." *Washington Post*, October 23, 2005.

Goodman, Melvin A. "America Is Safer since 9/11." *Christian Science Monitor*, September 18, 2006.

Grabo, Cynthia M. "Strategic Warning: The Problem of Timing." *Studies in Intelligence* 16, no. 2 (Spring 1972): 79–92.

Graham, Bob. *Intelligence Matters: The CIA, the FBI, Saudi Arabia, and the Failure of America's War on Terror*. New York: Random House, 2004.

Graham, Bradley. "Pentagon Crash Scenario Was Rejected for Military Exercise." *Washington Post*, April 24, 2004.

Gunaratna, Rohan. "Combating the Al-Qaida Associated Groups." In *How States Fight Terrorism: Policy Dynamics in the West*, edited by Doron Zimmerman and Andreas Wenger. Boulder, CO: Lynne Rienner, 2007.

———. *Inside Al-Qaeda: Global Network of Terror*, 3rd ed. New York: Berkley Books, 2003.

Gutman, Roy. "Examining Closely Why an Important Story Is Not Widely Told." *Nieman Reports* 61, no. 1 (Spring 2007). www.nieman.harvard.edu/reports/07-1NRspring/p31-0701-gutman.html.

Haass, Richard N. "Supporting US Foreign Policy in the Post-9/11 World." *Studies in Intelligence* 46, no. 3 (2002).

Haddick, Robert. "Strategic Error: When the Big Picture Misses the Point." ForeignPolicy .com, August 24, 2012. www.foreignpolicy.com/articles/2012/08/24/strategic_error.

Hamm, Mark S. *Terrorism as Crime: From Oklahoma City to Al-Qaeda and Beyond*. New York: New York University Press, 2007.

Handel, Michael I. "Avoiding Political and Technological Surprise in the 1980s." In *Intelligence Requirements for the 1980s: Analysis and Estimates*, edited by Roy Godson. New Brunswick, NJ: Transaction Books, 1980.

———. "Intelligence and Military Operations." In *Intelligence and Military Operations*, edited by Michael I. Handel. London: Frank Cass, 1990.

———. "Intelligence and the Problem of Strategic Surprise." *Journal of Strategic Studies* 7, no. 3 (September 1984).

———. "Perception, Deception and Surprise: The Case of the Yom Kippur War." In *International Violence: Terrorism, Surprise and Control*, edited by Yair Evron. Jerusalem: Hebrew University of Jerusalem Press, 1979.

———. "Strategic Surprise: The Politics of Intelligence and the Management of Uncertainty." In *Intelligence: Policy and Process*, edited by A. C. Maurer, M. D. Tunstall, and J. M. Keagle. Boulder, CO: Westview Press, 1985.

———. "The Yom Kippur War and the Inevitability of Surprise." *International Studies Quarterly* 21, no. 3 (September 1977): 461–502.

Hanley, Robert. "Suspected Terrorist Convicted in Bomb Case." *New York Times*, November 30, 1988.

Hanson, Victor Davis. *Carnage and Culture: Landmark Battles in the Rise of Western Power*. New York: Doubleday, 2001.

Hanyok, Robert J. "'Catching the Fox Unaware': Japanese Radio Denial and Deception and the Attack on Pearl Harbor." *Naval War College Review* 61, no. 4 (Autumn 2008): 99–124.

———. "The Pearl Harbor Warning That Never Was." *Naval History* 23, No. 2 (April 2009).

Hanyok, Robert J., and David P. Mowry. *West Wind Clear: Cryptology and the Winds Message Controversy—A Documentary History*. US Cryptologic History, series IV: World War II, vol. X. Washington, DC: National Security Agency Center for Cryptologic History, 2008.

Hastedt, Glenn P. "Organizational Foundations of Intelligence Failures." In *Intelligence: Policy and Process*, edited by Alfred C. Maurer, Marion D. Tunstall, and James M. Keagle. Boulder, CO: Westview Press, 1985.

Hathaway, Robert M., and Russell Jack Smith. *Richard Helms as Director of Central Intelligence 1966–1973*. Washington, DC: Central Intelligence Agency Center for the Study of Intelligence, 1993 (orig. classified "Secret").

Hayden, Michael V. "Prepared Remarks at the Council on Foreign Relations." New York, September 7, 2007. www.cia.gov/news-information/speeches-testimony/2007/general-haydens-remarks-at-the-council-on-foreign-relations.html.

———. "Statement for the Record by Lieutenant General Michael V. Hayden, USAF, Director, National Security Agency, before the Joint Congressional Inquiry." Washington, DC, October 17, 2002. www.fas.org/irp/congress/2002_hr/101702hayden.html.

Hedley, John Hollister. "Learning from Intelligence Failures." *International Journal of Intelligence and CounterIntelligence* 18, no. 3 (October 2005): 435–50.

Heinl, Robert D. *Marines at Midway*. Washington, DC: Historical Section, Division of Public Information, Headquarters, United States Marine Corps, 1948.

Heinrichs, Waldo. "The Russian Factor in Japanese–American Relations, 1941." In *Pearl Harbor Reexamined: Prologue to the Pacific War*, edited by Hilary Conroy and Harry Wray. Honolulu: University of Hawaii Press, 1990.

———. *Threshold of War: Franklin D. Roosevelt and American Entry into World War II*. New York: Oxford University Press, 1989.

Hempstone, Smith. "Embassies at Risk." *The National Interest*, September 22, 1998.

Heuer, Richards J., Jr. "Limits of Intelligence Analysis." *Orbis* 49, no. 1 (2005): 75–94.

———. *Psychology of Intelligence Analysis*. Washington, DC: CIA Center for the Study of Intelligence, 1999.

Hewitt, Christopher. *Political Violence and Terrorism in Modern America: A Chronology*. Westport, CT: Praeger, 2005.

Higgins, Andrew, and Christopher Cooper. "A CIA-Backed Team Used Brutal Means to Crack Terror Cell." *Wall Street Journal*, November 20, 2001.

Hill, Eleanor. "Joint Inquiry Staff Statement, Part I." Washington, DC, September 18, 2002.

———. "Joint Inquiry Staff Statement, Hearing on the Intelligence Community's Response to Past Terrorist Attacks against the United States from February 1993 to September 2001." Washington, DC, October 8, 2002.

———. "Joint Inquiry Staff Statement, the FBI's Handling of the Phoenix Electronic Communication and Investigation of Zacaria Moussaoui Prior to September 11, 2001 (as Supplemented October 17, 2002)." Washington, DC, September 24, 2002.

Hilsman, Roger, Jr. "Intelligence and Policy-Making in Foreign Affairs." *World Politics* 5, no. 1 (October 1952): 1–45.

Hoffman, Bruce. "Intelligence and Terrorism: Emerging Threats and New Security Challenges in the Post–Cold War Era." *Intelligence and National Security* 11, no. 2 (April 1996): 207–23.

Holmes, W. J. *Double-Edged Secrets: US Naval Intelligence Operations in the Pacific during World War II*. Annapolis, MD: Naval Institute Press, 1979.

Homeland Security Institute. *Underlying Reasons for Success and Failure of Terrorist Attacks: Selected Case Studies*. Final Report, June 4, 2007.

Honig, Or Arthur. "A New Direction for Theory-Building in Intelligence Studies." *International Journal of Intelligence and CounterIntelligence* 20, no. 4 (December 2007): 699–716.

———. "Surprise Attacks: Are They Inevitable? Moving beyond the Orthodox-Revisionist Dichotomy." *Security Studies* 17, no. 1 (2008): 72–106.

Horn, Steve. *The Second Attack on Pearl Harbor: Operation K and Other Japanese Attempts to Bomb America in World War II*. Annapolis, MD: Naval Institute Press, 2005.

Hudson, Rex A. *The Sociology and Psychology of Terrorism: Who Becomes a Terrorist and Why?* Washington, DC: Federal Research Division, Library of Congress, 1999.

Hulnick, Arthur S. *Keeping Us Safe: Secret Intelligence and Homeland Security*. Westport, CT: Praeger, 2004.

Hybel, Alex Roberto. *The Logic of Surprise in International Conflict*. Lexington, MA: Lexington Books, 1986.

Irons, Larry. "Hurricane Katrina as a Predictable Surprise." *Homeland Security Affairs* 1, no. 2 (Fall 2005). www.hsaj.org/?fullarticle = 1.2.7.

Isikoff, Michael, and Michael Hirsh. "What Went Wrong." *Newsweek*, May 27, 2002.

Isikoff, Michael, and Daniel Klaidman. "The Hijackers We Let Escape." *Newsweek*, June 10, 2002.

Isom, Dallas Woodbury. "The Battle of Midway: Why the Japanese Lost." *Naval War College Review* 53 (Summer 2000): 60–100.

———. *Midway Inquest: Why the Japanese Lost the Battle of Midway*. Bloomington: Indiana University Press, 2007.

Jackson, Brian A. *Breaching the Fortress Wall: Understanding Terrorist Efforts to Overcome Defensive Technologies*. Santa Monica, CA: RAND Corporation, 2007.

Jackson, Brian A., and David R. Frelinger. *Understanding Why Terrorist Operations Succeed or Fail*. Santa Monica: RAND Corporation, 2009.

Jacobs, Janice L. "Written Statement of Janice L. Jacobs, Assistant Secretary of State for Consular Affairs, Department of State, before the Senate Homeland Security and Governmental Affairs Committee." July 13, 2011.

Jacobson, Michael. "Terrorist Dropouts: Learning from Those Who Have Left." *Policy Focus* (Washington Institute for Near East Policy) 101, January 2010.

———. "They Trained, They Plotted, Then They Bailed." *Washington Post*, March 23, 2008.

Jacobsen, Philip H. "Foreknowledge of Pearl Harbor? No! The Story of the US Navy's Efforts on JN-25B." *Cryptologia* 27, no. 3 (July 2003): 193–205.

———. "Pearl Harbor: Who Deceived Whom?" *Naval History*, December 2003.

———. "Radio Silence and Radio Deception: Secrecy Insurance for the Pearl Harbor Strike Force." *Intelligence and National Security* 19, no. 4 (Winter 2004): 695–718.

Janis, Irving Lester. *Groupthink: Psychological Studies of Policy Decisions and Fiascoes*, 2nd ed. Boston: Houghton Mifflin, 1982.

Jenkins, Brian M. "Intelligence and Homeland Security." In *Transatlantic Homeland Security: Protecting Society in the Age of Catastrophic Terrorism*, edited by Anja Dalgaard-Nielsen and Daniel S. Hamilton. London: Routledge, 2006.

———. "Lessons for Intelligence." *Vanguard* (Canada), March 1, 2006. www.rand.org/commentary/030106VC.html.

———. "Prepared Statement for the 9/11 Commission." Washington, DC, March 31, 2003. http://govinfo.library.unt.edu/911/hearings/hearing1/witness_jenkins.htm.

———. "The Terrorist Threat to Commercial Aviation." RAND Corporation, Santa Monica, CA, March 1989.

———. *Unconquerable Nation: Knowing Our Enemy, Strengthening Ourselves*. Santa Monica, CA: RAND Corporation, 2006.

Jensen, Mark A. "Intelligence Failures: What Are They Really and What Do We Do about Them?" *Intelligence and National Security* 27, no. 2 (April 2012): 261–82.

Jervis, Robert. "The Politics and Psychology of Intelligence and Intelligence Reform." *The Forum* 4, no. 1 (2006). www.bepress.com/forum/vol4/iss1/art1.

————. "Reports, Politics, and Intelligence Failures: The Case of Iraq." *Journal of Strategic Studies* 29, no. 1 (February 2006): 3–52.

————. "Response to James Lebovic's Review of *Why Intelligence Fails: Lessons from the Iranian Revolution and the Iraq War*." *Perspective on Politics* 8, no. 4 (December 2010): 1169–70.

————. "What's Wrong with the Intelligence Process?" *International Journal of Intelligence and CounterIntelligence* 1, no. 1 (Spring 1986): 28–41.

————. "Why Intelligence and Policymakers Clash." *Political Science Quarterly* 125, no. 2 (Summer 2010): 185–204.

Johnson, Loch K. "Analysis for a New Age." *Intelligence and National Security* 11, no. 4 (October 1996): 657–71.

————. "Feature Review: An Elephant Rolling a Pea." *Diplomatic History* 30, no. 2 (2006): 327–33.

————. "A Shock Theory of Congressional Accountability for Intelligence." In *Handbook of Intelligence Studies*, edited by Loch K. Johnson. London: Routledge, 2007.

Johnson, Thomas R. *American Cryptology during the Cold War, 1945–1989, Book I: The Struggle for Centralization, 1945–1960*. US Cryptologic History, Series VI: The NSA Period. Washington, DC: National Security Agency Center for Cryptologic History, 1995.

————. *American Cryptology during the Cold War, 1945–1989, Book II: Centralization Wins, 1960–1972*. US Cryptologic History, Series VI: The NSA Period. Washington, DC: National Security Agency Center for Cryptologic History, 1995.

————. *American Cryptology during the Cold War, 1945–1989, Book III: Retrenchment and Reform, 1972–1980*. US Cryptologic History, Series VI: The NSA Period. Washington, DC: National Security Agency Center for Cryptologic History, 1995.

————. "American Cryptology during the Korean War: Opening the Door a Crack." *Studies in Intelligence* 45 no. 3 (2001).

Johnston, David. "Lack of Pre-9/11 Sources to be Cited as Intelligence Failure." *New York Times*, June 11, 2003.

Jones, R. V. "Intelligence and Command." In *Leaders and Intelligence*, edited by Michael I. Handel. London: Frank Cass, 1989.

Kahn, David. *The Codebreakers: The Story of Secret Writing*. Revised ed. New York: Scribner, 1996.

————. "The Intelligence Failure at Pearl Harbor." *Foreign Affairs* (Winter 1991–92): 138–52.

————. "Pearl Harbor and the Inadequacy of Cryptanalysis." In *Selections from Cryptologia: History, People, and Technology*, edited by Cipher A. Deavours, David Kahn, Louis Kruh, Greg Mellen, and Brian J. Winkel. Boston: Artech House, 1998.

————. "Roosevelt, Magic, and Ultra." In *Selections from Cryptologia: History, People, and Technology*, edited by Cipher A. Deavours et al. Boston: Artech House, 1998.

————. "The United States Views of Germany and Japan in 1941." In *Knowing One's Enemies: Intelligence Assessment before the Two World Wars*, edited by Ernest R. May. Princeton: Princeton University Press, 1984.

Kam, Ephraim. *Surprise Attack: The Victim's Perspective*, with a new preface. Cambridge, MA: Harvard University Press, 2004.

Kaplan, David E. "On Terrorism's Trail: How the FBI Unraveled the Africa Embassy Bombings." *US News & World Report*, November 23, 1998.

Karaball, Zachary, and Philip D. Zelikow. "Iraq, 1988–1990: Unexpectedly Heading toward War." In *Dealing with Dictators: Dilemmas of US Diplomacy and Intelligence Analysis, 1945–1990*, edited by Ernest R. May and Philip D. Zelikow. Cambridge, MA: MIT Press, 2006.

Katz, Samuel M. *Relentless Pursuit: The DSS and the Manhunt for the Al-Qaeda Terrorists.* New York: Forge, 2002.

Katzman, Kenneth. *Terrorism: Near Eastern Groups and State Sponsors, 2001.* Washington, DC: Congressional Research Service, 2001.

Keegan, John. *Intelligence in War: Knowledge of the Enemy from Napoleon to Al-Qaeda*, 1st American ed. New York: Alfred A. Knopf, 2003.

Kent, Sherman. *Strategic Intelligence for American World Policy.* Princeton, NJ: Princeton University Press, 1949.

Kernan, Alvin. *The Unknown Battle of Midway: The Destruction of the American Torpedo Squadrons.* New Haven, CT: Yale University Press, 2005.

Kerr, Richard J. "The Track Record: CIA Analysis from 1950 to 2000." In *Analyzing Intelligence: Origins, Obstacles, and Innovations*, edited by Roger Z. George and James B. Bruce. Washington, DC: Georgetown University Press, 2008.

Kessler, Glenn. "File the Bin Laden Phone Leak under 'Urban Myths.'" *Washington Post*, December 22, 2005.

Kifner, John. "US Fury on 2 Continents." *New York Times*, August 21, 1998.

Kirkpatrick, Lyman B., Jr. *Captains without Eyes: Intelligence Failures in World War II.* London: Macmillan, 1969.

Knorr, Klaus. "Failures in National Intelligence Estimates: The Case of the Cuban Missiles." *World Politics* 16, no. 3 (April 1964): 455–67.

Kovach, Gretel C. "Five Convicted in Terrorism Financing Trial." *New York Times*, November 25, 2008.

Krikorian, Greg. "Plot Posed a Real, Immediate Threat, Experts Say." *Los Angeles Times*, December 15, 2007.

Krugman, Paul. "A Can't-Do Government." *New York Times*, September 2, 2005.

Kuhns, Woodrow J. "Intelligence Failures: Forecasting and the Lessons of Epistemology." In *Paradoxes of Strategic Intelligence: Essays in Honor of Michael I. Handel*, edited by Richard K. Betts and Thomas G. Mahnken. London: Frank Cass, 2003.

Kurzman, Charles. *Muslim-American Terrorism in the Decade since 9/11.* Durham, NC: Triangle Center on Terrorism and Homeland Security, 2012.

Lance, Peter. *1000 Years for Revenge: International Terrorism and the FBI—the Untold Story.* New York: Regan Books, 2003.

Larew, Karl G. "December 7, 1941: The Day No One Bombed Panama." *The Historian* 66, no. 2 (June 2004): 278–300.

Laurie, Clayton. "The Korean War and the Central Intelligence Agency." N.d. www.foia .cia.gov/KoreanWar/EstimatesMisc/CSI/2010-05-01.pdf.

Layton, Edwin T. *Oral History of Rear Admiral Edwin T. Layton.* Annapolis, MD: US Naval Institute Press, 1975.

———. *Oral History of Rear Admiral Edwin T. Layton*, conducted by E. B. Potter. Annapolis, MD: US Naval Institute Press, 1970.

Layton, Edwin T., Roger Pineau, and John Costello. *"And I Was There": Pearl Harbor and Midway—Breaking the Secrets.* New York: William Morrow, 1985.

Leary, William M., ed. *The Central Intelligence Agency, History and Documents.* Tuscaloosa: University of Alabama Press, 1984.

Levite, Ariel. *Intelligence and Strategic Surprises.* New York: Columbia University Press, 1987.

———. "*Intelligence and Strategic Surprises* Revisited: A Response to Richard K. Betts's 'Surprise, Scholasticism, and Strategy.'" *International Studies Quarterly* 33, no. 3 (September 1989): 345–49.

Levy, Jack S. "Qualitative Methods and Cross-Method Dialogue in Political Science." *Comparative Political Studies* 40, no. 2 (February 2007): 196–214.

Lewin, Ronald. *The American Magic: Codes, Ciphers and the Defeat of Japan.* New York: Farrar, Straus & Giroux, 1982.

Lichtblau, Eric. "State Dept. Says It Warned about bin Laden in 1996." *New York Times,* August 17, 2005.

Lieberman, Joseph I., and Susan M. Collins. "We Could Have Stopped the Terror at Fort Hood." *Washington Post,* February 6, 2011.

Linder, Bruce R. "Lost Letter of Midway." *US Naval Institute Proceedings,* August, 1999.

Liptak, Adam. "Suspected Leader of 9/11 Attacks Is Said to Confess." *New York Times,* March 15, 2007.

Lipton, Eric, Eric Schmitt, and Mark Mazzetti. "Review of Jet Bomb Plot Shows More Missed Clues." *New York Times,* January 18, 2010.

Lord, Walter. *Incredible Victory.* New York: Harper & Row, 1967.

Love, Julia. "Alleged Al-Qaeda Operatives Indicted in New York Plot." *Los Angeles Times,* July 8, 2010.

Lowenthal, Mark M. "The Burdensome Concept of Failure." In *Intelligence: Policy and Process,* edited by Alfred C. Maurer, Marion D. Tunstall, and James M. Keagle. Boulder, CO: Westview Press, 1985.

Lundstrom, John B. *Black Shoe Carrier Admiral: Frank Jack Fletcher at Coral Sea, Midway, and Guadalcanal.* Annapolis, MD: Naval Institute Press, 2006.

———. "A Failure of Radio Intelligence: An Episode in the Battle of the Coral Sea." *Cryptologia* 7, no. 2 (April 1983): 97–118.

MacEachin, Douglas J. *Predicting the Soviet Invasion of Afghanistan: The Intelligence Community's Record.* Washington, DC: CIA Center for the Study of Intelligence, 2002.

MacFarquhar, Neil. "In Bombing Trial, a Deluge of Details." *New York Times,* March 19, 1995.

Macgregor, Douglas. "Remember the Blitzkrieg Before It's Too Late." *Washington Times,* May 10, 2010.

Mahle, Melissa Boyle. *Denial and Deception: An Insider's View of the CIA from Iran-Contra to 9/11.* New York: Nation Books, 2004.

Mahnken, Thomas G. "Gazing at the Sun: The Office of Naval Intelligence and Japanese Naval Innovation, 1918–1941." *Intelligence and National Security* 11, no. 3 (July 1996): 424–41.

———. *Uncovering Ways of War: US Intelligence and Foreign Military Innovation, 1918–1941.* Ithaca, NY: Cornell University Press, 2002.

Markle Foundation. *Nation at Risk: Policy Makers Need Better Information to Protect the Country.* Report of Task Force on National Security in the Information Age. New York: Markle Foundation, 2009.

Marks, Edward. "Terrorism in Context: From Tactical to Strategic." *Mediterranean Quarterly* 17, no. 4 (Fall 2006): 46–59.

Marrin, Stephen. "Evaluating the Quality of Intelligence Analysis: By What (Mis)Measure?" *Intelligence and National Security* 27, no. 6 (December 2012): 896–912.

———. "Preventing Intelligence Failures by Learning from the Past." *International Journal of Intelligence and CounterIntelligence* 17, no. 4 (December 2004): 658–59.

Marzulli, John. "Zazi, Al-Qaeda Pals Planned Rush-Hour Attack on Grand Central, Times Square Subway Stations." *New York Daily News*, April 12, 2010.

Matthew B. Ridgway Center for International Security Studies, University of Pittsburgh. "Anatomy of a Terrorist Attack: An In-Depth Investigation into the 1998 Bombings of the US Embassies in Kenya and Tanzania." Working paper, 2005.

May, Ernest R. *Strange Victory: Hitler's Conquest of France.* New York: Hill and Wang, 2000.

Mayer, Jane. "Junior: The Clandestine Life of America's Top Al-Qaeda Source." *New Yorker*, September 11, 2006.

Mazzetti, Mark, and Eric Lipton. "Spy Agencies Failed to Collate Clues on Terror." *New York Times*, December 31, 2009.

McCarthy, Andrew C. "Testimony before the US Senate Judiciary Committee, Subcommittee on Terrorism, Technology, and Homeland Security." Washington, DC, April 20, 2005.

———. *Willful Blindness: A Memoir of the Jihad.* New York: Encounter Books, 2008.

McCarthy, Mary. "The National Warning System: Striving for an Elusive Goal." *Defense Intelligence Journal* 3 (Spring 1994): 5–19.

McCollum, Arthur H. *Oral History of Rear Admiral Arthur H. McCollum.* Annapolis, MD: US Naval Institute Press, 1973.

McConnell, Michael. "Remarks by the Director of National Intelligence." Project on National Security Reform Conference, Washington, DC, July 26, 2007.

McCreary, John. *NightWatch*, January 8, 2010.

McFadden, Robert D. "For Jurors, Evidence in Kahane Case Was Riddled with Gaps." *New York Times*, December 23, 1991.

McKinley, James C., Jr. "In-Laws Say Bomb Suspect Led Quiet Life." *New York Times*, August 26, 1998.

———. "Key Witness in Bomb-Plot Trial Admits Lying about His Exploits." *New York Times*, March 8, 1995.

———. "Lawyer Forces Bomb-Trial Witness to Admit Trail of Lies." *New York Times*, March 23, 1995.

———. "Many Faces of Witness in Terror Trial." *The New York Times*, March 6, 1995.

———. "Security Flaws Left Embassy in Nairobi Open to Attack." *New York Times*, September 9, 1998.

———. "Trade Center Defendants Plotted to Bomb 12 Jewish Targets, Informer Says." *New York Times*, March 14, 1995.

———. "Trial Details the Selecting of Bomb Targets." *New York Times*, March 17, 1995.

———. "Witness in Bombing Plot Once Failed Lie-Detector Tests." *New York Times*, March 3, 1995.

McManis, David Y. "Technology, Intelligence, and Command." Incidental paper, Seminar on Intelligence, Command, and Control, Program on Information Resources Policy, Center for Information Policy Research, February 1993. http://pirp.harvard.edu/pubs_pdf/mcmanis/mcmanis-i93-1.pdf.

Memorandum for the Director of Central Intelligence, "Post-Mortem on Czech Crisis." November 22, 1968. www.foia.cia.gov/CzechInvasion.asp.

Miller, John, Michael Stone, and Chris Mitchell. *The Cell: Inside the 9/11 Plot, and Why the FBI and CIA Failed to Stop It.* New York: Hyperion, 2002.

Miller, Judith. "A Bullet Dodged." *New York Post*, September 26, 2009.

———. "Planning for Terror but Failing to Act." *New York Times*, December 30, 2001.

Mintz, John. "15 Freighters Believed to Be Linked to Al-Qaeda." *Washington Post*, December 31, 2002.

Mitchell, Alison. "Official Recalls Delay in Using Informer." *New York Times*, July 16, 1993.

MITRE Corporation. *Rare Events.* JASON Study JSR-09–108, October 2009.

Mobley, Richard A. "North Korea's Surprise Attack: Weak US Analysis?" *International Journal of Intelligence and CounterIntelligence* 13, no. 4 (December 2000): 490–514.

Morison, Samuel Eliot. *Coral Sea, Midway and Submarine Actions May 1942–August 1942.* History of US Naval Operations in World War II, vol. IV. Boston: Little, Brown, 1962.

———. *The Two-Ocean War: A Short History of the United States Navy in the Second World War.* Annapolis, MD: US Naval Institute Press, 1963.

Morris, Daniel R. "Surprise and Terrorism: A Conceptual Framework." *Journal of Strategic Studies* 32, no. 1 (February 2009): 1–27.

Mullen, Mike. "Why Midway Matters." *Naval History* 21, no. 3 (June 2007).

Mulrine, Anna. "CIA Chief Leon Panetta: The Next Pearl Harbor Could Be a Cyberattack." *Christian Science Monitor*, June 9, 2011.

Naftali, Timothy. *Blind Spot: The Secret History of American Counterterrorism.* New York: Basic Books, 2005.

National Commission on Terrorism [Bremer Commission]. *Countering the Changing Threat of International Terrorism.* Washington, DC: US Government Printing Office, 2000.

National Counterterrorism Center. *2009 Report on Terrorism.* Washington, DC: National Counterterrorism Center, 2010.

National Intelligence Estimate. "National Intelligence Estimate 2/1: "Chinese Communist Intervention in Korea," November 24, 1950. www.foia.cia.gov/KoreanWar.asp.

National Security Agency. *SRMN-005: File of Memoranda and Reports Relating to the Battle of Midway.* Washington, DC: National Security Agency, n.d.

———. *Special Research History (SRH) 147, Communications Intelligence Summaries, 1 November–6 December 1941, Commandant, 14th Naval District, United States Navy.* Washington, DC: National Security Agency, n.d.

———. *Special Research History (SRH) 152, Historical Review of OP-20-G.* Washington, DC: National Security Agency, 1944.

———. *Special Research History (SRH) 406, Pre-Pearl Harbor Japanese Naval Dispatches.* Washington, DC: National Security Agency, n.d.

New America Foundation. "Homegrown Terrorism Cases, 2001–2011." Available at http://homegrown.newamerica.net/.

Nolan, Janne E., and Douglas J. MacEachin. *Discourse, Dissent, and Strategic Surprise: Formulating US Security Policy in an Age of Uncertainty.* Washington, DC: Georgetown University Institute for the Study of Diplomacy, 2006.

Nye, Joseph S., Jr. "Peering into the Future." *Foreign Affairs*, July–August 1994.

Office of the Director of National Intelligence. *Vision 2015*. Washington, DC: Office of the Director of National Intelligence, 2008.

Ovodenko, Alexander. "(Mis)interpreting Threats: A Case Study of the Korean War." *Security Studies* 16, no. 2 (April–June 2007): 254–86.

———. "Visions of the Enemy from the Field and from Abroad: Revisiting CIA and Military Expectations of the Tet Offensive." *Journal of Strategic Studies* 34, no. 1 (February 2011): 119–44.

Pantucci, Raffaello. "Manchester, New York and Oslo: Three Centrally Directed Al-Qa'ida Plots." *CTC Sentinel* (West Point Combating Terrorism Center), August 2010.

Parker, Charles F., and Eric K. Stern. "Bolt from the Blue or Avoidable Failure? Revisiting September 11 and the Origins of Strategic Surprise." *Foreign Policy Analysis* 1, no. 3 (November 2005): 301–31.

Parker, Frederick D. "How OP-20-G Got Rid of Joe Rochefort." *Cryptologia* 24, no. 3 (July 2000): 212–34.

———. *Pearl Harbor Revisited: United States Navy Communications Intelligence, 1924–1941 (H-E32–94–01)*. US Cryptologic History, series IV: World War II, vol. 6. Fort George G. Meade, MD: Center for Cryptologic History, National Security Agency, 1994.

———. *A Priceless Advantage: US Navy Communications Intelligence and the Battles of Coral Sea, Midway, and the Aleutians, CH-E32–93–01*. US Cryptologic History, Series IV, World War II, Volume 5. Fort George G. Meade, MD: Center for Cryptologic History, National Security Agency, 1993.

———. "The Unsolved Messages of Pearl Harbor." *Cryptologia* 15, no. 4 (October 1991): 295–313.

Parshall, Jonathan B., and Anthony P. Tully. *Shattered Sword : The Untold Story of the Battle of Midway*. Washington, DC: Potomac Books, 2005.

Patton, Thomas J. "A Personal Perspective: Commentary on 'Two Strategic Intelligence Mistakes in Korea, 1950.'" *Studies in Intelligence* 46, no. 3 (2002).

Pellerin, Cheryl. "DIA Five-Year Plan Updates Strategic Warning Mission." American Forces Press Service, July 18, 2012, www.defense.gov/news/newsarticle.aspx?id = 117160.

Pincus, Walter. "Judge Discusses Details of Work on Secret Court." *Washington Post*, June 26, 2007.

———. "Mueller Outlines Origin, Funding of Sept. 11 Plot." *Washington Post*, June 6, 2002.

Pillar, Paul R. "Adapting Intelligence to Changing Issues." In *Handbook of Intelligence Studies*, edited by Loch K. Johnson. London: Routledge, 2007.

———. "Good Literature and Bad History: The 9/11 Commission's Tale of Strategic Intelligence." *Intelligence and National Security* 21, no. 6 (December 2006): 1022–44.

———. "Great Expectations: Intelligence as Savior." *Harvard International Review*, Winter 2006, 16–21.

———. *Intelligence and US Foreign Policy: Iraq, 9/11, and Misguided Reform*. New York: Columbia University Press, 2011.

———. "Predictive Intelligence: Policy Support or Spectator Sport?" *SAIS Review* 28, no. 1 (Winter–Spring 2008): 25–35.

———. *Terrorism and US Foreign Policy*. Washington, DC: Brookings Institution Press, 2003.

Pluchinsky, Dennis A. "A Typology and Anatomy of Terrorist Operations." In *The McGraw-Hill Homeland Security Handbook*, edited by David G. Kamien. New York: McGraw-Hill, 2006.

Porch, Douglas, and James J. Wirtz. "The Battle of Midway." *Strategic Insight*, June 2002.

———. "Surprise and Intelligence Failure." *Strategic Insight*, September 2002.

Posner, Richard A. *Preventing Surprise Attacks: Intelligence Reform in the Wake of 9/11.* Lanham, MD: Rowman & Littlefield, 2005.

Post, Jerrold M. "The New Face of Terrorism: Socio-Cultural Foundations of Contemporary Terrorism." *Behavioral Sciences and the Law* 23 (2005): 451–65.

Potter, E. B. "Admiral Nimitz and the Battle of Midway." *US Naval Institute Proceedings*, July 1976, 60–68.

———. *Nimitz.* Annapolis, MD: Naval Institute Press, 1976.

Powers, Thomas. "The Secret Intelligence Wars." *New York Review of Books*, September 26, 2002.

———. "The Trouble with the CIA." *New York Review of Books*, January 17, 2002.

Prados, John. *Combined Fleet Decoded: The Secret History of American Intelligence and the Japanese Navy in World War II.* New York: Random House, 1995.

Prange, Gordon W., Donald M. Goldstein, and Katherine V. Dillon. *At Dawn We Slept: The Untold Story of Pearl Harbor.* New York: McGraw-Hill, 1981.

———. *Miracle at Midway.* New York: Penguin Books, 1982.

———. *Pearl Harbor: The Verdict of History.* New York: McGraw-Hill, 1986.

Presidential Decision Directive 39. "US Policy on Counterterrorism," June 21, 1995. The directive was classified, but a redacted version is at www2.gwu.edu/~nsarchiv/NSA EBB/NSAEBB55/pdd39.pdf.

"Project Megiddo." *Terrorism and Political Violence* 14, no. 1 (Spring 2002): 27–52.

Quinn-Judge, Paul, and Charles M. Sennott. "Figure Cited in Terrorism Case Said to Enter US with CIA Help." *Boston Globe*, February 3, 1995.

Ranstorp, Magnus. "Introduction: Mapping Terrorism Research." In *Mapping Terrorism Research: State of the Art, Gaps and Future Directions*, edited by Magnus Ranstorp. London: Routledge 2007.

Rashbaum, William K., and Al Baker. "How Using Imam in Terror Inquiry Backfired on Police." *New York Times*, September 13, 2009.

Rashbaum, William K., and Kareem Fahim. "Informer's Role in Bombing Plot." *New York Times*, May 23, 2009.

Reeve, Simon. *The New Jackals: Ramzi Yousef, Osama Bin Laden and the Future of Terrorism.* Boston: Northeastern University Press, 2002.

Report of the Accountability Review Boards on the Embassy Bombings in Nairobi and Dar Es Salaam on August 7, 1998 [Crowe Commission Report]. Washington, DC: US Government Printing Office, 1999.

Report of the Secretary of State's Advisory Panel on Overseas Security [Inman Report]. Washington, DC: US Government Printing Office, 1985.

Ridgway, Matthew B., and Harold H. Martin. *Soldier: The Memoirs of Matthew B. Ridgway, as Told to Harold H. Martin.* New York: Harper, 1956.

Rimington, Stella. "'Humint' Begins at Home." *Wall Street Journal*, January 3, 2005.

Ripley, Amanda. "The Fort Dix Conspiracy." *Time*, December 6, 2007.

Risen, James. "CIA Said to Reject Bomb Suspect's Bid to Be Spy." *New York Times*, October 31, 1998.

Risen, James, and Benjamin Weiser. "Before Bombings, Omens and Fears." *New York Times*, January 9, 1999.

Robarge, David S. "Getting It Right: CIA Analysis of the 1967 Arab-Israeli War." *Studies in Intelligence* 49, no. 1 (2005).

Rochefort, Joseph J. *Oral History of Captain Joseph J. Rochefort*. From a Series of Interviews in 1969 with Commander Etta-Belle Kitchen. Annapolis, MD: US Naval Institute Press, 1983.

Rose, P. K. "Two Strategic Intelligence Mistakes in Korea, 1950." *Studies in Intelligence*, Fall–Winter 2001.

Rovner, Joshua. "Why Intelligence Isn't to Blame for 9/11." *Audit of the Conventional Wisdom* (MIT Center for International Studies) 5, no. 13 (November 2005).

Rovner, Joshua, and Austin Long. "The Perils of Shallow Theory: Intelligence Reform and the 9/11 Commission." *International Journal of Intelligence and CounterIntelligence* 18, no. 4 (Winter 2005–6): 609–37.

Rovner, Joshua, Austin Long, and Amy B. Zegart. "Correspondence: How Intelligent Is Intelligence Reform?" *International Security* 30, no. 4 (Spring 2006): 196–208.

Russell, Richard L. "CIA's Strategic Intelligence in Iraq." *Political Science Quarterly* 117, no. 2 (Summer 2002): 191–207.

———. *Sharpening Strategic Intelligence: Why the CIA Gets It Wrong, and What Needs to Be Done to Get It Right*. New York: Cambridge University Press, 2007.

Safford, Laurance F. *National Security Agency Special Research History (SRH) 149: A Brief History of Communications Intelligence in the United States*. Washington, DC: National Security Agency, 1952. www.fas.org/irp/nsa/safford.pdf.

Sagan, Scott D. "From Deterrence to Coercion to War: The Road to Pearl Harbor." In *The Limits to Coercive Diplomacy*, 2nd ed., edited by Alexander L. George and William E. Simons. Boulder, CO: Westview Press, 1994.

Sandia National Laboratories. "Osama Bin Laden: A Case Study." 1999. www.gwu.edu/~nsarchiv/NSAEBB/NSAEBB343/osama_bin_laden_file04.pdf.

Sanger, David E., and Thom Shanker. "Gates Says US Lacks a Policy to Thwart Iran." *New York Times*, April 18, 2010.

Schmidt, Susan, and Douglas Farah. "Al-Qaeda's New Leaders." *Washington Post*, October 29, 2002.

Schmitt, Gary J. "Truth to Power? Rethinking Intelligence Analysis." In *The Future of American Intelligence*, edited by Peter Berkowitz. Stanford, CA: Hoover Institution, 2005.

Schorreck, Henry F. *National Security Agency Special Research History (SRH) 230, Battle of Midway, 4–7 June 1942: The Role of COMINT in the Battle of Midway* [Orig. pub. in Cryptologic Spectrum, National Security Agency, 1975]. Washington, DC: National Security Agency, n.d.

Schwartz, Peter. *Inevitable Surprises: Thinking Ahead in a Time of Turbulence*. New York: Gotham Books, 2003.

Schwartz, Peter, and Doug Randall. "Ahead of the Curve: Anticipating Strategic Surprise." In *Blindside: How to Anticipate Forcing Events and Wild Cards in Global Politics*, edited by Francis Fukuyama. Washington, DC: Brookings Institution Press, 2007.

Shafer, Jack. "Don't Blame the *Washington Times*." *Slate*, December 21, 2005.

Shalev, Aryeh. *Israel's Intelligence Assessment before the Yom Kippur War: Disentangling Deception and Distraction*. Brighton: Sussex Academic Press, 2010.

Shane, Scott, and Eric Schmitt. "Qaeda Plot to Attack Plane Foiled, US Officials Say." *New York Times*, May 8, 2012.

Shellum, Brian. "A Chronology of Defense Intelligence in the Gulf War: A Research Aid for Analysts." Defense Intelligence Agency History Office, July 1997. www.gwu.edu/~nsarchiv/NSAEBB/NSAEBB39/document16.pdf.

Shulsky, Abram N., and Gary J. Schmitt. *Silent Warfare: Understanding the World of Intelligence*, 3rd ed. Washington, DC: Brassey's, 2002.

Shultz, Richard H., Jr. "Showstoppers." *Weekly Standard*, January 26, 2004.

Shultz, Richard H., Jr., and Ruth Margolies Beitler. "Tactical Deception and Strategic Surprise in Al-Qaida Operations." *Middle East Review of International Affairs* 8, no. 2 (June 2004). http://meria.idc.ac.il/journal/2004/issue2/jv8na6.html.

Shultz, Richard H., Jr., and Andreas Vogt. "It's War! Fighting Post-11 September Global Terrorism through a Doctrine of Preemption." *Terrorism and Political Violence* 15, no. 1 (March 2003): 1–30.

Smith, Brent L., Kelly R. Damphousse, and Paxton Roberts. "Pre-Incident Indicators of Terrorist Incidents: The Identification of Behavioral, Geographic, and Temporal Patterns of Preparatory Conduct." University of Arkansas, 2006.

Smith, Craig S. "North Africa Feared as Staging Ground for Terror." *New York Times*, February 20, 2007.

Solberg, Carl. *Decision and Dissent: With Halsey at Leyte Gulf.* Annapolis, MD: Naval Institute Press, 1995.

Southern Poverty Law Center. "The Second Wave: Return of the Militias." August 2009.

Spector, Ronald H. *Eagle against the Sun: The American War with Japan.* New York: Vintage Books, 1985.

Stein, Janice Gross. "'Intelligence' and 'Stupidity' Reconsidered: Estimation and Decision in Israel, 1973." *Journal of Strategic Studies* 3, no. 2 (September 1980): 147–77.

Stern, Jessica. "Review of Peter Bergen's 'The Longest War.'" *Washington Post*, February 20, 2011.

Stinnett, Robert B. *Day of Deceit: The Truth about FDR and Pearl Harbor.* New York: Free Press, 2000.

Strom, Kevin, John Hollywood, Mark Pope, Garth Weintraub, Crystal Daye, and Don Gemeinhardt. *Building on Clues: Methods to Help State and Local Law Enforcement Detect and Characterize Terrorist Activity.* Final Report. Durham, NC: Institute for Homeland Security Solutions, Duke University, 2011.

Studeman, Michael W. "Pacific Faces Crisis in Intel Analysis." *US Naval Institute Proceedings*, January 2003.

Subiri, Obwogo. *The Bombs That Shook Nairobi and Dar: A Story of Pain and Betrayal.* Nairobi: Obwogo and Family Publishers, 1999.

Sullivan, Patricia. "Roberta M. Wohlstetter: Military Intelligence Expert." *Washington Post*, January 10, 2007.

Sulzberger, A. G., and William K. Rashbaum. "NY Terror Suspect Admits Guilt and Cooperates." *New York Times*, February 23, 2010.

Sunstein, Cass R., and Adrian Vermeule. "Conspiracy Theories: Causes and Cures." *Journal of Political Philosophy* 17, no. 2 (June 2009): 202–27.

Symonds, Craig L. *The Battle of Midway.* New York: Oxford University Press, 2011.

Tabor, Mary B. W. "US Indicts Egyptian Cleric as Head of Group Plotting 'War of Urban Terrorism.'" *New York Times*, August 26, 1993.

Taleb, Nassim Nicholas. *The Black Swan: The Impact of the Highly Improbable.* New York: Random House, 2007.

———. "Learning to Expect the Unexpected." *New York Times*, April 8, 2004.

Taleb, Nassim Nicholas, and Mark Blyth. "The Black Swan of Cairo." *Foreign Affairs*, May–June 2011.

Temple-Raston, Dina. "Terrorism Case Shows Range of Investigators' Tools." NPR, October 3, 2009. www.npr.org/templates/story/story.php?storyId=113453193.

Tenet, George J. "Testimony before the Senate Select Committee on Intelligence." Washington, DC, February 6, 2002, transcript. http://intelligence.senate.gov/pub107th congress.html.

———. "Written Statement for the Record of the Director of Central Intelligence before the National Commission on Terrorist Attacks upon the United States." Washington, DC, March 24, 2004. http://govinfo.library.unt.edu/911/hearings/hearing8.htm.

Tenet, George, and Bill Harlow. *At the Center of the Storm: My Years at the CIA.* New York: HarperCollins, 2007.

"Thwarted Terrorist Attacks." *NYU Review of Law and Security* 7 (April 2006): 16–21.

Trachtenberg, Marc. *The Craft of International History: A Guide to Method.* Princeton, NJ: Princeton University Press, 2006.

"Transcript of Secretary Kissinger's Staff Meeting, October 23, 1973" (orig. classified "Secret"). www.gwu.edu/~nsarchiv/NSAEBB/NSAEBB98/#doc63.

Travers, Russell. "Statement for the Record of Russell Travers, Deputy Director for Information Sharing and Knowledge Development, National Counterterrorism Center, before the House Judiciary Committee, March 24, 2010."

Treverton, Gregory F. "Risks and Riddles." *Smithsonian Magazine*, June 2007.

"Two Months before 9/11, an Urgent Warning to Rice." *Washington Post*, October 1, 2006.

US v. Bin Laden 5(7) 98 Cr. 1028 (SDNY, 2001).

US Central Command. "Operation Desert Shield / Desert Storm Executive Summary, July 11, 1991" (Orig. "Top Secret," declassified and available from the National Security Archive). www.gwu.edu/~nsarchiv/NSAEBB/NSAEBB39/.

US Congress. *Hearings before the Joint Committee on the Investigation of the Pearl Harbor Attack [Pearl Harbor Hearings].* 39 vols. Washington, DC: US Government Printing Office, 1946.

———. *Report of the Joint Committee on the Investigation of the Pearl Harbor Attack [Pearl Harbor Report].* Washington, DC: US Government Printing Office, 1946.

———. *Report of the US Senate Select Committee on Intelligence and US House Permanent Select Committee on Intelligence (S. Rept. 107–351 and H. Rept. 107–792) [The Joint Inquiry Report].* Washington, DC: Joint Inquiry into Intelligence Community Activities before and after the Terrorist Attacks of September 11, 2001, 2002.

US Department of Justice. *A Review of the FBI's Handling of Intelligence Information Related to the September 11 Attacks (November 2004).* Washington, DC: US Department of Justice, Office of the Inspector General, 2006.

———. *A Review of the Federal Bureau of Investigation's Counterterrorism Program: Threat Assessment, Strategic Planning, and Resource Management (Report 02–38), Executive Summary Redacted and Unclassified.* Washington, DC: US Department of Justice, Office of the Inspector General, 2002.

US Department of State. *Foreign Relations of the United States, 1955–1957, Suez Crisis, July 26–December 31, 1956*. Washington, DC: US Government Printing Office, 1990.

———. *Patterns of Global Terrorism 1991*. Washington, DC: US Government Printing Office, 1992.

———. *Patterns of Global Terrorism 1992*. Washington, DC: US Government Printing Office, 1993.

———. *Patterns of Global Terrorism 2000*. Washington, DC: US Government Printing Office, 2001.

———. "Saudi Arabia: Meeting with ——— Re Bin Laden Threat." US Embassy Riyadh cable, June 16, 1998.

———. "Terrorism / Usama Bin Ladin: Who's Chasing Whom?" Bureau of Intelligence and Research, July 18, 1996. (Orig. classified "Top Secret," this document was declassified and released in response to a Freedom of Information Act request from the organization Judicial Watch.)

———. "The Wandering Mujahidin: Armed and Dangerous." Bureau of Intelligence and Research (INR), *Weekend Edition*, August 21–22, 1993. (This paper was written by INR analyst Gina Bennett, and has been released through the Freedom of Information Act.) http://blogs.law.harvard.edu/mesh/files/2008/03/wandering_mujahidin.pdf.

US General Accounting Office. *Combating Terrorism: Selected Challenges and Related Recommendations*. Washington, DC: US General Accounting Office 2001.

US House, Armed Services Committee. *Intelligence Successes and Failures in Operations Desert Shield/Storm*. Report of the Oversight and Investigations Subcommittee. Washington: US Government Printing Office, 1993.

US Navy. *Naval Doctrine Publication 2, Naval Intelligence*. Washington, DC: US Navy, 2001.

US Senate, Select Committee on Intelligence. "Unclassified Executive Summary of the Committee Report on the Attempted Terrorist Attack on Northwest Airlines Flight 253." May 18, 2010. http://intelligence.senate.gov/100518/1225report.pdf.

Vadlamudi, Sundara. "The US Embassy Bombings in Kenya and Tanzania." In *Countering Terrorism and Insurgency in the 21st Century: International Perspectives, Vol. 3, Lessons from the Fight against Terrorism*, edited by James J. F. Forest. Westport, CT: Praeger, 2007.

Vanderpool, Guy R. "COMINT and the PRC Intervention in the Korean War." *Cryptologic Quarterly* 15 (Summer 1996): 1–26.

Van Der Rhoer, Edward. *Deadly Magic: A Personal Account of Communications Intelligence in World War II in the Pacific*. New York: Scribner, 1978.

Van Evera, Stephen. *Guide to Methods for Students of Political Science*. Ithaca, NY: Cornell University Press, 1997.

Van Natta Jr., Don, Elaine Sciolino, and Stephen Grey. "Details Emerge in British Terror Case." *New York Times*, August 28, 2006.

Van Riper, Paul. "Reinventing War." *Foreign Policy*, no. 127 (November–December 2001).

Vick, Karl. "Assault on a US Embassy: A Plot Both Wide and Deep." *Washington Post*, November 23, 1998.

Villa, Brian, and Timothy Wilford. "Signals Intelligence and Pearl Harbor: The State of the Question." *Intelligence and National Security* 21, no. 4 (August 2006): 520–56.

Vistica, Gregory L. and Daniel Klaidman. "Tracking Terror." *Newsweek*, October 19, 1998.

"Waiting for Al-Qaeda's Next Bomb." *The Economist*, May 5, 2007.

Waldman, Peter. "Lapses in Handling Sergeant Mirror Larger Failings in FBI's Terror Policing." *Wall Street Journal*, November 26, 2001.

Waller, Douglas. "Inside the Hunt for Osama." *Time*, December 21, 1998.

Warner, Michael, and J. Kenneth McDonald. *US Intelligence Community Reform Studies since 1947*. Washington, DC: Central Intelligence Agency Center for the Study of Intelligence, 2005.

Warrick, Joby, and Joe Stephens. "Before Attack, US Expected Different Hit." *Washington Post*, October 2, 2001.

Watson, Russell, John Barry, Gregory L. Vistica, Michael Hirsh, Christopher Dickey, Mark Dennis, Steve LeVine, and Gregory Beals. "Our Target Was Terror." *Newsweek*, August 31, 1998.

Weadon, Patrick D. *The Battle of Midway: AF Is Short of Water*. Fort George G. Meade, MD: National Security Agency Center for Cryptologic History, 2000. www.nsa.gov/publications/publi00023.cfm.

Weiner, Tim, and James Risen. "Decision to Strike Factory in Sudan Based Partly on Surmise." *New York Times*, September 21, 1998.

Weiser, Benjamin. "Defense Psychiatrist Tells Jury of Embassy Bomber's Remorse." *New York Times*, June 28, 2001.

———. "Remorseful Terror Conspirator Gets an 11-Year Sentence." *New York Times*, October 16, 1999.

Weiser, Benjamin, and James Risen. "The Masking of a Militant: A Soldier's Shadowy Trail in US and in the Mideast." *New York Times*, December 1, 1998.

White, Mary Jo. "Prosecuting Terrorism in New York." *Middle East Quarterly*, Spring 2001.

———. "Statement before the Joint Congressional Inquiry into the September 11 Terrorist Attacks." Washington, DC, October 8, 2002.

White House. "Attempted Terrorist Attack on December 25, 2009: Intelligence, Screening, and Watchlisting System Corrective Actions." Washington, DC, January 7, 2010.

———. "Fact Sheet: Combating Terrorism: Presidential Decision Directive 62." Washington, DC, May 22, 1998.

———. "Fact Sheet: Plots, Casings, and Infiltrations Referenced in President Bush's Remarks on the War on Terror." Washington, DC, October 6, 2005, http://georgewbush-whitehouse.archives.gov/news/releases/2005/10/20051006-7.html.

———. "Summary of the White House Review of the December 25, 2009 Attempted Terrorist Attack." Washington, DC, January 7, 2010.

White House Commission on Aviation Safety and Security [Gore Commission]. *Final Report to President Clinton*. Washington, DC: US Government Printing Office, 1997.

Whitlock, Craig. "Trial Opens in Alleged Plot Against US Targets." *Washington Post*, April 23, 2009.

Whitlock, Duane L. "The Silent War against the Japanese Navy." *Naval War College Review* 48, no. 4 (Autumn 1995): 43–52.

Wildenberg, Thomas. "Sheer Luck or Better Doctrine?" *Naval War College Review* 58, no. 1 (Winter 2005): 121–35.

Wilder, Dennis C. "An Educated Consumer Is Our Best Customer." *Studies in Intelligence* 55, no. 2 (June 2011): 23–31.

Wildhorn, Sorrel, Brian Michael Jenkins, and Marvin M. Lavin. *Intelligence Constraints of the 1970s and Domestic Terrorism: Vol. I, Effects on the Incidence, Investigation, and Prosecution of Terrorist Activity.* Santa Monica, CA: RAND Corporation, 1982.

Wilensky, Harold L. *Organizational Intelligence: Knowledge and Policy in Government and Industry.* New York: Basic Books, 1967.

Wilford, Timothy. "Decoding Pearl Harbor: USN Cryptanalysis and the Challenge of JN-25B in 1941." *Northern Mariner / Le marin du nord* 13, no. 1 (January 2002): 17–37.

Winton, John. *Ultra in the Pacific: How Breaking Japanese Codes and Ciphers Affected Naval Operations against Japan, 1941–45.* London: Leo Cooper, 1993.

Wirtz, James J. "The American Approach to Intelligence Studies." In *Handbook of Intelligence Studies,* edited by Loch K. Johnson. London: Routledge, 2007.

———. "Déja Vu? Comparing Pearl Harbor and September 11." *Harvard International Review* 24, no. 3 (Fall 2002): 73–77.

———. "Epilogue: The Future of Intelligence." In *Intelligence: The Secret World of Spies, An Anthology,* 3rd ed., edited by Loch K. Johnson and James J. Wirtz. New York: Oxford University Press, 2011.

———. "The Intelligence–Policy Nexus." In *Strategic Intelligence, Vol. 1, Understanding the Hidden Side of Government,* edited by Loch K. Johnson. Westport, CT: Praeger, 2007.

———. "Responding to Surprise." *Annual Review of Political Science* 9 (2006): 46–51.

———. "Review of Ariel Levite, Intelligence and Strategic Surprises." *Survival* 30, no. 5 (September–October 1988): 478–79.

———. *The Tet Offensive: Intelligence Failure in War.* Ithaca, NY: Cornell University Press, 1991.

———. "Theory of Surprise." In *Paradoxes of Strategic Intelligence: Essays in Honor of Michael I. Handel,* edited by Richard K. Betts and Thomas G. Mahnken. London: Frank Cass, 2003.

Wohlstetter, Roberta. *Pearl Harbor: Warning and Decision.* Stanford, CA: Stanford University Press, 1962.

Woodward, Bob. *State of Denial.* New York: Simon & Schuster, 2006.

Wright, Lawrence. "The Counter-Terrorist." *New Yorker,* January 14, 2002.

———. *The Looming Tower: Al-Qaeda and the Road to 9/11.* New York: Alfred A. Knopf, 2006.

Zegart, Amy B. "American Intelligence: Still Stupid." *Los Angeles Times,* September 17, 2006.

———. "'CNN with Secrets': 9/11, the CIA, and the Organizational Roots of Failure." *International Journal of Intelligence and CounterIntelligence* 20, no. 1 (March 2007): 18–49.

———. "An Empirical Analysis of Failed Intelligence Reforms before September 11." *Political Science Quarterly* 121, no. 1 (Spring 2006): 33–60.

———. *Flawed by Design: The Evolution of the CIA, JCS, and NSC.* Stanford, CA: Stanford University Press, 1999.

———. Radio interview, KCET, Los Angeles, September 11, 2007, transcript. www.kcet.org/lifeandtimes/archives/200709/20070911.php.

————. "September 11 and the Adaptation Failure of US Intelligence Agencies." *International Security* 29, no. 4 (Spring 2005): 78–111.

————. *Spying Blind: The CIA, the FBI, and the Origins of 9/11*. Princeton, NJ: Princeton University Press, 2007.

Zeman, Ned, David Wise, David Rose, and Bryan Burrough. "The Path to 9/11: Lost Warnings and Fatal Errors." *Vanity Fair*, November 2004.

Zimmerman, John C. "Pearl Harbor Revisionism: Robert Stinnett's Day of Deceit." *Intelligence and National Security* 17, no. 2 (Summer 2002): 127–46.

INDEX

Information in figures is indicated by *f*. Information in notes is indicated by n between page number and note number.

CPSIA information can be obtained
at www.ICGtesting.com
Printed in the USA
FSHW010704171220
76817FS